LOCAL LIVES AND GLOBAL
TRANSFORMATIONS

Local Lives and Global Transformations

Towards World Society

Paul Kennedy
Manchester Metropolitan
University, UK

First published 2010 by
PALGRAVE MACMILLAN

Palgrave Macmillan in the UK is an imprint of Macmillan Publishers Limited, registered in England, company number 785998, of Houndmills, Basingstoke, Hampshire RG21 6XS.

Palgrave Macmillan in the US is a division of St Martin's Press LLC, 175 Fifth Avenue, New York, NY 10010.

Palgrave Macmillan is the global academic imprint of the above companies and has companies and representatives throughout the world.

Palgrave® and Macmillan® are registered trademarks in the United States, the United Kingdom, Europe and other countries.

ISBN: 978–0–230–22476–6 hardback
ISBN: 978–0–230–22477–3 paperback

This book is printed on paper suitable for recycling and made from fully managed and sustained forest sources. Logging, pulping and manufacturing processes are expected to conform to the environmental regulations of the country of origin.

A catalogue record for this book is available from the British Library.

A catalog record for this book is available from the Library of Congress.

10 9 8 7 6 5 4 3 2 1
19 18 17 16 15 14 13 12 11 10

Printed in China

For Jasmine M. K.

Contents

Part Three   Paths towards a World Society

Boxes

Acronyms

BRIC countries	Brazil, Russia, India and China
CAW	Committee for Asian Women
CIA	Criminal Investigation Agency
CNN	Cable News Network
ELN	National Liberation Army (Columbia)
EPZs	Export Processing Zones
ETI	Ethical Trading Initiative
EU	European Union
EZLN	Zapatista National Liberation Army
FARC	Revolutionary Armed Forces of Columbia
FATF	Financial Action Task Force
G7/8	The leading group of industrial nations (prior to including Russia, it was the G7)
G20	The expanded group of leading economies including some from the South
GATT	General Agreement on Tariffs and Trade
GDP	Gross Domestic Product
GINS	Globally Integrated Networks
GJM	Global Justice Movement
ICTs	Information and Communication Technologies
IGOs	Intergovernmental Organizations
ILO	International Labour Organization
IMF	International Monetary Fund
INGOs	International Non-governmental Organizations
IPCC	Intergovernmental Panel on Climate Change
IRA	Irish Republican Army
IWGIA	International World Group for Indigenous Affairs
MPI	Migration Policy Institute
MST	Landless People's Movement (Brazil)
NAFTA	North American Free Trade Association
NGOs	Non-governmental Organizations
NHS	National Health Service (Britain)
NWSS	New Wall Street System
OECD	Organization for Economic Co-operation and Development
OPEC	Organization of Petroleum-Exporting Countries
PGA	People's Global Action

PLO	Palestine Liberation Organization
SAPs	Structural Adjustment Policies
SEWA	Self-Employed Women's Association
TNCs	Transnational Corporations
TNCC	Transnational Capitalist Class
TNS	Transnational State
TRIPS	Agreement on Trade-Related Aspects of Intellectual Property Rights
UKIP	United Kingdom Independence Party
UN	United Nations
UNCTAD	United Nations Conference on Trade and Development
USSR	Union of Soviet Socialist Republics
VC	Via Campesina (The Peasant Road)
WB	World Bank
WHO	World Health Organization
WTC	World Trade Center
WTO	World Trade Organization

Acknowledgements

The list of colleagues, friends, fellow researchers, mentors and students who in different ways have influenced and stimulated my thinking about globalization, and to whom I owe a debt of intellectual gratitude, is too long to enumerate here. Many members of both the UK and North American Global Studies Association have provided a lasting and always enjoyable dialogue, but particularly: Barrie Axford, Marco Caselli, Jörg Dürrschmidt, John Eade, Elizabeth Grierson, Jerry Harris, Ray Kiely, Darren O'Byrne, Leslie Sklair and Gillian Youngs. Among valued colleagues and friends at Manchester Metropolitan University – past and present – working in the field of globalization and who always fed me useful ideas and criticisms are Shoba Arun, Jon Binnie, Tim Edensor, Robert Grimm, Angela Hale, Susie Jacobs and Gary Pollock. Over time, numerous third year, master's and doctoral students have also challenged ideas and suggested new avenues for investigation. Special thanks are due to Robin Cohen, Steve Edgell, Roy May and Phil Mole who over many years have provided in equal part, generous, quality friendship and powerful intellectual stimulation which I value enormously. The three anonymous reviewers of the manuscript offered invaluable advice and suggestions which I have tried to follow as much as possible. It goes without saying, however, that I am fully responsible for whatever flaws or mistakes may remain in this text.

Beyond academia, the team at Palgrave were always patient and helpful but I am especially grateful to Emily Salz for her unstinting encouragement and thoughtful guidance. Finally, my long-suffering family, and especially Sue, have provided more support than they can ever realize.

Introduction: Global *and* Local

1

Globalization does not simply refer to the objectiveness of increasing interconnectedness. It also refers to cultural and subjective matters…The world is not literally 'for-itself' but the *problem* of being 'for-itself' has become increasingly significant, in particular because of the thematization of humankind in a number of respects.

(Robertson 1992: 183, author's italics)

World society, the sum total of human interactions, is now of a shape where its history leaves it with uncertain and unclear organization, and its theory has yet to escape the confine of the Modern Age. It is not clear how far it is shaped by an incipient global society or how far such a society could extend its sway over the world.

(Albrow 1996: 114)

The key quotes which head this chapter point strongly and usefully to the main theme of this book; namely, the disjuncture between the mostly inward looking, local character of most people's primary concerns and their limited capacity to think, feel or act as if the world mattered very much in their lives and despite the often-threatening and all-encompassing nature of globalization processes and the interconnectivities to which they have given rise. It is striking and highly commendable that both these pioneer thinkers in the sociology of globalization, Robertson and Albrow, identified and drew attention to this central dilemma quite early in their thinking on this topic some years ago.

1.1 Setting the scene

A world not yet for itself

Albrow argued that for 200 years the project of modernity dominated the aspirations of people in many societies. Modernity was about the pursuit of material progress through harnessing rational thought especially in the shape of applied science and bureaucratic organization. Led by nation-states, and their political elites, the project was grounded in a clearly defined sense of territorial ownership and driven by the desire to defend and expand the nation's influence in a world of competing states. In stark contrast, Albrow is quite clear that unlike state-led modernization, 'globality is not a project' (1996: 95) of any particular agent or set of agents. Rather, although the multiple and cumulative actions unleashed by many elites have contributed to its making, over long periods, those involved rarely if ever intended that their actions would lead us to this uncharted and uncertain condition we call globalization. This condition of globalization means that a global logic has become paramount and inescapable. Accordingly, it is leading us rapidly into a global age where humanity and its needs have become the fundamental frame of reference for everyone. Albrow is also emphatic that although the arrival of the global age means a world society is emerging – consisting of the totality of social relations which one way or another assume a global scope and intention – these webs of worldwide social relations do not yet constitute a global society whose members have the capacity to think and act on behalf of all humanity. For Albrow and Robertson, a further consequence is that the multiple, unfinished, chaotic, contested and highly complex processes we associate with globalization create a situation where everything is possible and nothing is yet resolved.

Robertson's (1992) thinking is along similar lines. In a key discussion he develops an analogue taken from Marx's nineteenth-century work as a way of getting to grips with the reality of an increasingly interdependent world yet one where personal subjectivities remain to a considerable extent constructed around national, ethnic or religious affiliations and despite the rise of many forms of successful interstate cooperation including international laws, agreements, institutions and events (55 and 183). This analogy draws on the distinction Marx made between a class 'of itself' and a class 'for itself'. In the former case, members were not yet capable of acting together so as to produce a unified collectivity sharing a class consciousness. Eventually, however, the proletariat would overcome the constraints preventing them from taking this direction and would begin to act collectively to improve their situation through joint political struggles. Robertson applied this same distinction to the situation confronting humanity at the present time. Thus, currently the world exists in a state of being of itself where its people's lives and futures are increasingly bound together by common difficulties to which all contribute.

However, he also sees some evidence of an intensifying world consciousness which he refers to as globality. This is something entirely new in human experience. Thus, there is a 'coming into...conjunction of different forms of life...a heightening of civilizational, societal, ethnic, regional, and indeed individual, self consciousness' in respect to the relativization of all societies, cultures and peoples as they inevitably become compressed together and unavoidably exposed to each other (27). Sometimes, therefore, individuals are aware of themselves as being participants in a shared belief-system built around mutual respect for each other's cultural differences and not just as members of national or ethnic collectivities. Nevertheless, this situation remains 'problematic' (27). There is some way to go before the world begins to exist in a condition of being for itself and where the idea of a distinctive global interest has a chance of being taken seriously by an increasing number of social actors.

In Chapter 2 we explore the various concepts offered by global theorists that try to explain and define the essential characteristics of globalization. Chapters 3, 4 and 5 examine some of the key agents of global change and the macro-forces at the leading edge of globalization processes that are driving them but which also affect the lives of all humans. These chapters suggest that we are already living global as well as local lives in the sense that each individual's fate is bound up with those of innumerable others despite vast distances, cultural barriers and territorial boundaries. However, it is also apparent that we are often unable or unwilling to act as if these globalizing processes and interdependencies affected us.

One way of thinking about this huge disjuncture between the pressing need for much greater global collaboration alongside most peoples' preoccupation with their immediate lives and affiliations is to recall how much concern is dedicated to discussing what is or might be in the national interest. This can be loosely understood as all those events, changes and polices which are presumed or designed to benefit native citizens, institutions and businesses more or less exclusively. Such discussion often takes place within and by think-tanks, newspapers and TV documentaries, researchers and of course politicians. But members of the general public can also be heard in streets, markets or bars describing what they see as the decline of national strength, the threat to indigenous culture or government failures to prioritize citizens' needs over those of 'foreigners' or an assortment of international agencies. Beck (2000a) describes this un-reflexive and powerful urge to think almost entirely in terms of national spaces – as if land, people, country, economy and culture all neatly overlapped and coexisted behind territorial borders, in a state of virtual solitary confinement – as methodological nationalism.

Globalizing processes increasingly undermine much of this discourse on the peculiarities of the nation and render it partly redundant. Nevertheless, concerns and priorities shaped by methodological nationalism continue to dominate the perceptions of most individuals, governments and political elites. Thus, we rarely, if ever, hear individuals or groups speaking in terms of the world's interests or the interests of all the world's peoples. Merely, to raise this possibility would probably engender disbelief or incredulity. Putting this another way, we might ask who is either able or willing to mind the interests of all the world and not just those relating to particular nations, classes or tribes – or as Silver and Arrighi (2003: 328) ask: '[w]here are we to locate the effective agents of the countermovement for the self-protection of world society?' And, more specifically, in an era where markets have been freed from government restrictions across most of the world, who, they ask, can act so as to protect 'the common people of the world' from the consequences of an unregulated, free-market global capitalism.

An indication of how difficult it is for most people to think in terms of the world's needs can be gleaned from the fact that most are unable or unwilling to accept that the risks and insecurities they believe are threatening their lives are global as well as local in origin and that only by tackling both causes is the local situation likely to improve. Instead, people demand national remedies, displace blame onto local agents, usually politicians, and generally talk and act as if the problem they feared could be rendered innocuous by removing it beyond their country's borders through tough government action. Taking migration as an example and writing about Britain, Griffin (2007: 241–3) observed that 'xeno-phobic and racist anxieties concerning mass migration and national identity' are not only expressed in the tabloid press but are also 'extensively catered to politically' by the main political parties, sections of which have long appealed to the 'patriotic reflexes and insular instincts' of many in the population and especially in respect to immigrants from countries outside the European Union (EU). It seems that politicians and journalists as well as citizens assume they can live in a self-reliant, bubble container largely insulated from the rest of the world. Their government can solve all the 'problems' which beset its citizens, in this case migrants, by acting in isolation or simply by somehow removing the 'difficulty' far from their shores. It is as if action taken to stem the tide of entrants at the national level will by itself somehow cancel the crises – oppressive, collapsing states, environmental devastation, falling world com-modity prices, meagre and often declining aid and so on – which compel people to migrate legally or illegally in search of a better life in the first place.

Of course, there are many cooperative actions pursued by international institutions and these help to generate 'worldwide constructs' or scripts (Lechner and Boli 2005: 44).[i] These global institutions and movements share a 'deep structure' of understandings which underpin the actions of those who manage them. But their participants and those who try to influence them form a small percentage of the world's population. Also, these organizations tend to operate in very specialized areas such as health (the World Health Organization, WHO) or the environment (the scientists attached to the Intergovernmental Panel on Climate Change, IPCC). But negotiating inter-national agreements between nation-states and other key agents in respect to specialized problems or world regions such as Sub-Saharan Africa is different from calling for comprehensive action in respect to the interests of the world as one single entity. Of course, in the absence of a world government, it is not easy to see who or what could assume the equivalent role that govern-ments play – or try to play – in national affairs on behalf of their citizens' multiple concerns. Growing minorities in many countries are beginning to share one or other kind of global imaginary (Steger 2008); ways of thinking about the future of all or certain sections of humanity which move beyond the limitations of national imaginaries. Similarly, some individuals are developing Robertson's (1992) consciousness of the world as a single space. Yet, these are mostly tiny minorities and they tend to be massively drowned out by the loud chorus trumpeting the interests of localities, nations and/or ethnic groups.

The multiple ties binding the world together

Summarizing the previous discussion, it seems that we are beset by an alarming number of threats which require worldwide cooperation between the citizens of different nations and between governments. Yet, most of us remain relatively disengaged from such ideas most if not all the time. We are either more or less oblivious and uninformed – only dimly aware of exactly how our actions impact the lives of innumerable others or how their actions affect us – or we are relatively indifferent towards them and preoccupied, instead, with our own local life worlds. Here, we briefly list some of the most obvious ways in which nations and peoples are increasingly bound together through complex chains of interdependency. None of these situations or the dangers they create can be contained within or managed by single nations. Nor can their consequences be easily prevented from crossing territorial borders. The first three of these interdependencies are analysed in considerable depth in Part One and consist of the following:

1. The rise of a more predatory and mobile capitalism (Chapter 3).
2. The mutual interdependency of rich and poor countries in respect to migrant labour flows linked to demographic differences and growing inequalities between most countries in the Global South and the rich countries of the North (Chapter 4).
3. The increasing reach of transnational organized criminal gangs and the threat from terrorist groups networked across the world (Chapter 5).

There are, of course, a number of additional global interdependencies. Among the most well-documented and pressing of these we might include:

1. Climate change and global warming.
2. The widening gap between the most successful and least successful developing countries.
3. The imbalanced character of global trade, investment and credit flows between South East Asia and America coupled to the relative economic decline of America and the G7 nations and the ways in which this skewed global economy has helped to fuel the present financial crisis.
4. The risk of future scarcities in the supply of essential commodities, especially food and oil, and linked partly to the rapid economic growth taking place in China, India and other Southern countries with large, expanding populations but also – in the case of food – to climate change and the increasing unreliability of rainfall.[ii]

Unfortunately, space does not allow us to give these the attention they deserve and so the discussion only alludes to them briefly in the chapters that follow.

Nevertheless, some are also explored and given more focus in later Boxes, especially 1, 3, 4 and 5. At the same time Boxes 2, 7 and 8 also point to the growing inequalities between North and South, the resulting flows of poor people to the North and the social conflicts and tensions that sometimes occur partly as a result of these North-South linkages.

Box I   Recent evidence of climate change

The evidence that climate change is taking place continues to accumulate. In essence this is linked to global warming and the omission of greenhouse gases which are, in turn, the result of innumerable human activities taking place across the planet. A growing number of scientists working on climate change and global warming are now arguing that the window of opportunity available to humanity – for acting to have some realistic possibility of keeping the inevitable rise of average global temperature in future decades to somewhere at or below 2 °C – is probably now only a few years. Should the rise in temperature exceed two degrees most scientists believe that further environmental changes will be triggered as various crucial tipping points are reached. One example of this tendency for climate change to accelerate further and the risk that it will spin beyond our capacity to control is given below.

Melting polar ice caps.   In August 2008, satellite images revealed that ice at the North Pole was melting at an unprecedented rate due to summer storms over Alaska pulling in warm air streams. Scientists from the US National Snow and Ice Data Centre in Colorado have charted the thinning of the polar ice caps for some time and have accumulated evidence suggesting that instead of lasting till around 2070, as once predicted, the summer arctic ice cover cap may disappear by or before 2013 because the rate of melting has accelerated. This will have huge consequences including the diminishing capacity of the ice to reflect solar radiation back into the atmosphere, hence intensifying global warming even further, increasing the rate at which sea levels are rising but also the possibility of disrupting the Gulf Stream which keeps temperatures higher in Western Europe than they would otherwise be (McKie 2008).

However, there are equally serious implications across the world: for example, the risk of more frequent and intense hurricanes, floods and droughts – in 2008 Somalia was suffering its third year of drought – and therefore the spectre of growing food shortages, mass environmental migration as some regions become uninhabitable and the impact of rising sea levels on many cities, estuaries and sea boards including London and New York.

1.2   An outline critique of some globalization theories

Chapter 2 investigates the key concepts and theories developed by globalization theorists. Most of this material is essential for understanding the globalizing world. Nevertheless, it is also possible to criticize or modify some arguments. This section therefore indicates the direction my own analysis will follow by outlining some counter-arguments partly drawn from the work of other academics. I begin by focusing on one of the central themes of this text; namely, the continuing power of the local in people's lives and the need to reframe globalization theory so as to restore the local to a more central position. A second argument suggests that we need to take more account of how ordinary social actors perceive and experience globalization from 'below' rather than relying solely or mainly on academic theorizing which tends to overstate the impact of globalization on most people's lives. Third, global theory has tended to concentrate on identifying the broad parameters of globalization and frequently this means that attention is disproportionately given to the operation of vast structural forces and/or the role of powerful macro-actors. In contrast, much of the discussion in this book focuses on the central role played by micro-actors in shaping and coping with globalization, especially Chapters 7, 8 and 9.

Bringing the local back into focus

The argument developed in Chapters 6 and 7 is that the local is ubiquitous and commonplace despite globalizing processes. It absorbs, diverts and distracts us. It surrounds and envelops us, filling our lives with huge volumes of detail, information, attachments, pressures, expectations and demands, patterns, routines, responsibilities, pleasures, desires but also familiar routes and spatial-social niches. To summarize briefly, the definition of the local deployed in those chapters encompasses three overlapping experiences: our physical/bodily but also social emplacement in the locality we inhabit at any one time and the latter's particularities; the experience of everyday life through a round of multiple, repeated and sometimes trivial practices involving family, work, leisure and much else besides – some undertaken reflexively and others without much thought; and what Hannerz (2003: 26–7) calls the 'forms of life' relating to shared ethnic or national meanings and identities flowing through 'households, work places, neighbourhoods' and which provide the 'formative experiences' of early life. The following four points expand on this argument.

1. The ordinariness of the local and its powerful centripetal tendencies and attraction, pulling us inwards, affects everyone to a greater or lesser extent and usually the former. Of course, certain social groups – living perhaps on sink estates in the rich countries or in the shanty towns of the South in a condition of economic marginality or those whose livelihoods and ways of life are most threatened by unemployment and increasing job insecurity due partly to economic globalization – may be especially prone to cling to the local. Here, danger, threat and loss encourage people to endow the local and its certainties with almost a magical power to protect, replenish and restore. Sometimes, too, those most harmed by change may try to resist it and/or protect what they perceive as their threatened ethnic or national identities in

ways that involve violence or its possibility. Writing about the fragmentation of national societies, partly linked to globalization, Friedman (1997) described some people's determination to 'return to roots' and to 'fixed identifications' that can immunize them against change (71). He then identified likely responses to social fragmentation on the part of some members of the native populations; the reassertion of national identity through indigenization processes or attempts to revive certain regional or sub-national affiliations which flourished in the era before the national state. Migrants, too, may engage in such processes, for example, by attempting to re-ethnicize their affiliations endangered by living in the host society. However, the possibility that distressed groups may be more prone to invoke localness in overtly defensive and sometimes aggressive ways while most people avoid such behaviour does not detract from the reality that the local in all its manifestations constitutes the 'normal' condition for virtually everyone, irrespective of social class, age, gender, religion or ethnicity. The empirical material explored in Chapter 7 fleshes out this argument.

2. Some global thinkers assume that the local is now so criss-crossed with influences flooding in from other societies that its existence as a unique, coherent entity with its own more or less durable centre of gravity is now seriously in doubt. Indeed, it would be more appropriate to speak of the glocal because the numerous outside influences which flow across our social horizons are increasingly absorbed into the local. Certainly, too, our lives are caught up and often shaped by powerful global processes as Chapters 3, 4 and 5 demonstrate. The difficulty, however, is that many people either do not understand or acknowledge these forces. Thus, although under globalizing conditions the encounters which always take place between cultural elements originating in different societies have massively increased, and sometimes these are blended together, the cultural theorists who observe these processes of hybridization from the 'outside' understand them in ways that are strikingly different from ordinary societal members. For the latter it is the 'specificity' of their culture that is crucial and the way in which the various elements that have gone into its making have been 'synthesized' into a set of coherent, viable practices and meanings (Friedman 1997: 80–4). In this respect a culture is forged by its inhabitants and becomes a living but 'ethnically focused form of identification'. Those on the 'inside of a social world' experience 'cultural mixture...only as a phenomenon of self-identification' (81). To them, the various possible origins of these elements are of little significance.

3. In many instances when individuals do engage with others belonging to societies different from their own it is mainly because they are trying to protect their own local attachments and identities. Instead of trying to express globality – support for the predicament faced by distant others and/or the desire to register an involvement in a world consciousness – they are actually seeking to enlist the support of people who do not belong to their local as a strategy for perpetuating the latter's integrity against threats with which they

cannot cope alone. It is the need to preserve the local that motivates them. Chapter 8 examines some of the well-documented examples of this phenomenon. Some indigenous or tribal peoples in the South are highly vulnerable to land loss and other threats to their cultural integrity from national or foreign companies or because their governments are determined to open up forests, valleys or farming land to various modernizing projects. Despite limited resources some have turned to the outside world for support (for example, Castells 1997, Kekk and Sikking 1998 and Reitan 2007). Peasants and small farmers across the world have struggled to retain a degree of independence within their own locality or nation for generations but recent transformations, particularly the power of corporations and more open world trade regimes, have encouraged many to join transnational peasant campaigns. In the face of patriarchal dominance and poverty, women, too, in many countries have also mobilized political protest or action around their concern with place. In doing so, they have often joined or helped to construct networks linking them to women in other places and nations across ethnic, national and social class divides (Harcourt and Escobar 2005). In all these cases, while their experiences may alert those involved to the plight of others facing similar conditions, their primary goal normally remains the protection of their own local situation.

Many second or third generation migrants living in the cities of Europe and North America feel caught between their ethnic/national attachments to their parents' homelands and their partial assimilation to the host country where they grew up. Faced in many instances with discrimination, many turn to symbolic forms of protest through musical expression (Bennett 2000 and Sernhede 2005) and this may enable them to assert a political and aesthetic connection with migrants of different ethnic/national origin living in the same or other locales. Again, their concern is not global activism but asserting the importance of the local in the context of their own particular hybrid experience. In global cities based in the North, alliances are sometimes formed between sympathetic national non-governmental organizations (NGOs), anti-globalization activists, women acting as concerned mothers and migrant groups reacting to police brutality, and these are fundamentally concerned with local conditions (Sassen 2004 and 2007). There are of course numerous additional cases where people in the North resort to political action to preserve local identities. Just one random example was demonstrated in 2005 when a section of the local football fans supporting Britain's Manchester United football team – with its iconic global status – acted to protect what they saw as their team's local roots by breaking away from the main club in protest against its acquisition by an American businessman (Porter 2008). Then there is the minority but consistent support across many EU countries given to populist right wing political parties, as discussed in Box 7. Here, supporters vehemently and sometimes violently demand a return to policies designed to preserve and favour the national culture and economic interests of native people over those of immigrants, foreign businesses and international interests (Mudde 2007).

4. Drawing on these previous points, a final observation is that some theories engage in a kind of 'global overcoding' (Marston, Woodward and Jones III 2007: 52) in respect to their treatment of the local. Indeed, in some writing it almost seems as if globalization absorbs the local to the point where the latter becomes little more than a figment of our imagination (Giddens 1990). Thus, theorists endow global influences with a much greater capacity to reconstitute and dominate the local than they wield in reality (Amin 2002a, Castells 1996). Even more critically, in terms of the argument we are developing here, the evidence that global forces are constantly being absorbed by and into the subjective worlds of most micro-actors in everyday life is thin on the ground. Again, Friedman (1997) brings us back to earth:

> We read about ethnic violence, of demands for cultural rights, but also of global reach, internationalised markets... of disappearing company and state funds, of globalised drug trafficking, terrorist bombings, and so on... We are told that the world is one place, but for whom, one might ask! (70)

The reasons for being sceptical of such theorizations and for placing local life back into the centre of our analysis – though without falling into a similar trap of reifying its significance and autonomy – are explored in depth in Chapter 6.

Whose globalization? The view from 'inside' and 'below'

The way in which ordinary people perceive and experience everyday life, including globalizing forces, is likely to be very different from the views held by scholars and other informed observers whose job is to record and interpret social life from a broader, objective and 'outsider' perspective. Certainly, it is highly problematic to assume that the great majority of people, many with little or no education, share even a small part of the knowledge available to epistemic communities, aesthetic connoisseurs, journalists, politicians, international non-governmental organizations (INGOs), transnational campaigning groups – and of course academics – concerning how globalization impacts on our lives.

Here, a phenomenological perspective, as it has been developed in sociology by Schutz (1964 and 1974), might enhance our understanding of the continuing power of the local. Schutz argued that the social life of actors is only possible because they share a common-sense knowledge which is taken for granted and rarely reflected upon. This has several fundamental implications. Because this knowledge is shared, its members are able to understand and interpret each other's actions. But our intersubjective 'knowledge of trustworthy recipes for interpreting the social world' (Schutz 1964: 99) also allows members to make sense of their everyday actions and of the society around them and to engage in practical actions: it provides them with a life world (1974). The argument that social life is only possible because actors share common-sense knowledge might cause us to wonder whether sociologists, too, can ever escape the social life worlds to which they are exposed both within the professional sphere of personal interaction, trust and mutual collegiality and within their private life outside academia. At the very least, his argument invites scepticism concerning the attempts by sociologists to construct conceptual schemes claiming to explain 'society' and given that these are unlikely to be intelligible or useful to ordinary social actors. Bourdieu (2000: 142–3) also contrasted the knowledge on which ordinary people rely with the scholastic knowledge valued and sought by philosophers. The latter deliberately try to stand outside the everyday and to construct rational knowledge which is quite separate both from their own and the lives of those they are studying. However, ordinary people rely on knowledge which is practical, immediate, habitual, grounded in their bodily needs and taken for granted. It is also shared with other social actors through intersubjective communication and reciprocal trust.

Bourdieu's concept of the habitus is also germane to this argument (1990 and 1993). As a result of their childhood socialization and through their participation in a particular concatenation of situations and experiences based in the membership of national, class, locality, generational, religious and other kinds of structured affiliations, social actors acquire a set of dispositions and orientations or a habitus. Quite often the habitus impels actors to make choices and undertake actions, semi-consciously, which in effect reinforce and reproduce those same structures thereby endowing social life with a durability and sense of order. Yet, at other times, the social actor's capacity for reflexivity and for investing his or her life with meaning comes into play and this provides scope for exercising a degree of autonomy including the possibility of utilizing whatever kinds of capital they have acquired – social, cultural, economic and so on – to exploit the various overlapping power fields and sub-fields of social life operating all around them within their particular society.

Of course, globalization processes call into question the continuing all-encompassing quality and viability of Schutz's life world and Bourdieu's habitus because it is now much more difficult to live in self-contained social class, ethnic or national collectivities where all members share an entirely distinctive and separate reality. Nevertheless, Schutz and Bourdieu remind us that the world as seen through the eyes of ordinary people and as experienced by them at first hand is something quite different from the abstractions developed by social scientists. It occasions no surprise, therefore, to discover that many, and probably most, social actors remain locked into the horizons shaped by the sphere of the local with its immediate, familiar, near-at-hand and pressing responsibilities and even though the latter is increasingly criss-crossed by globalizing forces.

This gulf between the outsider character of much scholarly theory and the common-sense assumptions of the everyday life world is thrown strongly into relief by the argument that the central reality of globalization is its ability to increasingly generate multiple interconnectivities between societies. The difficulty, however, is that the basis, scale and impact of these interconnectivities vary a great deal. The force behind them also depends on the agency or agencies primarily responsible for driving them. These differences, in turn, may determine the extent to which most people understand and act upon them, if at all. Probably the most powerful sources of interconnectivity – in terms of their capacity to reach and re-shape many lives – involve 'abstracted' and 'disembodied' processes and flows (James 2005: 197), linked to market competition and a money economy but also the communications architecture provided by information technology. Because these are widely recognized and underpinned by an invisible infrastructure of international agreements and laws, it is possible for complex business arrangements to be established involving vast supply chains and the coordination of work teams, materials and components spread across many different companies and countries. But these webs of economic activity are highly complex, so much so that they almost defy understanding, even by experts. Also, the financial transactions between banks, suppliers, shippers, wholesalers, retailers and others on which they depend are mostly impersonal. Those caught up in such complexities across the world as workers, consumers and suppliers almost never experience face-to-face interpersonal contact outside their own locale. Interconnectivity is remote and detached from most people's lives. Turning to the local for support and/or displacing blame onto those who currently manage it seems, and actually is, infinitely more real and satisfying.

Focusing on the role of micro-actors in global life – bringing people back in

As we will see in Chapters 2, 3, 4 and 5, a good deal of globalization theory has focused on the global interconnectivities which are occurring with increased frequency and intensity at the macro-level. Without denying their overwhelming influence, it is equally useful to explore the role of human sociality operating through co-present and virtual interaction in bringing about global transformations. One reason why micro-relations in a global context have attracted less attention is that the vast distances involved and the continued strength of linguistic and cultural differences seem to validate the argument that the viability of any emergent or future global society would need to revolve primarily around mediated experiences and solidarities as well as the interlocking webs of international and global institutions. Here, a global imaginary would almost certainly provide the bedrock for shared experiences and meanings but would need to be transmitted constantly through knowledge and educational channels but also especially through the mass media and information technology – though global mega-events, tourism and so on would be important, too. The early modern nation also depended on the ability to conjure an imagined national community partly by utilizing education and the media as key instruments for bridging the deep gulf between citizens caused by physical distance and class, regional and other divisions (Anderson 1983). In the case of global society, visuality would be especially weighty in creating shared, easily accessible experiences that might cross and outweigh more grounded cultural differences. Moreover, although physical-bodily movement would contribute to this, the mass media, consumer culture and virtual forms of travel would provide the core conduits for disseminating cosmopolitan 'ways of thinking and perceiving' (Szerszynzki and Urry 2006: 127).

However, while acknowledging the strength of this argument, micro, inter-personal social interactions, including those involving co-presence, may be capable of playing an equal or even, at times, a larger role in helping to build a global society. First, as Robertson reminds us, 'globalization is as much about *people* as anything else...Once one has begun to appreciate this so-called micro dimension then one can very easily produce multitudes of examples of the "the local in the global"' (Robertson 2001: 465–6, author's italics). It is ordinary people in their everyday lives who cope with and sometimes react to the global forces penetrating their particular life spaces – threats to jobs, the casualization of work, the effects of climate change or the stresses of living in a multicultural city – even though they do not always understand or interpret them as global forces. Similarly, it is individuals as members of family, friendship, ethnic or lifestyle groups who select, reject, adopt, adapt or blend incoming cultural fragments and feed them creatively into their own shared cultural life worlds thereby contributing to the rise and fall of sport fanzines, fashions and styles in music, clothing, holidays, cuisines and much else besides.

Second, a more bottom-up, 'micro-level' approach to the study of global interconnectivities would give a more 'human face' to the idea of agency in global studies (Favell, Feldblum and Smith 2006: 1–3) as opposed to the more usual concentration on impersonal flows and vast institutional complexes. Moreover, a stronger focus on the niches where interpersonal micro-relations flourish in global life would reveal their role in lubricating the operations of large and often global organizations and institutions. Four examples of such niches are the following: the places in global cities where corporate directors and other elite members of the transnational class (Sklair 2001) meet to build trust, relay crucial information and construct deals (see Chapter 7); the reciprocal social bonds constructed around kinship, village or ethnic affiliations which enable poor migrants to survive in the host society, cope with discrimination and maintain multifaceted transnational networks with their homelands (Chapter 4); the dependence of transnational criminal organizations on the loyalties grounded in blood ties and ethnic, regional or national bonds despite their increasingly global and sophisticated mode of operation (Chapter 5); and the importance of conferences, assemblies, meetings and demonstrations which draw together transnational activists engaged in contesting globalization and provide sites where strong mutual understandings and affiliations can be forged (Chapter 9).

A key point to note here is that although poor, unskilled migrants and privileged transnational elites and classes (for example, Carroll and Carson

2003, Castells 1996, Sassen 2000, Sklair 2001) have attracted a good deal of scholarly interest, very little research has been conducted on the increasing numbers of individuals who are carving out an intermediate socio-economic space between the arenas dominated by the top corporate and economic policy elites and the vast and rather powerless majority. Favell et al. (2006: 8) describe these relatively under-researched groups as the 'middle classes' in pursuit of 'international migration opportunities linked to careers and education'. They form a heterogeneous category which includes many current and future professionals but also business people or simply educated young sojourners seeking temporary adventure and career improvement. They bring a freewheeling and culturally experimental style to the situations they encounter overseas and their numbers are growing rapidly. Moreover, unlike transnational elites, most individuals lack the power to shape global economic life or influence governments (Robinson 2001) and the media. Nor, contrary to the views of some writers (Calhoun 2002, Featherstone 1990), do they provide models of sumptuous global lifestyles that might tip yet others into seeking arenas for experimenting with cosmopolitan agendas.

A third way in which face-to-face relationships may contribute to the formation of a global society is where such exchanges take place across territorial and cultural boundaries. Such intercultural relations require and engender qualities very different from those that result from exposure to idea and media scapes (Appadurai 1990), global brands, the space of flows (Castells 1996) or the institutional rules and universal themes encoded in global 'scripts' (Lechner and Boli 2005: 44). The messages carried by these forms of media are often fragmentary and disjunctive as between different spheres of experience. More important, they do not require personal responses and commitments from those who receive them to function, though these may be forthcoming. However, as with all forms of human sociality, when co-present and cooperative interactions occur among social actors in global arenas they can only generate mutual satisfaction, and therefore endure, if both partners invest real involvement in the relationship. Meanings need to be communicated; personal responses, commitments and rules have to be negotiated and certain compromises may be required. Interpersonal interaction does not endure for long if actors act passively. Rather, they need to take up social space in the lives of others. However, globalization increases the likelihood that the lives of at least a minority of people from different national cultures will increasingly intersect as they cross territorial and cultural borders. But here, too, viable and mutual satisfactory relationships will work only if real personal involvement and commitment are forthcoming.

It may also be the case that those involved in intercultural relationships will convey to each other their own personal narratives drawn from their unique ethnic or national repertoires of knowledge and meaning. Thus, and just like any other socialization process, it may be through the learning experiences – underpinned by respect and affectivity – acquired in such directly interactive relationships, and not only through TV programmes, films, website exposure or adverts, that some people will come closest to attaining a glimpse of the real lives of distant others. If so, such individuals may also become more capable of empathizing with, and willing to discoverer more about, each other's conditions even to the point of taking ethical/political action on their behalf. In short, these relationships may provide an important source of globality, one that works through much smaller numbers of people than mass media imagery and visual stimuli but which is nevertheless more qualitatively intense and contains a potential multiplier capacity to spread horizontally through the rippling effect of sociality engendered by personal relationships. Chapter 9 examines some examples of these processes.

1.3   Fleshing out the idea of globality

Robertson's (1992) argument that more people are experiencing an intensifying consciousness of belonging to one world and humanity – or globality – provides the essential starting point for any quest which aims to evaluate the prospects for a future global society endowed with a capacity to act for itself. Moving on, though, the idea of globality needs to be fleshed out so that we can search more precisely for its possible forms. For example, we need to understand whether, in what circumstances and how ordinary people across the world might begin to follow the lead set by a few political, intellectual, artistic and other elites and the members of global social movements in seeking to engage more decisively in global actions rather than waiting, perhaps, for crises to push them in this direction. Of course, some people have long exercised their power as consumers, viewers, cyber-users and savers in the attempt to influence the global policies of investors and corporations. There have also been a number of salient protests by the members of an incipient global civil society especially since the late 1990s. We explore some of these themes and events in Chapter 9. However, these movements have appealed to rather small minorities of mostly young people although they have often attracted a media attention that is disproportionate to the numbers involved. The evidence for the expression of mass global concerns or actions is more difficult to discern. One obvious, but so far very scarcely used, channel through which people in everyday life could seek to express globality would involve them in using their political rights as voters and citizens to pressurize their national governments and political representatives from within their own country and urging the latter to engage more decisively in acts of interstate collaboration designed to reduce or avert global crises. The worldwide, coordinated mass demonstrations which took place in 60 cities against the second Iraq war in February 2003 certainly offer one very powerful example since those involved were clearly trying to send a message to their own and other governments concerning an issue of global significance. However, such events have so far been rare.

A number of additional questions arise when thinking about globality. The possible list, here, is long but it might include the following. To what extent do age, generation and education influence the capacity of individuals to express some concern for distant 'others' or to engage in acts betokening globality? Are those individuals who experience a degree of social displacement, in that they move by choice or necessity outside their early or original national, regional or social class position, more likely to become open to other cultures and/or prone to think and feel globally? One example might be 'marginalized professionals' (Watt 2007). These are middle-class individuals employed mainly in the third or public sectors as teachers, social workers or nurses. The combination of high education, working in highly responsible, caring jobs and being placed by low income outside their 'normal' social class location appears to leave many strongly disposed towards political actions and holding ethical values. Skilled, educated migrants who move overseas alone and without the support of an organization might provide another instance because by moving they place themselves outside the immediate control of their family, friends and home culture. Yet, arriving alone in a strange location they are equally compelled to find or construct a new social network and life space. There is some evidence that this situation may leave them exposed to a much wider range of potentially new socio-cultural influences – in the form of both host society members and other foreigners in the same situation – than they would be likely to encounter had they remained at home (Kennedy 2007a and 2008).

Yet, most people do not migrate to other countries nor do many move very far even within their own society. Perhaps, in contrast, this immobility engenders social conservatism, a lack of curiosity and a paucity of awareness concerning other cultures and the plight of distant, unknown others. On the other hand, it may be perfectly possible to always remain at home, largely encapsulated within a homogeneous social milieu, yet begin to think, feel and even act, at times, as if the lives of strangers in far away locations mattered. Even if some individuals do become much more open towards, and interested in, the lives and people from other cultures, perhaps through living overseas or marrying someone from a different country, this may not necessarily foster a sense of moral responsibility towards unknown others.

Possible links between cosmopolitanism and globality

Arguably, these and related questions have become much more compelling during recent years largely because of globalization. The discussion in Chapter 9 takes up some of these questions and tries to move the research agenda concerning globality a bit further along though it would require at least one entire book, and probably several, to explore these issues thoroughly. One very important way of pursuing the theme of globality further, and the kinds of issues and questions it raises, might be to look briefly at theories of cosmopolitanism. Indeed, the globalization discourse has helped to renew interest in theories of cosmopolitanism and has raised fresh questions concerning its origins, content and possible role in forging a global society (see for example, the contributions to Cheah and Robbins 1998, Vertovec and Cohen 2002, Nowicka and Rovisco 2009 and the special issues of the journals, *Theory, Culture and Society,* in 2002, and the *British Journal of Sociology* in 2006). The evolving debate has tended to pivot around two key ways of thinking about cosmopolitanism: either as an openness to ways of life very different from one's own or the willingness at times to assume a degree of moral responsibility for socially, and probably geographically, distant and unknown people. Both themes are highly relevant to the globalization debate and especially to the issue of globality.

Hannerz's (1990) highly influential approach tends towards the first of these. He defined cosmopolitanism as the willingness to engage with the cultural 'other' mainly through face-to-face social interactions encountered in the 'the round of everyday life in a community' (240). He contrasted this sharply with tourism or situations where individuals live in voluntary or compulsory exile but confine their social interactions to other expatriates like themselves. This emphasis on exploring cultural difference, however, has attracted criticisms. For example, it has been suggested that this version of cosmopolitanism focuses much more on aesthetic than social or moral concerns. In doing so it tends towards cultural elitism (Calhoun 2002) whereby only wealthy and highly educated individuals enjoy the leisure and – crucially – the linguistic skills required for engaging in deep cultural interactions with the 'authentic' life ways of 'true' locals. It has also been suggested that this approach appears to turn cultures into 'objects of artistic appreciation' and thereby highlights the 'general value and significance of the intellectual vocation' (Robbins 1998: 254–5) which anthropologists and scholars in cognate fields, including Hannerz himself, clearly exemplify. In any case, seeking aesthetic knowledge and insights into the cultural history and experiences of other nations is not the same as crossing socio-cultural borders and forging strong and enduring personal relationships with people from other countries. The latter requires 'a field of moral forces' (Turner 2006: 139) to underpin recognition, trust, respect and reciprocity. Moreover, as outlined above, this, in turn, assumes a willingness by participants to assume a degree of responsibility towards each other as a normal part of friendship while investing in relationships where complex and subtle differences of meaning, interpretation and intention will need to be negotiated.

Tomlinson's approach (1999: 183–6) is linked much more directly to the concept of globality because he suggests that the most important aspect of cosmopolitanism is people's willingness to demonstrate a sense of ethical responsibility with regard to global problems beyond their own society and milieu. But by using the term 'ethical glocalism' (194) he also injects an element of realism into the debate since he suggests that in displaying such wider ethical concerns we continue to remain embedded in, and concerned about, our own local sphere, too. Neither orientation needs to preclude the other. This is an extremely useful idea which we take up in Chapter 9. Interestingly, Tomlinson's realism concerning the likely limits to cosmopolitan behaviour can also be detected in the wider discourse. For example, Cheah and Robbins

(1998) suggested that many individuals and groups sometimes think, feel and even act beyond their immediate particularistic loyalties but this stops a long way short of identifying with all humanity and might exclude certain groups altogether. There is also a welcome inclination among some of the contributors to the book edited by Cheah and Robbins to focus rather more on empirical realities and concrete cases than ideal-type conceptualizations.

Finally, Beck's (2004) recent thinking is also quite circumspect concerning the prospects for cosmopolitanism. Thus, he insists on a clear distinction between 'normative' or 'philosophical' and 'real-world cosmopolitanism' (133). The former exists where rare individuals pursue the goal of 'harmony across national and cultural frontiers' (132) but the latter is much more common, is usually 'passive' and 'unconscious' (134) and is driven by the immediate compulsions of poverty and oppression or the side effects of modernization and globalization. Similarly, although Beck suggests that the border crossings and mixings intensified by globalization have been increasingly noticed and articulated self-consciously, in what is effectively a 'global public arena' (137), on the other hand, these changes really amount to a process of 'cosmopolitanization' rather than the genuine expression of cosmopolitan intentions designed to improve human relations. Thus, we have become exposed to a range of global cultural experiences, especially through the mass media, and to an extent we have subjectively absorbed these into our self-identities. But their impact on us is often shallow. They provide exotic resources with which we can enrich and diversify our bodies, private lifestyles, consumption profiles and self presentations – we feed them into our local lives – but they stop some way short of deepening our awareness and understanding of the 'other' or our determination to take moral responsibility for people far away.

1.4   The organization of the text

Quite simply, the remainder of the book is divided into three parts. Each of these is introduced by a brief introductory section which spells out the direction which the discussion will take, chapter by chapter, by sketching the main themes to follow. The introductions to Parts Two and Three also provide an outline summing up the overall discussion up till that point thereby linking the parts together and reminding the reader of the overall theme of the book as outlined above. Part One deals with three major global transformations and tries to show how they, and the actions undertaken by the agencies caught up in them, are more often than not mutually entangled. It also works through some of the main concepts, concerns and arguments developed so far by globalization theorists and offers a brief critique which is taken up and explored much more thoroughly in Chapter 6. Part Two deals with local lives, first, by considerably expanding the argument outlined in Section 1.2 on the continuing power of the local, second, by exploring a range of case studies which illustrate how and why most people remain socially and culturally embedded within their class, regional, national, locational or other milieu and finally by considering why those who do sometimes look outward to the world are driven primarily by their need to protect their local lives. Part Three consists mostly of one chapter and is highly tentative and exploratory. Nevertheless, it does take up and flesh out the discussion outlined in 1.3 and explores certain issues relating to globality and the prospect for a more meaningful world society – capable of acting at times for itself – which have not so far received much attention from some global thinkers while returning out attention to the equally neglected key role often played by of micro-actors and interpersonal relations in globalizing processes.

Part One

Global Transformations

Introduction to Part One

If there is one single idea that not only academics but also journalists, politicians, artists, celebrities and other public figures convey when talking about globalization, it is that the lives of people everywhere are becoming increasingly interconnected. Robertson famously referred to this process as the compression of the world (Robertson 1992). It is as if once separate social entities and actors are being increasingly squeezed together and are increasingly weaving dense webs of social ties and practices that cross social and geographical space. Here, the activities, needs and concerns of people everywhere are increasingly drawn together whether through the possibility of collaborative activities conducted over great distances, the enactment of concrete interactions and agendas or the shared burden of problems and experiences which intrude into the lives of people everywhere irrespective of territorial borders and ethnic or national loyalties. Held, McGrew, Goldblatt and Perraton (1999: 17–26) refer to the extension across distance but also the intensity and the accelerating speed with which social activities are being connected together as key attributes of globalization. When all three of these are high and increasing across all 'the domains or facets of social life from the economic to the cultural' then we find 'thick globalization' (21) as has been the case during the past two decades. As Beck (2006: 110) suggested, the other side of the coin to this process of growing interconnectivity is that 'the nation is leaving the container... The problem is not boundarylessness, but that boundaries are no longer being drawn solely along national lines'.

Chapter 2 unravels some of the most telling conceptual ideas and debates developed by leading theorists of globalization in their attempt to make sense of these central realities of globalization. Indispensable, rigorous and illuminating as this theorization has become, some of the arguments are open to criticism or re-evaluation. Accordingly, the final section of Chapter 2 and much of Chapter 6 attempt to open up these aspects of globalization theory to further scrutiny.

In Chapters 3, 4 and 5 we apply some of the theoretical material examined in Chapter 2 while drawing strongly on recent empirical material wherever possible. In these three additional chapters we then explore the impact of four overlapping yet very different transformations which have become central forces in our everyday lives: the rise of an increasingly integrated global economy, the growing migration flows mainly from the Global South to the developed nations, the rise and consolidation of transnational organized crime and the worldwide threat of terrorism. Each of these transformations, in turn, is being steered by a particular set of leading agents: denationalized capitalists, who can be said to form a transnational capitalist class (Sklair 2001), mostly rather poor and relatively unskilled migrants – though some are increasingly better educated – transnational criminal gangs and the worldwide webs being spun by those involved in some terrorist networks.

Drawing on Bourdieu's work (1990, 1993 and Bourdieu and Wacquant 1992) we can say that each of the four transformations and the activities they engender constitutes and creates a field of global power relations governed by its own rules of the game and specific goals. Thus, the actors involved in each of these fields are disposed to seek out particular spheres of activities and geographical regions of operation. They also try to convert one kind of resource into others that compensate for any deficits or insecurities which threaten the success of their activities. Examples of the latter might be the money laundering needs of criminal gangs – finding legitimate business niches for dirty money – or when poor economic migrants draw on their social capital in the form of assistance provided by kinship groups, village affiliation or wider ethnic/national affiliations as a route to overcoming poverty and their lack of economic resources (Faist 2000). But the actions undertaken by these agents frequently generate consequences, sometimes unintentionally, which penetrate relentlessly into our lives. In doing so they either create new insecurities and risks or help to sharpen or worsen existing ones. While these common dangers bind all humans together through ties of mutual interdependency, they also bring new, or intensify earlier, crises and conflicts. Thus, global economic life creates a situation where we are competing against each other for access to jobs and income security, for a share of dwindling facilities such as living space in urban slums (Davis 2006), or for water, oil and environmental safety and other scarce resources. Alternatively, by bringing our lives into close conjunction they have the potential to exacerbate existing misunderstandings and cultural meanings, as in the case of mass migration.

Of course, in the recent past other agents pursuing their own agendas also helped to create a stage on which these four sets of players could operate more effectively. Especially important here has been the role played by an increasing number of governments and national political elites in successfully creating the basis for state-led modernization and industrialization programmes. As new countries move in this direction and the productivity of their workforces rise so more and more people become sufficiently wealthy to expand the worldwide demand for goods and services, the proportion of humanity living in poverty in some countries falls and the variety of commodities available for enjoyment, by those who can afford them, increases. Yet, at the same time, as economic competition and trade rivalry intensify they bring the risk of greater employment insecurity for many and/or the feeling of being excluded from the global feast where government failure or unfair trade regimes marginalize rather than empower large numbers of less fortunate individuals. Some governments and political elites have also acted in ways that enlarged the stage on which our leading global agents operate because for 30 years they have deliberately implemented policies which were intended to deregulate capital, trade and investment flows, reduce the state's involvement in economic life, undermine the employment security and social entitlements which workers had won in the preceding period while at the same time increasing the restraints on labour's capacity to organize effectively (Standing 2007). Such state managers have been supported increasingly by a range of professional and political officials exercising influence through membership of various IGOs, INGOs and international think-tanks.

A further source of governmental or state agency originates in the system of international relations existing between sovereign nation-states. Here, each state guards its territory, tries to raise revenue from the movement of goods across its borders and is managed by deeply embedded laws, institutions and professions – the national police forces, customs and security organizations but also lawyers, accountants and other experts. Each of the latter, in turn, is governed by its own traditions, rules and customs, grounded in national history and long-established practice and tied into internal, hierarchical power systems and promotion structures. Consequently their members often find it difficult to collaborate with counterparts in other countries even where the increasingly transnational nature of environmental problems, financial disorder and disease but also crime, terrorism and migration flows, and the problems these generate, urgently require such collaboration.

However, there are additional causal influences feeding into globalization which are less often noticed and these are being driven by yet other agencies. Here, we might note the role played – again unwittingly – by the mass of ordinary citizens throughout the world. Here, whether as employees worried about their jobs, consumers buying cheap, smuggled and/or prohibited goods, culturally concerned 'natives' persuaded that migrant flows threaten the integrity of their national culture or second/third generation migrants who feel divided in their loyalties as between the host and their parent's homeland, many non-elite citizens make choices and engage in actions that also shape the global economy and enlarge the stage on which our four leading agents perform. The life choices made by numerous ordinary individuals living in the Global North in respect to family size also have unintended consequences because it creates a growing world demographic imbalance between the growing populations of many developing countries alongside the stagnant or falling numbers now evident in most of the highly developed nations.

Each of our leading agents of globalization, capital, migrants, criminals and terrorists is propelled by his/her own peculiar dynamics and demonstrate unique and evolving characteristics. Yet, equally, all are being driven by common causal forces and the worldwide contradictions these generate to a quite remarkable extent. In Chapters 3, 4 and 5 we identify and elaborate on these: neo-liberal ideology; the role of governments in pushing this and other policies; recent technological changes, particularly the revolution in ICTs; the end of the Cold War and its aftermath, including the huge increase in the potential supply of workers available to capital; intensifying world trade competitiveness linked to the widening web of rival industrializing nations, not least China and India, with their huge populations; and the growing tensions generated by the relative marginalization of large number of people particularly, though not only, those living within the least economically successful countries. Finally, each of these chapters explores some of the most interesting ways in which the needs and activities of these agents are becoming increasingly entangled and interdependent even while each retains certain unique features and trajectories.

Theorizing Globalization: Linking the World

2

In order to explore the origins, nature and consequences of the interconnectivities central to globalization we need to investigate some of the key concepts which different theorists have developed to identify and then explain both the intrinsic character of globalization processes and the ways in which these impinge on our lives. In doing so we soon find that there are different ways of thinking about globalization. Moreover, each author tends to construct or apply their own theoretical 'take' on the subject. Yet as Urry (2003: 15) suggests, the global 'is so immensely complicated that it cannot be "known" through any single concept or set of processes'. Bearing this advice very much in mind the discussion now works through some of the most important and interesting concepts provided by global theorists as vehicles for understanding this multidimensional phenomenon we call globalization.

Not surprisingly, some of the concepts we discuss, and their application by theorists, have been subjected to critical scrutiny. We examine these arguments in considerable detail in Chapter 6. For the time being, however, the concluding section takes the theme of interconnectivity – the central focus of this chapter – and reappraises it critically in the light of the book's main theme: namely, that people continue to live local lives despite, and perhaps partly because, of globalization.

2.1 The de-territorialization of social life

In the view of many theorists (for example, Scholte 2005) the central experience of life under globalizing conditions involves but also requires the diminished significance of place, geography, territory and borders. Indeed our understanding of spatiality and time are said to undergo a fundamental transformation because in effect time-space compression (Harvey 1989) shrinks distance and seems to accelerate the pace of events. More specifically, it has become possible to lift some social relations and exchanges out of particular locations while making them less dependent than formerly upon affective bonds to continuously co-present others, interacting in close physical proximity. Instead, such relationships can and are being formed and extended both spatially across distances and borders and qualitatively, in the sense that they may involve interactions with people we may never or rarely meet, who are from national or other backgrounds very different from our own and/or with whom we might share only a one-dimensional economic or cultural interest. At the same time this expanding possibility of forging diverse and multiple relationships across space also means that our lives are becoming mutually entangled. Thus, the social practices, meanings and needs of people living in their own unique geographical, cultural and political settings, increasingly encroach on the lives of distant others and vice versa.

This extension of social relations out of the immediate social and local is not new but was increasingly enhanced during the era of capitalist modernization from the late eighteen century onwards and for the most part within the territorial scale encompassed by the nation-state. Giddens' (1990) trio of concepts designed to illuminate this transformation in social life highlight the processes which not only made modernity possible but which also underpin de-territorialization and globalization. Time-space distanciation increased the capacity of humans to experience events in time and space separately from each other and to disconnect them from concrete places. It also became possible to disembed social relations from their former and virtually complete dependence on face-to-face interactions with concrete individuals through the increased use of symbolic tokens, expert systems and impersonal knowledge coupled to new forms of communication. Alongside these, social actors attained a certain reflexivity such that they were better able to gauge and if necessary alter their behaviour in the light of its impact on others and more capable of reconstituting incoming knowledge rather than merely interpreting it along the guidelines indicated by tradition. Of course, the historical extension of the capitalist relations of production across the world also contributed massively to making possible the increasing de-territorialization of socio-economic life, driven as they were by the compulsions of profit, the conflicts between labour and capital and continuous waves of technological changes rippling across the world.

The effects of de-territorialization

The overall result of these often taken-for-granted and overlapping transformations associated both with modernity and capitalist modernity have been many but in respect to globalization the following are especially significant. First, a great deal of economic life has been released from 'reciprocal exchange' (James 2005: 207) where cooperation between individuals worked because they were known and bound to each other through particularistic ties. Instead, such processes have been massively supplemented and increasingly replaced by an increasing volume of 'disembodied' yet 'patterned' and 'material' social relations capable of being extended, synchronized and coordinated over vast distances (James 2005: 207). Accordingly, a largely impersonal and abstract money-based economy, driven by capital's need to compete, but also by the information and images increasingly projected through and by 'networks of electronic communication' (201), is now said to provide the main – though not the only – basis for global economic life.

Second, many additional activities, not just economic ones, now operate as if distance or territorial belonging does not matter. Among these are mundane activities such as simply making telephone calls to friends overseas or joining Internet chat rooms with people across many countries. But practices and relations in many other spheres of human activity also now take place over distance with relative ease. Thus, political campaigns, shared lifestyle activities or family and friendship concerns, rituals or events are stretched through multiple spaces and places.

Third, it is not only social, cultural, political and economic relations and organizations which have been partly liberated from embeddedness in particular locations and affiliations. In fact, a growing number of more amorphous or generalized phenomena such as climate change and the spread of environmental wastes, the risk of nuclear annihilation or the spread of financial chaos from one nation or economic sector to others through instantaneous, computerized money markets, now encompass human beings irrespective of territory and as if the world was a single place (Scholte 2005).

Fourth, the concept of de-territorialization goes a long way towards enabling social theorists to jettison methodological nationalism. This is the formally entrenched tendency within the social sciences and nationalist discourses to define social relations within a 'state-centric epistemology' (Brenner 1999: 47) and to regard them as confined within a 'parcelized, fixed and essentially timeless geographical space'. In this way of thinking, territorial space was also seen as static and naturally determined rather than historically and socially constructed.

Fifth, the shift towards de-territorialization has also enabled capitalism and human activities generally to become extended across 'multiple geographical scales' (Brenner 1999: 43). In similar vein, a range of thinkers (for example, Amin 2002a, Basch, Schiller and Blanc 1994, Castells 1996 and Sassen 2002 and 2007) have pointed to the increased significance of alternative and reconfigured spatial forms and geographical networks that do not require territorial enclosure to operate. Among these are global city regions, transnational migrant networks and spatially optimized transnational industrial complexes. All these are explored in later chapters. Here alongside the familiar 'nested scales' (Sassen 2007) extending vertically through the local, subregional, national and supranational, but pivoted centrally around the authority and logic of the nation-state and the idea of the geographical as forming a container, we find proliferating horizontal extensions of social practices. These criss-cross territorial boundaries and may involve the pursuit of agendas not confined within the scope of national rules and meanings. They enable the actors involved to juggle relationships and agendas that are simultaneously grounded in their immediate micro-situations and neighbourhoods but which also extend to far away places across the world.

Contrasting experiences: disconnected contiguity and simultaneity

One mundane consequence of living in this way is that curious anomalies often arise. For example, people may live in close physical proximity to a large number of people, perhaps the co-occupants of a large block of flats. But despite being only a few metres away from many others, they may actually know almost no one in the block, nothing about their lives and hardly ever speak to them. This situation is especially likely in large urban areas where there is a high turnover of people including individuals attached to numerous small or large ethnic-migrant groups, including some very recent arrivals, but probably other strangers, too. These might include students seeking cheap, temporary accommodation and perhaps an exotic, cosmopolitan location in which to live for the time being, those who are old and isolated – left behind when friends and relations died or moved away – or the young professional, renting a room temporarily so as to be close to work. Albrow refers to this condition as 'disconnected contiguity' (1996: 157) because despite their physical proximity many in such a locality experience little or no social interaction with any one else. Their social lives 'scarcely touch each other' (1997: 51) and indeed may have become almost cut adrift from physical co-mingling of any kind. Yet at the same time these same individuals may participate in a rich and varied set of friendship networks spread across the world to, and with, whom they write, phone, email and visit as often as possible.

   Last, the reality of de-territorialized social relations also changes how we experience time. Partly this is because the compression of space appears to speed up temporal events and crowd in more happenings and items. In addition, electronic communications mean that more and more actions can be and are synchronized; that is, they take place more or less instantaneously in real time as with world news satellite coverage, the use of the Internet or the sale of debts or currencies through the world's linked money markets. Scholte (2005: 61) suggests that these two trans-world phenomena whereby events and connections occur both simultaneously and instantaneously also constitute qualitatively distinctive and new features of contemporary globalization which are equally as significant as supraterritorial relations. At a more personal level, our own capacity to stretch our relationships across the world means that we may become exposed to a far wider range of stimuli and more knowledgeable about a multiplicity of happenings than previously. This, coupled to our experience of the simultaneity of events and interactions, may encourage us to feel that we are living in a global village (McCluhan 1962) or one world. Certainly, and according to Anderson (1983), something very analogous to this helped to give rise to modern popular nationalism during the past two centuries because along with the establishment of universal educational systems, citizens were exposed every morning and evening to the same information from newspapers and later from radio and television reminding them of their shared history, institutions, problems and cultural uniqueness.

2.2 Global flows and scapes

Globalization processes also penetrate and connect social relations through the images and messages moving in and out of people's personal life spaces brought by a kaleidoscope of informational and cultural sources. At times the proliferation of influences and experiences they bring seem bewildering. Of course, modernization processes have been altering social life and individual subjectivity profoundly for some time. According to Berger and Kellner (1973: 63) modernity transformed social orientations because it meant that we no longer shared a 'common life world' constructed around multiplex social loyalties. Instead, we experience a 'plurality of life worlds' (62) and must constantly cope with 'widely discrepant...meaning systems' (75) and continuous changes which may create a feeling of 'homelessness' (77). However, globalization has further radicalized this subjective experience of a disjointed and homeless existence because it has massively increased the life worlds available to us (Magatti 1999).

Cultural fragmentation

One very evocative way of thinking about this exposure to new information and cultural experiences of all kinds can be gleaned from Appadurai's (1990, 1991) influential work. He suggested that globalization brings different 'scapes' which move across our line of vision, penetrate our consciousness and so enter our individual life worlds. These scapes flow around the world in a fragmented and disjointed way. Also, they do not neatly overlap, interrelate or move with equal force as they might have done in the previous age of nation-state led modernity. Indeed, today's nation-states are often weakened by scapes since while governments may seek openness to global technology, finance and tourist flows as valued resources fuelling economic growth, they may in other respects feel threatened and try to control other incoming flows such as ideas concerned with human rights, religious freedom or the rights of minorities to a degree of political autonomy (Appadurai 1990: 304–6). Moreover, all societies contribute to these global scapes, albeit unequally, so that models of the Western centre always dominating the subaltern, non-Western periphery are no longer valid. But, while the movement and disjuncture brought by scapes intensify cultural fragmentation and unevenness they also feed the imaginations of individuals and groups, for example global youth, and enable them to construct different 'imagined worlds' (Appadurai 1990: 296) or landscapes. By drawing from this moving repertoire of bits and pieces, which have often become detached from other people's lives, experiences and cultures, we can weave criss-crossing patterns of meaning.

Scapes may be carried by ethnic communities, probably through migration as ethno-scapes. They also travel in other forms. Finance-scapes involve the stocks, shares, currencies, derivatives and other financial instruments relating to debt and money liquidity coursing through global computerized electronic circuits. Techno-scapes bring the ever-changing need to adapt to evolving work processes but also innovations. Idea-scapes carry various discourses including that of human rights, democratization and neo-liberal economic individualism. However, the power of media scapes (Appadurai 1991) is probably the most intense and all-pervasive and they reach into virtually every geographical and experiential nook and cranny, rupture boundaries and bring fragments from different cultures and societies into constant juxtaposition. Because, the penetrative impact of the global mass media are so considerable it has become impossible for us to inhabit entirely localized worlds even if we wish to do so. Moreover, the media create a situation where 'fantasy is now a social practice' offering the possibility of imagining alternative ways of living (Appadurai 1991: 192). Thus, stirred by the mass media, even the lives of those trapped in the most demeaning and impoverished circumstances are now no longer experienced as 'mere outcomes of the givenness of things' (192). Migration in search of one or other of these imagined alternatives might be a direct result of such exposure and personal imagining.

In addition to our constant exposure to symbolic and alternative life worlds through migration flows and the mass media, the images of exoticity spread through worldwide 'consumption scapes' (Kenway, Kraack and Hickey-Moody 2006: 107) also provide rich resources from which to create imagined landscapes. Often these are attached to 'branded products and advertising' (Urry 2000: 185). All of this is readily found in every shopping precinct and mall, department store, eBay web site, magazine and glimpsed in every film and TV programme. Such worldwide experiences are said to also enable people to think of 'themselves as global' (Urry 2000: 185). In addition, the visuality of the global made possible by physical-bodily, media and virtual forms of travel (Szerszynzki and Urry 2006: 127) has become an additional, powerful, potential transmitter for spreading various cultural messages as well, perhaps, as cosmopolitan 'ways of thinking and perceiving'.

New cultural spaces and a nomadic life

Although cultures may never have possessed the degree of solidity and firm attachment to localities once attributed to them by some social scientists, there seems little doubt that they have become much less coherent than formerly. Everywhere, as Friedman (1994) argued, the items making up the global mosaic of cultures are leaking into one another and losing whatever distinctiveness they might have once possessed. Much of this is due to the fact that cultures have become unmoored from particular and familiar places and thrown into the maelstrom of the 'global post-modern' (Hall 1992: 302) – or de-territorialization. Globalization also generates 'new spaces' where cultures clash and mix both across and within nations (Featherstone and Lash 1999: 1). Similarly, national cultures are breached by diverse inward migrations so that several cultures then coexist in a given territory. Meanwhile, other transnational cultures are increasingly extending 'over large spaces without covering them completely' especially those defined by a strongly professional, business, scientific, artistic or political ethos though some national identities with a long diasporic history such as Jewish culture also belong in this group (Friese and Wagner 1999: 106). According to Welsch (1999), so profound have been the changes brought by cultural flows and scapes that we need to jettison the idea of interculturality and multiculturality since both presume we still live in a world of separate and internally coherent cultural 'islands or spheres' (197). Instead, there is trans-culturality characterized by 'mixes and permeations' (197) and the continuous 'interpenetration', overlapping and interconnecting of cultures through 'external networking'. Meanwhile, worldwide communications technology means that all information is 'identically available' everywhere and no cultural item can be either 'absolutely foreign' or exclusively owned any longer (198). With fragments of every culture implanted everywhere, hybridization also become inevitable and commonplace.

Additional possible consequences of living a life constantly exposed to scapes and flows are that sociality is based both on proximity and distance, presence and absence and it is simultaneously place bound and mobile. In addition, the flowing, networked, fluid and unmoored nature of much human experience under globalizing conditions and the reality that we are never completely rooted to one location, life world, identity or set of influences has prompted some sociologists and other commentators to refer to contemporary life as nomadic. Certainly, different kinds of migrants, but also seasonal workers, exchange students, backpackers and those whose work requires frequent travel, are less likely than formerly to have fixed, permanent attachments to particular places. Accordingly, they may end up with several place identities of varying degrees of significance. Driven by poverty and prejudice, first generation poor migrants are especially likely to build replica ethnic enclaves in the host society of their family and village life at home while constructing multifaceted transnational networks linking home and host society together (for example, Basch et al. 1994 and Vertovec 1999 and 2001). Thus, they live bi-local or bi-focal lives richly embedded in both situations. Yet other migrant communities maintain such transnational connections with relatives and other nationals dispersed over several countries and therefore conduct poly-local or poly-focal lives. Increasingly many other social collectivities – people who retire abroad, professionals employed by transnational corporations (TNCs) who rotate between companies based in several countries (Bozkurt 2006), people involved in cross-national marriages, artists and others – also negotiate such bi- or poly-local lives. An alternative way of viewing these social arrangements is to say that those involved build 'third spaces' (Pries 2001: 23) existing 'above and beyond the social contexts of national societies' and live unfixed and transnational lives (Featherstone 1990: 8, Ong and Nonini 1997: 11).

However, even without real physical or bodily mobility many people are exposed to so many flows of ideas, information, images, competing commitments and so on that, in effect, they have become nomads – forever searching and experimenting. Even when we are stationary, the world around us is swirling, flowing in all directions. The following quote from Beck's work (2000a: 74) evokes well the idea of the nomadic life brought by globalization:

> One's life is no longer tied to a particular place; it is not a staid, settled life. It is a life 'on the road' (in a direct and transferred sense), a nomadic life, a life in car, aeroplane and train, on the telephone and Internet, a transnational life media-supported and media-stamped.

The following brief extract based on the personal reflections of an Indian-born journalist contemplating the impact of a life spent in frequent travel also captures this theme perfectly:

> It is hard not to think that such quick transitions bring conflicts, and sometimes illusions that we haven't confronted before...the planes on which I travel are full of management consultants and computer executives and international aid workers and tribal backpackers who fly much more than I do...And what complicates the confusions of the Global Soul is that, as fast as we are moving around the world, the world is moving around us. (Iyer 2001: 27)

However, many others gain little or no advantage from the nomadic nature of global life. As Bauman (1998: 2–3) vividly reminded us, remaining 'local in a globalized world is a sign of social deprivation and degradation'. Moreover, globalizing influences supposedly undermine the ability to provide the meanings which localities could once provide. Thus, the mobilities which are central to globalization bring new freedoms to some but also put 'a new gloss on the time-honoured distinction between rich and poor, the nomads and the settled, the "normal" and the "abnormal"'.

Last but not least, Albrow (1997) outlined an additional way in which our exposure to a nomadic life of mobility and flows may impact on our lives. He suggests that we can conceptualize the totality of relations each person experiences under global conditions – spread over several places and distances and operated through various modalities, co-present, virtual and imagined – in terms of a sociosphere. Each person's sociosphere may incorporate many different kinds of people from a variety of situations. Also, many included in it may not know each other. Thus, our school and university friends probably are not the same and these, in turn, probably have no contact with the work friends made during a two-year period of employment in Australia, or while completing our studies on a student exchange scheme in Italy. Similarly, few if any of our present neighbours, work colleagues and weekend leisure friends will have ever met any members of the preceding groups. Given the apparent dispersed, flowing and mobile character of global life and the reality that to a greater or lesser extent the thinning down of social collectivities, including 'society', leaves each individual exposed to their own unique and constantly changing concatenation of experiences and contacts, the concept of sociosphere is an especially valuable one in helping us understand and explore the diverging and sometimes chaotic nature of contemporary experiences.

Albrow also adapted Appadurai's (1990) theory of scapes and added another to the original repertoire: namely the notion of 'socioscapes' (1997: 52–4). Wherever a cluster of individuals, each with their own sociosphere, happen to collect together in a particular locale we encounter a series of probably disconnected flows of social life. Together these form a social situation which perhaps most closely resembles a cavalcade – or a temporary conjuncture of people, incidents and passing emotions – rather than a dense, overlapping set of social interactions capable of invoking or sustaining permanent, shared meanings and affiliations. Examples of such situations might be people eating lunch in a café, those attending the same pop concert or the mélange of students, seasonal workers and multi-ethnic occupants streaming out briefly from several nearby blocks of apartment buildings to shop twice a week in a city street market. Interestingly, the places where socioscapes are most likely to occur probably share similar characteristics. Thus, Auge (1995; see also Ritzer 2004: 39–42) claimed that modern citizens spend an increasing amount of their time in supermarkets, train stations, airports, shopping malls and department stores, train waiting rooms and platforms, cinema queues and buses. He refers to such locations as non-places because they are emptied of any authentic, deep, community content which traditional places may once have contained, they are mass-produced, only suitable for very temporary sojourns and are unlikely to engender permanent or meaningful relationships among those who linger in their vicinity.

2.3 Managing spatiality – the power of networks

Writing on the topic of how geographers and others think about globalization, Massey (2005) summarized succinctly the main tenor of our discussion so far when she suggested that it 'calls up a vision of total unfettered mobility'. Moreover, in 'place of an imagination of a world of bounded places', as during the era of nation-state led modernity, 'we are now presented with a world of flows. Instead of isolated identities, an understanding of the spatial as relational through connections' (81). But in referring to the theme of spatiality and how we experience it with globalization she also highlighted an under-lying theme which has been weaving in and out of the analysis so far. Thus, she continued by arguing that the 'very word "globalization" implies a recog-nition of spatiality. It is a vision which in some sense glorifies...in the triumph of the spatial (while at the same time speaking of its annihilation)' (81–2).

Re-conceptualizing spatiality

There are many difficulties involved in re-conceptualizing spatiality and geog-raphers, perhaps more than sociologists, have found this task especially com-pelling but also theoretically demanding given the nature of their discipline as the study of how all aspects of social and natural life map onto and interact with the physical characteristics of the earth. In Chapter 6 we place conceptu-alizations of the global and local under a critical microscope and particularly notions of space and place. But for the moment it is useful to think about networks and their relevance to globalization by seeing them in the context of discussions about spatiality. This is because the idea of networks provides one of the possible escape routes out of the complex theoretical wrangles over the changing character of spatiality. At the same time they offer another way of understanding how social life operates when practices and meanings are apparently no longer confined to concrete relations and localities but are sometimes stretched between actors living in different places.

Amin's (2002a) thinking on these questions is particularly revealing. Drawing on the work of other theorists, he argued that we should stop thinking about space and place as separate entities, tied to different physical locations or territories. Similarly, it is not helpful to think about global con-nectivity as something which takes place within different territorial containers. Instead, we need to think about places 'as nodes in relational settings, and as the site of situated practices' (391) where social actors engage in and experi-ence a multiplicity of changing relationships, activities and feelings – of greater or lesser permanence – and requiring affiliations both to actors far away and others living in the same vicinity. But this, in turn, suggests that place rela-tionships may involve both presence and absence, proximity and distance at the same time. Moreover, as entities which are always being constructed and reconstructed through human action, place and space do not possess any onto-logical meaning in their own right but only that generated by the actors and social practices emplaced within them.

Putting all this together, Amin (2002a) suggests that under globalizing conditions networks are hugely significant because they enable us to 'make space' (390) work for us by linking different agencies, localities and sets of social practices in different ways. Indeed, globalization can be regarded as 'an energized network space' (395) characterized by the growing interdependence and connectivity of a constantly changing mélange of people and organiza-tions operating in many localities. At the same time, Amin (2002a) was clear that places have become so open and penetrated by flows and networks that it is no longer possible to distinguish meaningfully 'between local and global' situations or experiences. He used the following example to illustrate this point. Worker and migrant groups in cities have the potential to form political associations in allegiance with NGOs to campaign together over improved working conditions and legal rights. However, all the parties combining to pursue such activities, especially migrants and NGOs, are probably 'relying on international financial and other support networks' (388) as part of their strategy. In this situation, therefore, it makes little sense to identify these groups and their relationships as either 'local' or 'national' when in reality their actions and relations extend well beyond these situations (see also Sassen 2004).

Box 2   The debate on the causes of growing inequality in global cities*

One of the key debates on global cities arose originally from Sassen's 1991 argument that global cities were places of endemic inequality and growing socio-spatial polarization.

- The relative shift towards a high-service economy had led to the expansion of financial, managerial and specialized professionals serving global capital.
- In most Western cities, traditional manufacturing employment and sectors such as dock work have declined accompanied by the movement of skilled and semi-skilled native workers out of the city. Many small and medium local businesses have also disappeared as land prices rose.
- An expanding upper middle class and their employers needed high-quality housing, entertainment and company and private domestic services. This generated a demand for low-service jobs requiring few skills: cleaning offices, hotels, streets or the metro, but also domestic workers to look after the houses, gardens and children of two-career professional families. These jobs were increasingly filled by migrants. Meanwhile, middle-class jobs shrank.
- The skills of global elites are crucial to company profitability and presuppose high levels of education so they command salaries reflecting their scarcity value. But there is an abundance of low-grade service workers given the pressures propelling people to migrate. Also, many are women and undocumented entrants vulnerable to racism and police harassment (Sassen 2007, chapter 4).
- Last, not only did this skewed economy lead to growing inequality but also to the concentration of the privileged in preferred housing localities which created gentrification and rising land prices in certain areas and pushed the poorer groups into run-down city areas. Consequently spatial segregation was accompanied by social polarization.

Other researchers such as Hamnett (2003) and Vaattovaara and Kortteinen (2003), writing about London and Helsinki, argued that recent occupational changes were due less to globalization than the huge growth of a high-level business and professional class linked to the rise of symbolic knowledge economies. Thus, by 1999 business and professional services accounted for virtually one-third of all employment in London's 'post-industrial city'. This was a higher proportion than for any other occupational sector and was four times larger than manufacturing – a complete reversal of the situation in 1961 (2003: 2404). The very similar occupational transformation in Helsinki was linked to Finland's emergence as a world-class leader in IT businesses.

However, recent research on London (May, Wills, Datta, Evans, Herbert and McIlwaine 2007) found considerable evidence for Sassen's theory. Thus, since the early 1990s immigration into the city has increased sharply. By 2005 more than a third of London's working-age population were foreign born – higher than for New York. Moreover, jobs at this lowest end of the pay range grew substantially alongside those at the top level and this gap has been largely filled by migrants. For example, up to 60 per cent of London's jobs in hotels and restaurants are carried out by foreign-born workers, while nearly half of cleaning work, refuse collection, labouring and domestic services are also undertaken by these groups. In general, wages are very low, especially in catering and hospitality, and this largely explains why the native population are reluctant to take these jobs.

Note: * Further discussion of global cities can be found in Box 6 and the beginning of Chapter 7.

Network thinking

Turning briefly to a discussion of networks, it is useful to remember that social networks have been widely studied in their own right. They have also been employed as an analytical tool (Scott 2000) by sociologists and anthropologists, in social psychology and business studies, among other fields. Further, they have always played a central role in social life alongside more solid and possibly enduring social collectivities and institutions such as kinship, church, community or neighbourhood and particularly in modern societies experiencing a deepening division of labour and the rise of more contractual, specialized and dispersed forms of activity. Social networks consist of a collection of nodes and each of these, in turn, marks the social space where two or more members interact. But hubs also form around particular participants or agents who interact with a much larger number of members than their co-participants. In contrast to these highly involved central characters, around which the network might crucially revolve, there may be relative social isolates connected through only one other member. One of the characteristic of social networks which is often of special interest is their degree of connectivity or the density of the relations between members: to what extent do all or most participants know and also interact with each other (close-knit) or alternatively do most relations in the network involve a situation where each member is linked to rather few other participants (loose-knit).

Despite modernization, increased mobility and the tendency for many relations and activities to become de-territorialized because of globalization, a core part of most people's lives continues to revolve around small and fairly dense clusters of relations that exist within locales and among friends, work-mates and neighbours (though they may be involved simultaneously in others that are either relatively loose-knit and/or extended over distance such that co-present interactions are infrequent). Because most people, most of the time, are caught up in these relatively localized and dense networks it is extremely difficult for us to ever hope to meet everyone on the planet or even a tiny proportion of them. Employing Granovetter's (1983) terminology there is nor-mally a very large degree of separation between everyone on the planet (see also Urry 2004). However, if we take into account what Granovetter calls the strength of weak ties there may only be as little as six degrees of separation between everyone – the number of times there needs to be an intermediary link between any two individuals for them to be personally connected to everyone on the planet and vice versa. Such everyday dense and recurring networks, tied mostly to locality and/or long-established friendship groups, permit intensive flows of information that are useful and enjoyable. But much of what takes place is, in a sense, redundant because of its iterative and endlessly recycled nature within the network. Thus, becoming exposed to new items of informa-tion is something that is more likely to occur when people are linked into one or more entirely new networks as a result of meeting a stranger or a distant acquaintance by accident or randomly – for example at a conference, a party, while travelling or on holiday. It seems, therefore, that it is through relative strangers or casual acquaintances rather than close friends that we are most likely to hear about such things as new employment or business opportunities and indeed the possibility of forming additional social links with yet more new people (Granovetter 1983).

Networks and globalization

What, then, is it about networks that enables them to play such a significant role under globalizing conditions and which has made them the buzzword among many global thinkers? Certainly, many scholars of globalization have thought about global life and its possibilities in terms of a network metaphor. This emphasizes the relational character of social life under globalizing condi-tions whereby instead of co-presence, proximity and close affiliation being the pivots around which individuals, associations or organizations construct their life worlds and achieve their goals – though these remain significant – what matters most is becoming and remaining connected to appropriate networks. Here, Castells' (1996) work has been extremely influential. His argument can be summarized in terms of the following linked arguments.

Beginning in California in the 1960s, a technological revolution built up in a cumulative fashion (40–52) which involved the harnessing of a series of advances in the use of certain microelectronic tools, particularly the micro-chip. These made it increasingly possible, at very low cost, to store, process, share and project into social space unimaginably vast amounts of information irrespective of distance. Meanwhile, digitalization made it possible to fuse and interchange information between the various media – visual, aural, numerical, textual and so on. Additional and powerful influences also underpinned these technological changes including neo-liberal economic policies of deregulation, certain geopolitical changes, such as the end of the Cold War and the collapse of the former communist regimes, and the partial opening up of India and China to global market competition coupled to their rapid economic growth since the 1980s and 1990s respectively. Nevertheless, it is this accelerating technical transformation that has contributed more than any other single factor to the consolidation of the symbolic knowledge economy and the rapid rise of services as the main source of employment. But it has also played a key, if not the central, role in the galloping development of an informational society especially the rise of the Internet as perhaps a major form of communication now for many individuals, associations, businesses or governments. It has also contributed to the increasing though uneven spread of the alluring Western model of consumerism as the main path to self-realization for many people. In addition, the post-Fordist restructuring of capitalist businesses since the 1970s, which enabled them to attain greater flexibility and leanness while successfully globalizing their operations, were all partly dependent upon their ability to adopt a more 'horizontal' (Castells 1996: 164), decentralized organizational model. This made it easier for power to be devolved downwards and facilitated networking. However, achieving this substantial move away from their former vertical and hierarchical form of organization was also made very much easier because of the availability of Information and communication technologies (ICTs).

For Castells (1996) this revolution possessed several unique characteristics compared with previous technological paradigmatic shifts. One concerns the reality that whereas inputs of knowledge and information have always been central ingredients in economic and other areas of social life, the feedback loops intrinsic to ICTs enable the former to expand cumulatively thereby generating constant spirals of innovation. Moreover, this process amplifies and extends the scope of human activity so that a 'growing integration' (32) takes place between human minds and machines. 'For the first time in history, therefore, the human mind is a direct productive force, not just a decisive element in the production system' (32). Second, ICTs have obviously hugely magnified and intensified the potential strength of weak social links because it enables the members of localized or dispersed social networks to become more instantaneously, easily and effectively linked than ever before. But it also massively simplifies and eases the process of becoming connected to many other networks if members so wish, for example, through the Internet hubs that have been created during the past 15 or so years. Just one example of the rapid and creative deployment of virtuality is indicated by the fact that according to Friedman (2005: 230) between 2001 and 2005 the daily use of Google rose from 150 million searches to over 1 billion. While it is a characteristic of all networks that they are open and decentralized rather than hierarchical and inclusive, and therefore capable of being extended both geographically and qualitatively by absorbing new members, those enhanced by ICTs are likely to exhibit these features far more strongly. For example, the central relational aspect of networks – that in terms of the possibility of enjoying frequent and intensive interactions with other members distance, even vast distance, matters far less than not being connected at all – is clearly enhanced by electronic communication (Castells 1996: 470). Similarly the likelihood and the opportunities for integrating new nodes and networks, for sharing information among members and a network's capacity to be flexible and to innovate 'without threatening its balance' (470), all improve dramatically.

Third, Castells was quite clear that given their 'light-speeding' operations and their capacity to be highly 'dynamic' (470), networks based on information technology inevitably become the most 'appropriate instruments' for operating in the contemporary world situation irrespective of the type of activity. Consequently they increasingly 'configure dominant processes and functions in our societies' (470) and indeed provide the central architecture and modus operandi for arranging human affairs. Thus, a networking logic and model of operation is evident and advantageous everywhere including in the following fields: the weaving of enterprise webs (Reich 1991 and Castells 1996) by corporations or the professionals who work for them directly or indirectly through the pooling of design and other information across the boundaries of businesses or territories; the transnational social movements constructed by those trying to contest neo-liberal globalization; or the transnational criminal gangs who, despite their continuing dependence on ethnic/national loyalties as the basis of their operations, increasingly benefit from inter-gang collaboration (Castells 1998).

Fourth, electronic communication has become so all-pervasive and essential to human life across so many spheres and locations that Castells claimed 'a new spatial logic' (1996: 378) has become apparent whereby the space of flows takes precedence over the 'historically rooted spatial organization' we experience as the space of place. Similarly, he made the following now widely quoted statement; 'the power of flows takes precedence over the flows of power' (1996: 469). Here, he suggested that the networks made possible by ICTs and the huge volume of information they carry fundamentally dilute and dissipate the social relationships and meanings which could previously be shared by those occupying particular locations or societies. In effect the latter are swallowed up by, and merged into, gigantic information flows such that the origins, motives and ultimate destination of the ingredients being transported cannot be readily determined (see also Massey 1995: 54).

2.4   Global mobilities and global complexity

In view of the previous discussion, Urry's (2000: 2–6 and 22–6) insistence that we need new metaphors and concepts to make sense of contemporary life seems irresistible. Increasingly, therefore, we must rethink the idea that overlaying the intrinsic variation and volatility of all social life and human activity there flourishes a solidity and order provided by structures, systems, permanently internalized values and hierarchies of power which are inherently durable and which social scientists can analyse if they invent appropriate concepts. Similarly, he suggested that in place of spatial metaphors such as region, territory, nation, society, and similar notions which depict social life as more or less containerized, we need ones that point towards the capacity of all phenomena, events and processes, not just human sociality, to continuously flow or roam across the world while negating all territorial borders. Indeed, he insisted that we need a 'mobile sociology' (2003: 59).

Classifying global mobilities

Continuing this line of thought, James' (2005) identification of four kinds of mobility operating in global space is helpful. First, there is the movement of individuals, families and friendship or other groups. Examples would be migrants, tourists, backpackers, professionals working abroad, criminals or terrorists, airline pilots or long-distance truck drivers, sports or fanzine enthusiasts and perhaps political activists interested in various global events. James referred to this as 'embodied globalism' (201) because these connections are established by living people though of course the interpersonal connections they forge may also be supported by other modalities of social engagement especially virtuality or global imaginaries (Steger 2008). In James' view, embodied global activity is important but is no longer 'the defining condition of contemporary globalization' (201).[i] A second mobility concerns the movement of material objects and the means of transporting them across distances – ships, trains, trucks, planes, camels and so on. The goods conveyed might be components, finished goods, machinery, processed or whole foodstuffs or other raw materials such as various metal ores or unrefined oil.

Third, are the movements and alliances formed by powerful agents who represent institutions and organizations and who may belong to various global elites. Examples would be members of intergovernmental organizations (IGOs) such as the World Bank (WB) or World Trade Organization (WTO) or the directors of TNCs and the national participants in summit meetings of the Organization for Economic Co-operation and Development (OECD) or G8 nations. Through their various and sometimes combined actions – for example as members of international think-tanks (Carroll and Carson 2003) or participants in summit meetings of the OECD, G8 nations or the annual convention of the Economic Forum at Davos every January – all these agents contribute to knitting nations and their citizens together through various actions. James' (2005) fourth, and most important, source of mobility, in terms of what ultimately makes global life possible, is 'the movement of abstracted capital and culture through processes of disembodied interchange' (201) – and to which we referred earlier. These flow as images, information and the forms of money and liquidity moving through the global banks, stock, commodity and currency markets and often instantaneously via computers. Together they make it possible for innumerable economic actors who do not know each other personally to engage continuously in tiny or vast reciprocal exchanges, transactions, deals and payments thereby lubricating and sustaining huge volumes of global activity. We return to discuss the implication of this classification at the end of the chapter.

Global complexity, networks and path dependency

The central role of mobility in global life is also inextricably tied up with various kinds of complexity and here the attempt by Urry (2003) to link these together is fascinating. In order to develop his arguments he drew on the complexity theory developed not only by scientists engaged in the study of the physical world but also on the ideas of social scientists. In doing so Urry (2003) suggested that global relations reveal many of the same features of complexity and uncertainty that occur in the natural world. Indeed, and facilitated by the possibilities released by increased mobility, globalization processes probably require and necessarily lead to an ever-increasing range of interconnections between localities, events, individuals and organizations. Moreover, the innumerable agencies implicated in these processes both as recipients and contributors create what he calls 'global emergent properties' (40) whereby something much greater than the sum of the individual or discrete items feeding into this global order is generated. These emergent properties could not have been predicted or intended by the agencies involved. Examples of this would be the uncertainties and volatility of the world economy and environmental change and the de-territorialized nature of many global problems which cannot be said to exist in any single place.

Returning to networks, Urry made an interesting contribution to this theme while showing at the same time how certain types of networking also contribute to global complexity. He argued that the power of any network is largely shaped by its size – the number of nodes it contains – and its density and connections to other networks (52–4). Every time an additional node is added the network's scope increases exponentially. Consequently, networks exert effects that cannot be followed through a linear logic – where change happens in an orderly and incremental fashion. Instead, they can lead to dramatic outcomes as tipping points which were not expected are reached. He gave the example of the fax machine and the mobile phone. Those who adopted them did so initially because they did not wish to be left out of the growing communication loop. But they then discovered that the anticipated advantages were much greater than they had thought, both for themselves and everyone else, because the number of contactable individuals or organizations grew exponentially all the time as new participants joined, including themselves.

Urry (2003: 54–60) also discussed another factor which can magnify the power of certain networks. This arises where sometimes quite minor events or technical changes occur which were not necessarily intended to have any particular long-term influence outside the locale or narrow field of activity where they originated. However, and despite their contingent character, because they occurred at what turned out to be a rather appropriate moment in a sequence of developing socio-technical arrangements, their advantages came to be more widely perceived as beneficial. Thus, their positive feedback effects in one location or activity become widely dispersed and eventually lead to a situation of path dependence. Thus, whole networks of linked organizations and activities become locked into this pathway and come to dominate entire economic sectors, industries or lifestyles along with the institutions, interests and patterns of power which grow up around them. One example he gives here is the rise and rapid dominance of the petroleum-fuelled vehicle industry although equally appropriate and preferable vehicle fuel options existed and could have been developed at the time (55). Expanding on this argument, we know that in the early decades of the twentieth century, petrol-driven vehicles rapidly spawned a vast range of parallel and dependent activities: garages and repair firms, road-building and maintenance, industries producing components and accessories (paints, upholstery, electrical goods and so on) and so on. Similarly, the new industry also generated various business, labour, political and citizen interests while helping to consolidate a range of parallel social changes such as mass suburbanization and the rise of supermarkets.

Globally integrated networks and global fluids

The giant networks, such as those just outlined, will find it easy to interact with others and may form dense webs of nodes and hubs which may increasingly extend globally as well as across regions or nations. Urry (2003: 56–7) referred to these entities as globally integrated networks (GINs). Although they are not without certain vulnerabilities, their sheer size and the scope of the resources they can muster by virtue of their extensive links and connections across the globe gives GINs enormous advantages. These include the capacity to endure, to cope with the uncertainties they encounter and to exercise enormous influence over localized cultures and workforces, governments, IGOs and global opinion. Transnational corporations in all their various forms, including those which follow the business formula described by Ritzer (1993) as 'McDonaldization' – offering standard products, venues and cultural experiences through a worldwide network of largely franchised companies – provide the most obvious examples of GINs. However, organizations such as Greenpeace and Oxfam also belong in this category in that like TNCs they have developed vast worldwide networks of collaborating 'affiliates' and 'partners' as well as effective links to other GINs. These include various United Nations (UN) agencies, IGOs such as the WB, the mass media and other organizations engaged in trying to counter the current world economic system. In addition, they have evolved their own brand with worldwide circulation and which conveys texts, images and skills that are widely recognized and influential everywhere.

Urry (2000) went on to argue that given the flowing, mobile nature of globalization, network thinking cannot always convey the power and distinctiveness of some forms of global mobility. Drawing on the work of several researchers and theorists he argues (2000: 38–9) that some of the flowing quality associated with global processes is better understood in terms of the idea of liquids or fluids. Here he partly employs the description used by Deleuze and Guattari (1988, chapter 1) of certain human activities as tending to spread unpredictably and without any particular starting or ending point, rather like rhizomatic plants. These push horizontally and what appears to be randomly in sometime hidden directions at, near or under the surface of the soil. But by analogy, rhizomatic-like social phenomena 'can be connected to anything other, and must be' (Deleuze and Guattari 1988: 7). Thus, the 'fabric of the rhizome is conjunction "and…and…and"' (25). Urry also employs an analogy with blood and the way it moves along arteries and exudes different degrees of viscosity. Similarly, certain blood corpuscles can diffuse through artery walls and flow into endlessly tiny capillaries. Thus, like blood, global fluids flow in all directions. They spill and leak through and across all borders, they seep and percolate into territories, organizations and networks and they move unevenly and under their own momentum. Basically, they are extremely difficult if not impossible to resist, manage, contain or control, are unpredictable and they may mix with other fluids, join with different entities or spill into empty spaces in unforeseen ways. Moreover, they sometimes move very rapidly and cannot be distinguished easily from other social forms.

Examples would be pop tunes, the signs and symbols which define associations, blueprints and designs, fashions, advertising jingles, brand names and logos, consumer culture, icons, the Internet and the information it carries but also religious sects and social movements and the loyalties, sentiments, imagery and emotions they can engender and which may permeate to the four corners of the world. Above all, these fluids cannot be stopped or channelled along certain paths: rather, they have the capacity to flow and create momentum everywhere. One of the especially interesting examples he provided which demonstrates the often irresistible quality and potential power of global fluids concerns the collapse of communism in the former Soviet Union between 1989 and 1992. For example, as a mass consumer culture became consolidated in the West one of the main difficulties faced by these regimes was how to counter the 'fascination with consumer goods, with distinctions of taste and style and more broadly with shopping as an intensely pleasurable activity' (Urry 2000: 42) among their populations. For those living behind the Iron Curtain, various commodities attained the status of cult products, Western life was increasingly regarded as more enjoyable and travel by families, tourists and smuggling all helped contribute to a growing knowledge of, and desire for, Western life. Ultimately, these regimes lacked the 'social power to stem the inevitable march of goods, services, signs, images and people across some of the most powerfully policed of national borders' (42).

Hybrid agents – human dependence on technologies

As a key part of his argument, Urry (2003) also insisted that most human activity increasingly depends closely on various technologies and this further intensifies but also makes possible global complexity and mobility. Of course, human survival in the face of the natural environment and the ability to engage in various forms of cooperation have always been intimately tied up with our dependence on various technologies both as individuals and collectively. This would include everything from nets and spears to ploughs, boats and windmills although a shared language, norms and rules as well as cooperation constructed around a social and technical division of labour have also been critical. Nevertheless, modernization and now globalization have become predicated upon human actions that rely on an army of technologies to an extent and in ways that were previously unnecessary and indeed impossible. Consequently, global networks 'do not derive directly and uniquely from human intentions and actions'. Rather, humans 'are intricately networked *with* machines, texts, object and other technologies' so that there are no 'purified *social* networks' (Urry 2003: 56, author's italic). This intimate dependence on technologies takes us into the realm of post-social relations where modern and especially global life is literally unthinkable without this capacity to merge with machines. Quite simply, without our cars, mobiles, walkmans, heart-pacing machines, fridges and Internet chat rooms most people could not manage their personal lives nor could we obtain the food and other ingredients essential to everyday life (electricity and water, for example). Similarly, the economy, health systems, government regulation, crime prevention and control, international trade and much else besides could not function at all, and certainly far less effectively, without the computerization and sophisticated transport, communication and surveillance systems we now take for granted.

Among other issues, this human-machine form of hybridity calls into question the relevance of the agency versus structure debate which has been much debated by sociologists and others for decades. Thus, what ever human agency is, it is now inseparable from the role of inhuman hybrids or technologies; it is a joint agency. In the same vein, Urry (2003) described the various 'scapes' (56) which provide the grids and frameworks along and through which various flows of information, images, people, money, brands, values and ideologies, lifestyles and so on can move. Among these scapes he included the following technologies which together make possible the wiring or networking of the world: fibre optic cables, air planes, digitalized binary codes, satellite TV networks, the Internet, credit cards, an array of weapon systems and electric money and stock circuits working through instantaneously integrated banking and market systems.

2.5 Glocalization

One of Robertson's major contributions to global theory has been his analysis of glocalization processes (1995). Here, local and global realities interact and co-evolve through a series of mutual engagements and in response to various human actions. He explained how such processes have been associated with the decisions made by Japanese companies to engage in 'micro-marketing' (1992: 100) by tailoring their export-commodities deliberately to meet the local cultural preferences of the markets they wished to enter. Taking the case of a car, the following modifications might be appropriate: adapting a vehicle for countries where average family size was small, or building-in specifications to suit hot or cold climates, taking account of local colour preferences or even finding a model label that fits in with local cultural preferences. But glocalization also refers to a much larger and more general range of local-global interactive processes. Here, the incoming global – probably a cultural fragment or practice flowing in from another local – is examined by certain social actors, perhaps cultural entrepreneurs, artists or media performers or participants in a particular youth culture. Certain elements of this global experience are then selected on the basis of their appeal and/or relevance to existing cultural preferences and meanings. These appropriated elements are then indigenized or captured and built into existing local experiences. Ultimately, it may become difficult to identify and single out the original imported elements since, in effect, they are now absorbed into and regarded as aspects of the indigenous life world (Friedman 1997). Indeed, glocalization is not new. For example, Robertson (1992: 85–96) explored the case of religion in Japan where centuries before the drive for industrialization the ruling elites and population syncretized indigenous Shinto and shamanist religious practices with imported ones especially from China, India and Korea (94). Then, following the 'introduction of Confucianism and Buddhism an indigenous Japanese religion was "discovered"; and was given the name of Shinto'. No doubt this pragmatism later proved especially useful to modernizing Japan. Thus, after the 1868 revolution and like other modernizing political elites, the Japanese government examined the various institutional models already adopted by countries such as the USA, Prussia and Britain in respect to educational, legal, military and other systems and codes. They then adopted and embedded into Japanese government and society those models which they regarded as most relevant to their existing national culture and as part of their bid for successful industrialization.

Clearly, for all societies the sheer scope of glocalization processes and the number of items and/or experiences where these might occur have grown exponentially with the recent acceleration of globalization: music, food and cuisine, sport practices, health remedies, religious belief and practice, clothing and fashion and the formulation and evolution of abstract knowledge spreading through epistemic and educational communities, and so on. Urry (2003: 84–7) built on this analysis and used it as part of his argument concerning the inherent and growing complexity of global life. Thus, he explored various ways in which glocalization processes can be said to operate continuously. This is not only because new items flow in as well as out continuously but also that the interplay and momentum of evolving interactions may build up over a long period, result in numerous combinations and the process may never be complete. One possibility here is that when apparently new items flow into a given local (local 1), imbricated within them will be elements of local 1's own original culture which were earlier diffused to, and then glocalized by, yet another local (local 2) somewhere across the world. But what returns to the first local society (local 1) in the form of ingredients of its own culture has been altered in the meantime by members of local 2 as they, too, selected, captured and embedded these elements into their own culture and tried to make them their own. The returning elements are not the same as those that originally flowed out. Clearly, in this way of thinking the scope for escalating complexities seems endless.

2.6   The meaning of global interconnectivities for social actors

In different ways all of these concepts and approaches point strongly – and more often than not convincingly – to the reality that globalization leads human affairs in the direction of increasing interconnectivity. The reality that we live in a world of multiple interconnectivities and the interdependencies to which they often give rise cannot be doubted. In Chapters 3, 4 and 5 we examine some of the key agents in global life who play especially prominent roles in spinning these webs that bind our lives together. This includes the elites and organizations who have constructed the global economy as well as international criminal gangs, terrorists and migrants though there are many others whose causal influence is also weighty but whose impact probably stretches less far. However, it is crucial to think through carefully exactly what is involved in talking about global interconnectivities in terms of their actual content, how they operate and their likely impact on the everyday lives of micro-actors. In fact, global interconnectivities assume very different forms but this is mostly ignored by some theorists. This diversity is largely a consequence of their being either propelled or engineered by quite different kinds of agency. Moreover, the degree to which, and the ways, they impact on our lives also varies markedly whether in terms of their sheer global scale, the intensity of the processes that lie behind them, whether they affect some areas of life rather than others or operate intermittently or continuously. All these differences, in turn, help to determine whether and to what extent they are understood by social agents and therefore, what kinds of responses, if any, they are likely to provoke. In short, the global flows into our lives in a number of very different ways and we need to be aware of their likely variable impacts and implications for social actors. Here, we return to James' (2005) classification of global mobilities and deploy it as a useful framework for assessing and critiquing some of the global theory examined above.

1. Comprehending abstract flows.   First, global flows can and frequently do arrive as a series of abstract, disembodied processes (James 2005) especially the power of market competition and the compulsions of money. Certainly, if we lack the means of acquiring the latter, we and our families either die or have to resort to charity, crime, begging or reliance on state welfare. Several points can be made about the all-pervasive but also largely opaque nature of the interconnectivities produced by markets and a money economy. One is that these disembodied and abstract flows bind the fates of individuals and organizations together, creating the possibility of a 'world economy' which is 'a miracle of collective organization' where 'hundreds of millions of people unknowingly collaborate' to 'make it possible' (Harris 1983: 9). Yet, their very scale and complexity also mean that 'no single person can comprehend' them. Accordingly, it seems highly unlikely that most people across the world are able to cognitively grasp the intricate, diverse and multiple workings of these forces even though their everyday lives may be hugely shaped by their operation – for example, such things as job availability, the price of basic commodities or the safety of their savings – and despite the fact that their own micro-decisions and choices as consumers, savers, viewers and so on feed cumulatively into their world wide operation (Kennedy 2007a). Lacking much in the way of a clear understanding of how these forces operate and impact on their lives and divided, moreover, by differences of language, ethnic/national culture, religion, social class, gender, age and generation, it is hardly surprising that many people seem unable to construct shared systems of meaning which might enable them to respond by taking one or other kind of individual or collective action designed to shift the balance of these forces more in their own favour.

Moreover, when individuals do undertake such actions in response to their predicament they are much more likely to direct their anger and opposition at local or nationally based agents who they see as responsible for the chemical spills, rising unemployment, terrorist threats, illegal importation of drugs and other dangers they perceive as existing all around them. Doubtless, too, some political leaders, especially those with extreme right wing agendas (see Box 7) and who are specifically anti-pathetical to global concerns and international affiliations, are not averse to augmenting and crystallizing such fears where they are present among the general population (Liang 2007). For example, writing about the political tactics used by the right wing Flemish Vlaams Blok party, in Belgium, to win popular support, Swyngedouw, Abts and Van Craen (2007: 83–4) referred to this process as jumping scales. Here, global issues such as international migration, transnational crime and terrorism are 'redefined as national or local issues' and 'simplified to the all-embracing populist opposition between insiders and outsiders'. Not only is a local/national frame of reference much easier to comprehend but it is also the educational systems,

media and political processes operating at the national rather than the global
level to which citizens have been socialized into responding and where their
capacity to demand some kind of political accountability mostly lies. In any
case, while these abstract forces do impact on all global citizens, tying their
fates together into common structures and processes, this same integration of
the global economy and world labour market also propels them into a competitive struggle for survival against each other as we will see in Chapter 3.

2. Underplaying the power of leading agents.   Global influences also flow
into our lives as a consequence of the decisions made and strategic organizational actions taken by leading agents acting through and in conjunction
with various technologies but also with the support of certain networks, laws
and policy-making capacities they are able to influence or wield (James 2005
and Scholte 2005). They include governments, corporation directors and
financiers, journalists and other opinion makers, scientists and the members
of other epistemic communities and so on. Here, without doubt, many more
people across the world people do possess some grasp concerning how the
actions and decisions of these agents shape their lives. The rise of various
transnational social movements whose members aim to reform or undermine
globalization processes speaks strongly to this reality as do the micro-decisions
in daily life taken by growing numbers of individuals involving such actions
as engaging in ethical consumption or investment.[ii] Nevertheless, these remain
very much minority activities – though their significance is growing slowly –
and most studies bear this out. Keane (2003: 16), for example, has suggested
that perhaps only around 5 per cent of the world's population 'has an acute
awareness of the tightening interdependence of the world, its ecosystems, institutions and peoples' while another 25 per cent may be 'moderately or dimly
aware'. We consider additional empirical material which points in a similar
direction in Chapter 6.

    Arguably, there is a further difficulty here. As we have seen some theorists
tend to construct a picture of the global as something which is inherently
complex and difficult to control. By definition, globalizing processes cannot
be contained within or by nations and societies but operate across borders and
cultures. The processes involved are multidimensional, unfinished and interact on each other often in unforeseen ways and they are driven partly by and
indeed are intrinsically dependent on a range of technologies and inanimate
substances and entities of enormous power which are governed by their own
unpredictable dynamics. However, this scenario conjured up by theorists seriously underplays the role of the key, powerful human agents indicated above
whose decisions and actions – sometime intentionally and at other times not –
have hugely contributed to the construction and deepening of global processes
and structures. It also overlooks or says little about the many social, economic
and political inequalities which either preceded recent trends, but which globalization has done little or nothing to change, or which are a direct consequence of global changes. These are explored in Chapter 3. There is a danger

here, that if we believe we face such arbitrary and self-governing influences, wielded by a gamut of complex global forces largely beyond our control, then we may give up trying to resist or transform the decisions, ideologies and interests taken by certain leading human agents which have helped to make them happen. This surely plays into the hands of the powerful and has the potential to further enhance their ability to make decisions which consolidate their influence while giving them an excuse for not acting differently on the grounds that global complexity render any actions they might take as largely impotent. It would be ironic and absurd if far from empowering human agents, particularly those who are currently disadvantaged as well as those who struggle to assist them, globalization theory provided an ideological smoke screen behind which the privileged and powerful could defend their own interests while arguing that it would be pointless or impossible for them to change the way they operate.

As Beck (2006: 80) argued:

> [t]alk of 'streams' brackets the extent to which these structure- and boundary-undermining 'streams' themselves define the connection to *agents*, indeed themselves define actor's possibilities of action. The stream metaphor can thereby mislead us into neglecting the analysis of relations of power. (author's italics)

3. The neglect of interpersonal, micro-actions. A third way in which the global crosses into our lives and forges interconnectivities is through the actions of ordinary individuals or, indeed, even those undertaken by powerful elites in their private, informal lives rather than through their capacity as leading members of organizations. As we saw, James (2005) referred to these under the heading of 'embodied globalism' (201). But so far global theorists have mostly ignored micro-actions and their possible efficacy in contributing to globalization or relegated them to a minor role, preferring, instead, to think in terms of abstract generalities, remote processes and the actions of various elites as the key forces producing the overwhelming structural architecture and parameters of global life. Given the significance of such macro-influence in bringing about global transformations this primary focus has been perfectly reasonable and indeed essential. Nevertheless, the impact of micro-relations also deserves attention and may in some respects be more efficacious in generating or sustaining global change. One so far rather neglected area where this might occur concerns those situations where unlike first generation economic migrants, individuals do not merely cross territorial borders but also negotiate and engage in truly intercultural relationships with people with ethnic or national affiliations quite different from their own. Certain kinds of skilled migrants, for example, may find themselves in social situations where this becomes both possible and necessary (Kennedy 2004, 2007b and 2008). In addition to possessing the kinds of skills which equip them to seek and manage encounters with the cultural 'other(s)' they will also probably need linguistic skills[iii].

Currently, the scope of these micro-interconnectivities is small, though growing fast. Nevertheless, given that cross-ethnic and national interpersonal exchanges engender and indeed require recognition, respect and a kind of moral commitment as a basis for attaining mutual understanding, their potential to contribute to a global consciousness may be considerable. Here, obligations are negotiated and rules have to be accepted so that the partners to the relationship become part of each other's social lives. Such intercultural relations do not consolidate or recreate primordial loyalties. Moreover, while the emotions and exchanges that may be sparked off by the messages emanating from the mass media do not require personal responses and commitments from those on whom they impact as a condition for their operation – though these may arise – the opposite is the case with interpersonal relations. Without affectivity, mutual respect and dependency they cannot work. However, where these elements are in place between individuals from different cultures they may enable them to gain deep and empathetic insight into each other's unique personal narratives and ethnic or national knowledge repertoires. We return to this theme in Chapter 9.

2.7   Appraisal

Continuing the critique outlined in the previous section, I am arguing that global theory often fails to engage with the phenomenological lives of the world's multitudes of micro-actors and to take account of the overriding importance to them of the subjective meanings they construct, share and wield in everyday life. But this theoretical and empirical gap at the heart of global studies makes if difficult for scholars and policy-makers to understand the very concrete reasons why the great majority of world citizens often have little understanding of globalization and how it operates. We return to this theme in Chapter 6.

The Global Economy: Fragmented Workers – Mobile Capital

3

In many respects the rise of an increasingly integrated global economy forms the core driving force of change around which other agents, institutions, social movements, businesses and individuals increasingly pivot. Moreover, the leading agents of the global economy are increasingly able to operate not only as if the world was one vast arena where nations and their borders counted for little but, unlike criminals, terrorists and undocumented migrants, they can also do so legally and openly. In this chapter, therefore, we focus on exploring this central phenomenon of a global economy and examine how different observers analyse and evaluate its current and perhaps future implications. In doing so, our key theme can be summarized as follows:

> [t]he world has entered a long transition towards a single global economy and labor market...movement towards a global labor market will put many workers in many countries in a more precarious position than before with capital in the driver's seat. (Freeman 2007: 35–6)

The economic recession that has gripped virtually the entire world since 2007, and which accelerated markedly in the late summer of 2008, is widely regarded as having originated in the crisis of lending and confidence that swept through the linked global financial system. Notwithstanding this situation, the discussion focuses mainly on the changing character of the businesses operating in the 'real' global economy and which provide the main sources of employment for the great mass of workers across the world whether they are engaged in agriculture and fishing, manufacturing, mining or construction, transportation or a vast number of professional or low-skilled non-financial services.

3.1 How far does economic globalization shape our lives?

We begin by placing the arguments pertaining to economic globalization in a broader theoretical and substantive context. This suggests, first, that we need to remember the severe constraints which place limits, and always will, upon the extent to which economic globalization can take place and, second, that there are other strong factors at work in shaping our work lives in addition to the rise of something we might call a global economy.

The limits to economic globalization

On the first theme, several points need to be made. One is that economic globalization is far from being a new or a complete process though it has accelerated and intensified in recent decades. While its impact is increasing, this is nevertheless highly uneven both between regions, countries and social groups and in respect to the benefits and/or disadvantages it is bringing. We say more about this later. Second, taking just one crucial measure of economic globalization, namely, how much of the overall business activity undertaken by TNCs occurs outside their country of origin, we can say that many large businesses remain firmly rooted within and dependent upon local, regional or national resources, workers and markets. In addition, those which do have overseas operations often retain the greater part of their activities within their home nation whether for cultural and linguistic reasons or because the nature of their primary activities depends upon the relatively greater political security on which they can rely at home. Alternatively, investment in business may require secure and continuous access to extremely expensive and advanced infrastructure as well as high-level scientific and technical skills. These may be more readily available and of higher quality in their country of origin.

Thus, even huge corporations vary a good deal in terms of their degree of transnationality. This can be measured for each company by calculating the average of three ratios: its foreign assets as a percentage of total assets and similarly in respect to foreign and total sales and foreign and total employment. What results is a tool for calculating each company's transnationality index. If we then take data from United Nations Conference on Trade and Development's (UNCTAD) most recent table showing the world's top one hundred non-financial TNCs ranked in terms of the amount of their foreign assets, we find that even for the largest companies there is considerable variation in the degree of transnationality (UNCTAD 2007). Although 44 of these TNCs revealed a transnationality index of more than 75, in 18 instances this was less than 50. In addition, Dicken (2007: 125–6) has also shown that while the average transnationality index for the largest 100 TNCs in 1993 was 51.6 (the list of such companies slightly changes over time as some move up the global hierarchy while others move down), this figure had only risen to 57 by 2002. In addition, the degree of transnationality found among companies varies according to their national origins. Thus, companies with a home base in smaller countries such as the Netherlands tend to be quite highly transnationalized but Japanese and, to a lesser extent, American companies are much less so though in both cases this situation is changing. Clearly, cultural and historical factors as well as the availability of national resources can affect the inclination of businesses to spread their operations across the world.

In any case, and third, the fundamental materiality of nature and of humans, the need to find a livelihood and the entanglement in affective, social ties means that even in the case of a highly transnationalized company, every component of its 'production network – every firm, every economic function – is, quite literally, "grounded" in specific locations' (Dicken 2007: 18). Castree, Coe, Ward and Samers (2004) take this argument further when they argue that however much socio-economic relations become global, 'uneven geographical development and local specificity persist' (17). Moreover, despite the desire of some workers to migrate, the ability of firms to become mobile and the reality of time-space compression through the effects of communication technology, 'place still matters for production, reproduction and consumption' (17). Chapter 6 pursues this argument concerning the continuing influence of locality in more detail while extending it beyond those life experiences pertaining to work and economic production.

Parallel influences

Turning to the question of what additional possible explanations there might be for the economic transformation we are currently living through there are at least three major contenders. One concerns the possible impact of technological change on work and employment. This has certainly continued apace during the past two decades, running alongside increasing economic globalization, and has impacted strongly on long-term employment, job security and work experience (see, for example, Beck 2000b, Castells 1996, Lash and Urry 1987 and 1994, Rifkin 1996). Particularly important have been the following: widespread automation and robotization, the increased use of generic machinery – adaptable, long-lasting, lean, sophisticated and programmable – and of course the adoption of information technology across all economic sectors.

Second, in respect to the least developed countries and their populations, economic globalization is not the only reason for their relative failure to attain higher levels of economic growth and reduce poverty levels – despite the more open competitive world economy and heightened mobility of capital that it has brought. Thus, many observers (for example, Chang 2008, Gowan 1999, Stiglitz 2002, Wade 2001) argue that the unfair and skewed trade and financial regimes as well as policy choices that most developing countries have been compelled to accept since 1980 in effect created a world economy which has been biased towards serving the long-term interests of the already developed countries and perpetuating their leading position while saddling the former countries with disadvantages. One example concerns the trade rules imposed by the WTO which allow the rich countries to subsidize their agriculture but not the poor ones so that the former can export farm products at prices well below their real cost while the latter's farmers cannot compete. In fact, even before the rise of neo-liberal economic policies and their imposition on the countries of the South after 1980, the subsidies provided by Northern governments for their farmers tended to fuel vast crop surpluses which then led to falling world prices and the dumping of cheap grains on poorer countries. Then, there is the tendency for the advanced countries to impose steep tariffs on the manufactured goods exported by the developing countries – as they try to increase the value of their output – while exhorting the latter to reduce their trade barriers to Northern imports. Another impediment to development has been the reluctance of the advanced countries, especially America, post-1980, to accept the argument that a country in the early stages of economic development needs to protect its infant industries from foreign competition and endow its own burgeoning businesses with various advantages for a period even though virtually all the advanced countries once engaged in such practices themselves. Boxes 3 and 5 also try to throw some light on these issues.

Third, there is the argument that we are seeing the rise of a less accountable and more predatory form of capitalism compared with the recent past and that this partly explains the rapidly changing and perhaps worsening employment and work conditions experienced by people more or less everywhere. As will become evident, it is very difficult to disentangle this possibility from the reality and impact of economic globalization since both constantly interact and reinforce each other. Nevertheless, and for this very reason, it will be useful to expose this argument concerning the shift towards a much more rapacious capital to a thorough investigation by considering some possible reasons why this might have occurred.

3.2   The turn towards a more predatory capitalism

The argument here is that the needs of shareholders and the rewards due to company directors and managers have taken absolute priority over all other considerations in recent times and certainly compared with the supposed 'golden age' of the welfare state and social democratic government, rising incomes, full employment, strong labour organizations and relatively progressive taxation policies which prevailed across most Western countries roughly from the late 1940s to the mid-1970s. Thus, business leaders now do not hesitate to demand longer hours of work, to reduce the social benefits available to their employees wherever they can, to constantly squeeze and push down wages, to continuously cut employment levels, to reduce the contribution businesses make to social reproduction through tax and to play one workforce against another while showering financial rewards – bonuses, share options, final salary buyouts and very high pay – generously upon themselves and their shareholders. These contrasting scenarios of the rather 'benevolent' capitalist behaviour supposedly typical of many companies during the middle decades of the twentieth century compared with the apparently far more profit-driven and uncaring business mentality of today may seem merely to offer two caricatures of capitalist behaviour which are unreal at best and positively misleading at worst. After all, capitalism has always been driven by competition, the need to respond to market incentives and to maximize profits on pain of economic extinction for those individual firms caught up in its vortex. The key early twentieth-century observer and theorist of America's national-based industrial capitalism, Thorstein Veblen, for example, described and understood US capitalism, even then, as a system driven solely by pecuniary imperatives and therefore as inherently predatory in the sense that it damaged the long-term evolutionary possibilities of socio-economic life and the process of creative technological development (Edgell 2001: chapter 6).

Despite these provisos, there is some concrete evidence suggesting that at least compared with the recent past we are indeed living in an age dominated by a more demanding and less accountable capitalism which persistently heaps huge rewards on a few while conferring limited, if any, additional benefits on the majority. At the same time, there are some solid reasons for arguing that the balance of economic power between labour and capital has swung much more decisively than during earlier eras in the latter's favour.

One startling piece of evidence pointing towards the more rapacious character of today's capitalist economy consists in the fact that inequality has increased dramatically during the past two decades both between and within nations. Rising inequality within nations has been especially evident in the USA and the UK though it is generally the case in many additional countries including Germany and Sweden. According to Atkinson (2005), in the USA, between 1979 and 1999, after-tax, real incomes declined in the case of the poorest fifth of households, rose by only 5 per cent for the middle group of income earners but escalated by 250 per cent for the top 1 per cent of earners (54). In fact more than one-third of the benefits of economic growth during this period accrued to the richest 1 per cent of wage earners. This increase was even more extreme in the case of the top 0.01 per cent whose salaries were a mere 50 times larger than the average worker's income in 1970 but had become 250 times larger by 1998.

Atkinson cites several reasons for this increasing inequality including technological changes. These have generated increased employment in the poorly paid services and at the higher end of the occupational spectrum but produced a demise of many skilled manual and middle-class jobs especially those involving the routine processing of information (55–7). Another factor has been the export of many other kinds of work – including clerical work – to cheap labour havens in developing countries because of a more open global economy. But he suggests that 'non-market and institutional changes' (59) have also contributed to these developments. One is the changing cultural and political ethos in some advanced societies whereby there is greater toleration by voters and governments of grossly unequal incomes and an entrenched ethos of self-interest and individualism among the wider population (Beck and Beck-Gernsheim 2002). Second, globalization has intensified worldwide competition because there are now far more national players able to export quality goods and services and a much larger number of markets in which to seek customers. Consequently, the pace of competition between an increasing number of rival national as well as global companies has massively intensified. This, in turn, compels companies to attract the most creative and potentially productive employees while simultaneously cutting costs to the bone. In other words, they are driven 'to pay more at the top and less at the bottom'. At the same time, increasing the returns to shareholders and share values 'has become the overriding goal of most companies'. We have moved from a gentler era of capitalism, when firms tended to reward seniority rather than youthful high-flyers, valued and rewarded company loyalty and there was less market pressure to push down wages for those lower down the ladder, to one dominated by investor capitalism. Here, maximizing returns and profit for shareholders has become the only goal (Atkinson 2005: 59).

Hutton (2007: 26), too, argues that particularly in the USA and UK 'a business culture has developed where the share price is the be-all and end-all'. Two consequences follow from this. In order to deliver higher share prices, corporation directors are pursing what he refers to as 'the world's biggest takeover boom' of other companies and these generally result in job losses and downsizing but normally little increase in productivity (see also Gowan 2009: 24–5). Although this has happened before, we are seeing a drive to increase profits which is based not on the attempt to expand the productive output of the firm or the economy by investing in more and better skills, plant and machinery but rather an attempt to improve company returns by acquiring ownership of another company and stripping out its most valuable assets – a kind of predatory capitalism (see also Brenner 2002, Gowan 1999, Harvey 2003: 145–69). In this respect Hutton cites figures suggesting that in the USA alone between 1995 and 2005 the total value of such takeover deals reached $9 trillion. The other consequence has been the rise of a more greedy and demanding elite of corporation directors and financiers who by topping up their company's assets and their shareholder's gains through takeovers can also reward themselves with much higher returns (see also Elliot and Atkinson 2008: 215–16 and 222–4). He concluded by suggesting that rising inequality and corporate unresponsiveness is not due to globalization – which has brought the benefits of employment and cheaper goods to millions everywhere despite a parallel increase in job insecurity – nor to the rise of China and other industrializing nations with their vast low-paid work forces. In fact, and despite its fast growth and increased exports of manufactures, China's workers earn only 4 per cent of the wages earned by American and British workers, are far less productive than the latter and approximately 60 per cent of China's exports and patents are controlled by foreign companies. Rather, the real source of uncontrolled global capitalism lies in the weakening of all those forces which could once embed capital in 'checks and balances' including pressure from the media, the former ability of governments to regulate companies and the rules of competition, the existence of an ethos of long-term ownership and loyalty within companies and strong trade unions.

Turning to some of the possible explanations for the changing ethos of capitalism, Hobsbawm's argument (1994) is extremely suggestive. The end of the Cold War brought the final collapse of any realistic socialist alternative to capitalism but it also undermined whatever ideological credibility communist ideas might have possessed and their ability to influence people around the world. It also ended the fear that the military and economic power of the Soviet Union might one day prevail especially, for example, if a prolonged capitalist economic collapse plunged millions into unemployment. What Hobsbawm is suggesting here is that throughout much of the previous century, strong trade union and socialist movements directly challenged businesses and governments. Their ideas also gripped the imagination of millions of people living in industrial societies, and elsewhere, and offered the prospect of an alternative to capitalism's economic uncertainties and at a time when the benefits of economic growth seeped through to the masses slowly and unevenly. In addition, once the Soviet alternative became a reality following the success of the 1917 Bolshevik revolution in Russia the threat to Western capitalism was doubly reinforced: the ideals of communism now possessed an apparently credible, practical alternative and the Soviet Union could and did provide concrete support for socialist groups and parties around the world.

Hobsbawm argued (1994), further, that all this encouraged at least some capitalist interests and Western governments to accept the need to reform capitalist institutions. Gradually, therefore, trade unions were legalized and social insurance in respect to pension, sickness and unemployment rights was introduced. After the Second World War, additional welfare benefits were introduced in some countries along with the belief that governments ought to intervene in economic life to promote full employment. There was also a move towards more progressive taxation regimes designed to redistribute income from rich to poor – the era of Keynesian welfare capitalism. Of course, in part these gains for workers and the less well off were the result of the struggles pursued by ordinary people. However, Hobsbawm is suggesting that the impulse to reform also came from within the capitalist camp itself as a strategy for heading off the threat of a serious socialist alternative.

Almost certainly, there was an additional factor here. The two world wars in the first half of the twentieth century required the mass mobilization of citizens including huge numbers of women who were needed both in the armed forces and to replace male industrial and agricultural workers transferred into the armed forces. Similarly, citizens had to be persuaded to accept the privations and disciplines imposed by war: food shortages, the suspension of some leisure and social services, long hours of work, separation from family and so on. Without doubt, involvement in these two wars, especially the second, stiffened the resolve and the confidence of many ordinary people to demand major reforms but it also demonstrated that the capitalist market could be partly suspended and replaced by government planning. Moreover, at this time a far greater proportion of economic activity was owned by nationally based capitalist companies. Many, if not most, of these national capitalists were just as patriotic as the workers they employed and their children were also mobilized or sent abroad to fight for the greater patriotic good. Despite their superior wealth, their desire to keep their workers' wages and influence under control and the compulsions of competition which inevitably drove their business interests, many national capitalists were prepared to accept some degree of economic reform and realized that the presence of a secure, healthy, skilled workforce whose members could afford to buy the good they were helping to produce were guarantees of a strong economy and safeguards against the threat of socialism.

Returning to the present, this set of conditions has altered markedly. First, the end of the Cold War has largely removed the spectre of communism and the previous rationale for accepting reform. At the same time, it has exposed the new states which emerged from the collapse of Soviet Russia to market competition and inflows of capitalist investment. Second, the revolution in information technology and its fusion with the mass media during the past 20 years coupled to cheaper and more efficient transport systems have obviously enabled capital to spread some of its investments across the world in search of various market opportunities and other inducements and to do so without undermining the overall coordination and smooth running of their overall complex operations and activities (Castells 1996).

However, the shift worldwide towards a much more predatory form of capitalism is also related to economic globalization and especially to the growing dominance of neo-liberal economic policies since the 1980s. Indeed, these have probably done more to create the conditions for the rapid extension and deepening of economic globalization than any other single factor. Bienefeld (2007: 20), for example, argued that 'the fundamental structural difference between the "Golden Era" and the neoliberal models of global capital' comes down to the fact that 'in the former model, capital had an address'. Thus, the basic variables of economic life 'were largely determined at the national level through some form of tripartite negotiation between capital, labour and the state'.

In what ways and why did neo-liberal policies exercise these effects? When adopted by the advanced industrial countries neo-liberal economics opened their national economies much more to international trade and competition by deregulating many of the previous controls on the inward and outward flows of money, goods, ideas and investment while removing many of the previous constraints on the operations of capitalist enterprise including the ability to move around the world in search of short- or long-term profitable outlets (Kiely 2005a). Along with these moves to liberate market forces and encourage enterprise has been an emphasis on contracting the state's hold on economic life by reducing the subsidies, which once tried to protect local companies from decline or superior foreign competition, while privatizing state and national assets – including opening them up to acquisition by foreign interests. In addition, the fiscal burden on business has been reduced and spending on social welfare provision has fallen supposedly to reduce the over-dependence of individual citizens on state protection and create a more mobile labour force. Some of the previous legal and customary rights to free collective bargaining enjoyed by employees and trade unions have also been removed or cut. Neo-liberal policies were also imposed on many Third World countries during the 1980s and 1990s by the International Monetary Fund (IMF) and WB through the so-called Washington Consensus – the promise of debt relief and other advantages in return for swallowing the medicine of economic liberalism and national deregulation (Kiely 2005b, Stiglitz 2002). In addition to the influence exercised on the IMF and WB by the governments of the USA and G7 nations, many TNCs and other powerful capitalist interests, such as Wall Street's financial industries (Brenner 2002, Gowan 1999), doubtless played a key part, too, in pushing for Washington Consensus policies.

One striking symptom of capital's growing ability to reduce its obligations towards the social reproduction of those states and national populations where it makes profits is evident in the sphere of taxation. Thus, TNCs have been able to demand that governments reduce their contribution to national tax revenues. For example, Klein (2001: 33) provided figures for the USA which demonstrated that corporate taxes as a percentage of the total revenue received by the federal government fell from nearly one-third in 1954 to 11.5 per cent by 1998. Indeed, in the EU as a whole, companies are either able to avoid paying some of their taxes, or, to attract more foreign investment than rival countries, some governments are competing by conducting 'tax races to the bottom' (Martin 2007: 133). In 2007, Macedonia, for example, offered a low tax rate of 10 per cent on company profits and a zero rate where profits were reinvested. But this is also a country where the average gross monthly salary for citizens is approximately £280 or $560.

The net result of all these changes has been to allow capitalists to extend the frontiers of their activities much further than previously both spatially – by scooping up worldwide markets, labour forces, materials and any inducements provided by a growing number of governments and incorporating these into their operations – and qualitatively by altering the forms of their organization in the search for greater flexibility and reduced risks and costs. The reality that capital has become much more mobile has allowed it to disregard much of its previous sense of obligation to ordinary people and to the nation where it originally became established: whatever impulse to capitalist reform that may once have existed has dwindled markedly.

3.3   Competing in the world labour market

As the preceding discussion indicated, there is an increasingly strong case for arguing that few and in fact a decreasing number of individuals on the planet can now live outside the world labour market. Nor can most escape from its competitive and individualizing pressures on jobs and incomes or the constraints it imposes on the prospect for attaining a degree of lifetime or indeed any economic security. Similarly, a diminishing proportion of the world's labour force, especially, but not only, women and those with little education and few skills, can expect their governments any longer to provide much, if any, protection from global competitive forces and the constant pressure of lower and falling wage rates elsewhere.

A number of events and processes over the past thirty years or so have combined to push most individuals into this cauldron of endless competition, the casualization of work and therefore a condition of inherent work insecurity. We have already considered some of the main ones: the rise and spread of neo-liberal economic policies, the end of the Cold War and the communication and transport revolutions. But alongside these, several additional changes have been taking place. Freeman refers to these changes as the three 'drivers of the globalization of labor' (2007: 25): 'the great doubling' of the global labour force; the expansion of higher educational provision in many developing countries; and the rapid transfer of advanced technology to these same countries (25–7).

Increasing supplies of labour

It is worth examining in detail the circumstances surrounding the increase in the supply of world labour. Considered overall, Freeman (2007: 25–6) sees a doubling of the global labour force available to capitalism taking place between approximately 1980 and 2000. Thus, the numbers grew from approximately 1460 million workers in the years before 2000 (one-third in the developed countries and the remainder based in the non-communist developing countries) to a world total of approximately 3 billion by 2000. Interestingly, and for similar reasons, the IMF has recently estimated that the global supply of labour available to capitalism has risen approximately four-fold since 1980 (The Economist 2007: 84). How can increases of such dimensions be explained?

Although, during the past fifty years or so, and with differing degrees of success, a number of developing countries, such as South Korea, Taiwan, Malaysia, Brazil and Mexico had already taken steps to foster industrialization, thereby expanding the world's industrial-capitalist labour force; three more recent changes have hugely added to this process. First, since the late 1970s, China has successfully pursued policies designed to attract foreign investment, to raise the technical capacities of much of its labour force and to expand its share of world manufactured exports and to some extent in services too. Indeed, China's economic rise within the space of only 30 years has been spectacular and is often noted. Bolstered by many years of almost continuous high rates of economic growth, around ten per year, it is fast becoming the world's workshop for a wide range of high-tech as well as basic manufactures. For example, by 2005 IMF figures showed that China's share of world exports in both manufactures and services reached 7.2 per cent compared with Japan's 5 per cent and America's 9.8 per cent (The Economist 2007: 121). Similarly, its share of world GDP reached 15.1 per cent in 2006 compared with India's 6.3 per cent, America's 19.7 per cent and the EU euro zone's world share of 14.7 per cent.

Second, although India had already laid down the basis for a largely self-sufficient and advanced industrial economy in the years between the mid-1950s and 1990, its rate of economic growth had been relatively slow compared with that achieved in many South East Asian countries and the quality of its overprotected home products was often rather low by world standards. However, since India's government began to implement a series of economic reforms from 1991 onwards – designed to open its economy much more to foreign competition and investment – its rate of growth has accelerated and many economic sectors, especially in IT and various cultural services, have fared well in the global economy. This is because not only does India posses a population of rather more than a billion people but a large component of this consists of an educated middle class of approximately 300 million individuals whose ranks were swelled by decades of earlier government and family investment. Armed with this enormous cadre of educated people, India has been particularly successful in capturing a growing share of the world market for middle-level services – such as the processing of medical and other information or dealing with telephone enquiries. Here, a combination of relatively low wages compared with those enjoyed by high-level service workers in North America and the EU countries, the ability of information technology to cancel the constraints of geography and the growing relative importance of the symbolic knowledge economy have all enabled educated Indians to establish a growing niche in the world service industries. Thus, India's exports of IT-related services grew from $565 million in 2000 to $6.2 billion by 2006 (Paus 2007: 13). Much of this was also helped by members of the educated Indian diaspora who migrated to the USA from the 1960s onwards. Many eventually attained high positions in companies such as Intel and Motorola and later encouraged their American employers to establish research and business links with firms in India (Suri 2007: 165).

Box 3   Global imbalances: US-Asian economic symbiosis and the financial crisis

The global economy operates in a condition of fragile, skewed interdependency. This is particularly apparent in the case of the highly unbalanced flows of trade/export, debt, credit and even economic growth-dependency between the USA and South East Asia. (Nations such as Saudi Arabia also enjoy surpluses in respect to the US economy and either lend money to the US government by buying treasury bills or encourage funds to flow into various private financial enterprises).

US relative economic decline. America's world economic leadership is in relative decline as against the growing combined clout of the EU, East Asia and the BRIC economies and the latter's ability to equal or even out-rival the USA in most industries except biogenetics, pharmaceuticals, IT and communications, the media and cultural industries and financial services (Bello 2001 and 2002 and Gowan 2009). This changing balance of world economic power – not just between the USA and the South but also between the G7 countries and the leading economies of the South – was clearly evident at the G20 meeting in London in April 2009 because everyone recognized that overcoming the worst economic recession since the 1930s was only possible if far more than the G7 groups of countries were involved.

US trade deficits.   For decades America has piled up trade deficits despite its attempt to retain its influence by pushing a neo-liberal agenda on the rest of the world. However, because of (a) the Cold War and many nations' dependence on US military support (until 1991) and (b) America's ability as the world's largest economy to offer a huge export market, foreign investment and the use of the dollar as world money, most countries – for example, Japan, South Korea and Taiwan – tolerated these trade imbalances. More recently, China too, has accumulated vast dollar reserves partly because of its export surplus to the USA. For example, China's accumulated currency reserves reached nearly two trillion dollars by October 2008. China also held US treasury bonds to the value of $541 billion in 2008 (Wearden and Stanway 2008).

Mutual advantages.   Both parties nevertheless gain from these trade imbalances.

1.   On the Asian side – and especially in the case of China – their export surpluses with North America, Europe and Japan have helped to fuel rates of economic expansion which would have been far lower had these countries relied solely on their own home markets. Thus, virtually one-third of China's growth in GDP between 2005 and 2007 was fuelled by exports to the EU, Japan and the USA. This conceals a further global imbalance; namely, the reluctance of Asian consumers to spend more than they earn or to use credit cards as a path to consumerism and their preference for saving – the very opposite of the tendencies demonstrated by many Western consumers.
2.   Asia's governments, banks and businesses have recycled some of their surpluses back into the global economy, and especially towards the USA (Brenner 2002, Gowan 1999 and 2009) by either purchasing federal government treasury bills – thereby helping America to fund its military programme – or recycling surpluses through Wall Street.
3.   The funds recycled via Wall Street and London financial businesses have boosted the earnings of the US and British economies as these funds were partly moved into investment banks, hedge funds, derivatives and other financial instruments. They also swelled the loans and credit available to consumers, house buyers and businesses. Indeed, all this contributed towards the vast flows of unregulated credit swirling around the global economy during the past ten years.

In the case of South East Asia, including China – but also India – it is important to remember that despite the very considerable remaining inequalities evident within these economies, rapid economic growth in recent decades has contributed strongly to the overall decline of world poverty though the picture is complicated (see Cohen and Kennedy 2007: 198–201). Thus, on one hand, the percentage of the world's population living in poverty, as defined by the World Bank – living on less than one US dollar per day – fell substantially across the world as a whole during the main years of neo-liberalist policies and intensifying economic globalization between 1981 and 2001 (World Bank 2004). Moreover, this was especially true in respect to India's educated middle classes and also half a billion people in China, many of them living in that country's burgeoning industrial cities (World Bank 2004). On the other hand, and even in the latter case, the conditions available to the other half of China's population, most living in rural areas, appear to be either barely improving or actually worsening whether through local government corruption, sheer population size or the concentration of national investment in industrial city regions. Moreover, poverty, inequality, and often violent repression, remain the lot of large numbers of individuals and their families across much of Africa, Latin and Central America and in the former countries of the Soviet Union and Eastern Europe. What also needs to be said here is that while it has been in South East Asia, including China, that the most spectacular evidence of falling poverty has occurred, much of this poverty reduction was linked to state-led policies designed to produce rapid economic growth rather than neo-liberal policies. Indeed, the industrialization of countries such as South Korea, Taiwan and Malaysia was strongly underway well before the era of neo-liberalism took hold. In fact, according to some commentators it was the opening up of these South East Asian economies to neo-liberal policies from the early 1990s, mostly against their will and under US pressure, that largely accounted for the economic crisis that engulfed some of these countries, especially South Korea, in 1997–8 (Stiglitz 2002, Wade 2001).

Returning to the question of how we can explain the huge expansion in the global supply or labour, there is a third explanation. The end of the Cold War between 1989 and 1992 not only opened the former Soviet Union and its communist allies to global capitalism for the first time in over seventy years but it also simultaneously exposed the relatively well-paid workers in the industrialized Western nations, especially in Europe, to the job hunger existing among the mass of individuals living in these countries, many of them highly educated and technically skilled. Whether as eager migrants, willing to accept any job abroad, or as a cheap labour force at home which global businesses could incorporate into their worldwide holdings through foreign investment, these vast reservoirs of low-cost labour have also helped to swell the ranks of the world labour market and intensified the competition for jobs. Indeed for some time, many TNCs have been moving their plants into the former countries of Eastern Europe and the Soviet Union in search of cheaper but skilled workers and as a way of competing more effectively with the industrial economies of South East Asia. With current labour costs in Poland, the Czech Republic and Slovakia only one-fifth of those prevailing in Germany and other EU countries this is hardly surprising. For example, General Motors and Ford motor manufacturers have recently moved some of the operations to these countries – including Turkey – while shedding approximately 60,000 jobs in the USA plus many more in Britain and Germany. Toyota is engaged in similar operations (Gow 2006: 29).

Expanding higher education and technology transfer to developing countries

Freeman's (2007: 26–7) second driver for creating a global labour market concerns the increased investment in higher education undertaken by some developing countries thereby raising the value-creating potential of their workforces. Between 1970 and 2000, the number of college and university students rose by approximately 400 per cent and this process has continued. To take one crucial example, the numbers of people attaining first degrees in China between 2000 and 2005 increased to 4 million – a rise of 500 per cent. Similarly, if we include Chinese students studying for their doctorates in science and engineering in the USA, at current rates of expansion the Chinese economy will soon have at its disposal more people with such science-based doctorates than America (Freeman 2007: 26). Other developing countries such as Brazil and Peru also doubled their university students during the 1980s and 1990s. Freeman's third contributor to the emergence of a global labour force has been the increased transfer of advanced technology to many developing countries. This is the result of a combination of factors: the deliberate policies pursued by governments designed to facilitate this process including investing in higher education; the role of skilled migrants working in the advanced countries who have often helped this process by relaying information and skills back to their countries of origin; and the increasing willingness of TNCs to spread their technology to many developing nations by establishing advanced production and research facilities there, especially when they can find a sufficient quantity of specialized and high-quality workers at much lower cost than at home (Freeman 2007: 32).

Continuing this line of argument Freeman identifies two particular groups who are losers in this process such that not only is a global labour force emerging but it is also one which includes a growing number of widely dispersed graduates. One such group consists of those workers in Latin and Central America and some other countries such as South Africa where standard manufacturing plants producing generic goods such as clothing were established several decades ago (30). Here, workers remain low waged compared with their equivalent in the advanced countries but their earnings are now perhaps four times higher than those which companies need to pay their employees doing similar work in China or India. Moreover, some of these industries and firms are relatively easy and cheap to relocate to lower-wage economies. One consequence of this has been the need for increasing numbers of workers in countries such as Mexico, Peru, El Salvador and South Africa, to retreat into the urban informal sector in search of livelihoods where incomes and work conditions are often far more hazardous, insecure and poorly paid. Indeed, according to Davis (2006: 176) the urban informal economy already provides nearly three-fifths of the 'employment' available in Latin America for the economically active population and supplies most of whatever 'new' jobs are created. The second group in danger of losing out are graduates and those with equivalent technical skills currently living in the developed countries. This is linked both to the growing availability of educated workers – including people with a training in science – and the spread of high-tech facilities to the developing countries. In the past, it was always possible for governments and individuals in the advanced economies to upgrade national and personal skills through education and as a response to the rise of much cheaper but less-skilled workers in developing countries. However, this tried and trusted remedy for retaining a comparative economic advantage appears less likely to succeed as the world supply of graduates of all kinds increases, as countries such as China and India move up the technological ladder and as they expand their export of high-tech as well as generic products while retaining much of their low-wage advantage (Freeman 2007: 32–3).

The diminished bargaining power of labour has also been explored by Castells (1996). He argued that on one hand the spread of a leaner, more efficient but also globally networked form of capitalist enterprise – more empowered by ICTs than perhaps any other global actor – has massively contributed to strengthening business. But on the other hand it has also contributed to the 'disintegration of the workforce' (240). At the same time ICTs mean that many routine and repetitive jobs can easily be taken over by machinery. Accordingly, the particular capacities possessed by a group of workers in one country or region are less important to capital now than its access to a generic world labour force. The majority of workers, especially if they are poorly educated, find themselves in competition with millions of others around the world and at the very time when most programmable and mundane skills are being downgraded. Even the minority who possess the kinds of symbolic and knowledge-creating or disseminating resources possessed by professionals, such as architects, scientists, fashion or media designers, computer programmers or educators, who in the past found themselves wooed by businesses and enjoyed a strong bargaining position, now have to compete with others in low-wage countries and cannot be certain of having access to lifetime careers or permanent employment. Accordingly, while 'at its core, capital is global', in most cases 'labour is local' (475) and is normally constrained much more than top corporation professionals and directors by limited language skills, relative poverty and strong affiliations to particular cultures and places. Similarly, a network logic means that while 'capital is globally coordinated' (476) and converges towards a 'meta-network' (475) labour tends to become individualized, 'fragmented in its organization, diversified in its existence, divided in its collective action'. Increasingly these two entities, capital and labour, occupy different times and spaces.

Putting all this together, we can say that since the 1970s an era of massive worldwide restructuring largely focused around economic globalization has resulted in the 'total commodification or "marketization" of social life world-wide' (Robinson 2002: 217). At the same time while global corporate business has increased its direct control over nation-states, its power over labour has increased much more. Indeed this relationship has become fixed 'in a new global capital-labour relation' involving the 'global casualization or informalization of labour'. This has been accompanied by the return of all those forms of insecurity – for example, little or no protection against the risk of unemployment, fluctuating incomes, illness or unsocial working conditions – which had plagued most workers and their families across the industrial countries in the era before the Second World War (Standing 2007: 42–5). While globalization and the policies that accompanied it have allowed capital to escape from the earlier constraints that nation-states could once impose, labour has been turned into a 'naked commodity, no longer embedded in relations of reciprocity rooted in social and political communities' (Robinson 2002: 217) which were once largely outside capital's control. Here, nation-states now function as what McMichael (1996) called 'population containment zones' but while this containment does not apply either to highly skilled mobile labour or to global companies it does constrain nationally fixed and locally bound labour. Meanwhile, and in so far as something resembling a 'national' economy can be identified, nation-states operate increasingly to protect and foster their competitive edge or niche in the global market not by protecting local/national workers from foreign competition but instead by encouraging them to gain more skills, to be willing and able to operate as flexible, multitasked employees and to work longer hours. Referring to this situation, Teschke and Heine talk about the demise of the 'welfare state' and in its place the rise of the 'competition state' (2002: 176).

3.4   Living on the global assembly line – tying the world together

The creation of a global economy also means that most people now depend not just for their livelihoods but also for their very existence on a vast and complex world division of labour. As Harris observed (1983: 9), 'the world economy is a miracle of collective organization...hundreds of millions of people unknowingly collaborate to make it possible'. Thus, the well-being and futures of all peoples and nations have become mutually dependent, directly or indirectly, not only upon global money and investment flows, jobs and livelihoods linked to foreign companies, overseas markets and complex technologies but also on vast networks supplying food and raw materials, components and a multiplicity of goods and services between innumerable locations. Several key structural arrangements and collaborative activities stretched across socio-geographical space interweave and link together so as to support this world division of labour. In this section we examine each of the following in turn: the rise of numerous global commodity or supply chains; the growing practice whereby large companies subcontract or outsource much of their activities to large and small firms often spread across many countries; the tendency for TNCs with a portfolio of worldwide business activities and affiliate companies to spatially optimize their operations so as to maximize the benefits that each location, region or country can offer; and the orchestration of a powerful worldwide consumerist ethos, underpinned by the seductive imagery and promises of self-realization generated by the mass media and popular commercialized culture.

Global supply chains

A bewildering range of these contribute powerfully to the architecture of the global capitalist economy. They consist of long networks of interdependent producers, component suppliers and transporters – perhaps involving small, medium, large or huge businesses – as well as wholesalers and retailers, brought together to service each other's needs by the compulsions of money and profit but with roots in different countries. Ultimately at the ends of these chains are consumers of different kinds. These global supply chains may provide a variety of food products. For example, armies of linked suppliers may together ship grapes, mange touts or early tomatoes by airfreight or ship and according to the season from tropical farms to temperate city supermarkets. Alternatively, the numerous factories situated along a chain may contribute the component parts of a vast range of manufactured products from clothing and sports shoes to cars and computers. But global care chains have also become quite significant in recent decades. These provide for the care needs mostly of people in the rich societies. Here, mainly young women migrate from countries such as the Philippines, Thailand or Nigeria to work as nannies, housemaids, nurses and cleaners or they care for the elderly whether in the private homes of wealthy middle-class couples or in hospitals and nursing homes or for companies which contract to clean offices (Hochschild 2000, Yeates 2004).

Garment manufacturing is a key example of an industry which depends critically on the networking possibilities provided by global supply chains. This is because during the past 40 years production has spread rapidly to many countries yet many of the leading consumer outlets for clothing sales now manufacture little or no products themselves. For many developing countries, the garment industry offers a relatively low cost and technologically simple way of beginning the process of moving up their industrial learning curve while hopefully starting out on a path to export-led economic growth. Moreover, the world market for clothing is set to continue its upward expansion as China, India and other countries become richer. It is hardly surprising therefore that by 2002 the developing countries provided 70 per cent of world clothing exports (Hurley and Miller 2005: 17). In Bangladesh, for example, garment production accounts for three-quarters of export earnings and employs nearly two-thirds of the total industrial workforce. Worldwide an estimated 40 million people are employed in the garment industry and most of them are women (Wills and Hale 2005: 1). Especially in the South, they work in a myriad of networked firms, large, medium, small and tiny, and in situations and under conditions most of which are hidden from public view and which operate beyond the capacity of the larger more responsible Third World manufacturers or the large buyers in the developed world to properly regulate and control.

Returning to Bangladesh, by 2004 there were 3280 garment factories employing approximately 1.8 million workers – nearly all of them women. Less than 10 per cent were employed in the largest tier of factories providing reasonable conditions of work and wages. Spread across the remaining small factories and/or working in their own homes, it was impossible for most of these women to have much understanding of how their fragmented inputs contributed to overall garment output, or who controlled it and how it linked them into the global economy. At the same time – and like garment and other industrial workers in many other countries – the combination of oppressive national governments, the relentless demands of buyers and consumers for lower costs and the sheer complexity of an industry held together by world-wide chains makes it extremely difficult for them to organize workplace or national trade unions (Wills and Hale 2005: 10–11).

Outsourcing skills, components and services

A second key feature which contributes to the working of the global assembly line has gradually become much more evident and crucial since the 1970s and concerns the increased dependence of corporations on their ability to subcontract much of their business's activities to numerous suppliers. This is particularly evident in the case of supermarkets and companies supplying clothes, sportswear, accessories and household goods such as fridges or cooking aids. Typically these large and small subcontracting companies are spread across a number of Third World countries. Here, as we have seen with the garment industry, labour is usually cheap. Also environmental and other laws are frequently either weak or sparsely enforced. Worldwide downsizing by large companies has also been immensely helped by the falling costs and technological advances achieved in long-distance transportation, for example, containerization and the availability of ever larger tankers and ships in addition to low-cost airfreight for moving high-value but low-weight commodities.

An increasing part of international trade consists of the flows of unfinished goods around the world between the affiliate companies of TNCs and other companies. As Paus (2007: 4) suggests, this trade in parts and components is an indication of the extent to which world production as a whole is becoming fragmented and spread 'across national borders'. Research in the USA indicates that the share of imported inputs – parts, components and so on – as a proportion of the final output of firms based in America increased from just over 5 per cent in 1972 to approximately 23 per cent by 2003. Similar trends have been taking place in other developed economies. For several decades,

such outsourcing operations by mainly Western companies involved subcontracting the more labour-intensive aspects of their overall operations to
companies in developing countries where wages were much lower. Often, too,
the local businesses which won these contracts were based in special Export
Processing Zones (EPZs). These promised low costs and minimum regulation
and were set up specifically by governments to attract local and foreign investment. In the Maquiladora EPZ area in northern Mexico, for example, a large
American TNC might outsource some of its production to firms originating
in South Korea, Japan, Brazil, Germany or indeed in Mexico itself. However,
more recently the rising educational levels and technological capabilities now
available in the more successful developing countries means that outsourcing
to such firms increasingly involves not just low-value manufactured goods
and components but placing orders for high-tech parts inputs, too. As Paus
explained, the 'flip side of this deindustrialization process in developed countries has been increased industrial upgrading in some of today's developing
countries, especially in Asia' (4). Moreover, as we have already seen, outsourcing now involves the massive and hitherto unexpected growth in the
capacity to export many service activities to countries such as India. Here, it is
estimated that the opportunities to outsource future 'IT-enabled' service jobs
is considerable and estimates range from 20 per cent of employment in some
leading economies to a slightly lower figure of between 11 to 14 per cent for
the USA. However, Paus cited figures claiming that IT will probably enable
two or three times as many US service jobs to be outsourced in the coming
years as has occurred so far within the manufacturing sector (Paus 2007: 5).

Spatial optimization strategies

A third key organizational pivot around which the global assembly line is
being constructed concerns the activities of the largest TNCs. Whether as large
investors with direct or partial ownership of multiple subsidiary, affiliate and
partner companies spread across the world, or in their capacity as the sources
of market demand for huge volumes of outsourced components and finished
goods subcontracted to millions of smaller businesses, TNCs exercise a powerful influence over the global economy out of all proportion to the small percentage of the world's labour force they directly employ on their payrolls.
According to Klein (2001: 261), the latter figure amounted to only 5 per cent
in the late 1990s. Indeed, although the world's largest 100 TNCs increased
their assets by approximately 300 per cent between 1990 and 1997 their direct
employees rose only by 9 per cent during the same period (261).

In fact many of the largest TNCs own foreign assets through direct investments held in numerous countries and often this involves huge numbers of
overseas affiliates. Using UNCTAD's data for 2005 showing the world's top
100 TNCs with the greatest volume of overseas assets, General Electric came
out top in that year. More than three-quarters of its companies were based
outside the USA and numbered in total 1184 subsidiaries out of a total of

1527. Lower down in the same UNCTAD table at number 66, the Japanese TNC, Hitachi, owned nearly half of its companies outside Japan with 356 overseas subsidiaries compared with an overall figure of 752. The tendency for corporations to invest widely across the world is most obvious in the case of the largest TNCs and especially those engaged in oil and manufacturing. However, TNCs in mining, transport and the wholesale/retail sector are also important as are those operating in the field of producer services. The latter includes such businesses as management consultancy, advertising, finance and banking and business law (Beaverstock, Doel, Hubbard and Taylor 2002, Sassen 2002).

A key point to note about these TNCs is that they engage in spatial optimization strategies and these also provide an element of coherence to the global assembly line. Here, TNCs unscramble a portion of their original nation-based operations, often a very large portion, and then spread fragments of their portfolio of business activities across different countries according to location, resources and the inducements each can offer. In the case of a manufacturing company, for example, product research and design would be retained in the original nation and/or the leading markets, the manufacture of various components might be assigned to a battery of Third World countries with good labour skills while the assembling of the final goods and the main wholesale distribution points would be organized at a number of world regional centres as jump-off points for marketing. Here, each TNC's vast range of diverse business activities are matched to what each separate country can best offer: for example, low-cost but skilled labour, highly skilled design talent, raw material availability, advantageous government inducements, the concentration of high-quality scientific research opportunities in a particular city or micro-region, or geographical proximity to major markets, production centres or distribution points.

Robinson (2002) argues that because capital has reorganized production on this worldwide basis, in effect, national economies have become merely fragmented parts of 'globalized circuits of accumulation' based in companies (212). Of course, and at least since the early nineteenth century, many businesses have constructed world links. But until recently, these mainly took place through international trade (importing and exporting mostly finished goods or machinery) or capital flows involving either the search for raw materials and the setting up of colonies or funding overseas businesses by acquiring shares in foreign government or private activities. However, through the activities of TNCs and for the first time in history, production itself has become globalized thereby integrating nations organically and functionally across territorial borders as if they did not exist as separate entities. Moreover, what amounts to an overall unified world business logic from the perspective of each TNC may be experienced by a particular country as a process of being dotted with the many disarticulated fragments of business activities deposited by numerous foreign companies. In addition to spatial optimization, TNCs also link the world together because despite their immense wealth and reach, many increasingly engage in collaborative strategies such as joint research and investment funding or forming cross-border mergers. This is linked to the risks and enormous costs involved in developing new products for the world market since these often require tying up huge resources over very long periods before any returns are likely to materialize.

The culture-ideology of consumerism

According to Sklair (2001 and 2002) this is the fourth glue binding the global economy together. This compensates even the poorest for the work insecurities, growing inequality and other indignities and stresses that are likely to be the reality for most global citizens given the pressures that arise from our dependence on the world labour market and the need to cope with the complexities of living on a global assembly line. Indeed, the 'globalization of the capitalist system reproduces itself through the profit-driven culture-ideology of consumerism' (2001: 6). Moreover, it cannot thrive or expand without it. Thus, increasingly the same universally desired commodities are either produced or certainly sold and obtainable everywhere. Mostly these are branded goods where companies have invested huge amounts of money in product development, promotion and marketing, including the creation of a company logo, as a way of offering an instantly recognizable and seductive consumer aura that is available to all who buy-into its unique style. Frequently these brands involve capturing, imitating and then transmuting the cultures drawn from the non-commercialized social lives of ordinary people whether exotic Third World cultures or the idiosyncratic worlds created by ethnic, youth, black, street or other subcultures or minorities (Klein 2001).

Frequently, branded commodities out-compete local goods and despite being more expensive are purchased willingly by even poor consumers because they believe that possessing them opens the door to a distinctive and empowering life style which marks them out from others. Here, Castells' (1997) argument is useful. He suggested that in a globalizing world our only or primary meaning comes from identity and this is what we are all obsessively engaged in trying to construct. Following a similar line of argument Sklair (2002: 62) claimed that

> the culture-ideology of consumerism proclaims, literally, that the meaning of life is to be found in the things we possess. To consume, therefore, is to be fully alive, and to remain fully alive we must continuously consume, discard, consume.

Moreover, the proof that the culture-ideology of consumerism is highly successful can be found in the shopping malls of the world 'where now large numbers of workers and their families flock to buy, usually with credit cards, thus locking themselves into the financial system of capitalist globalization' (Sklair 2002: 109). Given its worldwide power and significance, therefore, the culture-ideology of consumerism can be regarded, perhaps, as the fuel that drives global capitalism but also the cultural cement that guarantees its unchallenged domination with little or no need for the exercise of political, military or extreme economic coercion to ensure its survival.[i]

3.5 Corporate power and the transnational capitalist class

Some observers have argued that economic globalization has been closely linked to the emergence of an elite of top corporation directors, managers, supporting professionals, financiers, media moguls and others who can be regarded as forming a transnational capitalist class (TNCC). Included among their number are a variety of leading contributors to global think-tanks, international associations and other influential agencies such as the World Economic Forum and the International Chamber of Commerce. The emerging TNCC has been progressively freed by economic globalization and the imposition of the worldwide deregulatory regime of neo-liberalism from its former historical embeddedness within, and dependence on, pre-capitalist and national-capitalist structures, class interests and social affiliations. For example, Ong and Nonini (1997: 9) referred to the 'new transnational functionaries of global capitalism' who provide certain 'integrative competencies' (11) required if businesses are to be effectively managed across vast distances although they also take account of local and national cultural practices. Similarly, Featherstone (1990: 8) talked about the 'coterie of new specialists and professionals' who work outside the 'cultures of the nation-state'. Castells (1996: 415) pointed to the dominant 'technocratic-financial-managerial elite' who, aided by ICTs and the key cities which act as the nodes and hubs of globally networked capitalism, direct the space of flows that now constitutes the world economy.

Sklair's work (2001) here is particularly useful. He argued that the transnational capitalist class have several things in common. They seek to exercise control over the workplace but also over domestic and international politics while monitoring the impact of the culture-ideology of consumerism. Like other observers, he also argued that the members of the TNCC tend to have global rather than local perspectives, they come from many countries, share similar luxury lifestyles and they increasingly think of themselves as citizens of the world. Sklair divided this TNCC into four class fractions.

First, there are the directors of the TNCs and their local affiliate companies scattered across the world. This is the corporate fraction of the TNCC. Its members are especially likely to be exposed to global experiences. Thus, increasingly, corporations train and encourage local/national managers to run their local affiliate companies while generally fostering cross-country movement and ties. A period of training abroad is considered as crucial in creating highly professional managers. This is because 'globalizing companies need managers with cosmopolitan outlooks' and TNCs increasingly 'train their top cadre of managers to expect to work in any part of the world' (Sklair 2001: 55–6). Beaverstock, Smith and Taylor (1999: 101), for example, described how some American law firms rotate partners between different overseas branches and seek to expose 'outstanding younger foreign lawyers' to the 'global finishing schools' provided by a spell in the home company. Sklair's second component of the TNCC consists of the globalizing state and interstate bureaucrats and politicians or the state fraction. These push for economic and other policies at state and international level, for example through IGOs such as the WTO or regional organizations such as the EU. The latter further the global activities and concerns of the TNCs.

The third element are the globalizing professionals or the technical fraction whose members provide a range of specialized, high-value skills. Their careers are either directly linked to the TNCs as 'in-house' employees or they work for independent producer service companies such as law, management consultancy and accountancy firms, which service the needs of TNCs worldwide. Some may also work for think-tanks with international orientations. These professionals provide 'world benchmarking' standards and 'best practices' appropriate to the particular technical activities of different companies. States, too, value these standards because it helps them to develop policies that might improve national economic competitiveness. These world standards enable TNCs to compete internationally by measuring their 'performance against actual competitors or an ultimate target' (2001: 114) and by providing standards of comparison allowing them to compete more effectively with other global players. In addition, attaining world-class technical standards helps companies to justify their profits and market success. Finally, there are the globalizing merchants and media people: the consumerist fraction. The in-house specialists or contracted producer services who provide these inputs play several key roles. They help to distribute a company's goods and services around the world, they trumpet the existence and superiority of its global brand and they popularize the message that self-realization through consumerism is the path to personal liberation.

Several valuable points emerge from Sklair's analysis. For one thing, each fraction needs the others. Running global capitalism requires the close collaboration of each component of the TNCC including the forging of 'alliances' between 'globalizing politicians, globalizing professionals, and the corporate sector' (2001: 113). In addition, while the four groups of functionaries he identified are analytically distinct from each other, in everyday practice they frequently overlap. Thus, not only do they work together on occasion and pool their various specialized inputs but some also move between corporations from one institutional arena to another and perhaps back again. For example, some leading politicians end up as directors on the management boards of large corporations, whether during or after their stint in government, while company directors often join prestigious international think-thanks or IGOs such as the IMF (Stiglitz 2002). Alternatively, their insider, commercial knowledge is increasingly consulted by governments. Moreover, the basis of hegemonic control over the global economy exercised by the TNCC as a whole lies in its members' access to various types of 'capital' – used here in the broad sense suggested by Bourdieu. Thus, it is not just ownership of shares and rights to bonuses that defines membership of the TNCC, nor even the direct control over commercial decision-making. Rather, in addition to wealth, their 'capital' is defined in terms of the acquisition of organizational and specialist technical knowledge, participation in global social networks connected to business and international politics, the ability to develop the skills necessary for engaging in 'inter-cultural communication' and becoming empowered by 'a new type of habitus' or cultural outlook (Featherstone 1990: 8). Finally, Sklair (2001) argued that many members of the TNCC are aware that deep contradictions exist at the heart of global consumer capitalism and they are trying to overcome these and the conflicts they generate by cultivating a sense of corporate social responsibility – though whether this produces significant results is open to question. Thus, he suggested (2002: 6) that

> the transnationalist capitalist class is working consciously to resolve two central crises, namely, (i) the simultaneous creation of increasing poverty and increasing wealth within and between communities and societies (the class polarization crisis) and (ii) the unsustainability of the system (the ecological crisis).

Other commentators have made similar observations concerning the TNCC though they are more sceptical concerning its members' predisposition to demonstrate a degree of ethical or practical responsibility towards the world. Rather, they stress the deepening divisions between these global elites and the remainder of humanity. Bauman (1998: 3), for example, suggested that economic globalization has further disempowered the poor while leaving elites unaccountable and 'emancipated from local constraints'. Similarly, Burbach, Núñez and Kargarlitsky (1997: 117–21) referred to the rise of a 'barbaric' global bourgeoisie since the fall of communism whose members adhere to few values which might incline them to demonstrate accountability to the remainder of the world's population. Here, they would include the top celebrities of sport, music, film and TV and the growing number of millionaires and billionaires. These individuals, including members of the TNCC, are largely unaccountable and largely parasitic upon the countries that educated them. As such, they can often avoid contributing towards the continuous costs of socio-economic renewal – which all societies face – through paying their fair share of taxes for investment in schools, infrastructure, health services and so. But this only places a harder burden upon locally bound citizens who now have to cover all or a disproportionate share of the cost of social reproduction. This further undermines democracy and national power as the masses buckle and protest under the strain.

3.6   The rise of the transnational state

Robinson (2002, but see also Robinson and Harris 2000) argued that in Marx's writing on the state, the economic and the political are 'distinct moments in the same totality' (214). Although state elites sometimes impose restraints on national capitalists to better serve the wider national interest, as during time of war, this does not mean that states operate according to a separate logic from capital or that they are independent of other classes. In contrast, Weber saw nation-states as driven by a quite different logic from capitalist markets since the primary concern of nation-state elites is not profit but the preservation of national sovereignty and therefore maintaining monopoly control of the legitimate right to use violence in defence of territory, borders and citizens. Robinson concluded, therefore, that whereas in Weber's theory there can be no transnational state (TNS), there is nothing in Marxian thought that says the state must be tied to a particular territory or national base.

Following this line of argument, Robinson then suggested that it should occasion no surprise to discover that a TNS apparatus is emerging from the core of the nation-state system and that its members are part and parcel of the TNCC. Thus, as capitalism breaks free of the nation so, too, the political institutions of the state become partly internationalized to serve the interests of an equally transnational capitalism. Accordingly the transnational state

> comprises those institutions and practices in global society that maintain, defend and advance the emergent hegemony of a global bourgeoisie and its project of constructing a new global capitalist historical bloc...The rise of a TNS entails the reorganization of the state within each nation...and it involves simultaneously the rise of truly supranational economic and political institutions. (216)

Certain sections/fractions of each nation-state's officialdom and political elites increasingly use national powers to service the needs of global capital and they do this in conjunction with the leading supranational institutions – especially the WTO, IMF and WB – and macro-regional organizations such as the EU and NAFTA. Increasingly, too, their concerns prevail over the more localistic elites and bureaucrats within each country who try to protect and further what they perceive as national interests. Here, the members of the TNS believe that the interests of their own nation-state are best served by linking them more closely to the global economy. For example, rather than protecting local labour and businesses from foreign competition through tariffs or subsidies, their policies are designed to attract inward foreign investment, to foster greater skill, discipline and flexibility among local workers and to help both national and foreign companies within their territories to become ever more effective in responding to international trade opportunities. Clearly, this includes pursuing the entire neo-liberal agenda of deregulating capital flows and markets, the privatization of national assets and so on. For them, therefore, prioritizing 'national' capitalist and worker interests over those of foreign companies, whether through imperialist ventures or minimizing foreign capital's access to local markets, are no longer options.

At the same time, nation-state functionaries increasingly collaborate with the officials who run supranational institutions and as such they are becoming a component part of this emerging larger transnational whole. Both national and supranational officials, politicians and experts share similar world views. One piece of evidence for these processes can be found in the work of Carroll and Carson (2003). Their research involved mapping the overlapping networks formed by the five leading intergovernmental organizations engaged in formulating world economic policy-making – such as the Paris-based International Chamber of Commerce – and the top interlocking company directors drawn from the leading 350 corporations. They identified a core nexus of approximately 620 individuals within this already powerful group (39). Many move between corporate positions and elite policy-making IGOs from time to time while cementing ties and reinforcing each other's ideas. They also liaise with governments, global think-tanks, corporations and with each other. The authors suggest that together these individuals form a 'global corporate elite'. Clearly they appear to constitute a major core of Robinson's TNS apparatus as well as being participants in the TNCC.

In effect, the rise of the TNS signals an 'epochal shift' (211) where the national members of the TNS become 'proactive instruments for advancing the agendas of global capitalism' (220). This, in turn, further empowers the TNCC in their drive to become the 'hegemonic class fraction globally' (221). Like Sklair (2001), Robinson argued that this process is intensifying the contradictions of world capitalism specifically, the crisis of over production and under-consumption – or 'over-accumulation' – along with 'world-wide social polarization' (226). Finally, the nation-state is not so much losing its power, nor is it disappearing. Rather, it is undergoing massive transformation as it takes on new global perspectives and goals.

3.7 Appraisal

An increasingly integrated global economy is emerging along with the rise of relatively mobile capitalist elites. Unlike the national-capitalist classes of an earlier era, it is argued that the former do not feel accountable to any particular nation nor can citizens or governments do very much to alter this situation. This relative freeing of capital from previous constraints and its ability to often dominate local economies were partly made possible by the willingness of Northern governments, encouraged by IGOs, to liberalize financial and trade flows and retreat from many spheres of public and social life. It also seems that fractions of national political elites are becoming increasingly transnationalized and are now unwilling to impose constraints on the market or to resist the demands of capital on behalf of their own citizens.[ii] All this has given rise to a world risk economy (Beck 2000a). Here, whether labour is engaged in agricultural, industrial or service work, the experience for most is one of fragmentation, disempowerment and dependence on casualized employment. All but a small minority of elite professionals are being sucked into, and compelled to compete in, a precarious world labour market that offers little or no security or social protection.

Much of this has been rendered even more fragile by the rapid industrialization of China and India. This is because despite the advantages their rapid development confers on the world economy – cheap commodities and a growing demand for advanced goods and services – their vast, low waged but also increasingly educated populations contribute massively to what seems tantamount to a race to the bottom in terms of wages, job security and welfare provision for workers at nearly all skill levels. In these conditions, economic globalization and predatory capitalism reinforce each other and contribute to worsening inequality within and between nations. Ultimately, these inequalities threaten to destabilize capitalism itself as widespread poverty and underconsumption deprive many of the means to acquire the symbols of identity and belonging. But in a world where media images of self-realization and personal freedom through consumerist bliss penetrate everywhere, inequalities, insecurities and economic marginalization seem likely to lead to social disorder and disintegration at many levels while fostering terrorism, crime and mass migration. It is these additional forces, and the ways they interact with economic globalization and with each other, that we explore in the next two chapters.

Yet another consequence of growing economic insecurity and inequality has been the increased dependence of many individuals on debt as their primary or even sole means of buying into consumerism. Indeed, the collapse of global finance in 2007 and 2008 and the deepening economic recession which then spread rapidly across the world – as the supply of bank loans and credit shrank and inter-bank lending became frozen – were partly caused by the growing over-dependence of economic growth on vast increases in bank, business, household and consumer debt during the previous fifteen or so years, especially in America and the UK. This, in turn, was linked to several other economic changes which took place from the 1980s onwards and which accelerated from the mid-1990s.

One was the growing importance of what Gowan (2009) calls the 'New Wall Street System' (NWSS). This involved an attempt by successive US governments to compensate for its declining industrial hegemony in many fields by bolstering Wall Street's inherent global business advantages in the sphere of financial products. Thus, the financialization process – the increased relative importance of financial products, financial institutions and the channelling of resources into this business sector (Elliot and Atkinson 2008: 195) – intensified especially in the final years of the twentieth century. Here, earnings from financial business increased as a source of GDP. Moreover, instead of providing one of the main forms of funding to enable businesses to expand and create jobs for the majority (for example, Elliot and Atkinson 2008 and Gowan 2009) the NWSS became an increasingly dominant influence in sucking wealth out of the 'real economy'. Much of this paper or virtual wealth was diverted by the deregulated investment banks and hedge funds into the realms of financial speculation including blowing up the price of various assets – shares and securities or commodities such oil or cereals – during periods of intense purchasing to create a financial bubble and then selling while prices were high. Often this was followed by a collapse in values. Similar activities included funding company takeovers and creating the conditions for an immense housing boom by urging Americans either to take out mortgages on second homes or to buy a first home they could not afford. The latter became the main source of the now infamous toxic debts which were bundled up with other debts into securities, or collateralized debt obligations, and widely sold across the world banking system. A second change was the tendency for the big investment banks and the unregulated, non-transparent 'shadow banking' system (Gowan 2009: 13) – especially the hedge funds – to find numerous ways to increase the supply of profit-earning assets they could lend while reducing the share of the assets they retained against the demands of depositors. In addition to expanding their lending activities generally they also attracted resources for yet further lending from the pension funds and from the Asian trade surpluses recycled via Wall Street into financial investments (see Box 3). But much of this increased lending to other banks, to businesses, for speculation, to individual consumers via credit cards for household spending and car finance or mortgages ended up in huge amounts of unsecured borrowing. Together these practices created a crisis of confidence which nearly sank the global financial system in October 2008 and required huge interventions by governments in the attempt to limit the likely global economic damage. Clearly, these practices, which have become endemic to the financial system, further intensify the insecurities already tied into the workings of the real global economy that we have discussed in this chapter.

Migrants: Key Agents of Globalization

4

This chapter continues the theme that we increasingly live in a globalizing world which is linking the lives of all world citizens together in a myriad of ways. Here, we look at migrants while the next chapter focuses on transnational criminals and terrorists. In each chapter the discussion first outlines recent estimates of the size of the phenomena under consideration. Then we examine in what ways each is changing in response both to globalization and the opportunities created by global corporate power but also the opportunities, contradictions and conflicts generated by additional factors such as nation-state policies, growing global inequality and technological change. Finally, each chapter explores some of the most striking ways in which the needs and activities of these agents are becoming increasingly entangled and interdependent even while each retains its own unique character and trajectory.

4.1 The extent of migration

According to Jordan and Düvell (2003) current rates of migration are not especially high. There is no world 'migration crisis' except in the minds of politicians, media moguls and right wing nationalists. Moreover, many migrants are living in developing countries rather than in the developed ones. In 2000, for example, there were 32 million living for more than one year outside their country of origin in Sub-Saharan Africa, 51 million in Asia and another 9 million in other developing countries. Most of these migrants moved from adjacent countries. These figures included refugees and asylum seekers whose numbers reached 19 million worldwide in 1993 – following the collapse of the USSR – but fell to 12 million in 2002. Jordan and Düvell concluded that the proportion of people leaving their homelands today is much smaller than in the nineteenth and early twentieth centuries when the populations of both sending and receiving countries were considerably less than they are today. Held et al. (1999: 304–12) reached similar conclusions. During the entire nineteenth century, Britain's home population grew by 31 million but 18 million people left the UK during this same period so that a large proportion of this natural population increase emigrated. For Europe as a whole almost 40 per cent of the population growth in some decades went overseas, most to North America though some also went to Australasia and South America (Jordan and Düvell 2003: 65).

Jordan and Düvell (2003: 66) and Faist (2000: 3–4) suggested that the total number of individuals living outside their country of origin in the early 1990s was approximately 2 per cent of the world's population. In actual numbers this amounted to 120 million people in 1990 but the flows increased during the 1990s so they estimate that by 2000 the number probably reached approximately 150 million. In the context of Western Europe much of this migration took place in the post-Second World War decades of acute labour shortages and rapid economic growth between the later 1940s and the early 1970s when countries such as the UK and France absorbed large numbers of migrants from their former colonies. There were also huge migrations into the Middle East oil countries after the OPEC oil price rises of 1973 and 1979 and followed by rapid industrialization and building programmes which sucked in huge numbers from South Asia, the Philippines, Islamic African countries and elsewhere.

Turning to more recent figures based on UN data, the total number of foreign-born individuals in 2005 residing outside their country of birth was estimated at approximately 191 million (Migration Policy Institute or MPI 2007). Of these the largest absolute number by far had migrated to the USA (more than 38 million), followed by the Russian Federation (approximately 12 million), Germany (over 10 million) and France, Saudi Arabia and Canada with between 6 and 7 million each. Considered in terms of their share in the total host population, however, other countries were far more dependent on migrant labour. To give a few examples, the percentage of foreign born in the United Arab Emirates was 71 per cent in 2005, in Singapore it was 43 per cent, in Saudi Arabia 26 per cent while Switzerland, Australia and Canada contained 23, 20 and 19 per cent respectively (MPI 2007). As a percentage of the world's population in 2005, the MPI figure of 191 million migrants works out at approximately 3 per cent – a slightly higher figure than that provided by Jordan and Düvell.

Recent world migration flows: a complex scenario

However, some important qualifications are needed to compile a more accurate and recent picture of migration flows. First, such estimates are based on calculations of the documented flows of migrants across borders: that is those who enter countries more or less legally. But without doubt the number of illegal migrants is also high and has grown in recent years either because of human smuggling by criminal gangs – where illegal migrants seek work on farms, in sweatshops or in similar poorly paid work – or through the trafficking of enslaved or captured individuals sold by their families or as a result of debt bondage, including children and young women. In fact, flows of undocumented migrants are nothing new. The USA, for example, is an especially notable case and has always experienced very high numbers of undocumented migrants (see Cohen 1987). Shelley (2007: 200) gives a figure of over 10 million illegal entrants living in the USA at any time but other estimates point to at least 12 million, probably half of them from Mexico. Although by definition it is impossible to arrive at any safe estimates of the extent of illegal migration, if we aggregate such figures to the world as a whole we can suggest that the 'real' numbers of migrants – legal and illegal – is probably somewhere between half as much again and perhaps even double these official estimates for legal migrations. This might give an overall figure of approximately 5 per cent of the world's population though using a similar calculation Harris (2002: 18–19) arrived at an estimate approaching 7 per cent.

A second qualification is that the number of countries whose citizens are now involved in migration as sending and/or receiving countries has increased considerably during recent years. One obvious region where this has occurred concerns the former territories and allies of the Soviet Union. Thus, since the end of the Cold War there has been a huge increase in the movement of people between the countries of Eastern Europe and Central Asia, especially into the Russian Federation, but also very large numbers into Germany and other EU countries (approximately 38 million people between 2000 and 2003) as well as to more distant countries including North America and Israel (20 million during the same period) (Mansoor and Quillan 2006: 35). Another factor here is that the mass migrations that took place between the 1820s and 1914 involved a situation where most people moved from a small number of historically long-established European societies to a cluster – the USA, Canada, Australia, New Zealand, South Africa, Brazil and Argentina – of societies which were relatively new and which possessed small populations in relation to their large territorial size. Moreover, they desperately needed migrants to provide the labour power for fuelling the early stages of industrialization. However, the situation during recent decades has been very different in that migrant flows have involved streams of mostly poor, not very highly skilled, people moving from a large number of relatively impoverished countries in the South and East into the already highly developed countries of the North with relatively large and long-established native populations. In addition, most of today's migrants come from religious and ethnic cultural backgrounds and from societies with histories – including colonial ones – that are markedly different from the host societies where they are trying to settle.

These realities have several important implications which we discuss later. But the main point to make here is that there has been a globalization of migration flows and in at least two ways: it involves people from far more host and receiving countries; and second, contemporary migrations flows – particularly those found in global cities – bring into close physical proximity mixtures of people from a far greater number of backgrounds/nations who are also very different from each other and not just from the native populations encountered in the host societies. It has been claimed that London, for example, contains migrants from just about every nation (Benedictus and Godwin 2005) and it is also where most or large majorities of Afghans, Zimbabweans, Albanians, Iranians, Americans and French people – among numerous others – are likely to settle. Thus, since 1991 there has been a large increase in the numbers of non-traditional immigrant communities from countries other than former colonies including China, the countries of former Yugoslavia and Sweden (Vertovec 2007: 1029–31).

Third, the numbers involved in recent migrant flows and the alleged difficulties migrants create have often been grossly exaggerated by politicians, media people and others. This has helped to fuel a series of moral panics and political backlashes across EU countries such as Austria, France and the UK but also in the USA and Australia. Nevertheless, a combination of factors has definitely pushed up the numbers of migrants, including political refugees and asylum seekers, seeking entry to the more developed countries in the last decade. The number of legal migrants alone entering the USA and Britain between 2000 and 2005, for example, jumped by approximately 18 and 32 per cent respectively compared with the preceding five-year period (MPI 2007) and less dramatic increases occurred elsewhere. In the case of London, for example, census data indicate that the proportion of its population who were born overseas rose from approximately 18 to approximately 25 per cent between 1991 and 2001 (cited in www.bbc.co.uk/bornabroad) and according to May et al. (2007) this had risen to more than a third of the city's population by 2005. In fact the numbers of immigrants born overseas increased dramatically as a proportion of the working population as a whole. By 2006, they made up approximately 13 per cent of Britain's total labour force compared with approximately 7 per cent in 1997 (Travis 2007). The mass arrival of Polish migrants following Poland's 2004 accession to the EU was especially spectacular and provoked a great deal of controversy – though many have since returned partly because of the recent recession. Between 1997 and 2007 a total of approximately 2.7 million new jobs were created in the British economy and though different government departments give varying figures it seems likely that 80 per cent of these were taken by migrants (Smith and Montague 2007).

Last, migration flows have not only increased in recent years and become much more complex in terms of the sheer numbers of nationalities and ethnic cultures involved but they have also changed their character in two other ways. First, women now make up virtually half of the migrant population and increasingly they move in search of employment rather than for family reasons (Aviveros 2008). Some, particularly in South East Asia, have already become familiar with modern life, having previously left their rural origins to live in cities where they worked in factories or similar commercial activities before migrating. Thus, when they arrive in Los Angeles or Paris they have already acquired the familiarity and skills preparing them for work in laundries and sweatshops (Sassen 1991) or as maids, nannies, care workers in nursing homes or perhaps as sex workers (Ehrenreich and Hochschild 2003, Parreñas 2001). Second, a rising proportion of migrants are highly skilled. They are increasingly required to lubricate and valorize the global service industries and especially that component which concerns the symbolic knowledge economy. Accordingly many governments have altered the laws and reduced the restrictions on the inward flow of skilled people even while they have been attempting to tighten their control over poor economic migrants, asylum seekers and refugees.

4.2 Transnationalism – the changing nature of migration and its causes

Most experts agree that the recent character of migration has changed compared with earlier waves. Many nineteenth-century migrants to North America, Brazil and elsewhere retained strong connections through letters and visits to their families back home, sent cash to help their kin and some returned one or more times before finally deciding to remain in the host society. Nevertheless, the aim of those who did eventually choose to settle was to become more or less fully assimilated into the new society though, of course, this did not preclude the retention of a sense of cultural affiliation with fellow nationals both back home and in the new country often over several generations. In contrast, recent migrants are said to be less interested in prioritizing assimilation to the host society's values, goals and behaviour patterns. Obtaining full citizenship rights is one thing but becoming fully British, French or whatever in a cultural sense and relinquishing feelings of national identity and involvement in relation to their country of origin is something quite different. Contemporary migrants mostly have no intention of forgoing the latter to attain the former nor do they need to do so. Thus, instead of the 'melting pot' societies of the past where cultures eventually mixed and formed a dominant American or Canadian national culture, we find a 'salad bowl' society of cultural pluralism. Here each incoming group strives to retain much of its transported culture though school attendance and exposure to media influences means that second and third generations are likely to develop a more hybrid identity and perhaps experience a conflict of loyalty and values between their parent's culture and homeland and their society of birth. Other writers have referred to this situation slightly differently by talking about 'switching board' societies (Zhou and Tseng 2001). Here the host societies of today operate like aircraft carriers on which the ethnic/cultural airplanes of many nations land and take root but not completely and not necessarily forever. Instead these switching-board host societies operate in effect as bases from which numerous multiplex social networks branch out in all directions with their owners simultaneously continuing to nourish their links with their nations of origin, perhaps to family or friends who have migrated to yet other host societies but while also putting down roots of some kind in the host society.

Where migrants follow this pattern, they are engaged in constructing a form of transnationalism. Here, irrespective of whether they act individually, in families, village groups or through regional or national networks, migrants do not just cross territorial borders but they also construct 'multiple ties and interactions linking people or institutions across the borders of nation-states' (Vertovec 1999: 2). These multiplex linkages may encompass economic, family, cultural, religious and political ties and projects. On one hand, the result is the building of 'third spaces' (Pries 2001: 23) which cannot simply be understood as the consequence of home and host society interactions. Instead, distinctive life patterns are generated which demonstrate dynamic emergent connections and properties existing 'above and beyond the social contexts of national societies' (Pries 2001: 23). Nevertheless, despite living bi-focal lives or even multi-local ones – if their overseas diasporic ties to fellow nationals are dispersed to several countries (see Cohen 2008 for an in-depth analysis of diasporas) – most transnational migrants are also likely to remain strongly influenced by and dependent upon their own transplanted home cultures.

This 'new' transnational migration is causally linked to a number of recent parallel changes taking place both in the host societies to which economic migrants are most likely to move and their countries of origin. Both, in turn, are associated with globalization.

1. The impact of neo-liberal policies.   The imposition of neo-liberal policies in the form of structural adjustment programmes on most developing countries by the IMF and WB since the 1980s has been a particularly strong force propelling transnational migration (Basch et al. 1994, Jordan and Düvell 2003, Portes 1997, Massey 2005). These policies have often led to increases in the price of imports as currencies were devalued, governments were pushed into reducing public sector employment, welfare provision and subsidies – for example on foodstuffs and fuel – while the liberalization of trade and capital flows along with the privatization of some state enterprises were often standard requirements. All of this tended to reduce employment, undermine local businesses, including farmers, and increase poverty and inequality. The impact of neo-liberal economics, especially on the poorest groups, has compounded the additional economic problems already faced by many developing countries, namely, debt servicing costs, falling exports prices for raw materials and general economic stagnation and underemployment. One such case in point is Mexico which in the mid-1980s was encouraged by the IMF to eliminate agricultural subsidies and remove the previous legal constraints on the sale of peasant communal land holdings. This made it easier for private foreign investors to make inroads into commercial farming – but also forests and other national resources – thereby making it even more difficult for peasant farmers to compete with the import of cheap subsidized foodstuffs from the USA. In fact, this situation deteriorated further after the onset of the North American Free Trade Association (NAFTA) in 1994 which opened Mexican borders even more to trade flows from its Northern neighbour. As we will see in Chapter 5, one result was the tendency of some Mexican peasants – like their counterparts in several other Latin American countries including Bolivia,

Columbia and Peru – either to turn to coca cultivation or to seek migration as a strategy for basic family survival. Indeed similar patterns and processes have been evident across much of Sub-Saharan Africa, Central and South America and elsewhere.

Some writers (Basch et al. 1994, Jordan and Düvell 2003: 63 and 73–5, Portes 1997) wonder whether transnational migration by poor migrants constitutes a form of 'globalization from below' which parallels and partly negates the obstacles resulting from the globalization from above imposed by TNCs, IGOs, G7 governments and so on. Others (for example, Smith and Guarnizo 1998) disagree and argue that this celebratory view disguises the hard reality that most transnational migrants are engaged primarily in a struggle for economic survival, one in which they sometimes rely strongly on support from their home governments. However, this argument is pitched, there is little doubt that such migrants are finding ways to exploit the many niches created in the world economy by globalization and neo-liberalism and in doing so they turn the overwhelming power of global capitalism somewhat to their advantage and those of their family and/or fellow villagers at home. But this can only work if they keep a foothold in both host and home nation and harness the socio-cultural networks that bind both societies. Moreover, such micro strategies require migrants to draw on the reservoirs of social capital embodied in the norms of reciprocity and cooperation existing between individuals who know each other and/or who participate in the same social collectivity (Faist 2000: 100–8). Such norms and the expectation of giving and receiving help are especially likely to be strong in the case of friends and family. Thus, the migrant can hope to obtain assistance both from people at home – who may club together to raise the cost of their fares or invoke personal contacts among those already established in the receiving society to assist the migrant on his/her arrival – and their fellow migrants in the host society. In the case of the latter, relatively abundant social capital is converted into scarce economic capital: for example, the provision of accommodation, help in finding employment but also perhaps, access to credit, technical advice, business contacts and markets. Symbolic capital held in common by members of the ethnic collectivity, and not just immediate relatives and friends, can also be drawn upon in the form of 'shared cultural meanings, memories, future expectations' and collective feelings of identity or what Faist refers to as a 'we'-consciousness (Faist 2000: 102 and 109). Accordingly, this alternative economic globalization from below does not depend on treaties, laws, international institutions, deregulated capital markets, stock and money markets and corporate power but rather upon micro social networks and ethnic ties.

2. Time-space compression. The revolution in ICTs – especially emails and the interactive possibilities of Skype, but also mobile phones, faxes, making home movies of family celebrations and so on – plus the opportunities provided by frequent jet travel – all render frequent communication and reciprocal home visits increasingly accessible, simple and cheap. Here, transnational migrants are employing the same technologies as capital: the international banks, the money/currency markets and the TNCs. In doing so the aim of migrants is not to maximize 'company' profits but to construct and maintain long-term cross-border social networks.

3. The changing nature of migrant work.   Portes (1997) argued that in the nineteenth and early twentieth century most migrants could expect to eventually find secure, regular, manual or other work – whether unskilled, semi-skilled or skilled – on a long-term basis in the industrializing host economy. Often such employment involved the construction industry including railways, docks and various public sector buildings. Alternatively many migrants to New York, Chicago or Toronto worked in the sweated industries or joined the emergent Fordist manufacturing enterprises which depended critically on eager immigrant labour during the 1920s and 1930s. In contrast, Portes suggested that today's economic migrants not only possess limited economic resources, few skills that find a ready market in rich countries and face the risk of racism and discrimination, but the likelihood is also that much of the employment available to them is casualized, low grade, temporary and exists primarily in the service sector: cleaning, catering, entertainment, domestic service and so on. Often such work is not only poorly paid but it also offers limited or non-existent long-term prospects whether for men or for women. Other kinds of income-earning opportunities may involve fully- or semi-criminalized activities including drug dealing, prostitution, theft, dealing in counterfeit goods and so on. Westwood and Phizacklea (2000), for example, described how in New York and other cities it is commonplace to see or to discover accounts of second generation ethnic youth gangs fighting and competing with each other for scarce, badly paid jobs and carving out criminal territories in the cities along with young Afro-Americans.

The dearth of regular, long-term income possibilities and the risk of never attaining a reasonably comfortable economic life has at least two consequences for first generation migrants. One is that an uncertain economic future coupled, perhaps, with experiences of rejection and prejudice at the hands of host institutions and citizens may strengthen the desire, but also the need, to retain strong links with family and friends so that an escape route remains available. The willingness to provide assistance for those at home and to remain involved in local activities then become not just a moral or political obligation but a rational survival strategy. Second, the precarious nature of economic prospects provides an incentive for migrants to build a livelihood based on entrepreneurial activities which exploit the niches and opportunities provided by the transnational networks linking home and host economies. This might involve employing family or neighbourhood labour, whether at home or in the host situation, while catering not just for the local ethnic market but host consumers as well. Mostly, such businesses are likely to be small-scale and might encompass one or more of the following: exporting and importing foodstuffs, craft goods, cultural artefacts, second hand or cheap 'luxury' goods and cultural items whether for migrant and/or host markets in the receiving country or for people back home; providing travel, banking or media businesses or broking services which handle the moves of migrants and their families; running restaurants; or engaging in activities linked to the 'underground economy'. These might depend on child labour or sweatshops that break environmental and health laws, petty crime and so on, or employing cheap, family or child labour in the homeland to manufacture, export and market products in the host society.

Of course, some ethnic or family businesses which straddle two or more countries involve huge investments, technically complex activities and the utilization of highly educated and trained kin. For example, the threat posed by the impending absorption of Hong Kong into mainland China in 1997 encouraged many members of its business elite to spread their accumulated investments into Canada, USA and elsewhere. In order to do this some businesses planted a son or other close relative overseas and placed him/her in control of the family business there, perhaps strengthened by forging joint ventures with more established ethnic Chinese companies already operating in Vancouver, Los Angeles or wherever (Mitchell 1995). Alternatively, during the early 1990s, some hypermobile, 'astronaut' Hong Kong elite business owners, settled their wives and families in the host country – often in North America – to manage the business while husbands shuttled back and forth across the Pacific, attempting to juggle contracts and deals within and between the two countries (Chan 1997).

4. The contribution of nation-states. Waldinger and Fitzgerald (2004: 1187) argued that it is the actions of states and not just of immigrant communities that determines whether and under what terms transnational migration will take place. States do this by trying to control the exit and entry of individuals across their boundaries, including their own nationals, by raising issues of what constitutes citizenship and deciding when and on whom to confer the right to live in their territories (1185). In the context of contemporary transnational migration, the power of nation-states and nationalist affiliations are also demonstrated by the fact that many developing countries actively engage in what Schiller (1999: 110) described as 'transnational nation-state building': that is, they foster numerous policies deliberately designed to encourage their citizens to migrate and to build multiplex relations with the home society. Such policies include the following: passing dual citizenship laws, encouraging participation in national politics by allowing overseas citizens to vote in home elections, subsidizing communication and media flows from home to host society – so that, for example, home TV and radio stations are easily accessible in the host society – simplifying the procedures which allow overseas citizens to invest in national land or other business ventures, and so on. Governments do this because of the economic and other benefits which may accrue to the home society including regular flows of remittances, increased exports of local produce and skill acquisition and transfer. Some governments also wish to promote the presence and prestige of their nation by cultivating images which suggest the existence of a worldwide community of nationals, sharing the same cultural meanings and identities. For example, Smith (1998: 228) talks about the creation of an immediately recognizable 'Mexican global nation' abroad shaped by a gamut of signifiers denoting 'Mexicaness' and which overseas nationals also enjoy. In total, therefore, such policies often serve to consolidate rather than weaken nationalism and state coherence. Moreover, migrants contribute to this strengthening nationhood through their continued home affiliations and involvement in helping to fund local political struggles for the election of officials in their home town or by clubbing together with other migrants to finance village school or hospital improvements and similar actions.

Box 4   Increasing migration to the Global North: some consequences

As explained in the main text for Chapter 4, recent years have seen a rapid rise in the numbers of migrants attempting to enter the EU, North America and other prosperous countries. Many of these migrants are coming from regions, mostly in the Global South, characterized by endemic poverty, economic stagnation, a deteriorating environment and recurring political crises including civil wars and genocide (see also Box 5). So long as the countries from which they come remain in this condition, many of their citizens, especially young people, will continue to plan escape routes through migrating to the rich countries.

Migrants from Sub-Saharan Africa

Everyday many hundreds or even thousands of young Africans try to reach Europe in dilapidated boats, travelling via the Canary Islands to Spain, crossing into the EU from Libya via Italy or moving from Somalia to Yemen and then Europe (Rice 2008). Many are destined to drown during their voyages or have to be rescued by European coastguards. For example, it is estimated that 4 million of Mali's 12 million citizens are living abroad (Traynor 2008). Alternatively, others will succumb to diseases such as HIV/AIDS, with the associated tendency for these to escalate into uncontainable epidemics which then spread across the world through various vectors, or they may become willing or reluctant accomplices in armed militia gangs or in transnational criminal activities – with the capacity to wreak harm on those far beyond, as well those within, their national borders.

Native responses

■ Increased migration has given rise to moral panics among the media, some politicians and sections of the host population in many recipient countries.

■ Much of this concern focuses on the supposed pressures migrants place on housing, educational, health and employment resources – although the evidence for this is often limited. Moreover, on balance, migrants' economic and social input far outweighs any costs they engender, not least because most are young, their educational costs were paid by their home society, they are keen to work and their tax contribution is considerable.

■ However, many host-society citizens express anxieties concerning the threat that continuing inward flows of migrants allegedly pose to the survival and authenticity of native cultures. These tensions have helped populist radical right wing political parties across Europe, Australia and elsewhere to widen their support among sections of the general public.

■ For example, the Danish People's Party (DF) gained 12 per cent of the votes in the elections of 2001. Entering mainstream politics as part of a coalition they enabled other right wing parties to form a majority in parliament without needing the support of centre parties (Andersen 2007: 103). The DF's manifesto clearly states that 'Denmark is not a country of immigration' and it would not accept 'a transformation to a multi-ethnic society' (107).

Interestingly, the chains of human need tying the fortunes of rich and poor countries together through migration are not driven solely by the deprivations existing on the migrant-supply side. Strong demand pressures are also pulling migrants towards the host societies.

5. Tolerance of ethnic diversity. It has been argued that despite strong anti-immigrant sentiments, it is easier for economic migrants today to retain or even enhance their sense of nationalism when living abroad because in general host cultures are now much more tolerant of ethnic diversity, dual identities and the retention of some aspects of home culture than was the case a hundred years ago (Levitt 2001). In America, for example, the pressures to conform to a 'standardized notion of what it means to be "American" have greatly decreased' (Levitt 2001: 27). Values have also changed in other ways compared with the nineteenth and early twentieth century. Thus, during the past 60 years, decolonization, the establishment of the United Nations and the nurturing of universalistic ethical assumptions concerning human rights have all helped to legitimize and encourage the idea of migration from poor nations and the entitlement of those involved to exercise some choice regarding their identities and affiliations (Smith and Guarnizo 1998).

6. Cultural capital. Many poor migrants today possess more cultural resources than earlier generations. This is partly because access at least to primary education has become widely established in most developing countries. In addition, exposure to the mass media endows many migrants, including those with limited education, with a 'TV imaginary' (Westwood and Phizacklea 2000). Among other things this equips migrants with considerable knowledge about world events, some experience of cities and modernity and considerable understanding of commercial forces even before they have departed for foreign lands (Sassen 1991). All these skills and orientations probably facilitate the transition to life in the host society but also increase the confidence to juggle two identities and sets of loyalties.

4.3   Some consequences of transnational migration for host and home societies

Because the multiple, transnational networks forged by migrants of many different regional, ethnic and national origins criss-cross the world and spread in many directions, the activities in which their participants engage generate important consequences for their various home and host societies but also for globalization. While some of these are positive and contain the potential to foster economic development in the South, to enhance cosmopolitan understanding and deepen globality, others are more worrying in that they seem to either intensify existing divisions or create new ones.

One very positive consequence is that transnational networks create avenues for capital flows and for sustained cross-border entrepreneurial activity. As we have seen, the latter may involve a wide range of activities. In addition, transnational networks provide channels through which legal or illegal, unrecorded remittances are sent home to family members perhaps to assist educational costs, to pay for a funeral or to enable a parent or brother to buy farm land. In many instances remittance are larger than the value of inward flows through foreign direct investment, overseas aid, tourist income or even all of these. Often, too, they constitute a huge proportion of the incomes and GDP of some developing countries, for example, Jordan, Albania and Morocco. The World Bank suggested that the total world value of remittances to developing countries for the year 2004–5 amounted to $164 billion and reached an estimated $305 billion in 2008 (Ratha 2009). But it is likely that at least another 50 per cent is not recorded. In the case of migrants from Central America and the Caribbean, for example, a total of $48 billion was sent to their home countries in 2004 and this represented approximately 70 per cent of the value of foreign direct investment (Office of the Chief Economist, World Bank 2008).

Second, migrant linkages stitch very different societies together through the many flows and links of socio-cultural activity. Moreover, because most societies now contain a number of socio-cultural enclaves which have been transplanted and reconstructed within their borders by a variety of migrant groups, there is a sense in which no society can any longer retain whatever uniqueness and autonomy it may once have possessed. Rather it is as if each society is a continuation of, and/or overlaps with, many others simultaneously so that the far away is 'here'. Yet, at the same time, 'here' – our national members living in other countries – is also present far away. As Welsch (1999) suggests, we have internal complexity and difference caused by cultural 'interpenetration' while lifestyles 'no longer end at the border of national cultures' but 'are found in the same way in other cultures' (197–8). One possibility here is an increase in cultural hybridity and bricolage as the fragments from numerous ethnic and national repertoires – in music, dance, cuisine, dress and fashion, health practices, marriage customs and much else besides – are brought into close juxtaposition with cultural entrepreneurs finding ways to mix and merge them in new ways (Vertovec 1999). However, while this interweaving of world societies and cultures intensifies globalization and has the potential to increase cultural understanding, many native inhabitants in the host societies – who perhaps face similar problems of multiple disadvantage to those experienced by migrants – may feel threatened by what they perceive as a series of 'invasions' from people apparently indifferent to their own culture. Instead of hybridity and border crossings therefore we find re-territorialization, a retreat into local affiliations and social fragmentation (Friedman 1997 and Liang 2007).

Third, as we have seen, and partly because of the difficulties they are likely to encounter, economic migrants often desire and need to retain their imported culture while finding ways to continue their involvement with families and villages at home. But this, in turn, may create certain conflicts and tensions in relation to the host society, its native communities and its government. For one thing, migrants may import and re-establish some of the religious or sectarian, regional, ethnic, class or caste divisions and conflicts that are prominent in their home country along with established expectations concerning the continuing appropriateness of various customary standards of behaviour with respect to gender, generational or community relations. This is likely to generate misunderstandings and tensions in relation to migrant communities from other nations and with members of the host society. As has recently been apparent with Britain's participation in the wars in Iraq and Afghanistan, such difficulties may be exacerbated where the host government decides to pursue foreign policies which give rise to conflicting loyalties on the part of some migrants – in this case those with Muslim religious affiliations and/or who were originally from Pakistan, Afghanistan or the countries of the Middle East. Here, the combination of widespread antipathy towards Western and especially American intervention in Arab and Islamic countries and elsewhere over many years along with a sense of alienation felt by some second generation immigrants with respect to the character of British socio-political life, as against their 'home' societies and world Islamic identity, have fuelled considerable resentment, confusion and deeply divided loyalties. Similar divisions are evident in France, the Netherlands and other countries. Here, the problems, divisions and conflicts of the South, sometimes intensified by Western policy and intervention, become deeply embedded in the countries of the North.

Fourth, not all the conflict and misunderstanding which may arise in host societies are associated with difficulties between host and migrant communities. Rather, conflicts and tensions are also likely between the different migrant groups themselves and especially where they live in close proximity and are competing for scarce resources and jobs as in large urban conurbations.[i] As

Waldinger and Fitzgerald (2004: 1178) suggested, the 'highly particularistic attachments' that economic migrants seek to transplant to the host society more or less replicate the primordial sentiments and affiliations found at home. Indeed, migrants are engaged in the 'spatial extension' (Friese and Wagner 1999: 106) of their ethnic/national affiliations across borders. But these run counter to those aspects of globalization, such as an emergent global civil society and a widening consciousness of human unicity, that many would like to see. Moreover, in so far as transnational migration leads to the construction of multiple ethnic/national mini-societies in the host situation which are largely continuations of many distant home societies, what occurs is the 'stacking up' of completely separate social spaces within the same small physical location (Pries 2001: 3). Others have pointed to similar effects. Sennett suggested (2002: 47) that instead of globalization through migration leading to 'a flexible social world' it seems to be creating one 'that produces social relations of indifference...a regime of differences that are non-interactive' as in global cities.

4.4 Migrants and their linkages to other agents of globalization

We have seen some of the reasons why current forms of migration frequently take the form of multiplex transnational networks straddling home and host societies. However, transnational migration is also a response to several striking but also overlapping contradictions at work in the global economy and we now discuss each of these in turn. Finally, we consider some of the niches, legal and illegal, which migrants exploit in the host economies and show how these depend upon the collusion of other powerful global agents.

The contradictions of economic globalization

First, the neo-liberal policies of trade and capital liberalization and state retrenchment reluctantly adopted by many developing countries during the past 25 years strengthened the impact of an increasingly mobile corporate capitalism partly by freeing it from nation-state control. This intensification of the forces of economic globalization created a situation whereby both poor – and other – migrants and different kinds of capitalist interests are driven by the same overall global market parameters to a quite remarkable degree and despite their very different needs and capabilities. Thus, both are responding to the differential distribution of jobs, wages and market opportunities in various parts of the world and to the pressures and possibilities generated by economic globalization. Similarly, both contribute to deepening these same processes. In this sense, transnational migration is not just a cultural and political process but it also acts as a central agent of economic globalization in its own right.

Second, in theory this much more open, liberalized economy requires an equally open labour market where workers and migrants can move just as freely as capital, adapting rapidly to the flows and counter-flows, openings and closures in market opportunities, to new and declining niches and needs in different macro-regions over time. Here, however, a conflict exists between the needs of capital and the political priorities and responsibilities of nation-states which propel the latter to demonstrate a fundamental concern with preserving their sovereignty over territory, borders and citizens. Even if the transnational fractions of nation-states (see Chapter 3) are more inclined to encourage a considerable loosening of control over the movement of labour in and out of their territories, anti-immigrant campaigns orchestrated by sections of the mass media and some politicians along with moral panics among ordinary citizens render this problematic. As Massey (2005: 86–7) suggested, while 'a geography of borderlessness and mobility' is being created for capital there remains 'a geography of border discipline' for labour migrants. Moreover, in the face of inward migration from the poor regions of the world, the citizens of the rich countries suddenly rediscover their right to protect their own local culture and places from strangers by insisting on the 'smack of firm boundaries' (86). Thus:

> in this era of 'globalisation' we have sniffer dogs to detect people hiding in the holds of boats, people dying in the attempt to cross frontiers, people precisely trying to 'seek out the best opportunities'. That double imaginary...of the freedom of space on the one hand and the 'right to one's own place' on the other, worked in favour of the already powerful. Capital, the rich, the skilled...can move easily about the world...and at the same time whether it be in the immigration-controlled countries of the West, or the gated communities of the rich in any major metropolis...they can protect their fortress homes. Meanwhile, the poor and the unskilled from the so-called margins of this world are both instructed to open up their borders and welcome the West's invasion in whatever form it comes, and told to stay where they are.

Thus, numerous obstacles to mass migration and free labour movement remain in place despite the fact that the commitment to neo-liberal free markets and a borderless trading world ought, logically, to produce an equal concern with the free movement of labour. But, as Jordan and Düvell explained (2003: 87), the pronounced nomadic tendencies which are now endemic to global companies 'have outstripped the capacities of national migration management systems to adapt to the requirements of international capitalism'.

One of the curious contradictions resulting from this failure of governments to cope with migration was explored by Harris (2002: 20–41). He observed that for many migrants their move across borders is 'essentially a journey to work' (30) or in search of work. Moreover, many migrants only wish to remain overseas sufficiently long to be able to help their families at home while accumulating the savings and skills which might enable them to live a better life on their return. It is not the intention of many to acquire citizenship in the host society. However, closed borders and the imposition of ever tighter restrictions on immigration create a situation where many migrants are criminalized. Moreover, this threat and the need to avoid it encourages, indeed compels, migrants to seek legal citizenship and to settle permanently so that their access to work can become more secure. If borders were more open and migrants could come and go according to their own changing economic needs and in response to rising and falling employment opportunities in different countries, most would not attempt to stay permanently or to become host citizens. Rather their primary orientation would be to retain their roots and citizenship in their country of origin and returning home whenever possible.

This brings us to a third contradiction which in some ways brings the needs of capital and migrants into conjunction. Thus, the widening inequality, diverging economic opportunities and the degree of political security and freedom from oppression prevailing in the rich countries, compared with the situation confronting individuals living in the peripheralized poor nations, create a sharp disjuncture between the North and some countries in the South. This, in turn, gives rise to economic and political 'cliffs' (Jordan and Düvell 2003: 77) which motivate and drive many individuals living in the latter to attempt to scale these by engaging in transnational migration strategies. At the same time, much of the recent increase in migration has been due to the 'grave economic and political situations' existing in many parts of the world (Shelley 2007: 196): for example, population growth in many Third World regions alongside the growing economic disparity between the rich and poor worlds; political conflicts and collapsing states in many parts of Africa, the Middle East and South America; and the spread of corrupt, incompetent and oppressive governments whose elites channel scarce national resources into their personal accounts in offshore or Western banks. Additional factors propelling poor migrants northwards and westwards have been the collapse of the former USSR and the eruption of regional conflicts that followed, notably in the Balkans, but also the entry of a cluster of East European countries into the EU in 2004 and again in 2007. Thus, we find various forms of legal migration being encouraged for 'top-level and high-skilled' nomadic professionals in the global economy but alongside a parallel need for 'adaptable, biddable, low-paid, seasonal, temporary and service workers' coming from the weakest economies (Jordan and Düvell 2003: 74). Unlike their skilled, elite counterparts, welcomed everywhere, such poorly rewarded, often illegal and deeply insecure migrant workers move to escape from multiple disadvantages at home only to encounter more such insecurities and inequalities in the host society. Nevertheless, they are able to survive and sometimes even prosper because as we have seen they can usually utilize the informal ethnic enclaves and fluid economic niches which thrive in the rich countries. These, in turn, are built around personal trust and the reciprocal kinship ties, 'cultural solidarity' and perhaps religious sentiments shared by fellow members (Jordan and Düvell 2003: 75–6).

Last, strikingly different sets of work and life expectations exist within the rich as opposed to the poor countries in addition to very different demographic profiles. In the poor countries, we find high rates of population growth combined with a young population, the majority of whom are under 25, alongside low or non-existent economic growth, high rates of unemployment and poverty. In stark contrast, the demographic profile of most advanced economies demonstrates a dependent, ageing population, rising life expectancy and declining birth rates. This creates a situation where vacancies for a wide range of domestic and care workers are left unfilled. But in addition, in North America, Western Europe and Japan, even lower-paid native workers have experienced years of relatively good wages, social wage entitlement and therefore access to a comfortable lifestyle. They now hold high certain expectations concerning their entitlement to continue enjoying a reasonable lifestyle.

Migrant niches and colluding 'legal' agents

The overall result of these contradictory processes is that they create openings for different kinds of migrants as they respond to the various worldwide legal and illegal, blocked and relatively free market niches and opportunities generated by the combination of an open world market for capital and a rather closed one for labour. But the interests of some private businesses and public organizations as well as those of certain middle-class individuals living in the rich countries, and not just those of migrants, may also be served where the latter are successful in navigating this global game of snakes and ladders set within a terrain of unequal opportunities, dangers and resources. Thus, the political economy of globalization requires not just more effective channels whereby elites and highly skilled workers can move more easily around the world but also conduits for transporting and funnelling cheap, willing, less-skilled labour into certain work niches within the developed countries. What are these niches?

1. One occurs where high expectations among the native population have fostered the belief that they are justified in shunning certain kinds of menial, dangerous, unpleasant, or seasonal work, requiring unsociable hours and/or which are above all poorly paid (May et al. 2007). The labour shortages that result may attract some migrants especially, perhaps, those who have recently arrived or who have no legal residency or work rights. Among the economic sectors where migrant labour often plays this key role of providing a substitute for host workers are the following: certain aspects of agriculture especially fruit and winter vegetable picking; some aspects of tourism; building and construction work; catching, cleaning and sorting fish (Harris 2002: 27–31); some dangerous and unpleasant cleaning work, for example maintaining underground sewers or water ways, or clearing streets and metros; and the armies of people often working at night who come on stream, especially in global cities (Sassen 2007: 183–6), to service, clean, repair and remove rubbish in and from

hotels, restaurants, museums, stations, airports, supermarkets, thousands of offices in company buildings, colleges and other places of work. As one young Mexican migrant living in South Carolina declared when interviewed in January 2008 by two journalists:

> Yes I am here illegally. But we work the hardest. We are doing the jobs Americans will not do. We are building their homes, washing their dishes. We do all the work and they do not like us. (MacAskill and Glaister 2008)

2. A second niche exists where governments open up their public sectors enterprises – particularly hospitals, prisons and residential-care homes – to private investment including from foreign companies and/or require them to compete for customers by offering improved but also low-cost services. Alternatively, fundamental shortages of native skilled workers may exist temporarily in certain key sectors. In both situations, local and foreign companies need to attract the cheapest yet appropriately skilled labour available in the global economy. This, in turn, might compel both publicly owned and private service providers to develop pathways for avoiding or circumventing citizen laws, residence and work permit laws to obtain or retain workers from abroad. Alternatively, they might place pressure on the host government to turn a blind eye to contraventions of time limits on migrant residency or demand the modification of existing immigration laws so as to permit increased flows of certain categories of migrant worker. To take one example, the acute shortage of trained nurses and doctors in the UK National Health Service (NHS) combined with the expected long-term increase in the demand for health care led to an increase in the number of internationally recruited medical staff to the NHS. Thus, in 2002 and 2003 the annual admission of non-UK trained nurses rose be several hundred per cent compared with the 1960s. These mainly came from the Philippines, South Africa, India, Zimbabwe, Nigeria and Australia. It seems likely that other kinds of businesses might also engage in such practices to retain foreign professionals whose contribution or overseas connections are highly valued but whose legal right to remain has expired. Examples here might be dotcom or media companies, businesses engaged in various creative or design sectors or perhaps some producer service firms with complex networks of overseas clients, suppliers and partners.

3. A third niche arises where the interests of migrants and those of capital coincide – or, rather, the needs of those middle-class individuals employed on the higher rungs of business and other organizations based in the rich countries. This possibility takes us to the realms of 'the globalization of child care and housework' and the 'global redivision of women's traditional work' (Ehrenreich and Hochschild 2003: 11). Several changes have converged to make this possible and likely. An increasing number of women in the developed countries have taken up paid work since the 1970s. In the

USA, this proportion rose from 49 to 69 per cent between 1970 and 1990 (Beck 2000b) and reached 70 per cent by 1994 (Castells 1997: 159). Many of these women are now also employed as highly skilled professionals and exist with their equally well-paid partner in two-career families. As these changes have taken place, these Western women have had to find other caretakers – nannies, domestic servants and residential-care workers – to look after their children at home, to clean their houses and the institutions where their elderly relatives live, and to watch over the latter living in residential-care homes. Moreover, much of this work requires affection and the supply of emotional resources and not just physical labour and attentiveness. To some extent this also applies to the growing trend for migrant female labour, legal or illegal, to provide sexual services for men living in the rich countries. In addition, some women find employment in the thousands of cleaning and laundry companies now operating especially in North America. Alongside this, the feminization of migration has meant that a very high proportion of those moving to the developed countries end up filling this care gap one way or another. In doing so, such women have largely replaced the native domestic workers who once undertook these roles. For example, North African women now undertake the work as domestics in the households of middle-class French urban families that native girls from rural France once did. Similarly, in the USA, Hispanic maids, cleaners and nannies from Mexico and the countries of Central America have mostly replaced the African Americans who undertook three-fifths of such work 60 years ago (Ehrenreich and Hochschild 2003). Many of these foreign care workers do not enjoy the same welfare rights as native workers and face uncertainties over visa and work-permit renewal. Indeed, a large proportion are illegal and are likely to experience even greater risks and disadvantages than legal employees in the same occupation including very long hours of work and levels of pay far below the legal minimum.

Several factors propel women into migration including the following: the reality that an increasing number are now living in female-headed households and are largely responsible for family income; the lack of education and therefore poor job prospects and low wages available to their actual or potential husbands; the continuing low levels of economic development and widening inequalities prevailing in the countries from which they come; and the possibility of being able to find female relatives to look after their children while they are away. This, in turn, often creates much unhappiness for all concerned (Chang 2000, Ehrenreich and Hochschild 2003, Yeates 2004) while displacing the care deficit from host to home country. In addition, some governments in the South have also deliberately encouraged their young women to migrate because they see them as an important kind of export given the remittances most will send back home. This is especially true of the Philippines where approximately two-thirds of migrants are women, most of whom take up work as domestic or care workers overseas (Parreñas 2001).

Driven by the huge disparities in wealth and market opportunities between North and South and the potential gains from seeking entry to the rich countries, many migrants are prepared to seek entry illegally despite the costs and risks entailed. Here, once ensconced in the host country innumerable strategies and devices may be deployed in the attempt to remain such as using illegal visas, work permits or passports to remain after legal visas have expired. Other strategies involve finding marriage partners in the host country or buying such partners in the attempt to gain citizenship or hiding within the host society once official documentation has expired with the help of available social networks linked to kin, friends and community help. Then there is the possibility of resorting to criminal activities or becoming dependent upon criminals to survive and remain concealed.

Migrants and transnational crime connections

Before resorting to the kinds of strategies previously discussed, the illegal migrant first has to cross the world and gain entry to the host country. This, in turn, gives rise to another form of entanglement between the different agencies struggling to make a living in the global economy: namely, that between migrants and transnational criminal gangs which engage in various forms of people smuggling and given the constraints imposed by nation-states on the free movement of people across their borders.

It is important to distinguish carefully between the different types of criminal activities involving people. One involves the smuggling of 'free illegals' (Shelley 2007: 201) who cross borders illegally in search of work with the help of smugglers. Sometimes these are paid a fixed sum in advance by the migrants concerned but increasingly the latter are left with debts which must be paid back from their earnings over a period. The leading example of free illegals is the movement of mostly young males into the USA from Mexico and the Central American countries, mostly for economic reasons. Many join their families in America. Approximately 70 per cent of illegal migrants from Mexico use the services provided by professional smugglers. There are said to be up to 120 smuggling rings in Mexico and some provide a comprehensive service including transportation, the provision of safe houses during transit and links to possible employers. A variation of this pattern occurs where illegal migrants negotiate voluntarily to be transported abroad but where the price demanded by the smugglers is so large that to pay the costs incurred illegal migrants are locked into a condition of debt bondage for many years once overseas. This usually means that they enjoy little freedom of movement and remain largely under the direct control of the criminal gangs involved until the debt is paid. They probably also endure unpleasant living conditions to pay their debts and are compelled to accept long hours of dangerous or unpleasant work in sweatshops, factories, farms or restaurants (Shelley 2007: 201–6). The illegal Chinese migrants who go to the USA usually have to pay much larger 'fees' to criminal gangs – up to $50,000 in some cases (204) – because the distances involved are so vast, the officials of several countries have to be bribed, including Chinese officials, and the time and number of transit points involved are considerable. Clearly few migrants or their families can afford to pay such amounts in advance so the smugglers agree to receive part of their fees later and paid as debts over a period. Again most of these migrants are young males.

A third form occurs where criminal gangs engage in human trafficking and those involved are either captured or sold against their will prior to being smuggled abroad. Alternatively, they believe they are going to enjoy some freedom and access to reasonable employment once they reach the host society but then discover they have been tricked and in fact end up in conditions of slavery, perhaps for ever. The largest source of these victims of forced migration is in Asia, especially in South East Asia, and much of this is closely related to the market for illicit sex associated with sex tourism and prostitution in countries such as Japan and Thailand. Increasingly, too, this trade in illegal migrants who are largely victims, taken against their will or under false pretences, has become established in the former communist countries of Eastern Europe, the Balkans, Russia, the Ukraine and elsewhere (Miko 2007: 40–1). Many of these young women end up providing sexual services to other migrants or to host society members living in cities and towns across the EU countries. They also live under appalling conditions including the threat of retaliation against them or their families should they attempt to escape their condition.

This form of organized transnational crime is said to be among the fastest growing of all criminal activities at the present time (Miko 2007: 39, Shelley 2007: 198). Partly this is due to all the factors we have already discussed: a more open global economy with increased flows of people, goods and money which render concealment easier; growing inequality and poverty in many parts of the South; and disintegrating states and regions where war and crises are constant dangers. However, people smuggling is also less risky than crimes such as the drugs trade because typically it earns lighter punishment from courts, requires less investment and technical knowledge – though providing transport, bribing officials and arranging border crossings, transit points and so on does demand organizational skills – and is more lucrative. Estimates concerning the worldwide earnings from people smuggling vary but the Federal Bureau of Investigation in the USA suggested that this was equal to 9.5 billion dollars in 2005 (cited in Shelley 2007: 198). In terms of the numbers of people smuggled worldwide, the US government suggested that this amounted to between 600,000 and 800,000 individuals annually. However, the International Labour Office (ILO) in Geneva has estimated that if those who are forced into overseas migration are included, then, at any one time there may be over 12 million people worldwide who have been trafficked across borders and 80 per cent of these are women (Miko 2007: 40).

4.5   Appraisal

What seems clear, above all, from this discussion is the quite extraordinary extent to which there is a 'fit', or a multiple set of complementarities, between the unmet needs of the developed societies of the North and the diversity of human resources available in the poorer economies but which are not being utilized effectively because of widespread poverty, a history of underinvestment and sometimes dangerous internal conflicts and weak, incompetent states. Whether it is the paucity of responsible, low-cost carers to look after the aged, the ill or the infirm – both in public and private sector institutions – the unwillingness of local citizens to undertake many kinds of badly paid and unpleasant work, the skill deficits within some high-tech businesses and research establishments or the need of successful two-career families for reliable, domestic childcare support, migrants of all kinds can usually find niches to fill in the rich economies – though this is rarely matched by a corresponding recognition or appropriate rewards. Moreover, despite the anti-immigration sentiments that invariably accompany increased inflows of migrants, and once the current recession ends, this situation seems set to continue far into the future if for no other reason than the stagnant population growth and demographic imbalance that now characterizes virtually all Northern societies; though, paradoxically, the tendency for migrants to buck this trend by having more children may partly cancel out this discrepancy. Because migration processes lock the fates of the Global North and South together, those who participate in them, and the families and communities in both host and home society who support them, are key agents of globalization despite their often impoverished and desperate situations.

A second reality operating at the heart of increased world migration flows is the striking degree to which both migrants and capital are being driven by the same forces of economic globalization and the opportunities and hardships they bring. Among these are a more open but also more competitive and unequal world economy and the creation of a proliferation of new niches as between different economic sectors and localities coupled to huge differentials in profit and wage levels, job vacancies and market opportunities. Moreover, because nation-states cling to their sovereign control over territories, borders and citizens a glaring contradiction exists between an open global market for capital, money and goods alongside the relatively closed one for labour. However, this, in turn, creates additional opportunities for certain kinds of migrants and the national and transnational criminal gangs who make a living out of transporting or concealing them.

Transnational Criminals and Terrorists: New Insecurities

5

At the end of the Cold War in 1989, it was widely believed that a new world order of relative peace and spreading prosperity would follow. Globalization would contribute to this process by bringing the possibility of markets and democracy to far more countries and people than ever before (Thachuk 2007: 5–7). In reality, however, global economic inequalities as well as wide disparities between countries in their capacity to offer relatively stable, competent government with minimum levels of corruption have actually widened rather than diminished and much of this has either been exacerbated or caused by globalization. At the same time, the more open borders and the liberalization of finance, trade and investment associated with economic globalization, along with technological change and the weak capabilities of many states, have made it far easier for drug traffickers and other kinds of organized criminals, money laundering activities and terrorism to thrive and move with relative ease across borders. In short, as Thachuk stated in stark prose:

> Along with the rapid movement of people, money and information have come the criminals, terrorists, and thugs who cross international frontiers undetected, who peddle human beings, who steal weapons intended for mass murder, who conduct illicit monetary transactions in mere minutes, and who may carry disease and death in a suitcase. (2007: 6)

According to Thachuk all this has generated at least three consequences. One is that whereas the influences wielded in the international arena were once primarily within the remit of states, whose governments acted in accordance with certain recognized rules and procedures, recent changes have led to a situation where the power exercised in the global arena has become dispersed among many non-state actors to the point of anarchy. In addition, this has occurred to such an extent that often states can no longer hope to contain or deal with the problems that result. Second, the agencies which have increasingly moved into and indeed helped to create this much more open and less controllable global terrain tend to be either individuals or small groups.

They employ not just the new technologies to further their ends but also rely on interpersonal relationships and traditional sources of affiliation including ethnicity, religion and national identities.

Third, what we mean by national security has undergone a transformation and no longer pivots solely or even mainly around issues relating to the threat or possibility of armed conflicts between nations. Instead, threats to security today press in on people everywhere from many directions and sources and pose greater challenges than ever before (8). This chapter focuses on two of these threats to national and indeed individual security, namely, transnational organized crime and international terrorism. Certainly, both have increased alarmingly in recent years. They not only influence the lives of people everywhere but their impact also undermines the licit global economy and the effectiveness and sometimes the very existence of some nation-states. Each uses violence, intimidation, extortion and other drastic measures as part of their modus operandi, though for different purposes. Indeed, while the 'business of terrorists is terror, or asymmetrical violence; the business of organized criminals is business, albeit in conditions of violence' (Berdal and Serrano 2002: 201). Similarly, both rely on their ability to corrupt states, officials, security forces and various professionals as an instrument for weakening the criminal justice system, for obtaining information and hidden support for their operations and for weakening the legitimacy of political systems (Williams and Baudin-O'Hayon 2002: 134). At the same time, recent globalization processes have provided new resources, routes and fields of operation which both groups have proved highly adept at exploiting. More often than not, as well, this ability to respond with considerable resourcefulness to the possibilities and the tensions brought by globalization coupled to their willingness to collaborate across ethnic/national lines has enabled criminals and terrorists to frequently outmanoeuvre the more entrenched, locally bound and hierarchical institutional practices in which national-based protective agencies are steeped. Nevertheless, despite their similarities and occasionally overlapping global influence, transnational criminals and terrorists are also different in important ways and we consider these in the second section.

As with the previous two chapters, this one does not attempt to provide a thorough coverage of the vast literature relating to transnational crime and terrorism. Instead, in respect to crime we look at some recent estimates of its growing extent and changing methods of operation and consider the causal factors which explain these transformations. Then, discussion focuses on some key examples showing how the operations of transnational criminals overlap with, depend on and mesh into the activities and needs of other leading agents of globalization. In the case of terrorism we examine some recent attempts to identify and explain its contemporary forms. We also explore some of the major ways in which it feeds on the weaknesses of certain states, forges links to transnational crime and depends for its survival partly on legitimate and familiar social institutions.

5.1 Transnational crime – illicit pathways in the global economy

Crime organized across territorial borders has always existed but there is wide agreement that its scale and scope have increased rapidly during the past two to three decades. Along with this has grown a perception that this burst of transnational organized crime increasingly threatens to destabilize not just parts of the legal economy, democracy, law and order, health and much else besides, but also that it undermines the much needed attempts to improve forms of global governance which are urgently required as a response to the centrifugal forces of disorder generated by globalization (Williams and Baudin-O'Hayon 2002: 127–8).

Clearly, it is inherently impossible to calculate the value of global crime accurately and given that there can only be approximate estimates. Caution is therefore needed in attempting to identify its possible impact on, and place within, the world's legal economy. Nevertheless, according to Castells (1998: 172) the United Nations estimated that the value of the global drugs trade was approximately $500 billion in 1994, larger than oil. When considered overall the annual profits from all forms of global crime were estimated at approximately $750 billion but he reported that other reputable bodies such as the IMF put these figures somewhat higher. Certainly by the end of the last century such estimates were being raised. In 2002, for example, the IMF and WB estimated the value of illicit global money laundering – from the perspective of criminals, a necessary adjunct to their activity – at approximately $1 trillion (Thachuk 2007: 17 and 20) while an Australian academic put this figure much higher at $2.8 trillion (Walker 1999).

The sheer range of activities now pursued by organized crime groups, and which involve moving, coordinating and selling illicit goods between two or more countries, is also astonishing and grows all the time. Thus, as fast as technological change creates new commodities and markets, facilitates their move or eases the risks involved, so new kinds of crime open up. In addition to the familiar trade in drugs, weapons of all kinds and nuclear material, body parts, people, counterfeit goods, antiques and art items, money and currencies, a host of 'new' commodities are increasingly being stolen, smuggled and traded transnationally: for example, mobile phones, laptops, rare animals, babies, Mercedes and other makes of quality cars, petrol, computer data, credit cards and pornography to name but a few (Taylor 2002). Moreover, it is often the case that emerging nationally based criminal organizations which are struggling to carve out a niche for themselves often take the lead in developing new products, routes, methods of working and products. Examples here would certainly include the criminal gangs which emerged from the countries of the former Soviet Union and its Eastern European allies after 1992 but also Nigeria (Castells 1998: 175).

5.2 Explaining the upsurge of transnational crime

To a remarkable degree the deepening scope of transnational criminal, capitalist, migrant, and to a lesser extent, terrorist activity across the world have often been caused by very similar changes. However, each agent has also faced specific changes and pressures unique to them. What factors have mainly contributed to the growth of transnational crime?

Geopolitical transformations

A particularly crucial and recent geopolitical transformation was the end of the Cold War between 1989 and 1992 and the collapse of the USSR which followed. The reunification of Germany and the establishment of the EU single market were also important events since both simplified the movement of people, money and goods across national borders. Similarly, although the majority in fact moved to mainland China (Dombrink and Huey-Long 1997, Kong Chu 2002), the reunification of Hong Kong with China in 1997 (Carter 1997) led to a worldwide dispersion of some Hong Kong Triad groups especially to countries and regions with established Chinese ethnic communities such as the North American Pacific and East Coast seaboards.

The collapse of the USSR and the emergence of a number of new states proved to be particularly crucial in contributing to increased global crime (Castells 1998: 183–95, Williams and Baudin-O'Hayon 2002: 130–1) because its borders were opened up and the previous barriers to the movement of goods, money and people were either lifted or could now be manipulated much more easily. This allowed not just legal but illegal commodities to flow in and out of the countries of the former Soviet Union. These increased illegal flows often on a vast scale – of currencies, foreign and IMF loans (Castells 1998: 193) flowing outwards and into Western banks, but also cigarettes, stolen cars, women trafficked for illegal sex, weapons and nuclear material and other commodities – were facilitated by at least three additional factors. One was the inexperience and sheer ineptitude of the new states and their officials and the failure to produce appropriate regulatory regimes and mechanisms for controlling the new business and market opportunities that arose as state enterprises were privatized and former controls on the distribution of goods were removed. Second, the pressure from the West, spearheaded by the IMF, to impose the 'short sharp shock' of privatization and market liberalization extremely rapidly on Russia in the early 1990s flooded the country with dollars and facilitated the takeover of state enterprises by former communist officials, often in collusion with criminals. At the same time all this contributed to the collapse of the former economy in addition to the rise of crime (Stiglitz 2002). Indeed these almost certainly fed into each other. For the mass of ordinary citizens, unemployment rose, everyday commodities became scarce or rocketed in price and living standards plunged while a tiny minority became extremely rich. Third, a number of new local mafias linked to different ethnic or national groups quickly emerged in response to the new economic opportunities and engaged in widespread smuggling or imposed protections rackets on the new businesses. But in addition, organized global criminal gangs, particularly the Sicilian and Camorra mafias, established collaborative ties with local gangs to gain from the wholesale privatization of state assets. The former also participated in smuggling and linked the emerging Russian groups with drug gangs in Columbia.

Cold War American support for criminal gangs?

According to Woodiwiss (1993 and 2003), from the later 1940s through to the 1980s the Cold War struggles for military but also political and ideological supremacy waged by the USA against its Soviet enemy also helped to nurture the rise or consolidation of various criminal groups around the world. Thus, Woodiwiss argued that certain deliberate US policy measures, taken as part of its policy to contain communism, helped to lay the foundations for the later activities of several global criminal drug gangs. This involved a sequence of covert activities conducted by the US Criminal Investigation Agency (CIA) which were designed to sabotage or destabilize communist parties or militias by arming, financing or otherwise assisting various local criminal groups who were usually involved in some way in the drugs trade whether as manufacturers or smugglers. These were specifically groups which were perceived by the CIA as potential or likely allies in the fight against communism. Often they were highly nationalistic and right wing as well as opportunistic in their pursuit of criminal activities. Woodiwiss cited and explored a string of such alleged instances of collusion including the following. In the late 1940s, he suggested, the CIA enlisted the support of Corsican drug gangs to destroy the communist trade-union control of the Marseilles dockland by providing the former with arms and money. Similarly, he suggested that the CIA tolerated and encouraged the smuggling of heroin by gangs in Burma, Thailand and Laos during the Vietnam War in the 1960s as part of a strategy for undermining the communist offensive in South Vietnam but also to provide help with funding the war. He also pointed to the collusion that may have taken place between the CIA and right wing authoritarian regimes in Panama, Bolivia, Peru, Columbia and Nicaragua during the 1970s and 1980s. Here, anti-communist army leaders were probably receiving drug money and cooperation from criminal gangs to assist in the fight against communist insurgents with the covert support of the American government.

The impact of neo-liberal policies

The worldwide implementation of neo-liberal economic policies has probably done more than any other single factor to create new opportunities for transnational criminal activities. But economic liberalization and the deregulation of trade, investment and banking combined with policies designed to ensure government retreat from the economy have also exacerbated, or created, several deep contradictions that have shaped transnational crime. This has occurred in four ways. To begin with, organized crime can be regarded as 'the continuation of business by criminal means. And just as business has become transnational in scope as part of globalization, so has organized crime' (Williams and Baudin-O'Hayon 2002: 129). Indeed, there are a number of ways in which the activities of transnational criminals not only mirror those of corporate capitalism but also sometimes depend upon or interact with the latter and we examine some examples later.

Second, Andreas (2002: 37) suggested that in some ways transnational crime can be regarded as the 'quintessential expression of the kind of private-sector entrepreneurialism celebrated and encouraged by the neoliberal economic orthodoxy'. This is because the latter encourages individuals and businesses to become more responsive to price signals. This is exactly what peasants are doing when they turn to the cultivation of coca or opium in response to falling world prices for their legal crops or when underemployed city dwellers become involved in lucrative drug trafficking or marketing. Indeed, the production, processing, transport and sale of illicit drugs are a few of the activities where many developing countries and their citizens enjoy a genuine comparative economic advantage over rich countries. Thus, an unintended side-effect of market reform has been to encourage drug production, trafficking and money laundering (Andreas 2002) though violent threats and pressures from criminal gangs have played a role in pushing ordinary individuals into crime as well.

Third, led by the USA and supported by many governments and the United Nations Convention Against Illicit Traffic in Drugs, agreed in 1988, an ever tighter local and worldwide regime of drug control has been set in place during the last 20 years. Yet, while governments have attempted to collaborate in prohibiting drugs and enforcing restrictions on its production, trade and use they have simultaneously been engaged in loosening their control over flows of investment, trade and capital. Deregulation in one economic sphere has been accompanied by a concerted drive towards achieving more statist control in another but the former has almost certainly and partly undermined the effectiveness of the latter. Last, and following from the previous point, a more open global economy, rising international trade and therefore the growing flows of finished goods, components, parts, materials, machines and so on across many borders have all massively heightened the opportunities for transnational criminals to conceal and smuggle shipments of illegal goods whether these consist of people, stolen or counterfeit goods, drugs and so on. This increased ease of movement is especially pronounced with respect to money flows and has been enormously helped by the deregulation of global finance.

All these contradictions were clearly evident in the case of Mexico during the 1980s and 1990s when its government implemented a massive neo-liberal reform programme in response to US and IMF pressure and in respect to its vast international debts and supposed mismanagement of the national economy (Andreas 1999). Of course, very similar processes and results also occurred in other Latin American economies during the same period. However, since 1994 and the advent of the NAFTA, Mexico's degree of openness to the global economy through its economic links to the USA and Canada has further intensified. Among other things the reforms associated with Mexico's structural adjustment programme (SAP) increased the flow of direct foreign investment into Mexico while privatization brought further enterprises under the control of foreign capital. Part of the SAP also included opening up some peasant communally owned lands for sale to national and foreign agribusinesses thereby ending the protection from alienation which had been extended to them by the Constitution of 1917 (McMichael 2000: 271).[i] These made up approximately 70 per cent of Mexico's cropland (Andreas 2002). The government also made cuts to the subsidies peasants had previously received for credit, electricity, water and fertilizers while price supports for their crops were reduced. Instead of leading, as anticipated, to greater farm efficiency and independence from government through the benefits of intensified market competition, living standards fell in rural areas. For many peasant families the alternatives were either migration to the cities, illegal migration across the border into the USA or resort to cultivating illicit crops in whole or part as the only way to survive (Andreas 2002: 43–5).

Thus, the same changes which opened and liberalized Mexico also encouraged the expansion of an illicit economy and this, in turn, formed a central part of the deepening integration of the US and Mexican economies. Consequently, during the 1990s Mexico became not only a main world supplier of cocaine (between 20 and 30 per cent) and marijuana but also a major route whereby these drugs find their way into the US market – though this is also linked to attempts by the USA to extend its control over Columbian drug traffickers, thereby driving the Mexican/Columbian cartels to collaborate in finding an alternative route. The US Drug Enforcement Administration estimated Mexico's overall earnings from the drugs trade at approximately $7 billion per year in 1994 but the Mexican government put this figure much higher at approximately $30 billion (cited in Andreas 1999: 129). In fact, by 1994 some government officials in Mexico were suggesting that drug trafficking had become a driving force for economic growth. At the same time it has been estimated that during the 1980s up to 300,000 Mexican peasants were earning money through illegal drug cultivation (Serrano and Toro 2002: 162). Similar numbers of peasants were drawn into drug cultivation during the same period in Bolivia and Peru (161). These increasing flows of illicit goods into the USA have also been facilitated by NAFTA and by the deregulation of Mexico's trucking industry in 1989 – a further consequence of neo-liberal policies. Both have given rise to a vast increase in the number of trucks crossing the border: up to 220,000 vehicles per day, along with 3.5 million railcars and trucks per year in 1996. It is quite impossible for US customs to thoroughly inspect this huge volume of traffic and perhaps only approximately 3 per cent is properly examined (Andreas 1999: 134). But all this has increased the possibilities and the ease with which illegal goods can be smuggled across the border.

Technology

Exactly the same technological revolutions in ICTs and transportation that have empowered legal capitalist business by widening and cheapening the possibilities brought by economic globalization have also underpinned the proliferation of transnational criminal activities. There are several aspects to this. For example, computerization and electronic banking mean it is relatively simple for dirty money from criminal activity to be laundered by depositing and moving it rapidly and secretly through several national banking systems before it is invested in legal enterprises. Similarly, offshore banking havens such as the Cayman Islands, Luxembourg and Antigua provide secrecy, low tax regimes and minimum restrictions on cash deposits. These, too, facilitate the concealment, mobility and eventual legal transfer of illegal earnings into legitimate outlets (Andreas 2002: 45–6, Williams and Baudin-O'Hayon 2002: 132). In addition, technological change in the shape of Internet facilities, mobile phones and laptops has obviously accelerated and simplified the ability of criminal gangs to coordinate their activities over distance, pass on information and warnings to members of their own or other gangs – perhaps concerning impending police raids in one location or the need to change supply routes or storage depots – and keep track of their various transactions (Castells 1998: 198).

Economic liberalization and the fostering of more intensive market competition have also encouraged governments and companies to improve, extend and cheapen transport networks. Consequently, technological innovations in respect to the transportation of commercial cargo by rail, sea and air have reduced the costs of moving goods around the world. At the same time increased international trade flows linked to liberalization and outsourcing arrangements helped to boost world exports. Indeed, these doubled in a decade and reached $4.1 trillion by the mid-1990s (Andreas 2002: 41). But, again, these same processes have heightened the opportunities for smuggling illicit goods across borders and over large distances. The huge increases in the carrying capacity of ships coupled to containerization have proved especially significant. By the mid-1990s some ships were able to carry up to 6000 sealed containers each 20 foot in length. During the 1990s in the USA it required five customs officials and three hours of inspection to examine one such container effectively. Thus, approximately 90,000 person hours are needed to thoroughly search one ship carrying 6000 units (Andreas 2002: 41). Adding to the difficulties here is the fact that it would presumably be difficult to separate legal from illicit cargo within any of these containers especially in the case of drugs. It is hardly surprising therefore that only a very small percentage of shipping cargo is likely to receive proper examination.

Considered overall Castells (1998) suggested that the ability of criminal organizations to take advantage of the opportunities provided by transport and communication technologies enables them adopt very similar production and profit-maximizing strategies as those pursued by legal businesses. These include: outsourcing some of their supplies to and from other gangs; locating certain activities in currently low-risk areas where they can more effectively control the environment in which they secure their goods; and targeting their preferred market outlets in yet other locations thereby minimizing risks and maximizing returns. Accordingly they strategically juggle their various sites of production and marketing. Such activities can also be boosted by forming inter-ethnic criminal alliances. These enable gangs to cooperate by seeking joint ventures, subcontracting arrangements and carving out agreed zones of distribution and sourcing rather than constantly fighting over the control of different areas. Again such collaborative activities strongly resemble those conducted by legal corporations and demonstrate the similarity of the legal and illegal global economies – both furthered by technological change, neo-liberalism and globalization and both driven by entrepreneurial and highly commercial considerations (Findlay 1999). At the same time such measures and tactics give criminal gangs a worldwide reach as well as flexibility and relative security.

Box 5   The widening economic gap in the Global South

A widening economic gap is apparent between the most – the so-called BRIC countries, especially Brazil, Russia, India and China – and the least successful economies of the South. According to De Rivero (2001), for years, perhaps 130 or more Southern countries have experienced negative, very low, or merely average growth rates that barely exceed population growth. Also, in 1997 the IMF reported that the number of countries with a GDP falling within the lowest 20 per cent of global income distribution increased from 52 to 102 between 1965 and 1995 (cited in Munck and O'Hearn 2001: xiv).

- Many are small, in terms of population, land size or sometimes both, most lack oil or other valuable resources and remain highly dependent upon exporting raw materials whose prices fluctuate widely or have tended to fall in real value terms over time.
- Their manufacturing capacity, if any, is mostly concentrated in sectors such as textiles and garments where there are many rival exporting nations, skill levels are plentiful and the value-added generated by factories is low.
- Most Sub-Saharan African countries fall into this category of 'non-viable economies' (De Rivero 2001: 118) but others exist in North Africa, Central America, Central and South Asia and Eastern Europe.

The consequences

1. Extreme poverty and inequality, vast mega-cities, where many lack proper employment (Davis 2006), along with growing environmental crises, especially water

shortages and droughts, all tend to push these countries into political as well as economic crises while impelling numerous individuals to attempt migration to the rich
countries.

2. Collapsing states occur widely in these nations. They often demonstrate failing, corrupt and/or highly oppressive governments and/or the rise of rival, armed
militias competing for control of certain regions, key minerals or other resources.
Some have degenerated into genocidal wars or have become zones from which
transnational organized criminal gangs run their drug and other illicit supply routes
into the markets of the developed countries. Examples include Sierra Leone,
Liberia, Somalia, the Sudan, Zaire, the Democratic Republic of the Congo, Rwanda,
Zimbabwe, Angola, Columbia, Peru, Afghanistan, Pakistan, Sri Lanka and the former
countries of Yugoslavia.

3. Weaponry of all kinds has spread to these states either through various transnational criminal networks or it has been dispersed to armed groups where states
are ineffective. All this has further aggravated these violent conflicts.

Causes

These are many and are discussed in Chapters 3, 4, 5, 7 and 8. However, leading
explanations include: (a) the imposition of neo-liberal economics policies and SAPs
articularly by the USA and the WB, IMF and WTO; and (b) with the exception of
economies such as South Korea until the end of the Cold War, and China and India
today, the developed countries prevented these poor countries from operating the
kinds of policies which they practised during their own periods of rapid industrialization: namely, to protect their infant industries until they reached an advanced
point on their technological and managerial learning curves. Some observers see
these policies as nothing less than a deliberate attempt to thwart successful economic transformation in the poorest countries (Bello 2001 and 2002, Chang 2008,
Wade 2004).

Prohibited substances and activities

There is considerable agreement that in different ways the political decisions
states pursue and how they implement these – perhaps partly in response to
the moral and cultural demands of their citizens – largely set the parameters
for different types of criminal action. We have already emphasized the role
governments played in implementing neo-liberal economic policies and the
impact this often had on the fortunes of their countries including the links
with crime. We examine more examples of this in the next section. But here we
focus briefly on the legal prohibition and consequent criminalization of some
activities enforced by states. Here, several observers (see Castells 1998: 177
and Grayson 2003: 162–5) suggested that '[p]rohibition is at the nub of organized crime' (Serrano 2002: 16) and when such policies are generalized to the
international environment it cannot fail to sustain transnational criminality,

too. The drugs industry is the paramount example because 'demand drives supply', and given the refusal of most societies and governments to legalize and/or officially regulate their use, these decisions unwittingly create a vast global industry with deep roots percolating down into the micro-relations active in innumerable locales. As Castells pointed out 'the legalization of drugs is probably the greatest threat that organized crime would have to confront' (1998: 177). Moreover, legal prohibition not only creates vast clandestine and often dangerous markets but the value of the products traded is also increasingly augmented by their very prohibition. This stark reality does not apply only to drugs: the illicit market value of nuclear materials, body parts, weapons, art objects, immigrants, dangerous wastes and so on are all enhanced by legal prohibition.

In respect to the world drugs trade and US efforts to suppress it in Latin America, it is clear that the tighter the controls introduced, and the more determined the efforts since the early 1980s to control and stamp out the drugs trade in Columbia, and elsewhere, the larger, more vicious and elaborate the drugs trade has become. In Columbia, drug money fuelled the spread of weapons and this in turn led to kidnapping and extortion as well as increased attempts to corrupt and intimidate the police, judges and other officials along with increased violence between armed gangs. In fact, not only in Columbia but in several Latin American countries, governments responded to the increasing breakdown of civil law and the ineffectiveness of the judiciary by attempting to tighten controls, obtain the assistance of America and increase the role of the armed forces (Walker III 1999). In each case, however, the result was a further general escalation of violence among criminal gangs, more armed movements, an increased blurring of the border between criminal and police ranks and a deterioration of government efficacy (Serrano and Toro 2002: 170–7). A further consequence of attempts at eradication has been the spreading of the drugs industry to other areas of Latin America (Ronderos 2003). For example, in March 2008, the United Nations Narcotics Control Board (Campbell and Bowcott 2008: 19) reported that as the attempts to eradicate coca cultivation in Columbia have partially succeeded so the incidence of drug farming has grown in Bolivia and Peru. The same report also observed that governments are still concentrating on policing small local users in their countries and consequently they are failing to control the major global drug cartels while the latter continue to operate flagrantly across the world – including shifting their major European supply routes into West Africa.

5.3 The changing nature of transnational crime

Having considered the key factors which have caused the huge increase in transnational crime we now consider some of the additional and significant ways in which criminal organization is changing in response to globalization. In fact, law enforcement agencies across the world have increasingly recognized these changes (Carter 1997: 144). One such change has already been alluded to; namely, the sheer escalation since the end of the Cold War in the number of countries and regions which now provide the home bases for criminal activity and whose members quickly learned to push across borders and establish niches in other countries. Many, though not all, of these originate in the countries of the former Soviet Union: for example, Chechnya, Serbia, Albania, Poland, Ukraine, Rumania but also Nigeria and Somalia, to name but a few. In each case, these fledgling organizations had to carve out spheres of business activity and operational territories both in relation to the established mafias of Italy, China, Japan, North America, South America, and so on, and in respect to each other. Frequently, this involved the initial resort to extreme violence as a way of demonstrating their determination to find a niche and/or taking up the new illicit products being generated by the legal economy. Carter (1997) points to a second change whereby transnational criminals have become more entrepreneurial, calculating and responsive to changing market opportunities. Thus, criminal gangs are more likely to seek targeted commodities and to pursue specialization at any one time. They are prepared to outsource some of their operations to others on occasion – for example contract killing – and they are less inclined than in the past to remain committed to maintaining particular activities or affiliations for long periods. In short, they have become more flexible in their range and methods of activity (Carter 1997).

Third, blood ties and wider kinship affiliations, birthplace, cultural heritage, shared religion or customs have all remained significant sources of bonding and loyalty. As Castells observed (1998: 177): 'from these local, national, and ethnic bases, rooted in identity and relying on interpersonal relationships of trust/distrust (naturally enforced with machine guns), criminal organizations engage in a wide range of activities'. Yet at the same time, other relationships are increasingly accepted, negotiated and put to work alongside the older ones and as we have seen strategic inter-gang collaboration is increasingly taking place. Indeed, this is essential if transnational criminal gangs are to respond effectively to the new opportunities created by economic globalization while finding ways to reduce the risks of being caught. Such collaboration and communication can facilitate the sharing of information concerning future police operations in a given country and help gangs to shift their supply routes or establish new, safer storage depots when these seem threatened. Just one of many examples of inter-ethnic collaboration involving transnational criminal organizations is demonstrated by the links forged in the early 1990s between Italian mafia organizations and their then infant counterparts in Russia. Thus, the former provided counterfeit goods and in return Russian groups supplied various weapons and sophisticated equipment which had been partly stolen from the Russian military. These contacts also enabled the Italian groups to establish inroads into a range of new criminal ventures in Russia including money laundering, drugs and weapons smuggling (Williams and Baudin-O'Hayon 2002: 130).

What all this points to is the reality that transnational criminals have been able to achieve much greater flexibility and versatility – just like their business counterparts in the legal economy – by resorting to the network form of operation (Castells 1998: 182) both in respect to their internal and external relations with other gangs. Of course, the ingredients making up the modus operandi employed by all organized criminal gangs throughout history retain their fundamental usefulness: namely, the willingness if necessary to resort to intimidation, kidnapping and other extreme measures; and constructing a paid network of supporting inside figures (182–3), including judges, police officers, customs officials and politicians, who provide protection from the law, items of information and the ability to evade national rules and borders. Nevertheless, as Castells (1998: 183) also suggested, it has been the continued ability of transnational criminals to draw on the strengths provided by traditional local loyalties while combining these with 'flexible networking' and strategic inter-ethnic cooperation that has endowed them with the 'organizational strength' to engage successfully in global crime.

5.4   The links between transnational crime and other globalizing agents

In this section we explore two of the many possible ways in which the activities of transnational criminals depend upon and interact with those of other agencies often to their mutual advantage: the legal corporate economy – including its professionals, managers and consumers – and transnational migrants. Each type of interaction provides many examples but space allows only a brief examination of a few key themes. Linkages between transnational criminals and international terrorists obviously constitute a third and highly significant possibility but we explore this at the end of the chapter in a separate section.

The connections and overlaps between the legal and illicit global economies take multiple forms. Partly these arise because in the final analysis all organized crime is really 'the continuation of business by criminal means' (Williams and Baudin-O'Hayon 2002: 129). Similarly, as Findlay (1999: 138–42) reminded us, both crime and legal business are driven by and organized around the goal of achieving material gain through obtaining a profit on their operations whereby the revenue from 'sales' exceeds the financial 'costs' incurred. Similarly, both pursue market opportunities, are engaged in competition and are likely to seek profitable and safe outlets for their returns through wise investments. But this, in turn, requires the ability to launder the dirty money from crime by finding ways to convert it into legitimate business activity and in this way it seeps into the licit economy. Moreover, crime often operates alongside legitimate business, is grafted onto the latter or sits inside it. Accordingly, the demarcation line between the two is often much less clear-cut than governments, the media and members of the public would like to believe (Beare 2003: 183, Findlay 1999: 127–9, Ruggiero 2003). In all these ways criminal organizations provide a mirror image to legitimate businesses though of course there are also key differences such as the need for the former to employ violence and intimidation, to corrupt officials of various kinds and their willingness to specialize in trading commodities which have been prohibited. We now look briefly at some of the ways in which the illicit underside of the global criminal economy interacts with and depends upon a range of situations and agents supposedly operating in a perfectly legal, moral way.

Consumers preferences and actions

We begin with just three ways in which ordinary members of the public contribute to the creation of an illicit economy in their capacity as consumers who are rationally engaged in reducing their expenditure while maximizing their lifestyle interests. For example, the value of the illegal drugs industry is said to be equal to almost 1 per cent of global GDP, or a value higher than the GDP earned by 88 per cent of each of the world's countries. Moreover, the industry is estimated to cater for the drug needs of approximately 5 per cent of the adult world population over the age of 15 though much of this involves cannabis rather than cocaine or heroine (United Nations Office for Drug Control and Crime Prevention 2005). Although many of those who consume narcotics live desperate lives and do so as a compensation for their hardships, the considered use of drugs for regular leisure purposes by much wealthier consumers is also widespread and probably growing. Second, it is thought that approximately one-third of the cigarettes smoked in the UK were smuggled into the country (Thachuk 2007: 15) and similar cross-border activities by criminal gangs involving cigarettes have also been widely reported elsewhere, for example in Canada (Desroches 2003). A third example of consumer complicity in transnational crime is revealed by the rapid increase in the production, sale and smuggling of pirated or counterfeit goods. One estimate suggested that this probably forms approximately 7 per cent of world commerce (Thachuk 2007: 17). Partly, this involves luxury commodities such as watches and handbags but the trade in fake medicines has also risen markedly and this presents a much more dangerous threat. Here, medicines may contain only a small proportion of the essential ingredients for improving health (Thachuk 2007: 15). Clearly some consumers are prepared to satisfy their needs by buying cheaper goods when available despite their illegal origins.

Moving higher up the hierarchy of 'legal' activities and personnel, we can note that there are many sectors where the legal production and sale of certain goods may depend upon and merge with illegal activity at some point. The four examples we discuss here are weapons, body parts, cigarettes and money laundering but there are several others including people smuggling by transport companies (see Ruggiero 2003: 174–6).

The production of weaponry of various kinds, especially sophisticated equipment, often requires long periods of development, substantial investment and a key dependence on governments as the main buyers (Ruggiero 2003: 176). Clearly, however, the companies involved need to obtain the economies of large-scale production, if they can, while finding work for their highly skilled workers even during periods where perhaps armament contracts from legal buyers temporarily dry up or diminish. In addition, some governments and companies are more scrupulous than others in their willingness to respectively ignore or agree to sell their products to terrorists, criminals, warlords or regimes not sanctioned by the international community. According to Ruggiero (1993: 55), Fiat in Italy provides one example of a major company engaged in arms manufacturing which was linked to the Camorra in Italy and was implicated in illegal arms sales. It is also thought that in the mid-1990s several countries turned a blind eye to certain national companies which exported semi-legal armaments overseas including France, Spain, China, Israel and the Czech Republic (Castells 1998: 177–8). The illegal trade in body parts provides another such instance where it can be supposed that some degree of complicity is involved. Thus, removing a kidney, eye retina or other organ from a healthy person in, say, India or Russia who agrees to this operation for reasons of poverty, and its transfer in a fit condition to be reinserted into the body of a wealthy private individual in Saudi Arabia, Germany or Brazil, obviously requires the involvement of a range of professional organizations and individuals. These are likely to include properly trained surgeons and supporting staff at both ends, the availability of suitable hospital or clinic premises and equipment, or their equivalent, and the ability to transport the organ across a considerable distance by using appropriate transport and equipment so that it arrives in a fit state to be used. At all these points and across two or more countries a number of medical experts, hospitable administrators, bribable government officials and aircraft crews need to be complicit if this activity is to be successful (Castells 1998: 181).

A third example concerns the smuggling of cigarettes. As cigarette sales have fallen in the more developed countries, tobacco companies have increased their marketing efforts in the South. Here, there is a strong suspicion that though the big companies are not directly involved they have often been aware that some of their wholesalers and distributors, wittingly or otherwise, have on occasions sold cigarettes to drug gangs who then transport and sell the products, illegally across borders. For the latter this is not only an additional source of revenue but also provides one way to launder their earnings from the drugs trade (Campbell 2004). But such activities are not confined to poor countries. Thus, Beare (2003: 185–94) explained how in the early 1990s, the duties on cigarette sales were much higher in Canada than the USA and this was linked to various smuggling rackets whereby the cheaper American cigarettes were moved illegally across the border into Canada. A number of different agents were involved in this including the members of some Aboriginal Indian communities, various banned motorcycle gangs and certain crime families from Montreal. In 1993, the Canadian manufacturers increased their export of cigarettes to the USA by 300 per cent compared with the same period in 1992. Ostensibly this was designed to expand their export market and even though they knew that American consumers mainly smoked national products. However, Beare argued that they did this in the knowledge that 'others would commit the crime of tax evasion by smuggling the cigarettes back into Canada' (192) where the legal price of locally produced products was so much higher.

Legal business and money laundering

Finally we turn to money laundering which Castells (1998: 181) described as 'the matrix of global crime'. It is also the area where the legal and illicit global economies are most likely to become directly entangled. Thus, the liberalization of financial institutions, economic globalization and rising international trade together mean that far greater volumes of liquid resources now flow around the world legally through computerization as well as those which are the result of face-to-face transactions. All this has increased the opportunities for criminals to avoid state controls, move their earnings abroad and engage in illicit financial activities (Helleiner 1999, Schroeder 2001). Money laundering is essential for criminal gangs. First they need to push their earnings into the financial system – for example through the banks found in offshore financial havens such as the Cayman Islands which have lax regulatory regimes and offer secrecy. Then they must find ways to conceal the origins of funds by blending it with legal money before finally rendering it safe by converting a large proportion into legitimate investments. However, the huge increase in flows of dirty money and finding ways to ensure these are absorbed in the world financial system raises the possibility of worsening or triggering economic turbulence. Partly this is because criminals frequently move these flows around the world between banks, currencies, stock exchanges and different investments in the attempt to avoid being tracked and this can destabilize financial institutions and even countries (Castells 1998: 207). In addition, a large proportion of dirty money comes from the drugs trade and this has particularly damaging consequences for social life. Indeed, this is one major reason why governments have tried hard to introduce legislation and technologies designed to reduce the volumes of dirty money being laundered (Helleiner 1999: 60). But the stable working of financial institutions also relies critically on the confidence members of the public feel they can place in the trustworthiness and incorruptibility of those who handle their accounts, deposits, investments and loans and this is undermined by money laundering activities (58–9). Last but certainly not least, a major cause for concern in respect to money laundering, especially since the destruction of the twin WTC towers in New York in September 2001, has been the dependence of terrorists on various kinds of funding to carry out their exploits and therefore the desire to uncover the links that may exist between the money laundering activities of criminals and other agencies and whether and how these feed into terrorist networks.

Several strands of activity and layers of relationships are involved in money laundering. It certainly requires either the assistance of legitimate businesses, and some of their employees, officials and professionals, and/or the ability of criminals to deceive such businesses. This means that since 'any business is run to make a profit' (Lilley 2006: 65), in theory, virtually the entire capitalist economy and its innumerable legal contributors could be involved, unwittingly or willingly, in helping criminal organizations. Second, therefore, money laundering need not be oriented primarily towards bank services. Indeed, in recent years in the attempt to reduce transnational crime and terrorism some governments have introduced regulations designed to increase the degree to which bank officials monitor incoming deposits. Among the measures introduced or toughened up are the electronic tagging of currencies and insisting that banks record and investigate the origins of money flows whose origins appear suspicious. These heightened regulatory regimes have compelled criminal gangs to depend even more on wider business practices as vehicles for money laundering. One likely possibility occurs where dirty money is used to place orders for quantities of goods with factories or wholesalers thereby avoiding the banking system and turning tainted cash into goods that can then be resold for clean money (Lilley 2006: 64). The constant difficulties faced by most businesses in persuading their legal buyers to pay their invoices quickly and the cash flow problems this creates help to explain why they might be prepared not to ask too many questions. Alternatively, having acquired legal goods criminals may barter these for yet others before finally selling them for clean money which can be placed safely in banks.

Nevertheless, third, despite the tougher regulations that have been imposed on banks the latter remain 'commercial institutions whose primary aim is profit' (Williams and Baudin-O'Hayon 2002: 142). Thus, while the success of government regulations aimed at reducing the extent of money laundering requires banks to 'become adjuncts to law enforcement' this may conflict with the pressures from shareholders and others to maximize profits. Indeed, one of the ways in which this conflict between business – and employee – interest and regulatory requirement evidently come into conflict concerns the reality that some professionals appear unwilling to report suspicious financial transactions to the relevant authorities. Moreover, criminals are normally able to find many other professionals and reputable businesses other than bank officials, equipped with detailed financial expertise and contacts, to help them launder money including accountants, investment advisors and lawyers. For example, Lilley (2006) described how the UK National Criminal Intelligence Service has commented on the practices of certain London-based law firms though there are other instances. Allegedly, they exploit their own long-standing relationships with banks and their reputation for probity and respectability to open accounts on behalf of various criminal gangs. Among the examples cited by Lilley are Columbian and East European gangs and the Italian mafia (77–8).

Having acquired legal accounts, criminals can also open their own front companies and receive and send illegal funds around the world through electronic transfers (76). Money laundering also occurs where criminals evade the restrictions now operating in many countries by employing the facilities provided by stock exchanges or a large range of legal businesses – such as building companies, restaurants, hotels, casinos, antique dealers and nightclubs (72–3) – where the need to deal with continuous inflows of real money form a staple part of the enterprise. Finally, offshore banks are particularly useful for criminal money laundering. These are based in locations such as Luxembourg with very low levels of economic regulation and almost no tax obligations.[ii] Such banks are often merely shell organizations which exist either for the purpose of providing safe financial havens and money laundering conduits for criminals or for legal businesses anxious to evade taxation in their country of registration. Such banks are licenced to deal with foreign customers. One possibility here is that legal banks based in the developed countries establish relationships with these offshore banks and create an avenue whereby criminal gangs can then transfer their funds from their offshore accounts into legal accounts opened in the USA or the bank of another developed country.

Migrants and transnational criminal activities

We have already seen how transnational crime is crucial to the recent increase in illegal migration especially when it involves poor migrants trying to escape from poverty, underemployment and even political crisis in their home countries. But without intending to do so both legal and illegal migrants may help to create the conditions which enable criminal organizations to enter and flourish in host societies. There are several possible processes involved. One occurs where certain cultures which have traditionally bred criminal activities in the home society are exported overseas through the sheer process of reconstructing viable ethnic enclaves and social relations in the receiving society. Among numerous examples of this are the Triad societies which flourished in pre-modern China as secret organizations though not all were, or are today, involved in crime (Kong Chu 2002). Active Triad elements are now found living within the overseas Chinese communities which flourish in many countries and cities across the world.

Closely related to the above, a second important connection occurs where criminal elements deliberately follow earlier immigrants to the host society once the latter have become established (Castells 1998: 209, Friman and Andreas 1999: 12, Williams and Baudin-O'Hayon 2002) and then persuade them to accept protection in return for regular tribute payments. This promise might involve protection from discrimination at the hands of local officials and employers and/or from the 'unfair' competition offered by other migrant groups. Many migrants probably fear reprisals if they do not accept this 'godfather' role. However, others probably feel insecure and marginalized within the host society and threatened by native or other ethnic-migrant businesses and so may reluctantly accept the pressures imposed by ethnic criminals.

Where this happens, migrants collude in providing a sphere of market activity, a relatively secure ethnic base within which their criminal members can hide and support structures which allow criminals to develop additional activities. For example, according to Williams and Baudin-O'Hayon (2002: 133; see also Köppel and Székely 2002: 130–2), to

> understand the global rise of Nigerian criminal networks, or the importance of Turkish and Albanian criminal clans in heroine trafficking in Western Europe...it is necessary to examine the transnational distribution of ethnic communities within which and from which they operate.

They make similar observations concerning the trails of Russian and Ukrainian criminal networks moving into Israel, America and Western Europe. Of course, none of this is new. Many who formed part of the earlier waves of migrants to North America before 1914 were almost certainly exposed to such practices whether by the local branches of the Sicilian mafia, Chinese Triads or others. Nevertheless, what is distinctive about the current era is the sheer number and variety of exported criminal gangs seeking concealment within their own ethnic group overseas and who exploit their connections and use them as a home base for branching out into other criminal enterprises. Examples include Albanians, Russians, Nigerians, Croatians, Turks, Kurds, Jamaicans, Moldavians and many others (Friman and Andreas 1999: 12).

A third route into local and transnational crime occurs where the transnational networks between host and home society form part of a much larger worldwide diaspora so that migrants have affiliations through kinship, intermarriage, business links or village ties to people in several countries simultaneously. The existence of such vibrant diasporic connections obviously provides yet another way in which criminals can gain entry to several countries by utilizing these networks as pipelines and social vehicles of infiltration. Often, too, such worldwide links offer much better access to guns and other means of violence, a larger range of illicit products and field of operations and the possibility of forging inter-ethnic collaborative activities. However, the ability of criminals to gain access to host societies by exploiting ethnic-migrant affiliations may also lead to increased 'turf wars' between new, incoming national/ethnic gangs and those who were already established and therefore to waves of violence and growing attempts to corrupt and buy influence with officials, police, lawyers and others.

5.5 Contemporary terrorism in a globalizing world

The overwhelming sense of shock and insecurity after September 2001 provoked by the terrorist destruction of the twin WTC towers in New York has reverberated round the world ever since among both governments and ordinary people. From the perspective of governments not only did it become a pretext for unleashing wars in Afghanistan and Iraq and for bolstering security and surveillance measures, for tightening borders and making inroads into civil liberties in some countries, but it also provoked a call for worldwide collaboration against the threat of global terrorist conspiracies, led by America. The ability of those involved to penetrate the security systems of the world's most powerful military state and to wield terror by utilizing readily accessible technologies also highlighted the weakness of states and international institutions as against the potential threats presented by amorphous networks of hidden criminals and terrorists relentlessly eating away at the safety and viability of the legal global economy (Thachuk 2007). In an attempt to counter such threats, governments have also increasingly searched for the links they assume must exist between organized crime, the corrupt practices of many weak states, money laundering activities and terrorism (Beare 2003: xii–xv). We return to this theme later.

In this discussion we are not interested in state terrorism. Here autocratic governments unleash arbitrary regimes of fear and oppression against their own people, as during the French Revolution or in Stalin's Soviet Union, as a mechanism for stifling dissent or consolidating power. Rather the focus here is on the unilateral or one-sided deployment of intimidation involving the threat or use of violence by non-governmental groups. Moreover, the latter use violence not in individual or domestic situations – though of course violence here is very widespread – but in an organized way against governments or other civilians in the pursuit of some kind of imagined moral or political objective. This definition therefore excludes the numerous other situations where violence and intimidation are used either by individuals or by collectivities against others, such as in riots, street gang fighting, vigilantism or serial murders, where there are no clear, predetermined political or ethical purposes (Senechal de la Roche 2004). Following this line of argument we can explore several further characteristics of contemporary non-state terrorism.

The nature of non-state terrorism

First, terrorism is different from warfare since it does not accept any rules of engagement and is covert and unilateral rather than open and reciprocated (Black 2004: 16). Also, whereas armed guerrilla movements usually attack military targets and conceal themselves in remote rural areas, contemporary terrorists attack civilians and to that end are prepared to move into urban areas, the better to strike against their targets by adopting various measures of concealment and disguise (17). The latter, of course, render terrorists extremely difficult to track or counter and help to explain the panic which their presumed presence generates and therefore the extreme measures governments are prepared to adopt, often with considerable public support, in the attempt to regain control. Second, Black also argued that the moralistic or political intentions of terrorists involve them in deploying violence, or its threat, as a way of gaining a government's or society's compliance with its demand to restore something they believe they have lost. This might be a traditional way of life, territory or political independence as in the cases, respectively, of the Muslim demand for an end to Western interference in the Middle East and its traditional culture, the Palestinian demand for the return of land from Israel and the determination of the Tamils to become a state separate from Sri Lanka (18).

Third, increasingly with globalization, terrorists have been crossing national borders and their actions seem to be directed against enemies perceived as foreign. As such, they demonstrate a strongly transnational dimension (Bergesen and Lizardo 2004). Indeed, in the post-Cold War era and corresponding to the intensification of globalization processes, many observers have suggested that there has been a noticeable increase in terrorist incidents expressing global rather than solely national or regional concerns as was mainly the case during the 1970s and 1980s – for example, the Irish Republican Army (IRA) in Northern Ireland, Palestinian groups and the Marxist groups in Italy and Germany (Bergesen and Lizardo 2004, Black 2004). This global shift also seems to be associated with an increased reliance on networking as the primary means whereby contemporary terrorists organize their activities. Moreover, terrorism has spread to encompass more regions and countries, moving from Europe and the Middle East to include Africa, Latin America, South East Asia and mainland USA. Similarly, terrorist demands have either become more vague and difficult to determine or have drifted towards religious concerns (Bergesen and Lizardo 2004).

Some explanations for increasing global terrorism

We now consider what might be the reasons for the recent increase in global terrorism. One argument developed by Bergesen and Lizardo (2004) revolved around certain similarities they describe between the wave of 'anarchist terrorist' incidents that took place between 1880 and 1914 and those that have occurred since the early 1990s (41). The earlier period, for example, witnessed assassinations and bomb throwing involving a number of countries, such as Serbia, Macedonia, Croatia and Bosnia, whose members were struggling to gain independence from the autocratic and imperial control exercised by the Russian, Ottoman and Austrian empires. But these attacks also spread across territorial borders to other countries, including America, Italy, France, Spain and Russia and sucked in people of several nationalities. The Islamic Mahdi revolt in the Sudan during the 1880s against British imperial rule also bears some parallels with al-Qaeda's determination to resist contemporary American economic and cultural power (45–6). A second similarity is that during both periods terrorists were – or are – attempting not only to resist imperial aggression but also the dominant social transformation working its way through many societies and perhaps the world. In the earlier period this was the drive to modernity and industrialization though also associated with globalization processes. More recently it appears to have been directed against the much larger thrust taking place through a syndrome of economic, financial, techno-logical and cultural forces which are moving the world even more markedly in a globalizing direction. Here, terrorism appears as a 'defensive, reactionary, solidaristic movement' against the threat that globalization presents to trad-ition, 'local authority and a sense of place' (Bergesen and Lizardo 2004: 43).

Moreover, just as in the years between 1880 and 1914, when Britain as the world's hegemonic power was entering a period of relative economic decline, so America today faces this same prospect. But in the same way that Britain tried to counter this decline by engaging in 'defensive maneuvering' (46), which was designed to protect its waning economic power through imperi-alistic military actions, so, today, America is trying to follow the same road. Thus, in both cases a period of apparent imperial expansion actually coincides with – but unintentionally hastens – a loss of world economic leadership by the main imperial power. But this hegemonic decline, in turn, undermines world order by leaving a vacuum of power and an increasing uncertainty concern-ing the enforceability of international rules. In doing so it creates openings for new forms of instability though these tend to get displaced to periph-eral world regions where struggles against local despots are also continuing. Examples of these today might be the Sudan, Kenya, Saudi Arabia, Indonesia, Ecuador, Venezuela, Columbia, Serbia and others. These instabilities are likely to involve international terrorist acts by various non-state groups who can exploit interstate conflicts of interest and the insecurities to which they give rise but also the grievances of those who are disempowered or threatened by the exercise of imperial military power or intensified globalization. These eruptions of non-state violence may also serve as a portend of further instabil-ity to come in the world order.

Black (2004) developed a rather different argument concerning the recent outburst of international terrorism but one which complements the above and which also sees globalization processes as central to what is occurring. He suggested (16–18) that a key feature of 'pure terrorism' is that it is a form of social control involving self- or group-directed attempts to deal with a grievance by exercising mass violent aggression. In doing so the aim is not to harm particular individuals but rather entire collectivities or their unfortunate representatives who happen to be in the wrong place at the time of the attack. The 'rationale' for this is that these social groups are believed to be jointly liable for, and vulnerable to, punishment because of the wrongs they have committed against the principles upheld by the terrorists. In considering these alleged wrongs what is also at stake here – and what makes acts of terrorism possible and justifiable in their own eyes – is some form of social polarization whereby the collectivity whose interests the terrorists claim to champion are experiencing social, cultural or political distance from their enemy (Senechal de la Roche 1996). This distance might mean there is little or no possibility of social or economic contacts and relationships occurring between the two civilian populations or it may mean they live by cultural or religious pre-cepts which are totally alien to one another. Alternatively, the considerable degree of vertical distance, or inequality of power, status and wealth, existing between two collectivities effectively shuts down any possibility of genuine mutual understanding or reciprocity.

Black (2004) also argued that for most of human history, physical geometry, or distance, kept such potentially conflicting social collectivities far apart. This, in turn, meant that their deep social differences, and/or the capacity of one collectivity to exploit or humiliate another from afar, prevented such inter-collective grievances from erupting into mass violence against the civilian populations held to be responsible for whatever sense of oppression or threat was believed to prevail. Of course, steep social distances coexisted with close physical proximity in pre-modern conditions including in peasant societies where various forms of oppression on the part of landlords or feudal lords against the subordinate rural population were endemic (Black 2004: 20). However, these were usually – though not always – relatively homogeneous societies whose members shared more or less the same ethnicity, language and religion. If mass violence did occur in such agricultural societies it usually involved peasant revolts or, in more recent times, guerrilla warfare directed against ruling elites, governments and their representatives – the police, army or officials – but not normally against civilians. On the other hand, terrorism was deployed during the twentieth century against colonial governments and foreign nationals living in the colony. Examples here are Kenya and Algeria. In these and other instances, those attacked were socially and vertically distant – both in terms of their alien culture and their vastly superior power and wealth – in relation to the local population but were also easily accessible for terrorist acts given their close geographical proximity.

Black (2004: 20–2) then continued his argument by observing that recent changes have substantially altered these parameters. Clearly, violence perpetrated upon civilian collectivities, whose members and way of life are held to be socially very different from, as well as a threat to, that of their attackers presupposes physical contact as in cities, towns and neighbourhoods. Without such contact there can be no violence taking the form of terrorist acts. Accordingly, terrorism *'arises only when a grievance has a social geometry distant enough and a physical geometry close enough for mass violence against civilians'* to become possible (Black 2004: 21, authors italics). But, the recent intensification of globalization processes coupled to faster, cheaper transport and electronic communications have largely removed the former constraints of distance and accessibility. Thus, the time needed to reach distant locations where enemies live has been massively shortened and the risks and costs incurred in doing so have diminished. Similarly, ICTs permit terrorists to interact with others far away, to decide targets, plan attacks and to pool information and resources. The technology of weaponry also continues to become more deadly and sophisticated but portable and readily assembled from ordinary ingredients. As Black suggested, technology 'both globalizes the possibility of terrorism and magnifies its destructive capability' (22). At the same time globalization assembles increasing numbers of civilian enemy targets into easily accessible locations where they can be attacked – airports, stations, hotels, tourist locations and so on. On the other hand, Black (22) also claimed that these same forces of globalization, which bring people of different societies and cultures into increased physical proximity through travel, migration, the Internet and so on, are also creating 'global intimacy' and 'cultural homogeneity'. In the end, therefore, it is likely that these will weaken the social and cultural distances which currently divide and alienate different peoples.

5.6 The dependence of terrorism on global disorder

In this section we look first at the nature of the links that appear to exist between contemporary terrorists and transnational organized crime and assess their significance. We also try to establish the similarities and degree of overlap but also the clear differences between these two global agents. Then we consider some of the main ways in which, just like the players in the legal global economy, terrorism today is grounded in, and partly depends upon, certain political and social institutions which are often perfectly legitimate.

Transnational crime and terrorism

Some observers have pointed to two key characteristics of the terrorist groups which dominated the headlines during the past three decades of the twentieth century. One was that they were primarily concerned with nationalist goals and therefore confined their activities to attacks against governments, military forces or civilians within particular regions or nations. Key examples are the IRA, the Palestinian Liberation Organization (PLO) and the Taliban's focus on liberating Afghanistan from Soviet rule during the 1980s. But in addition, they all depended partly on the proceeds from crime to fund their activities and over a long period (Lilley 2006: 135–8). This link has continued in recent years as many terrorist groups have increasingly shifted their networks, activities and targets to include the global arena and not simply national domains.

This link between crime and terrorism has certainly flourished in respect to al-Qaeda's worldwide network of cells and 'colonies of terror' which together form what Napoleoni (2004: 198) referred to as a 'living transnational conglomerate of organisms'. Among the concrete instances of al-Qaeda's apparent dependence on crime as one source of finance for funding both immediate terrorist acts and its permanent activities are the following. Diamonds stolen from Sierra Leone and Angola were used to fund wars in Africa but some of the illegal revenue seeped into the al-Qaeda network (Williams and Baudin-O'Hayon 2002: 134). Indeed, precious gems and gold are ideal resources for funding terrorist activities because they are highly portable, easily concealed and once melted or broken down into different forms they become extremely difficult to trace (Thachuk 2007: 15). Moreover, al-Qaeda is also reputed to have relied at times on various drug trafficking activities as a source of funding and not only through its links with the Taliban and opium cultivation in Afghanistan. Similar claims have been made for other terrorist groups. Thus, according to the US State Department, approximately 12 of the world's largest 25 groups including al-Qaeda, Hezbollah, the Tamil Tigers and the Kurdish Worker's Party are said to have benefited from such connections to organized drug gangs (cited in Thachuk 2007: 16). In fact in some instances, the capacity to buy weaponry and to function as an armed organization over long periods probably depended almost entirely on illegal trading activities. According to Napoleoni (2004: 102), this has been the case with Columbia's two Marxist armed groups, the Revolutionary Armed Forces of Columbia (FARC) and the National Liberation Army (ELN) both of which have operated largely as 'self-financed armed organizations' through the production and smuggling of cocaine but also via illegal trading in oil, gold, precious stones and opium (see also Serrano and Toro 2002). Moreover, as Thachuk (2007) suggested, terrorists gain much more than profit from this involvement since over time narcotics smugglers have also 'established reliable underground networks that enable the almost seamless movement of money, goods, and people quickly and reliably' (16).

Nevertheless, most observers also insist that the links between transnational crime and contemporary terrorist activities need to be placed squarely into a wider context. Although there are strong similarities between these two activities – their increasingly transnational scope, use of violence, ability to generate loyalty from their members, capacity to attain high degrees of organization and their threat to local and global stability – they are also quite different in important respects. This includes the extent to which and the reasons why they resort to criminal activities.

Clearly, the link between these two sources of global violence exists and should not be overlooked (Thachuk 2007: 16). Indeed, since the events of 9/11, governments have been especially prone to point to the overlap between terrorism and crime and to emphasize its significance (Berdal and Serrano 2002: 201–2). However, conflating them together and failing to acknowledge the distinctiveness of terrorism serves no useful purpose because it undermines our ability to understand and ultimately deal with the threat each poses. Similarly, the reality that terrorists sometimes resort to criminal activity and may, on occasions, engage in 'ad hoc cooperation' with transnational gangs does not mean that 'there is an organized crime terrorism nexus' (Williams and Baudin-O'Hayon 2002: 134) or that cooperation is continuous, permanent and pivotal to the very existence of terrorists (Lilley 2006: 36). As we will see later, contemporary terrorists actually depend on a much larger array of everyday support mechanisms and revenue sources than just crime. In fact, to become too dependent upon this source would gravely weaken terrorist claims to be fighting for wider political, ethnical or religious goals and on behalf of oppressed peoples (Berdal and Serrano 2002: 8). It might also expose them to much greater risks of being caught when in fact their success and longevity depends on their ability to cover their tracks and ensure they remain protected by, and embedded within, numerous communities and micro-relationships across their various zones of world activity (Lilley 2006: 137).

Second, as we have already seen, there is general agreement that trans-national criminals and terrorists are pursuing very different goals. While criminal gangs are interested in accumulating wealth – pursuing 'the logic of profitability and economic gain' (Berdal and Serrano 2002: 7) – terrorists are engaged in political and moral projects, ostensibly on behalf of others, and for which they are often prepared to sacrifice their own lives (Berdal and Serrano 2002: 201, Black 2004: 16–18, Senechal de la Roche 1996). Of course, as with other forms of violence which are conducted for political ends, contem-porary terrorism aims to destroy. But in the eyes of the terrorists involved this is part of a larger project designed to create a new and more just social order (Berdal and Serrano 2002: 7). Last, and growing out of the previous point, while terrorists engage in money laundering activities in the same way as criminals, they do so for very different reasons. When criminals engage in this activity they are trying to convert dirty funds gained by illegal activity into clean money or legitimate business activities. However, when terrorists launder money they are mostly utilizing funds which have come from many origins, not just crime. Also much of the former stems from legitimate busi-nesses and fund-raising activities whose donors often had no idea their money would end up reaching terrorist groups. Thus, when the latter actually spend their funds to commit terrorist acts by using credit cards to withdraw funds from banks or simply smuggle cash across borders – to pay air fares, buy the ingredients for making bombs or cover their living expenses while preparing their conspiracies – they are actually deploying what is mostly clean money for 'dirty' ends (Lilley 2006: 128–33); the reverse of what criminal gangs do.

Weak, authoritarian and shell states

We now turn to the question of how contemporary terrorism is embedded within socio-economic and political systems most of which are partly or even completely legitimate. Here, there is wide agreement that certain kinds of states willingly or otherwise provide an environment that is propitious for terrorists though of course the same also applies to transnational criminals. Such states are usually described as 'weak' though Williams and Baudin-O'Hayon (2002: 139–40) also described them as corrupt and criminal states. An example they give of the latter is Serbia during the rule of Milosevic when he, his family and cronies, monopolized the import and export of key commodities while smug-gling and dealing in contraband goods across the Balkans. Weak states are characterized by political and legal systems – or a lack of them – which play into the hands of terrorists. Thus, they lack legitimacy in the eyes of their citi-zens because their rulers place their own interests or those of their kin, ethnic group, region of origin or political faction above those of the public interest.

In addition, they do not possess an autonomous and fair legal system, are unable to police their borders effectively and are incapable and/or unwilling to implement economic and social policies and regulations which might empower their citizens. Such states provide a 'greenhouse' where criminals and terrorists can cultivate their nefarious activities as well as 'excellent sanctuaries' (139) or safe havens where both can hide and from which they can mount local and global criminal or violent activities directed at other states and their civilians.

Of course, as we have seen, the need and ability of criminals to corrupt a bevy of officials, professionals and politicians and place them within their pay is an endemic aspect of criminal activity everywhere. However, Thachuk (2007: 9–11) suggested that in the case of weak states this capacity for terrorists, as well as criminals, to more or less capture large swathes of government officialdom through a mixture of threat, menace, violence, extortion, deceit and the manipulation of supposedly shared ideological concerns, while offering monetary and other inducements, may reach a point where they can effectively 'mold' such states and the latter's institutions to suit their needs. In extreme cases, states are unable to guarantee the most fundamental security for their citizens and local police, military, judicial and governmental systems either become demoralized and largely ineffective or sections within these organizations function on behalf of the terrorist or criminal groups operating within their boundaries. By the same token it becomes perfectly possible for terrorists, and criminals, to plot their future moves, recruit and train activists and maintain active communications and networks with groups in other countries (Thachuk 2007: 10–11). With particular reference to terrorism, there have been many examples of such weak states during recent years but Afghanistan, Pakistan, Columbia, the Sudan, Liberia, Sierra Leone, Angola and some of the Balkan states are among the most notable cases.

According to Lilley (2006) and Napoleoni (2004) in addition to weak states there is a second and third type which bolster global terrorist activities. The second occurs where states are not so much weak as highly authoritarian and oppressive though they may be internally divided and/or penetrated by partly foreign conspiratorial groups as well. This type has been particularly relevant to al-Qaeda's ability to survive as a world network of quasi-autonomous cells each of which breeds its own recruits, plans its separate conspiracies and largely runs its own affairs while simultaneously drawing upon the external support provided partly by authoritarian Islamic states (Napoleoni 2004: 196–9). The prime examples here are Saudi Arabia and the Gulf Emirates though to a lesser extent other Middle Eastern and Central Asian states including Syria, Iran and Egypt approximate to this type. In addition to being Islamic states, though with varying sectarian traditions, they are all highly dependent on various forms of oppression to maintain the privileged position enjoyed by their landowning classes or others who control the foremost sources of national wealth. In most instances they are also oil producers enjoying vast revenues. There are several reasons why these states tend, willingly or not, to provide various resources for terrorist groups. Their Muslim religious traditions obviously help to fuel Islamic fundamentalism and provide some converts. The Wahibist version of Islam which originated in Saudi Arabia, with its insistence on a very strict, disciplined interpretation of Islam, is one example of this. For whatever reason, certain citizens are willing to divert some of their immense wealth towards terrorist channels. Deep internal inequalities also fuel conflicts and hatreds which terrorist groups can harness in the form of popular sympathy for their cause. This is hugely magnified by the reality that these regimes are often heavily dependent on Western military and other kinds of support, Saudi Arabia being the classic example. Without this they would be liable to collapse so creating the opportunity for radical and purist Islamic groups, including al-Qaeda, to try to play a leading role in introducing more equitable and traditional societies and polities.

The third type of 'state' which underpins terrorism is described by Napoleoni as the 'terror state-shell' (2004: 85–106) though Thachuk's (2007: 10) reference to 'semifeudal fiefdoms' provides an alternative definition. These rely on violence and corruption to build autonomous zones and to exercise a controlling influence over the 'real' national state in their vicinity. The main examples Napoleoni provided of state shells are the PLO and its more democratic but also militant and fundamentalist rival, Hamas, both the Christian militia and the Muslim Hizbollah in Lebanon and the three Columbian armed groups, FARC, ELN and the government backed right wing organization – the Peasant Self Defense Group. All of these demonstrate some of the functions and powers exercised by genuine states: control of territory and a monopoly of the means of violence, the ability to impose tax or tribute on their populations and the construction of a bureaucracy. However, they are shell rather than real states because they lack international recognition – they possess no sovereignty – do not provide the rule of law or non-arbitrary and accountable government nor can they provide citizenship rights (88). The purpose of these state shells is to engage in permanent armed struggle and all are run by political/military elites. In order to survive and fund their struggle they construct some kind of economy and a 'socio-economic infrastructure' (87) which is capable not only of financing terrorist activities but may also offer employment and perhaps the resources to fund social benefits such as education and clinics for the subject population under their control. The Columbian shell states seem to have built their war economies primarily around drug trafficking, smuggling, extortion, kidnapping and other violent criminal activities. In contrast, the PLO and Hamas rely not only on crime but have also developed factories, farms and exports, levied taxes on their populations and draw on the outside financial support provided by sympathetic or unwitting individuals and charities existing outside Palestine. A further difference of some significance between the Palestinian shell state and the other examples is that many governments across the world are sympathetic to their goal of becoming a sovereign separate state in their own right, free from Israeli interference, and to their land claims. Moreover, they also enjoy a good deal of mass support from those living within their zones of operation and from many Muslims and non-Muslims across the world.

Terrorism and everyday socio-economic institutions

Lastly, contemporary terrorists, and particularly violent forms of Islamicism and al-Qaeda, depend not just on crime, legal businesses and states for their survival but also utilize the support provided by much larger local and/or global systems and institutions into which they are embedded worldwide through multiple diffuse social relations and obligations. Often, moreover, these protective and supporting frameworks are quite legitimate in that they flourish in their own right as legal associations or systems and their members are unaware of the ends to which at least some of their funding are directed. In the case of Hamas, one such support system has been the levies or tribute, equal to approximately 5 per cent of their incomes, which it has extracted from members of the Palestinian diaspora living abroad (Napoleoni 2004: 88). Then there are the charities dedicated to helping disadvantaged Muslims which flourish among the migrant populations and diasporic communities found in Europe, North America and elsewhere. Here, the Islamic religion and value system reinforces such charitable activity both within the Arab/Islamic world and among those living outside it because of the moral obligation to donate a portion of one's income or business earnings to help those in need of assistance. No doubt, too, some Muslim migrants willingly provide funding even though they suspect or know that it will end up serving terrorist aims just as some members of the Irish community in the USA knowingly raised funds for the IRA over many decades. One such charity is the Holy Land Foundation for Relief and Development established in 1992 and which has supported Hamas (Napoleoni 2004: 97; see also Lilley 2006: 137–40). Its official charitable status makes it even more attractive to donors because it provides tax advantages. It also draws funds from yet other charities in North America. In 2000 alone it collected an estimated $13 million across the USA and Canada. Although this flow of funds does not move directly into terrorist activity, but is used to support clinics, schools, community centres and refugees, by helping to generate popular support for Hamas it indirectly underpins the ability of the latter to pursue political goals partly through violent means. It seems probable that these charitable and social support systems also operate at times as vehicles through which finance gets funnelled to the al-Qaeda network and its many cells with or without the recognition or overt support of their contributors. Following the events of 9/11, it was certainly this fear which led the American government to direct the Financial Action Task Force (FATF) – established precisely for this purpose – towards investigating all the possible financial trails feeding into al-Qaeda's terrorist activities including those which might originate in certain Islamic charities across the world.

Two further possible avenues through which money may flow towards terrorist activities, mostly without their participants being aware of this, are the remittances which many migrants send home and the unofficial *hawala* banking system. Based on trust and person-to-person transfers of cash via brokers, a client can arrange to transfer money to someone living in another country. This might be linked to business deals, family assistance or other activities. For those involved, the *hawala* system seems to provide a quick, cheap and reliable way of engaging in monetary transactions and it is widely used by Muslims and others. However, the absence of formal bureaucracy means that there are no official records of transactions and no means for governments or security services to scrutinize the amounts involved or their purposes. Accordingly, there is a suspicion that *hawala* may be open to abuse by terrorists and criminals and/or terrorist financing (Lilley 2006: 146–7). In the attempt to severely limit the money laundering and other activities of al-Qaeda, since 2001, the American government's FATF, as well as other governments and IGOs, have concentrated on finding ways to ensure that banks are much more careful with regard to how they scrutinize and regulate the money flows and other forms of cash transaction which pass through their remit. However, as we have seen much of the finance that reaches al-Qaeda and other terrorist groups comes not through the official banking system or as a result of crime but originates rather in local and global social institutions and everyday cultural practices. Moreover, according to Lilley (2006: 134) the actual cash used to fund concrete terrorist acts is often delivered by hand through a courier rather than being taken from a bank account. Ultimately, therefore the task of depriving terrorist groups of the funds they need cannot be stopped entirely through using intelligent technology to monitor the movements of groups and individuals or by formulating techniques and regulations designed to track money flows through financial systems.

5.7   Appraisal

As in the case of migrants, there is a clear sense in which the activities of transnational criminals and terrorists are often deeply entangled with, and driven by, more or less the same logic and processes as those which impel businesses and other perfectly licit agents operating within the legal global economy. Thus, both sets of actors depend upon, respond to or find ways to manipulate, to their advantage, the resources, contradictions, institutions and policies that are grounded either in the global economy and/or the imperatives of nation-states. In addition, this intertwining is sometimes mutual and intended in that charities and religious foundations, certain kinds of businesses or formally 'legal' agents – such as lawyers, police personnel, accountants, bank managers customs officials or politicians – sometimes act in ways that further the goals of illicit global agents. Second, and again as in the case of migrants and indeed legal businesses, transnational criminals and terrorists depend strongly on interpersonal relationships and trust based on mutual liking and shared ethnic, national, religious or other values. But such everyday social interactions are deeply embedded within the mainstream, everyday affiliations found in all societies as well as the socio-cultural affiliations and institutions which inevitably stretch in all directions across borders and continents in a globalizing world. Without the support and cover provided by these wider social relations – more often than not without the knowledge or intention of the participants – contemporary transnational criminals and terrorists would find it hard to flourish. Thus, micro-relations remain enormously effective in shaping global events and processes, including in ways that sometime endanger us all.

Part Two

Local Lives

Introduction to Part Two

Globalization has deepened the multiple ways in which the lives of humans everywhere have become bound together by shared employment and income insecurities, the threat of environmental devastation and pandemics, the growth of mass migration, rising transnational crime and terrorism, and other problems. Nevertheless, despite the intensity and ubiquity of these forces, the evidence often seems overwhelming that most people remain only partly aware, if at all, of the forces and perils which now penetrate their lives. Where some kind of understanding surfaces, the fears engendered and desire to discover who is responsible are invariably deflected onto the national stage and especially local politicians. For example, the G20 meeting in London in April 2009 can probably be judged a success from the perspective of international government cooperation and the degree to which there was agreement concerning what nations needed to do in concert to tackle the global recession and avoid the return of a similar crisis. However, as one British political commentator observed: 'many voters...will have felt that the summit meant little to their lives...To the voter enduring the daily struggle to pay the bills and stay in work, the G20 will have appeared a distant event' (Rawnsley 2009: 27).

Indeed, relatively small numbers of individuals appear to possess a sense of globality – a consciousness of the world as a single space and of its peoples as one common humanity deserving, at times, consideration and support in their own right. Those who do reveal such a consciousness often find it hard to make the transition from cognitive awareness towards feeling empathy for the plight of distant others. In short, although we are already living thoroughly global lives beset by powerful forces, much of the time our actions are governed by our private, immediate phenomenological experiences. These seem to inhibit us from thinking, feeling and acting as if the global had much significance and certainly as if it could ever possess more than a fraction of the importance we attach to our local situation. We elaborate on this argument in Chapters 6 and 7. Moreover, the local remains significant in the face of globalization in another way because, not all, but a large element of the actions and processes that contribute towards, and indeed constitute, global processes consist of the cumulative exchanges, interactions and collaborations conducted by social actors who inhabit the spaces of many locals but whose actions are either intentionally or unwittingly linked in various ways to those of actors situated in yet other locals. In other words, a large part of what we label the 'global' is formed out of the fabric provided by innumerable locals plus the different interactions that join them together.

Returning to the disjuncture between local lives and global transformations, we need to examine the local's power and explore why and how it continues to exert such a compelling attractiveness in the face of powerful globalizing influences. In doing so it is also important to recall to what extent the activities of global actors and their capacity to operate effectively, or indeed at all, especially in the case of migrants, transnational criminals and terrorists, depend crucially on their micro-interactions and loyalties grounded in thoroughly local (kinship, village/region, ethnic, national or religious) affiliations. Thus, the local provides a large part of the resources which enable many kinds of global interactions to take place because only these are capable of sustaining the levels of interpersonal trust and the protection, information and material support without which those involved could not navigate global space in the pursuance of their various objectives. Micro-relationships grounded in local situations are central to globalization.

Following on from this argument, I suggest that it is useful to make an analytical distinction between three different but in reality overlapping elements which can be said to encompass the local. One concerns the centripetal pull of place, or the locale we inhabit at any one time, and the accompanying webs of social relations for which it supplies a stage. Second, there are the enveloping, minute micro-routines, rhythms, social and other responsibilities which engulf but also form our everyday lives. Then, third, the local is also constituted by the seductive certainties and continuities associated with the primordial cultural affiliations we absorb first in childhood and which continue to surround us through family, ethnic or national life.

Of course, the degree to which these three elements are fused together at any time in someone's life varies a good deal and much depends here on mobility and probably social class and education. Having recently moved to an unfamiliar location, for example, the primordial identity which the stranger transports to the new situation clearly 'belongs' somewhere else even though s/he will need to take some account of the concrete social relations endemic in this new locale. Thus, Simmel (1950: 402–8, in Wolff) described the predicament of the recent, lone stranger living in the industrializing German cities of the early twentieth century who was unable to find a replica home support system of fellow national or ethnic members; they find themselves in an outsider situation. Alternatively, the stranger may become absorbed in an ethnic/national enclave shared with other members of the same cohesive homeland culture as in the case of first generation poor immigrants today. This may mean that s/he remains bound and empowered by a definite set of primordial values and affiliations but these are out of kilter with the dominant local/native one though eventually some of the latter's richness and the minutiae of its everyday life will embroil the migrant so that s/he forms at least some new attachments.

However, in the more contemporary setting of global cities and for certain kinds of people, the situation may be different again in that the three elements making up the local may remain only loosely bound together in their private life worlds. This was apparent in some of the case studies discussed by the contributors to the book edited by Eade (1997) on London as a global city. Here, some native individuals worked in London's city centre and rented accommodation in a metropolitan borough where they enjoyed only shallow relations with neighbours and colleagues. At the same time their personal sociospheres contained rich affiliations to family and friends in other locations through visits, emails and other forms of communication. They felt and retained 'the emotional gravity of place' (Lovell 1998: 1) more strongly in relation to the one or several distant locations from which they had previously moved. Moreover, for such individuals, who were single, cosmopolitan and probably only short-term residents, their socio-ethnic and cultural references might remain strong but shaped by membership of social groups scattered across several distant localities.[i]

Nevertheless, even under globalizing conditions, for most people, the experiences and social ties clustered around and generated by locality, the rhythms of everyday life and shared primordial meanings and affiliations are probably lived and dealt with – at least during some or most phases of their life course – as forces which merge to form a seamless whole. In Chapter 7, we explore several case studies which tend to bear out this argument. Of course, globalization means that the local defined in this compound sense increasingly cannot encompass *all* the connections, meanings and identities which flow through our life space. Indeed, in the developed countries the earlier process of modernization had already separated home and work, generated growing occupational differentiation, rapid urbanization and many other changes which increasingly loosened family and individual life from their former, primary dependence upon concrete places and fixed, particularistic relationships.

In Chapter 6, the discussion also interrogates the relationship between the local and the global found in the discourse on globalization and where the interaction between them is presented as largely asymmetrical with the local apparently subordinate to the hegemonic global. This is unsatisfactory and we need to reframe the argument so that the local is repositioned and given a much more central and autonomous role. Second, I suggest that the local also operates as a contradictory social space. Although it is where and how we live most of the time, it is also the site from which we cope with the globalizing forces which intrude upon our lives while simultaneously undertaking microactions which mesh with globalization and contribute to the transformations engulfing the lives of distant others. A third theme considers the reasons why it is much more difficult for some people to resist or overcome the local's inward pull on their lives than others. For example, those who experience severe socio-economic disempowerment may be drawn by these circumstances even further into the life world of the local including, perhaps, building potentially aggressive trenches of resistance (Castells 1997) against the 'other(s)' who they believe are threatening their identity and way of life. In contrast, for yet other social actors, the same site of the local, and the experiences and resources it generates, may provide a platform from which, alone or in collaboration with others, they eventually try to contest, resist or reform globalization by seeking allies in other local situations who face similar problems. We examine this latter situation in Chapter 8. Accordingly, it is important to unravel the very different situations experienced by social actors in respect to the local's power in so far as they are shaped by social class, gender, region of origin, education, ethnicity and nationality or even the current stage of their life course.

The Resilient Local: Critiquing the Idea of the Hegemonic Global

6

It has become virtually impossible for anyone to place themselves outside the experiences brought by globalization though not everyone is equally engulfed. Global studies have created a whole new lexicon of concepts, theories, typologies and debates designed to make sense of what is happening – as we saw in Chapter 2. The difficulty, however, is that much of this theorizing has created a methodological and ontological dilemma since whether intentionally or not the terms employed and the meanings given to them have tended to conjure a binary divide between the so-called 'global' and the 'local'. In this chapter we first try to unravel and redress this dichotomy before going on to affirm the continuing power of the local, in its various forms, over most people's lives by examining both theoretical arguments and empirical materials.

6.1 Escaping from the local-global binary divide

There have been various attempts to delineate the presumed contrasting characteristics of these two entities: the local and the global. Gibson-Graham (1996: 125), for example, argued that capitalism tends to be understood as transformative, masculine, irresistibly powerful and free from the 'boundedness of identity' (9). But this hegemonic 'capitalocentrism' (41) – which sees no alternative possibility of conducting economic life – has recently become fused with ideas of the global. Here, and along with capitalism, the latter is seen as 'inherently spatial and as naturally stronger' (125) while those who exist in the local and who depend on alternative non-capitalist ways of economic survival are doomed to be victims who will eventually become 'subordinated to capitalism'. Ley (2004: 154–5) outlined the contrast between the supposedly rational, masculine, open, cosmopolitan and dominant global, propelled by dynamic economic and technological practices, and the local imagined as authentic, community-oriented, cultural but ultimately stagnant, weak/feminine and struggling to defend itself futilely against the intruding global. It is hardly surprising that this binary divide encourages us to believe that the local

141

and the global are pitted against each other in some sort of battle for survival or supremacy which the former will inevitably lose.[ii]

In this discursively created view of the local-global, the latter somehow exists 'out there', separate, external and hegemonic in shaping the local's destiny and character. But this idea essentializes both the local and the global (Dirlik 2001, Escobar 2001, Marston, Woodward and Jones 2007), and presents them as if they were 'things in themselves' (Gibson-Graham 2002: 31) – real objects or structures – when they are merely ways of thinking about the world which allow us to make sense of different contemporary human experiences. Indeed, these terms are only meaningful in so far as they are thought about in relation to each other and if we recognize that they do not refer to 'any specifically describable spatiality' (Dirlik 2001: 16). In any case whatever the 'global' is, it does not impact equally on all parts of the world to the same extent. All we can say is that it refers to 'something more than national or regional, but it is by no means descriptive of any whole' (16).

Several additional problematic ways of thinking tend to follow if this binary model is used unreflectively. For one thing, the 'privileging of the global' (Dirlik 2001: 17) has led to a situation where place, and those who struggle to engage in the place-making activities appropriate to it, are at best regarded as marginal and, at worst, the locations they inhabit and the lives they create are in effect discursively erased (Escobar 2001: 140). But there are compelling reasons for resisting this tendency to relegate place to a minor role. Thus, each locality possesses a materiality; a particular geography and topography of hills, valleys, plains, the presence or absence of waterways and transport routes and these sit alongside a specific spread and arrangement of human activities and habitations with their own history. Every locale also possesses a unique ecological environment – a microclimate plus a concatenation of flora and fauna coexisting with social life.

Then, too, humans themselves have bodies and it is only through our bodily experiences that we can understand and experience the world around us (Merleau-Ponty 1962). But our inescapable corporeality also generates continuous material as well as aesthetic, affective and sexual needs. Our ability to satisfy these bodily and other needs requires emplacement (Casey 1993); that is, we have to engage with place to live and maintain the processes necessary to life (Swyngedouw 1997). Bourdieu (2000), too, asserts that it is through our bodies that we obtain practical knowledge so that the world becomes 'comprehensible, immediately endowed with meaning' (135). But he goes further and reminds us that not only are we biological individuals, who must 'occupy a position in physical space', but we also live in a social space. Moreover, everyone 'is characterized by the place where he is more or less permanently domiciled'. Not to have such a place is to 'lack social existence' (135). Putting this all together Escobar (2001: 143) explains that 'place, body and environment integrate with each other' and 'places gather things, thoughts, and memories in particular configurations'.

If we allow the global-local binary to dominate our thinking a second difficulty arises because as Marston et al. (2007: 47) explain we are left with the task of developing 'a language for reconnecting them' through a terminology which evokes and explains spatiality and the ability to articulate human activity across distances. As we saw in Chapter 2, one way of doing this is through theorizing the idea of multiple, overlapping networks and flows which link together and make possible the otherwise dispersed lives of many social actors. Alternatively, it is necessary to construct a scalar logic whereby under globalizing conditions people's lives are both shaped by, and in turn influence, activities and processes taking place simultaneously in the multiple spaces of the local, micro-regional, national and perhaps continental or global. It is certainly true that today our lives do operate at a multiplicity of scalar levels. Manifestations of this are evident everywhere as the following brief examples illustrate. The actions of over six billion people worldwide – felling trees, driving to work, breeding cows, turning up their air conditioning and so on – contribute continuously to climate change and so another unusually fierce tornado strikes Florida, Bangladesh or Burma. Similarly, European and North American consumers choose to purchase prohibited substances or cheap, contraband goods and unwittingly fuel transnational criminal activity across several South American and Asian countries.

However, we must avoid endowing 'scale' with an ontological importance it does not possess. The scales at which human activity takes place, nearby and/or far away and everything in between, must not be regarded as 'pre-given geographical configurations' which determine and situate the motives of those who demonstrate those actions; scale per se is purely an abstraction. Rather it is the 'struggles between individuals and social groups' through numerous concrete activities which create scales and geography not the other way round (Swyngedouw 1997: 141–2). Similarly, it is unhelpful to think about global connectivity as something which takes place within the different territorial containers of place and space since this, too, inclines us towards viewing people and their lives as existing 'out there' in the global as opposed to we 'in here' situated at the national or local level. Instead, we need to think 'of places in nonterritorial terms, as nodes in relational settings, and as the site of situated practices' (Amin 2002a: 391) where social actors engage in, and experience, a multiplicity of changing relationships, activities and feelings, of greater or lesser permanence, including the forging of affiliations both with people far away and those living in the same vicinity.

Flusty (2004: 40) points to a third adverse consequence arising from the tendency of academics to employ abstract conceptualizations of global formations including the discursive invention of the scalar categories of global and local – up there and down here. Not only are these then 'taken for granted and inscribed back onto lived worlds' (55) but they also divert our attention away from what is happening on the ground. Here, people, not reified configurations, are making the global happen through a myriad of different exchanges and actions including some which are intended to stretch out and engulf other actors across the world. Also, employing a discourse which presents the global as involving 'higher order' and 'aggregate' (Flusty 2004: 40) processes and then contrasting these with the more mundane and emplaced nature of local human life devalues individual social life (41–55). Not only that but real experience is felt as a whole; all of a piece and this also gets overlooked. Indeed, it is individual social actors and the interactions in which they engage which provide the glue that meshes together those diverse and fragmentary experiences brought by globalization into one lived entity, not abstract de-spatialized or disembodied forces.

6.2   Rediscovering the power of place/locality

The need to avoid reifying the global applies equally to the local including, in the present context, place or locality. Instead we need 'a progressive sense of place' (Massey 1993: 63) where boundaries are open and social actors are continuously engaged in constructing place-ness out of a changing combination of internal differences and the influences reaching them through their entanglement with other places (66). With this definition there is no danger that we will regard the uniqueness of a particular place as the product of 'some long internalized history' (Massey 1993: 66), preserved by its parochial inhabitants as a fixed, stagnant identity, indifferent to the world outside. Robertson's (1992 and 1995) concept of glocalization also allows us to think about how local and global processes are being meshed together. Thus, companies shape their products so as to appeal to the cultural preferences, climatic and other particularities embedded in unique communities while locals select those incoming global influences which appeal most and then embed them into their own life worlds often changing their meaning in the process. So ubiquitous and widespread have such processes now become that it is tempting to talk of the 'glocal' rather than the local. Yet Robertson is certainly not suggesting that through glocalization processes the local loses much of its identity: quite the contrary.

On the other hand, some thinkers have taken this argument concerning the increased openness of place to external influences too far by suggesting that localities and their inhabitants have now become so caught up in the flows and networks permeating from outside that it is no longer possible to distinguish meaningfully between 'local' and 'global' situations or experiences (Amin 2002a). Perhaps, too, these globalization processes have reconstituted place to such an extent that it makes little sense to take the local seriously as an entity possessing any real influence in its own right. In Giddens' (1990: 140) words places have become more 'phanatasmagoric' than real. In effect, the global has hijacked place because as the space of flows becomes more crucial so the significance of concrete places will not disappear but 'their logic and their meaning' will 'become absorbed in the network' (Castells 1996: 412).

Marston et al. (2007: 52) refer to this type of thinking as 'global overcoding' whereby global influences are being endowed with much greater causal weighting than they actually do, or ever could, possess. In the case of flows, scapes and networks, for example, it seems that the lines drawn on a map or depicted in a diagram which show how local actions in different places are joined or linked in various ways take precedence over what is initiated by the real social actors operating at those places where the actual lines begin and end. A procedure or technique for illustrating the cumulative, linked consequences of numerous human interactions is imbued with far more meaning and causal significance than those actions themselves. Of course, global flows and networks are empowering because armed with various kinds of inflowing knowledge people can extend their activities across space and incorporate the resources available to others far away if they choose. Nevertheless, each participant remains grounded in their own specific situation and place with its own parameters, demands and distinctiveness during the time when such trans-local projects are being mutually enacted. Similarly, while it is vital to map the direction and intensity of the links connecting social actors across social space, it is equally valid and indeed necessary to investigate the additional, emplaced, phenomenological lives, needs and motives of the people who were responsible for dispatching, passing on or receiving the exchanges they represent in the first place. This is particularly appropriate where social actors do not imbue that portion of their lives which have global implications with the same significance as globalization theorists.

Considered overall, therefore, we need to restore a more central role to the local: to bring place back into focus. To do this we now draw on some important counter-arguments and empirical examples. These point to the stickiness of place and indicate how the rhythms it calls into action and engenders (Lefebvre 2004) absorb much of our attention and time and significantly distract us from wider, global concerns though it does not stop this altogether. Thus, like everyday life and primordial culture, locality exerts a powerful countervailing logic of its own despite – and perhaps sometimes precisely as a reaction to – the globalizing influences tugging us to acknowledge their presence. In effect, the local operates very much as a default position returning us continuously to its orbit. What arguments and evidence can be adduced for this assertion?

1. The continuing particularity of place despite global influences. Although globalization intensifies the likelihood that every locality becomes a point of intersection where both internally generated and external global meanings and interactions merge together (Massey 1993: 66), none of this undermines the specificity of each particular locality. This is because this very blend of co-evolving and co-responding internal and external interactions will be unique to that locality. Accordingly, 'each place is the focus of a distinct *mixture* of wider and more local social relations' while 'the juxtaposition of these relations may produce effects that would not have happened otherwise' (68, author's italics).

Many of the comments provided by youngish postgraduates from EU countries concerning the things they liked about living and working in Manchester vividly bear out Massey's argument here. This research was carried out by the author in 2005 and involved in-depth interviews with 61 skilled migrants from 13 EU countries.[iii] Some had only lived in the city for less than a year but others had been there much longer. The average length of residence was six years. The following not untypical comments indicate a strong sense of the awareness of Manchester as a unique locality but at the same time its very specificity was partly defined by the mélange of indigenous and foreign cultural elements bustling for self-expression. Thus, a Greek man who came to study in Manchester in 2002 and who later worked as a dental nurse insisted that

> *Manchester is not too big...it has everything you want, a nice commercial centre, a busy night life...many different kinds of nationalities. It's also culturally good – not just theatre and operas but festivals in summer and winter, for example the German and European markets.*

Similarly, a young Swiss man aged 29 who ran his own business observed that

> *Manchester has everything London has but without the hassle – bands will always come if they are in the UK– huge music possibilities and atmosphere...My visitors can't believe the curry mile (an area near the city centre with numerous South Asian restaurants and stores) and the many different kinds of feelings available in various parts of the city.*

2. The global consists of many locals.   We can also invert the argument concerning the directionality of globalizing flows and suggest that in reality the lines of causality move as much if not more from the local to the global as the other way round. In short, from one perspective, the 'global' actually consists of the sum of all the locals which are linked together through numerous connections spreading across territorial borders to form trans-local linkages forged by the actors living in those particular localities (Flusty 2004: 60). Of course, this notion of the global does not fully cover all aspects of what is normally referred to as the 'global' and we explore this at the end of the chapter. However, this viewpoint helps to shrink some of the unwarranted claims concerning the power of globalization processes over local lives.

3. Global flows presuppose their re-embedding.   Following from this, we can put the local, including place, back into the centre of our analysis by revisiting the concept of de-territorialization. Brenner (1999) suggests that this concept has been crucial because it enables us to escape from methodological nationalism – seeing social relations as defined by a 'state-centric epistemology' (47) and regarding them as confined within a 'parcelized, fixed and essentially timeless geographical space'. However, Brenner is also critical of the tendency for theorists to set up territory and concrete places as existing in opposition to the new timeless, distance-less global spaces. As the latter become more important, it seems, so the former diminish in relevance. But he insists that despite the increased importance of de-territorialized relations in global social life these only make sense in so far as spatial fixity and concrete places continue to provide locations through which such 'global flows can circulate' (Brenner 1999: 62). Accordingly, the de-territorialization of social relations 'hinges intrinsically upon their simultaneous re-territorialization' by social actors living in concrete localities. Mobility implies and indeed requires immobility and fixity. Putting this another way, it is clear that while globalization compels those who inhabit particular places to continuously reconstitute their locality in the light of incoming flows, the latter are only significant to local people to the extent that they endow them with meaning and incorporate them into their lives (Archer, Bosman, Amen and Schmidt 2007: 133). Moreover, they do this in very different ways according to the particularity of each place.

In similar vein, Latour (1993: 117–18) argued that it was partly the invention of technologies such as electric communications that allowed us to believe we have become truly modern because it facilitated the stretching of social networks across much longer distances and the deployment of human activities at numerous scales. But we should not conflate the ability to construct longer networks with some kind 'systematic' globalizing totality which we then imagine has generated universalizing tendencies governing all human life. For example, talking about the railway, he observed that while it can transport people and goods across borders and great distances, and in that sense it possesses certain global propensities, on the other hand, the railway is also 'local at all points'. Its workings rely on a continuous line of grounded objects and actions from sleepers and iron rails to signal systems, stations and the numerous workers who operate them in each location. Other technological networks display similar possibilities but also evince clear limitations and materialities. As he suggested: 'electromagnetic waves may be everywhere, but I still have to have an antenna, a subscription and decoder if I am to get CNN' (117). Similar points could of course be made in reference to the Internet.

4. Places remain essential facilitators of co-present relations in global life. If networks and flows begin, flow through and end in localities, then as Gibson-Graham (2002: 32) suggest, 'scratch anything "global" and you find locality – grounded practices in factories, stock exchanges, retail outlets, and communities'. Despite the parading of statistical information concerning their profitable worldwide transactions, even the operations of transnational corporations depend on many multi-local activities rooted in a series of real places. Here, we might add that the success of these scattered but integrated economic activities also depends on the continuous collaborative activities of numerous employees, who mostly live in close proximity to such economic units, are driven by economic pressures, bound by local or national legal institutions and hierarchical power arrangements and supported by informal and/or domestic bonds, shared cultural, linguistic codes and much else besides (Kennedy 2007a: 275). We should also recall the point made by Castree et al. (2004: 17) to the effect that it is the very specificity of local geographical features and the availability of particular resources in certain locations – for example, oil or other minerals, the presence of special kinds of labour or a flourishing business culture – that attract investment to some locations rather than others in the first instance.

Indeed, and paradoxically, economic globalization has, if anything, increased the relevance of social relationships dependent on co-presence tied to particular places even among business elites. This is because the increasing tendency for many corporations to disperse their activities across vast distances places an even greater premium on the ability to effectively coordinate and manage these complex and far-flung empires. Here, regular interpersonal interactions are required and these need to be re-grounded in particular localities. Further, the recent massive uptake of information technology by businesses worldwide has not fundamentally altered the significance of co-present intimacy and 'personal micro-networks' (Castells 1996: 416) in business life though clearly the former has brought enormous advantages. Moreover, successful global businesses require the kind of economic reflexivity that produces innovation, continuous learning and the ability to deal with complexity (Storper 1997). But again this requires sites where it is possible to gain access to 'ensembles of localized relations' (Beaverstock, Smith and Taylor 2000: 98) and where a 'mix of talents and resources' (Sassen 2002: 23) can be brought together thereby permitting companies to draw upon specialized information and to make appropriate 'interpretations and inferences' and evaluations (22). Global businesses also need to tap into local/national as well as wider knowledge if they are to deal with the needs of clients and cope with national regulations and cultures. Beaverstock et al. (1999 and 2000), for example, researched the worldwide connections between law firms based in London and New York and discovered that in addition to collecting talented transnational employees the success of these firms also depended on the ability to deliver a 'customized service built on local understandings and contacts' (100). This is because legal codes are ultimately tied to very local/national situations and histories.

Box 6 Homogeneous global cities? A debate

Global cities function as key locations from which business elites manage their de-spatialized world empires. Such cities therefore are said to form a trans-urban network tying the world economy together. They also supposedly share markedly similar characteristics such as the increased segregation of poor, middle-class and rich groups into distinctive districts. Also, while global cities draw resources from their surroundings – electricity, foodstuffs and commuting workers – they are said to have become relatively disembedded from local and national forces. These assertions have not gone unchallenged. Counter arguments include the following:

- All cities, including smaller ones with less obvious global characteristics, are exposed to globalizing processes (Marcuse and van Kempen 2000).
- Not all the changes shaping global cities are due to globalization.
- Global cities are partly influenced by national history and the ideologies and politics of state power prevailing in different countries especially the different provision of welfare regimes offering protection against unemployment and economic insecurity.
- Global cities vary also because their countries of origin draw on unique cultures and have evolved their own patterns of economic development, different modes of earning a national livelihood in the world economy and unique skills among their populations.

All of these have bequeathed a legacy of different patterns of economic and cultural path dependency (see Chapter 2) which are not easily discarded.

In their study of social exclusion in 22 neighbourhoods located in 11 **European cities**, Murie and Musterd (2004) found enormous variations. While Amsterdam and Paris possessed particularly high proportions of service workers, in Antwerp, Milan, Berlin and Birmingham – cities with a stronger manufacturing history – this was less evident. Unemployment levels also varied with high youth joblessness in Naples and Paris but much lower levels in Rotterdam and Amsterdam. The distribution of groups exposed to social exclusion – migrants, single mothers and long-term unemployed males – also varied even between different neighbourhoods in the same cities. Also, some poor neighbourhoods coped with social exclusion much better than others especially where local social networks were strong, often linked to the presence of relatively socially homogeneous populations and patterns of social 'interaction and mutual support' – for example, where recent migrants could rely on fellow ethnics for support.

Japanese cities are different again from those found in Europe or North America. Despite Tokyo's importance in the global economy, vast size and domination by decades of 'unfettered corporate advance', it retains clear Japanese characteristics (Waley 2000). These include a strong sense of social order, low crime levels, a relatively limited foreign presence, including among those employed at the top levels of Japanese companies, and a tendency for property to be owned predominantly by nationals. Moreover, gentrification levels are much less evident than in other global cities: 'the newly wealthy do not deem it necessary to lock themselves in behind iron gates and high walls' (Whaley 2000).

Immigrant entrepreneurs to Vancouver from Hong Kong, South Korea and Taiwan (Ley 2004) quickly grasped the very different business and economic circumstances in Canada compared with their homeland cities, especially much higher taxes and levels of business regulation. Such differences made it much harder to succeed in Vancouver and the social costs to family life were often problematic. They also alluded to the key role of local knowledge and the inability to transfer the rules of the business game acquired at home to their new situation.

Another example demonstrating the dependence of global companies on particular localities can be found in the contemporary experience of architects and other professionals employed in global building-design firms. Many of these increasingly cater for clients across the world (Kennedy 2004 and 2005). Further, many such clients – national banks, TNCs, international organizations, global theme parks and so on – have ambitions to use their buildings as a way of winning world acclaim and attention. Yet, it is never possible to avoid the demands of national, regional or city building regulations and bureaucratic practices, the reality of local climatic restrictions and conditions, the typical and traditional ways in which suppliers, surveyors, artisans and others have always worked in each country or region nor the defining influence of the work cultures prevailing in different offices. Also, dealing with all this requires the advice and support of local people even when the client and their project possess clear global ambitions. This was expressed particularly well by a 40-year-old British urban planner.

> *A large company can plan the construction and design of a project in London but they still have to work with the local architects of the country concerned ... deal with the local detail. The implementation is essentially local ... by contrast urban planning remains conceptual and strategic ... it comes before the architecture and so flows around much more. Architecture does have global, flow aspects too– design ideas and knowledge etc ... but further down the line it becomes more concrete. This is also where the ability to work in partnership with other nationalities comes in.* (Kennedy 2005: 238)

Even those localities which exist specifically as transit points, as places of embarkation and disembarkation, in the space of flows – such as airports, railway junctions and harbours – operate as specialized hubs or nodes which need to be organized and run by agents with local ties and who provide distinctive functions. Without the presence of these agents and the services they offer mobility would be impossible to plan or manage. Just one of many examples is shown by Belsunce, a zone in Marseilles mostly populated by immigrants (Grimm 2008). It has long operated as a Muslim ethnic enclave whose occupants facilitate the intercontinental inward and outward flows of migrants, and their merchandise, from North Africa and then their onward movement into the French and European interior. However, Belsunce is increasingly attracting migrants with business interests from South East Asia and other world regions. Here, we find specialized institutions run by more or less permanent ethnic residents who simultaneously retain their business, cultural and family links to North Africa while providing the numerous localized support systems in the enclave needed by other incoming and outgoing migrants, including the possibility of providing temporary legal or illegal employment for those too poor to move on immediately. Among these institutions are hotels and makeshift lodging houses, bars, restaurants and food vending stalls, markets for second hand and other goods, financial systems including money lending facilities, taxi services, Internet cafes and businesses which help the mobile to arrange their shipping, bus, car hire, air and other transport needs. The idea, never mind the reality, of something we might designate as the 'global space of flows' is inconceivable without the existence and of course the support provided by clusters of social actors working to sustain flourishing and interlocking localities.

6.3   The demands and attractions of everyday life

Looked at from a phenomenological-sociological perspective the knowledge on which most people rely is inextricably derived from, and embedded within, their actual everyday lives. It is not something they obtain from 'the intellectual schemes dreamed up in academe' (Jackson 1996: 4) but rather it is predominantly 'commonsensical'. Bourdieu (2000: 142–3), too, asserted clearly that the scholastic knowledge valued by philosophers is established by a 'knowing consciousness' and is set up as deliberately external to their lives. In sharp contrast, the knowledge on which ordinary people rely is quite different. Here, the social agent 'knows it, in a sense too well...takes it for granted, precisely because he is caught up with it; he inhabits it like a garment'. Moreover, the life world held in common by societal members, their shared habitus, is also essentially concerned with and constructed around a set of everyday practices which are pressing and immediate, grounded in habit and repetition, coloured by idiomatic imagery, symbols and meanings and are more or less unique to, or only fully understood by, those particular regional, class, ethnic or community members. This knowledge shared by other societal members through intersubjective communication is also based on mutual trust and reciprocity. Turner calls this 'the hermeneutics of social action' (2006: 145). Much of the time, too, everyday life is thought about and exercised in a relatively un-reflexive manner.

Of course, globalization has opened up the local life world described by these authors to flows coming in from other societies and peoples. The local needs to be understood as open, changing and always in the process of being reconstructed (Massey 1993). Hannerz (2003) also reminds us that the local was never as closed and resistant to external influences as we may once have supposed. Further, recent developments in the technologies of mass communication are contributing to the formation of a global ecumen (Hannerz 2003) where, rather like the different Christian churches and sects, members retain their differences but also establish their commonalities. Applying this more generally, individuals from different societies are exposed to each other's meanings and may share certain common understandings by participating in images carried by film, art, television and so on and without being bound to the same degree as previously by the constraints of language or the need for face-to-face interaction.

The continuing power of everyday local life

Yet, Hannerz also insists that the local's influence remains strong and should not be ignored. Accordingly, he explores three main processes which continue to underpin the local's power: language differences, the close association of the local with the repeated and unavoidable practices of everyday life and the continuing hold of shared ethnic/national cultural affiliations or what he calls the forms of life – which we explore in the next section. On the issue of language, he argues that despite the visual intensity and easy communicability of many media forms and their ability to partly override language difficulties, these still tend to define and guarantee cultural continuity. But along with this goes a sense of nationhood, citizenship as well as boundaries since among other things a shared language provides a sense of 'we-ness' (21) based around the private codes, secondary meanings and trusted recipes for making sense of our surroundings, described by Schutz (1964).

Hannerz's second set of processes concern the local's ability to provide an arena where social actors engage in the everyday practicalities and imperatives of work, leisure, household survival, building dependable neighbourhood and other social networks and much else besides. But these everyday activities are endlessly repeated; ensnared in daily routines and the minutiae of existence. They also both depend upon and take place within such 'enduring settings' (Hannerz 2003: 26) as bus routes, shopping malls, supermarkets, offices or factories, familiar paths and alleys, the children's school or the parks where they play and many sites of pleasure and leisure such as the gym, football ground, garden fence, pub or cinema. Here, we return again to the central significance of emplacement. Then, too, the sheer compulsion to continue performing everyday acts means that people develop a 'trained capacity' (26) to cope with life and do not need to reflect very deeply on their actions. In addition, the conduct of everyday life involves at least some face-to-face relations among immediate family and locally present kin but also workmates, neighbours, fellow commuters and shoppers, members of the pub quiz team, people met at the library, the Internet cafe, parent's evening or health centre and so on. But in so far as these relationships continue, are inclusive and engender shared colloquial understandings, jokes and memories, they also make possible mutual surveillance and control among participants. Moreover, because everyday life also involves the body and the self it engages all our senses, immerses us in its embrace (Hannerz 2003: 27) and creates strong emotional affiliations among members. It is through such everyday practices and interpersonal relations most people gain their earliest experiences of, and exposure to, deeper cultural meanings. Hannerz concludes that although local life has lost some of its all-encompassing character due to globalization, it remains significant as 'an arena in which a variety of influences come together...in a unique combination' (27). Like place, everyday life sucks social actors into its orbit and commands the greater part of our attention.

Evading macro-influences: Lefebvre and De Certeau on everyday life

A similar view concerning the hold of everyday life can be discerned in Lefebvre's mammoth work on how social space is produced (1991). In *The Production of Space* (1991, originally published in 1974), Lefebvre argued that although modern economic life has produced the 'abstract space' of capital, driven by vast business networks, worldwide money and dominated by commodity production (or economic globalization), the space of social life remains vital to human existence and here we express our identities and needs. Moreover, these social spaces are multiple and highly variable and they contain and generate numerous social relationships. These 'interpenetrate' (86) each other and through them we develop and become linked by numerous networks and pathways to other social spaces. Yet, the particularity of the local can never disappear, it is never 'absorbed by the regional, national or even worldwide level' (88). Despite the power of abstract space through capitalism, 'the worldwide does not obliterate the local' (86). These social spaces involve the actions undertaken by individuals and social collectivities who live and suffer in the sphere of the local. Here, every room, apartment, street corner or shopping centre possess a particular use and engenders social life (16). At the core of this social life lies the family with its immediate relationships which bind individuals to the cycle of procreation but also to nature and the earth. Yet society would disappear if it only encompassed the family so social space also moves outwards and embraces multiple additional social relationships (34–5). In short, all 'subjects are situated in a space in which they must either recognize themselves or lose themselves' and which they can 'both enjoy and modify' (35) through their everyday lives.

Similarly in *Rhythmanalysis* (2004: 95–6) Lefebvre provided a powerful account of the interplay of different rhythms in giving context and shape to our everyday lives.

> In and around the body, the distinction between two sorts of rhythm is found as in movements…mannerisms and habits: and this from the most everyday (the way one eats and sleeps) to the most extra-everyday (the way one dances, sings, makes music, etc.)…No more than the linear and the cyclical can the rhythms 'of the self' and the rhythms 'of the other', those of presence and those of representation, be separated. Entangled with one another, they penetrate practice and are penetrated by it. This seems to us true of all times and spaces, urban or not.

As their titles suggest, the first volume of De Certeau's, *The Practice of Everyday Life* (1988 but first published in 1984), and the second written with his collaborators (De Certeau, Giard and Mayol 1994) explored how the mass of ordinary people go about their daily lives. Like Lefebvre, De Certeau was interested in the myriad ways through which 'the ordinary man', the 'common' and 'anonymous' heroes, 'walking in countless thousands on the streets'

(1984) deal with, counter and often subvert the 'strategies' imposed on them by the leading agents of modern capitalist societies. These 'strategies' consist of hierarchical power structures, systems and rules and they are designed to configure the places and experiences of everyday life by circumscribing certain activities while formalizing, legitimizing and directing others. Thus, a range of life spheres, including work, shopping, education, reading and telling stories, moving around and so on are ordered, prioritized, tamed and directed by local and central governments, businesses, scientific bodies, universities and other powerful agents. But in response to these 'force-relationships' (xix) ordinary people develop a series of 'tactics' in everyday life which are designed to evade, neutralize or modify the impact of elite strategies and the latter's capacity to control, survey and regulate the institutionalized places of social life.

While these tactics can only be temporarily insinuated into the places controlled by power holders and although ordinary individuals can never develop a base of their own, they can manipulate time, seizing whatever opportunities are offered by 'propitious moments' (xix) to develop tactical advantages. Here, in innumerable ways everyday life provides a rich storehouse of opportunities: introducing private and local idiosyncrasies into the formalized national language during conversations; the experience of shopping where the housewife waits or bargains for the cheapest deal; the ways in which the tiniest details concerning the layout of streets and alley are used to save time or evade surveillance; or stealing time from an employer to produce an item for personal consumption when unobserved at work. Another example might be recounting traditional stories and legends. Such stories 'frequently reverse the relationships of power' and 'ensure the victory of the unfortunate in a fabulous, utopian space' (De Certeau 1984: 23).

Thus, the daily repeated acts of millions of ordinary and relatively powerless people can release what Certeau (1984: xiv) calls 'the procedures of everyday creativity' including deflecting or resisting established rules, disciplines, 'technocratic structures' and power centres, even while seeming to obey them. Alternatively, tactical moves allow people to subtly redefine meanings and codes. Indeed, in these ways, a cumulative space for the 'clandestine' and 'microbe-like' counter activities of numerous individuals is re-appropriated in and through everyday life.

Irrespective of whether we think about everyday life as a vehicle through which the powerless continuously challenge the controls exercised by macro-agents or we simply recall its ability to immerse us in routines, responsibilities, events, affections, worries, conflicts, details and numerous patterned activities, it manifestly constitutes a core element of the local. As such it is readily accessible and understandable in a way that global influences are often not. It also offers multiple, immediate and highly absorbing distractions as well as compulsions and it neutralizes both our ability and our need to pay much attention to threats and possibilities emanating from outside – though of course it does not preclude these altogether. Drawing on a recent empirical study, we now briefly explore an aspect of everyday life which is often ignored or sidelined by global theorists: the street life of global cities and how individuals use its resources to construct a sense of shared cultural identity.

Case study: the street life of Hispanic people in an American city

In 2006, Price (2007) studied the annual street festival of Calle Ocho, in the Little Havana district of Miami. This is just one of numerous Hispanic cultural events taking place across those American cities which have become increasingly Latinized. These events tend to bring together a heterogeneous range of Hispanic peoples with different nationalities, migration histories, social class backgrounds, legal statuses and so on. Although ethnic, linguistic and religious roots provide key sources of cultural solidarity, the Latin community in Little Havana is more diverse in terms of countries of origin than the Hispanic population of most other US cities. Moreover, there are additional reasons for suspecting that such a sense of shared affiliation might be problematic: the impact of divisive neo-liberal economic policies on many migrants, both those in America and their families back home; the general increase in inequality; and the exposure of everyone to the fragmenting cultural experiences presumed to be carried everywhere by globalizing processes and especially when they impact on global cities. Nevertheless, Price identified three key resources – one enacted during and ignited by the festival itself – which enabled this diverse group to construct and/or reinforce an enduring sense of Latino cultural coherence in the face of social divisiveness and globalization.

First, she argued that life under globalization is not solely about 'flow' but is also constructed around what she called 'pauses'. Here social actors work through the vicissitudes and insecurities but also the pleasures and certainties of the everyday. Thus:

> we still go about our daily lives...To be sure, folks certainly do grapple with malnutrition, stress, ill health, exploitation as laborers...and a host of other maladies exponentially increased under the auspices of 'globalization'. But they also dwell, raise families, break bread with one another, joke, beautify themselves and their surroundings, and appreciate a sunrise or a baby's smile. The lives of the vast majority of the planet's inhabitants are not only flow and abstraction but also pause and connection. (86)

Such shared experiences help to reinforce Latinidad as a sense of pan-ethnic cultural continuity and affiliation.

Second, and drawing on other scholars, Price (2007) explored how public spaces in all cities create opportunities for daily social interaction. Calle Ocho is just such a main street as it passes through Little Havana. Here, the 'very local scale' (87) provided by the main streets and their sidewalks but also cafes, parks, plazas, street corners and markets are particularly crucial in allowing and indeed inviting people to engage in pauses where they can express their everyday lives and concerns. Thus, sidewalks enable people to watch the passers by and participate in the buzz and profusion of local activities, to shop and eat, to show-off and enact their own personal identity projected through their choice of dress or demeanour but also to begin, renew or improve social ties. However, third, the occasion of the festival vastly augmented such opportunities because every nationality and the devotées of numerous aesthetic genres displayed their musical rhythms through bands and dance events while every variety of craft good, national and regional souvenir and food delicacy were on sale in innumerable booths and stalls as every group engaged in 'self promotion' (91). At the same time, people poured onto the streets in far greater numbers than normally and sat for long period on the sidewalks, talking, recounting ethnic or national stories, evoking memories, perhaps of exile, but also, of course, renewing acquaintanceships and friendships or discovering new ones. They also imbibed a powerful ambience and sense of socio-cultural unity as they watched the social interactions taking place and pulsing all around them. Thus, out of the place and situationally specific events of everyday social encounters, but also magnified here by a festival, an imagined sense of Hispanic cultural coherence is made possible and renewed.

6.4   Surviving primordial cultural affiliations and identities

Hannerz discusses a third set of processes which help to sustain the power of the local in most people's lives; namely, the role of culture. In doing so he identifies four cultural frames operating in social life (2003: 69–70) which offer possibilities for shared meanings: those emanating from the exercise of state power; the signifiers contrived for commercial reasons through popular culture; the meanings proclaimed by social movements; and a cultural frame Hannerz denotes as the forms of life. The first two are essentially asymmetrical – deliberately managed and imposed by powerful agents pursuing their own agendas – while the third is rarer. All of these underpin the local, especially the laws, policies and propaganda disseminated by nation-states. However, it is the fourth frame which is of most interest here. This is because by definition forms of life are rooted in the interpersonal, learned, continuously transmitted and everyday social life of ordinary individuals. Also, unlike state and commodified cultural sources their transmission depends on equalitarian relationships, reciprocity and mutual enforceability. They also generate powerful resonances which draw fellow members together while tending to exclude strangers or at least rendering it very difficult for non-members to participate on equal terms.

The forms of life flow within the intimate places which bring people together in close interpersonal relationships. Thus, they are found within 'households, work places, neighbourhoods' (69). They are continuously repeated, are routinized and always present through social interaction and they enable participants to share and to solve the problems of everyday life. They are 'massively present' and usually provide the 'formative experiences' of early life (69). As such they are likely to remain with individuals as they move through their life course. Hannerz stops short of identifying the forms of cultural life with primordial affiliations, embedded in ancient, ethnic or national histories, in myths of continuous blood lines and land rights and the memories of critical defining battles (for example Smith 1995). Yet, Hannerz does regard the forms of life as retaining considerable influence in shaping the relatively exclusive socio-cultural life of people in many countries. Thus, he suggests that 'for a great many people the idea of the nation...still encompasses virtually all their social traffic' (90). Moreover, this remains the case even in the 'heartlands' of the advanced Western nations where globalizing influences are the most pronounced.

European national-cultural differences

Other researchers, too, have suggested that despite globalizing influences national loyalties and institutions remain resilient. Our survival and that of the planet may depend on our ability to begin thinking and acting as if globality mattered but merely saying this does not render such a goal any easier to pursue or attain. Favell (2001), for example, criticizes what he regards as the speculative and untested interpretations of globalization constructed by recent global theorists and which he describes as 'globaloney'. Even in Europe, he suggests, after decades of economic unification and the removal of most barriers to the free mobility of businesses and citizens within the region, the resilience of national institutions and informal cultural preferences remain strong. For example, established rules and procedures for renting or buying property, transferring pension rights across borders and overcoming informal barriers to entering certain national, professional hierarchies on equal terms with locals, all remain strongly in force. Indeed, constructing a transnational life as if territorial borders no longer existed remains a questionable project because the 'still dominant, if partially challenged national "order of things" ... continues to exert an overwhelming pressure on the socialization of new migrants' (2003: 405).

The continuing stamina of national affiliations in Western Europe is surprising for other reasons besides their decades of exposure to EU regulation and global capitalist pressures, including American popular culture. Thus, its peoples and countries draw upon the cultural and intellectual legacies bestowed by centuries of shared Classical, Christian and Enlightenment discourses. They have also been through similar experiences arising from two hundred years of nation building, capitalist modernization and imperialist ventures. More recently, too, though to differing degrees, the past 50 years have also brought many migrants from the South who have established alternative ethnic life ways, especially in the urban heartlands. Despite all this, palpable and surviving differences are clearly evident between each nation and we can hardly avoid noticing them when visiting these countries.

For example, research into the long-term effects of economic globalization on young European adults (Murie and Musterd 2004, Middleton, Murie and Groves 2005 and the contributors to Blossfeld, Klijzing, Mills and Kurz 2005) have demonstrated the continuing influence of national institutional practices in respect to welfare provision and job protection across the EU. Thus, the contributors to Blossfeld et al. (2005) insist that the open world market, intensifying competition for jobs and products and the mobility of capital we associate with intensifying economic globalization, are combining to create highly precarious employment experiences for Europe's young people. While these forces are certainly helping to produce an underclass with very limited life prospects, even those who are highly educated are not immune from insecurity. Moreover, all this is compelling young adults to become more self-reliant and individualistic. One consequence is that across Europe young adults are delaying marriage and postponing or forgoing parenthood. Yet, governments still differ in the extent to which they try to insulate their citizens from world economic forces. For example, they identify countries with similar welfare regimes including Sweden and Norway, Denmark and Finland. In different ways these governments have deliberately tried to use the public sector as a vehicle for job creation much more than other countries, such as Britain, while simultaneously offering generous unemployment benefits, including to young people, helping individuals to retrain and move between jobs and prioritizing gender equality in the workplace (Mills and Blossfeld 2005: 12–13).

Surviving national institutional differences in regard to education systems also remains important along with the extent to which family traditions in different countries continue to influence the decisions young people make concerning extramarital relationships, the age of marriage and the incidence of divorce. For example, the authors identify Italy, Spain and Portugal as possessing socially conservative and relatively traditional 'family-oriented' welfare regimes where limited state support is often supplemented by the 'strong ideological and indeed practical involvement of family and kinship networks' which seek to protect members from economic risks (Mills and Blossfeld 2005: 13, but see also Murie and Musterd 2004).[iv]

Anecdotal evidence from the micro-impressions of ordinary people, migrants, travellers, journalists, novelists, television programme makers and politicians also point to the continuing hold of often subtle regional and national cultural differences. In Chapter 7 we examine case studies which explore the resilient local/national in detail. For the moment, however, here are three glimpses which suggest that personal experiences sometime lead individuals to believe that intra-European national-cultural characteristics and affiliations are not in any immediate danger of disappearing. These were provided by respondents in the 2005 Manchester study and are far from being untypical.

Talking about the impact of European and global influences on traditional and national ways of life a Finnish professional working in an IT company, aged 29 and married to a British woman commented as follows:

Take the UK as an example...we have all these people from all these different nations but if you travel within Lancashire, how many different local accents do you have and this is a small area...I think people will always need some traditions, they will evolve but they will not disappear.

Similarly, a German doctoral student who had lived in Manchester for three years suggested that

It takes a lot to take your roots out of you. Although I don't feel particularly German I am aware of that...and Italians are always Italians no matter where they are, the French are always French, so you have some sort of roots that will not be taken out of you. I hope tolerance will increase and you will mingle with other groups as well – increasingly with migration. But it is not necessarily the case that you will lose your roots. Italians will always love their wine, the French will love their food, Germans will always be more organized.

A final example comes from a French-speaking Swiss national working as a manager in a Manchester-based company. Before seeking work in northern Britain he studied at a London university.

In London everyone tells you 'oh my God it's so cosmopolitan'. But it used to strike me every time I used to go into the university bar, it was always the same every night. You get a table where all the Greeks were together playing backgammon, all the French were together as well at a different table talking French to each other, all the Germans were standing at high table and all the English were at the bar, close to the bar. And again at uni I had a very bad experience with the French people, French being my first language...These people were just refusing point blank to talk to English people...and I remember this French fellow...coming up to me and saying to me in French in front of this English fellow. 'What are you doing wasting your time with him?' So I had a bit of an argument with him...and since that day French people refused to talk to me and I wasn't accepted in the French circle any more.

Additional worldwide evidence for the strength of national, ethnic loyalties

Of course, it does not follow that the resilience of ethnic and national institutions and affiliations inevitably inhibit the development of sentiments of globality. In fact in Chapter 8 we consider how and why attachments to their local life worlds helps to explain why some people develop a greater sense of place-ness while simultaneously deciding to look outwards in search of global allies who might help them defend their local life from changes they perceive to be threatening. Similarly, for most people remaining firmly entrenched in the national or ethnic forms of life they have always known may provide the only safe standpoint from which they can begin to develop a global consciousness (Appiah 1998). In any case, as Cheah and Robbins (1998) suggested, many individuals sometimes do think, feel and even act beyond their immediate particularistic loyalties but this often falls a long way short of identifying with all humanity and might exclude certain groups altogether. Even taking all these qualifications into account, however, the evidence supporting the argument that across the world most people, not just a small cosmopolitan minority, are able or willing to express at least some glimmers of a global consciousness is perilously thin on the ground. Alternatively, such expressions are often inconsistent, skewed, ambiguous and infrequent. Empirical studies and/or informed estimates by experts tend to support this argument.

Turning, first, to evidence drawn from a particular micro-region, Savage, Bagnall and Longhurst (2005) discovered that only 4 per cent of the respondents in their study in North West Britain were able to demonstrate 'global reflexivity'. They defined this as the ability 'to look at their lives, thoughts and values from a perspective that did not take English referents as the implicit frame for judgement, but...a broader global comparative frame' (191). Interestingly, too, most of this tiny group had migrated to England having been brought up elsewhere (197). However, comparative data obtained from worldwide studies paint a similar picture. For example, drawing on the World Data Survey from 1996/7, which covers the opinions of citizens in 70 nations, Norris (2000: 161–4) found that only one-sixth of the sample pointed to their continent or the world as a whole as their primary geographical unit of identity, rather than nation, region or immediate locality. After reviewing UN and empirical material from other IGOs she concluded that globalization has 'not yet destroyed local ties' and there is little sign of the 'erosion of nationalism' (175).

Slightly more recent comparative data extracted from the World Values Survey (www.worldvaluessurvey.org) again reinforce these conclusions. Thus, one of the questions in the survey relating to issues of national identity asked respondents which of the following geographical groups they identified with 'first of all': their locality, region, country, continent or the world. One finding that stands out is the propensity for people in many – not all – countries in the South to rate the world as rather low in their hierarchy of geographical belonging compared with their locality or country. The figures relating to world identity for the following countries were the following: China, 4.4 per cent (2001), India, 4.2 per cent (2001), Morocco, 3.8 per cent (2001) and Tanzania, 3.2 per cent (2001).[v] In respect to the countries in the North, data are available for earlier periods enabling us to look for changes in the 20-year period between the early 1980s and the end of the twentieth century. Here, identification with the world rose quite markedly in Canada (from 2.4 to 12.5 per cent) and the USA (from 1.7 to 19.1 per cent), increased slightly for countries such as Spain, France and the Netherlands (averaging at approximately 10 per cent by 2000), remained the same in the case of Japan (at a relatively low level of 1.2 per cent) and actually fell slightly in the case of Britain, from 8.6 to 6.9 per cent. However, in some Northern countries and over the same period these small yet significant upward movements in world identity were accompanied by a parallel increase in the numbers of individuals who claimed that locality constituted the first claim on their identity. In France, for example, this figure rose from 36.2 to 43 per cent, changes of similar dimensions occurred in Denmark, the UK and Spain while in Japan this figure rose massively from 32.5 to 53.9 per cent – probably linked in part to the long period of financial uncertainty and economic stagnation through which Japan passed during the decade of the 1990s.

In any case, it is difficult to avoid noticing the often-trenchant character and continuing outbursts – often violent – of surviving ethnic-national-religious identities and loyalties in the face of global influences. Indeed, sadly, examples jump out at us from TV news screens, newspapers and Internet sites every day: in the Olympic year of 2008 alone, conflict and violence either continued or erupted in Tibet, the Sudan and between Russia and Georgia to name but a few of the most prominent cases. Another powerful expression of inter-ethnic and racial misunderstanding can be seen in the rising tide of hostility towards all kinds of immigrants – including asylum seekers fleeing from genocide, starvation and oppression – that has been evident in most nations within 'Fortress Europe' for some time, including the rise of extreme right wing movements in countries as diverse as Denmark, Hungary, France, Bulgaria, Italy, Austria, the Netherlands, Switzerland and Poland, among others (Liang 2007, Mudde 2007). Box 7 explores the incidence of right wing populism in EU countries in more detail. However, similar sentiments and movements are evident in countries such as Australia, South Africa and Russia.

Even when cultural identities and alliances are forged across national boundaries, they often flourish within racialized, pan-ethnic or religious spaces rather than reaching out to a genuinely global audience. Again, the study by Savage et al. (2005) illustrated this point well. The researchers compiled all the cultural references to music, cinema, TV, film, books and the visual arts which formed the diet consumed by their British North West respondents. This revealed that 70 per cent of these references were to English sources and three-quarters of the remainder involved the USA. In fact, only 7.5 per cent of such references involved products originating neither in the UK nor the USA and most of these related to European, Canadian or Australian sources (173). The authors concluded that 'global reflexivity' among their sample basically involved a 'white English speaking diaspora' (202) – perhaps, even more so, a white Anglo-Saxon one – rather than anything resembling a wider cosmopolitanism. Parallels can readily be found within 'global black popular culture' (Frederiksen 2002: 56–7), which appeals to and primarily caters for young black urbanites in America, the Caribbean, African countries such as Kenya and the African diaspora. But similar pan-ethnic solidarities are also evident within Chinese business networks spanning North America, Pacific Asia and of course in global Islam.

Yet, as we saw above in the case of Castells (1996: 412) and Giddens (1990: 140) and in Chapter 2 (Appadurai 1990 and 1991, Featherstone and Lash 1999, Kenway et al. 2006, Szerszynski and Urry 2002, Szerszynski and Urry 2006, Urry 2000, Welsch 1999 to name but a few) many scholars have argued that images, ideas and cultural meanings bring a vast new repertoire of lifestyle possibilities into people's local lives. This is particularly the case through the visual and communicative power of the mass media but it is supposed that information technology, travel, tourism and above all consumerism are also highly influential. For example, Appadurai (1991: 192) suggested that the lives of some oppressed individuals are empowered by the glimpses of alternative ways of living available in distant cultures which they obtain through the media. Consequently, 'fantasy' may become a 'social practice'.

It is only a small leap from such assertions to arguing that popular commercial culture can also help to dissolve or neutralize ethnic/national affiliations and contribute to building a shared sense of global unicity. But there are dangers incurred by making such assumptions. Talking about the difficulties involved in extending the notion of citizenship into a world setting, Turner (2006: 147), for example, suggested that although the 'global neo-liberal revolution has converted the citizen into a passive member of the consumer society...these changes in the global economy have not produced the global citizen'. Beck (2004 and 2006) also developed a careful line of argument on this issue. Capitalist modernization has been weakening the boundaries between peoples and creating a 'compulsory mélange' (2004: 137) of cultural experiences for two centuries. Moreover, the recent surge of globalization processes has further intensified border crossings and led to the piecemeal internalization of a growing range of fragmentary cultural experiences flowing in from outside our own ethnic or national groups. This amounts to a 'cosmopolitanization' process. Yet, this was not something in which most people freely chose to engage. Further, some aspects were thrust upon them by forces and dangers which were 'a side effect' (134) of economic, technological, environmental and other changes on a global scale. So we are dealing for the most part with a kind of 'passive' cosmopolitanism which does not 'emerge as love affair between all social actors'. Rather, 'it consists of a perception of global situations of danger' (Beck 2004: 138).[vi]

Similarly, in *The Cosmopolitan Vision* (2006), Beck described his book's thesis in the following terms: '*cosmopolitanization means the disappearance of the closed society for good*' (author's italics). Nevertheless:

> this is not felt as a liberation by the majority of people, who instead see their world in decline. People...are now suddenly faced with the contradictions of a tolerant form of society and a liberty they can neither comprehend nor live with, and which reduces them to strangers in their own land...the nation is leaving the container...But the human need for closure, identity and integration does not thereby simply disappear. (109–10)

In short, we should be wary of giving too much causal weight to global cultural flows as vehicles which change people's lives by rendering them less tied into primordial affiliations and ways of thinking. By the same token, the cosmopolitanization process outlined by Beck seems perfectly compatible with a strong surviving local/national mentality.

6.5 Appraisal

The analysis in this chapter has revolved around the following themes. First, global influences constantly invade our lives but from the perspective of most people they do not necessarily alter the distracting and more often than not absorbing pull of place, made more compelling by our own inescapable human corporeality and the needs this create. Similarly, the power of everyday life and its responsibilities and routines command our attention just as much as, and sometimes far more than, globalization. Certainly, too, Hannerz's forms of life preceded global flows and continue to frame most people's life-long identities during the moments when the global is breaking through their local spaces and afterwards. Our individual lives and needs continue to define who we are and our primary concerns though they cannot remain unaffected by globalization. The local not only survives but it also sometimes thrives partly in response to the global, as we will see in Chapter 8.

Second, partly what we mean by the global consists of the total of all those innumerable social interactions forged both by ourselves and the others living in many different local situations and which cross boundaries. In fact, viewed from within this theoretical frame, a considerable slice of what is being called the 'global' could be said to actually consist of numerous locals (L1+L2+L3+Ln) plus the sum of all those processes through which they become and remain linked together. Instead of viewing these as 'global' in character it might be more appropriate to regard them as trans-local or local-to-local interactions. Nevertheless, it remains crucial to acknowledge and identify the growing number of more amorphous or generalized phenomena which operate in a genuinely global fashion. Among these are the risks of climate change, the kind of financial chaos that swept across the world in the autumn of 2008, the possibility that epidemics will spread everywhere almost instantaneously, the diffusion of knowledge concerning nuclear and other weaponry with their attendant global impact if utilized and the inflationary pressures caused by worldwide competition for scarce food, mineral and other resources. Here, Scholte (2005) clarified our understanding of what is unique and common to all these global processes. Thus, each is almost totally de-territorialized or supraterritorial in their nature and impact: that is, they operate without restraint across all borders and as if the world was a single space. In addition, potentially or actually they encompass and threaten human beings everywhere irrespective of their physical location. In effect, therefore, such global events and processes 'may be situated anywhere or, conversely, nowhere (in virtual space for example) (Caselli 2006: 19).

Third, even the most powerful agents who exercise a truly global influence need to localize or domesticate their operations. For example, TNCs take account of the unique conditions they find in each country such as the historical conflicts between ethnic groups or social classes or the presence of a multicultural work force equipped with particular skills, cultural attitudes and work disciplines. Indeed, very often the global tends to become localized such that its global origins or character remains hidden or unrecognized. Friedman (1997: 80–4) helps to clarify what may be happening here. Under globalizing conditions the encounters which always take place between cultural elements originating in different societies have massively increased and sometimes these are blended together. However, the cultural theorists who observe these processes of hybridization from the 'outside' understand them in ways that are strikingly different from ordinary societal members. For the latter it is the 'specificity' of their culture and the way in which the various elements that have gone into its making have been 'synthesized' into a set of coherent, viable practices and meanings that is crucial. In this respect a culture is forged by its inhabitants and becomes a living but 'ethnically focused form of identification'. Those on the 'inside of a social world' experience 'cultural mixture ... only as a phenomenon of self-identification' (81). To them, the various possible origins of these elements are of little significance.

Of course, last, the opposite process whereby the local is globalized is equally present.

Here, according to Dirlik (2001) while there seems to be a semblance of symmetry in that the global is localized even as the local is globalized (2001), the losses incurred by the local are not fully compensated by the gains it makes from absorbing and grounding elements of the global because the latter's power is greater. Nor can this asymmetrical exercise of power be entirely explained away by emphasizing the ability of the natives to capture and glocalize the meanings brought by the global as just outlined. One of Dirlik's examples of this unequal exchange occurs where the managers of TNCs become part of the local when investing overseas. While the company takes account of local demands, idiosyncrasies and interests and although local agents remain largely immersed in their own affiliations and wield their own trans-local linkages, these cannot match the sheer 'geography of power' enjoyed by the vast networks in which the members of the TNCC participate and for whom the places in which their companies invest are 'mere inconveniences' (2001: 29).

Here, Dirlik's insistence on the unequal relationship between the local and the global chimes with much of the argument developed in Chapters 3, 4 and 5. Thus, at the present time all humans, including the powerful and their families, are now engulfed by a runaway world (Giddens 2002) of globalizing processes. Moreover, whether intended or not, these were mostly unleashed or intensified – over a very long period – through the deliberate actions and policies undertaken by corporate directors, governments in both North and South, by IGOs, the members of global think-tanks and professional elites and other key agents. These globalizing processes did not just happen by themselves. However, recognizing this inequality does not undermine the main argument pursued in this chapter and indeed throughout this book. This is because it is precisely the disjuncture between the mostly inward looking, local character of most people's concerns and subjective life worlds and their very limited capacity to display globality, despite the often-threatening nature of global problems, that we are trying to understand.

The Continuing Appeal of Local, Bubble Lives: Case Studies

7

In Chapter 6 it was argued that irrespective of social class, ethnicity or nationality, the lives and social affiliations of most individuals are confined within the various spheres of the local even though globalization means that the local can no longer monopolize our lives. Here we explore this theme by focusing on empirical studies which have investigated the lives and habitats of five social groups. First, we examine the lifestyles and attitudes revealed by the transnational elites who often work and live in global cities. Second, the lifestyles and orientations of 'average' middle-class suburban individuals are placed under the microscope. The third section considers the continuing reliance on certain 'traditional' or territorial notions of group affiliation and/or the tendency to seek social or neighbourhood enclosure within inclusive ethnic homogenous communities often evident among the majority of both working-class native citizens and second/third generation migrants living in the developed countries. Fourth, the discussion turns to those who have been either by-passed by globalization or marginalized by its most destructive aspects. Here, we refer to perhaps a third of the world's population most, though by no means all, living in the least developed regions of the South. We also consider reasons why globalization processes may actually strengthen some people's localism and/or inhibit or even close down the possibility of demonstrating a global outlook. Finally we look briefly at the sociology of football. Like other sports, for some of its supporters it provides a vehicle for the performance of underlying and competing local/national allegiances. However, equally, in other situations it helps to create or crystallize new identities and divisions which may diffuse into other aspects of daily life.

7.1 Transnational business elites

Global cities are among the leading haunts where members of the transnational capitalist class and other elites congregate. Over the past 30 years a range of TNCs and the leading producer service industries, which cater for the former's needs, have set up their headquarters in cities, such as London,

New York, Tokyo, Hong Kong and Singapore (Friedman 1986, Marcuse and van Kempen 2000, Sassen 1991, 2000, 2002). From these sites corporate businesses manage their far-flung empires while interacting with other companies, governments, think-tanks and others. This concentration of economic power in global cities has created a 'new geography of centrality' (Sassen 2007: 98). Because global cities are so crucial they attract numerous activities and act as sites of agglomeration: capital markets and financial services, media companies, hotels and entertainment, auction houses, galleries and businesses catering for sexual needs among many others. The importance of communication for transnational elites means that global cities have become focal points where dense airline and cyber traffic flows cluster. Of course, global cities vary in size and significance. Research conducted by Taylor (2004) and his colleagues deciphered the distribution and hierarchy of global cities by tracing the networks of partner companies established by leading producer service businesses across the world. For example, they looked at the leading 69 companies in law, accountancy, advertising and banking and finance and identified the cities in which they had branches across 263 cities between 1997 and 1998. They then ranked cities in terms of their numbers of company connections. This indicated that London, New York and Tokyo top the global city hierarchy.

In the literature on transnational business and professional elites, there is often a presumption that they neither can nor wish to put down roots since their high-powered careers in global companies require them to move frequently between cities and businesses. Their high earnings buy a privileged lifestyle which includes the ability to purchase quality real estate in the gentrified areas of global cities. Also, exposure to multinational experiences requires them to shed some of their national orientations and socializes them into coping with a transnational life. Thus, Featherstone (1990: 8) pointed to the importance of 'inter-cultural communication' among today's global professionals and their empowerment by 'a new type of habitus'. Sassen (2000: 24) claimed that global businesses require elites who are comfortable with reduced 'national attachments and identities'. Also, their presence in global cities brings a critical mass of commercial resources and networks which accelerate the 'denationalization' of 'deeply rooted' (Sassen 2000: 25) institutional areas that have hitherto obstructed global capitalism. Sklair (2001: 55–6) suggested that 'globalizing companies need managers with cosmopolitan outlooks' and described how TNCs increasingly 'train their top cadre of managers to expect to work in any part of the world' (55). Similarly, Beaverstock et al. (2000: 101) described how American law firms rotate partners between different overseas branches and expose 'outstanding younger foreign lawyers' to the 'global finishing schools' provided by a spell in the home company. Contreras and Kenny (2002) described how Mexican managers are sent out into the 'wider "social world"' of their industry and company so that they will engage 'in a network whose skills and values are defined by a transnational community of experts' (137).

These are large claims, but what is the evidence that these elites really do move comfortably between nations and cities and that their work enables them to acquire an outward-looking cosmopolitan habitus which helps to weaken nationalist interests and sentiments while insulating them from the ordinariness of local life?

Beyond place and the everyday?

Recalling the argument developed in Chapter 6, we know that the transnational elites employed by global companies or international organizations depend just as much on frequent co-present relationships and social interactions as do other kinds of workers. Thus, only interactions involving 'facial gestures, body language, voice intonation', and so on can generate forms of human exchange and the effective contextualization of meanings that are sufficiently nuanced to allow business people to achieve 'complex understandings, arrange informal trade-offs, and deal with unanticipated tensions' – among other processes (Boden and Molotch 1994: 272). Consequently, business leaders seek co-presence and 'flock together' (272) at conferences and in courtrooms, offices, work sites and boardroom meetings in key business districts while collecting informally in city bars, hotel lobbies and restaurants. In these concrete locations, activities are planned, coordinated and executed. But in any case global businesses and their top employees cannot operate by insulating themselves from local/national resources, laws and cultures. Rather, the ability to deal with the needs of clients and to cope with national regulations and cultures often means they must tap into local knowledge.

The study by Zhou and Tseng (2001) concerning Hong Kong business elites who have built up substantial investments in California clearly illustrates this need for localization. These overseas Chinese diasporic business networks were able to span continents precisely because they could embed their firms in family and ethnic connections overseas. However, business profitability also depended on being able to ground their companies in locally oriented 'ethnic economies' (132) constructed around Chinese immigrants who had sometimes lived in Los Angeles and run family businesses for generations. These provided not only a valuable local client base but also essential linguistic and 'bicultural' skills as well as knowledge of the 'regulatory framework' for business and how to operate in the 'local commercial environment' (148). Indeed, paradoxically, it seems that increasing competition, economic globalization and neo-liberal policies have created tensions that enhance the relevance of strong social relationships and frequent interactions within global sites and workplaces (Beaverstock et al. 2000, Mitchell 1995, Riain 2000, Sassen 2002) and not just among Chinese diasporic networks. Indeed, social scientists have always been aware of what Mitchell (1995: 365) calls the socially and historically 'embedded quality of economic activity' such that 'specific local traditions actively coproduce and rework global systems'. It is only the dominant discourse of neo-liberalism that has temporarily sidelined this insight in recent years along, perhaps, with some globalization theory.

The amount of time transnational professionals spend overseas and how often they move obviously varies. But even when the period overseas is short, they nevertheless need to form locally established social connections. The pull of the locale and everyday life are strong and perhaps especially so because of the disruption associated with moving and the compression of emotional needs into a short period. The impact of these forces is likely to be particularly strong when an individual goes abroad alone and unmarried and is not part of a pre-existing company team as is the case with professionals working in the global building-design industry. In Kennedy's study of such professionals (2004) several respondents discussed the emotional stresses involved. A Finnish architect, remarked that *'living abroad is always disturbing ... You can't be truly involved in the country where you are living except if you stay over a long time period'* and often this is not possible. A New Zealander who had worked in Hong Kong, Thailand, Abu Dhabi and London suggested: *'when you live abroad, your friends come from working there ... you build up a social life ... you could and do call upon them for help, for example, in talking with prospective clients'.*

Two other factors are likely to underpin this tendency: the difficulty of penetrating established local social networks – discussed in the next section – and the intense work pressures characteristic of such projects, given their high costs and narrow time scales. Thus, several respondents in this same study described the long hours of work required for overseas projects, up to 80 hours a week and often until late at night. This gave little time for building a social life outside the firm. Indeed, late-night meals, drinking bouts or clubbing with fellow workmates or visits to cinemas provided the most accessible avenues into a non-work life and often led to meetings with other professionals employed in different companies but placed in similar situations (Kennedy 2004: 165–8).

More typical is the situation where a group of professionals are moved overseas by their company en bloc or individuals join other members of the home company in an overseas posting, as in the studies conducted by Beaverstock et al. (2000) and Beaverstock et al. (2002). Here, legal, management consultancy and similar companies with worldwide branches and partners often provide financial and other support mechanisms enabling their professionals to move accompanied by their families. Consequently, children are sent to the same school or colleagues alternate barbecues and family dinner parties at weekends. Here, non-work life flows largely within expatriate networks. For example, professionals in Singapore relied heavily on maintaining close connections with local Singaporeans, both within their firms and outside, since business success required the ability to train local staff and to bring localized knowledge into the workplace. Yet, when it came to social life, most expatriates lived within 'very well defined expatriate enclaves' (534) and participated in clubs, sports and weekend socializing that 'rarely included locals' (Beaverstock et al. 2002: 529–34). Beaverstock et al.'s (2000) study of British skilled professionals in New York found a similar situation. Those who were married with children – more than half their sample – were again strongly involved in social networks that revolved around other UK members, especially in the case of weekend socializing.

Further, some highly sophisticated businesses straddling several global cities flourish by depending on kinship or ethnic, religious or national identities. Probably the most famous examples of global ethno-national enterprises are the diasporic networks formed by the overseas Chinese. Mitchell (1995), for example, explored how some wealthy Hong Kong business families moved capital to Vancouver as a way of reducing the risks associated with the impending transfer to China in 1997. Often this involved placing a son or other close relative in control of the Canadian investment but with the assistance of other Chinese companies as advisors and joint partners in land purchase deals. These arrangements were held together by friendship, clan membership or *guanxi* ties of mutual trust constructed around shared Chinese-ness. Thus, the relative planted in Canada regarded these partners in Vancouver as their 'uncles'. The trust and information-sharing underpinning such ventures supported 'international articulations' (379) across vast distances but also provided capital or long-term loans at below-market interest rates and with few penalties incurred where payments were delayed. Such flexibility may give Chinese entrepreneurs a strong competitive advantage over Western rivals particularly in this highly competitive era of globalization.[i]

Summarizing these findings, it appears that transnational professionals need and quickly build a localized, emotionally intense but 'circumscribed' (Ley 2004: 157) social life in the cities to which they move and irrespective of their length of stay. This revolves around specific locations, clubs, bars, sports centres and frequently rotates closely around expatriate networks. Here, Hannerz's (2003) forms of life are either directly exported or rebuilt abroad. Consequently , overseas life worlds end up being the very 'opposite of the expansive and inclusive networks' supposedly associated with these de-territorialized elites (Ley 2004: 157).

A cosmopolitan global outlook in question

Transnational professional elites enjoy high levels of educational attainment, lifestyles rich in cultural, social and economic capital and apparently move quite often between cities. Also their work may involve some mixing with people from other nations. Does this mean they demonstrate cosmopolitan outlooks?

In a recent study of highly paid professionals living in inner-city locations, one in Sydney and the other in Newcastle, Australia, Rofe (2003) discovered that almost three-quarters of his sample believed strongly that they were members of a 'global community' (2519). They also claimed that their lifestyles reflected a 'global persona' (2521). Further, they saw themselves as increasingly remote and alienated from the rising tide of xenophobia, anti-immigration demands and resistance to globalization they believed were evident among fellow mainstream Australians at the time of the research. They lived in gentrified neighbourhoods which they had often helped to create. These possessed a mélange of signifiers indicating cultural pluralism and an ambience suggesting a knowledge and interest in distant 'others': art galleries, restaurants and cafes sporting a wide range of international cuisines, craft shops selling exotic and authentic world products and so on. However, it transpired that these aspirations to belong to a transnational elite sharing sentiments of globality and cultural sophistication were often linked to a strategy for maintaining a distinctive and superior position while creating social distance with respect to newer elites moving into their neighbourhoods. In fact, their chosen path of looking 'to the scale of the global' and equating their consumption patterns with the 'extraordinary and the exotic' (2524) mainly provided a way of 'maintaining a distinctive identity' while labelling the 'local' lifestyles of the newcomers to their neighbourhood as mundane and pedestrian.

Butler's study (2003) of upper middle-class professionals living in gentrified neighbourhoods in Islington, in North-Central London, reached similar conclusions. Partly through their actions, this particular location became 'a global space, servicing the international service-class diaspora' (2474). Accordingly, there were numerous indications of a cosmopolitan lifestyle and the preference for cultural diversity and social integration as against parochialism. Yet, Butler's research also revealed how these elite live within a carefully constructed 'bubble'. This included manoeuvring their children's secondary school education to ensure they mix only with those from exactly similar backgrounds and pursuing leisure activities which presupposed high incomes and expressed their distinctiveness. Further, this group was exclusively white, despite the reality that in London in 2005 fully 29 per cent of its total population were not just second or third generation migrants but were foreign born (May et al. 2007: 155). Meanwhile, although the presence of the remaining lower middle- and working-class residents in the same neighbourhood was apparently valued by these respondents as a source of authenticity, in practice this upper middle-class elite had 'simply blanked out those who are not like themselves' (2484) and lived completely separately from those who did not share their lifestyle. Their claims to be living a global lifestyle were little more than thinly disguised attempts to legitimize privilege.

Calhoun's (2002) overall assessment of transnational professional elites offered an even harsher view. He argued that their lifestyles reveal a fake 'consumerist cosmopolitanism' (105) based on searching the world for cultural knick-knacks with which to adorn their expensive lives. Moreover, their rootlessness and mobility detach them from national affiliations and responsibilities. But this means their symbiotic relationships to the global economy equates 'cosmopolitanism' with a particularly exclusivist and divisive form of neo-liberal capitalism (2002: 106). Despite their undoubted ability to appreciate cultural diversity these elites are unable to assume the responsibilities we

once associated with cosmopolitanism: taking a lead in reforming global capitalism while supporting the extension of global civil society and democracy
(108). It seems, therefore, that mobility and sharing a thirst for world cultural
diversity do not guarantee a genuine desire to reach-out to other people or
assume some sense of global responsibility. These elites seem just as driven
by narrow class and individual career interests, tied by everyday family and
work anxieties, and dependent on localities and bound by ethnic and national
allegiances, as everyone else.

7.2   Embedded, national, middle-class suburbanism

We now consider a broad swathe of people living in the developed societies
who can be described as middle class and who often live in suburban settings. They are reasonably well educated and are neither wealthy nor living
on incomes considerably below the average for their country. Some of the job
securities they once possessed may be diminishing but they remain fairly comfortable, most hold jobs requiring considerable education, depending on the
country in question, some own their own residence, may be able to help their
children with their education and can usually save for old age. In assessing
recent evidence and debates we focus on the following themes: attachments to
localities as against more distant places; geographical mobility; the willingness
to admit strangers into social networks; and cosmopolitan openness to different cultural experiences and/or a willingness to assume moral responsibility
for distant others.

Place attachments – near and far

In the developed countries, the long period of modernity, now compounded
by globalization, has markedly altered most people's sense of attachment to
their locality and the social life that takes place within its space. Consequently,
community relations are constructed as much around symbolic meanings
(Cohen 1985) – notions of borders, unique cultural events, representations of
the area – as they are through the co-present interactions conducted by members supposedly typical of local life in an earlier era. Indeed, in late modern
societies most people's affiliations reside in networks and socialities which are
often highly dispersed (Giddens 1990, Wellman 1999).

   A study conducted by Savage et al. (2005) in the mid-1990s explored how
people experience belonging and identity within the localities where they
lived in an age of globalization. They concentrated on four localities in and
around Manchester containing mostly ' "middle class" neighbourhoods' (17).
A central finding was that their respondents no longer saw local identity and
the existence of 'true' localness as dependent upon a majority of individuals
remaining within the same location all their lives. In fact, these characteristics only applied to around one-quarter of their respondents although this

proportion varied between localities. Thus, the overwhelming majority were neither 'true' locals in the former sense nor incomers from distant regions. Consequently, most experienced their attachment to locality as based on a freely chosen and constructed 'elective belonging' not an inherited one and this enabled them to link their own particular life biographies to these same areas. They also regarded their locality as a 'residential space' (53) where they could construct a rich everyday life while retaining connections and meanings to other places. Nevertheless, their respondents did have a very strong sense of being at home in their localities. Possessing an elective belonging did not detract from its importance: 'fixed places' continued to 'play crucial roles within globalizing processes' (53).

Savage et al. (2005) also investigated their respondents' sense of attachment to more distant locations. Here, apart from those living in Chorlton – an area undergoing gentrification with a high proportion of graduates – most respondents had little or no interest in London whether as a source of cultural reference or emotional identity. Indeed, many felt antagonistic towards the capital because of the supposed transient nature of its inhabitants, high crime rates, dirtiness and large population (94–9). Instead, many evoked sentiments suggesting 'local patriotism' towards Manchester (98) and a desire to champion its position in competition with London. Those who demonstrated a strong affection for rural landscapes were mostly interested in northern regions: the Lake District, Yorkshire Dales, North Wales or the Scottish hills. Few displayed much knowledge of, or inclination to visit, the countryside of southern England (101). Thus, whether these respondents were primarily interested in urban or rural spaces they basically formed a 'northern middle class' (104). They had built their lives around a strong sense of northern identity though this did not extend to believing in the significance of a northern English regional grouping in some kind of wider political sense.[ii]

Limits to geographical mobility

Even in an age of globalization, increasing migration flows, international tourism, rising student exchanges, gap years and so on, the vast majority never actually leave their countries of origin on a long-term basis. This is certainly true of the European situation where, despite recent increases in cross-border movements (King and Ruiz-Gelices 2003, Recchi 2006), approximately 98 per cent remain in their country of origin (Favell 2003: 401). Also, where movement across borders is short term – perhaps for work or study purposes – this often leads to a dependence on expatriate networks during the time spent abroad (Kennedy 2008). Such moves are also unlikely to require a transfer of national affiliation to the host society (Favell 2003). But there is also considerable variation between the developed nations in respect to internal mobility. For example, Europeans in general are apparently much less likely to move within their country than Americans (Favell 2003: 412). Such mobility also tends to remain tied to limited areas or specific regions. Again this was illustrated by the Manchester study (Savage et al. 2005). Most of their respondents evinced complex feelings concerning their attachments to places and most had moved during their lives. Yet, the mobility displayed by approximately four-fifths of their sample was confined to the Manchester area or neighbouring regions and had occurred within an overall area of approximately 100 miles from the city centre (45–7). In contrast, migrants from another part of the UK or abroad formed only 10 per cent of the sample. Further, although in most cases immediate family member lived some considerable distance away, most respondents – between one-half and two-thirds – reported that at least some of their immediate family were living in 'regional range'; that is, in other parts of the north or the midlands (46). These individuals and their families displayed geographical mobility but within a fairly limited area.

Strangers and local social networks

Another way of exploring the intensity of local attachments involves investigating how far people are willing to accept strangers into their social networks. 'Strangers' are defined here as people who are nationals from other regions or foreigners. In his research on EU migrants living in the three 'urban epicentres of European mobility' – Amsterdam, London and Brussels – Favell (2003: 414) explored whether his interviewees had been able to break into national professional employment spheres and housing markets. He also considered whether they managed to penetrate the welfare, legal, financial, banking and other national bureaucracies dominant in each country. On the whole his respondents reported few examples of discrimination in respect to these areas though there were exceptions such as the opaque and secretive rental housing market in the Netherlands; nor had they been exposed to overt anti-foreign sentiments. Yet it had proved more difficult to penetrate local social networks based on shared nationality. Here, the experience of resistance to entry was more 'informal' and 'subtle'. Thus, the majority had formed friendships with expatriates met while abroad or with groups of other foreigners who faced the same social indifference from locals. Favell (2003: 421) argued that this disinterest was also evident among politicians and local government officials and despite the fact that these three cities were in the forefront of the European experiment.

Young professionals living in Helsinki and Stockholm, employed by TNCs engaged in the mobile phone business (Bozkurt 2006), more closely resemble the elite professionals explored above. However, their perceptions of Finnish and Swedish society tally with the argument here concerning middle-class culture. Thus, these TNCs tended to operate their own internally circulating labour markets and built portfolios of highly skilled employees from across the world. Bozkurt's respondents (2006: 239–41) stressed how much they appreciated working in these international teams. But by the same token, they felt 'disembedded' from the surrounding societies (239). They also commented on the 'homogeneity of these national societies' and the dominant parochial concerns prevalent among their populations.[iii]

Young EU skilled migrants working in Manchester also reported difficulties in penetrating local social life (Kennedy 2008). Partly this was because neither locals nor migrants have much incentive to invest in developing long-term social relationships where the latter intend only a short stay. Similarly, while the grasp of local language remains limited the vast store of private, localized colloquialisms and common-sense understandings (Schutz 1964: 95) locked within it may bar the migrants from full participation. But social conservatism, especially among those who never moved far outside their city or immediate region, may also be important factors. Here are some examples of the experiences recounted by individuals in the Manchester study.

Elvira was a Norwegian student who had been in Manchester since 2002 but she also worked part time for a clinic. She observed:

> In my first year I lived in halls and so I have a few British friends from there who are still close friends but they are all Londoners. I hardly know a single Mancunian... The only time I really interact with Mancunians is when I go to work for the physiotherapist job.

This connection with British people who were not from Manchester or the North West but from the 'Celtic fringes' – Scots, Welsh and so on– was mentioned by several respondents. Later she continued:

> I feel I belong to a set of international people. I've lived in many places, I have friends from all over the world. So whenever I encounter Mancunians they've lived here all their lives. Those that go to university here they'll stay here. Hence I don't have much in common with them. I get along fine with them... but to make friends with them is a lot harder because when I start talking about things I'm interested in, they're not necessarily interested.

Such difficulties are not confined to Britain. Frederik was a German doctorate student. He had previously studied and worked in the Netherlands and Sweden.

> For example in the Netherlands, at the university in The Hague there actually was no mix as far as I could see between the Dutch students and the exchange students from abroad... When I was in Sweden, in Stockholm for the first time... it happened that I lived in a student flat... for exchange Erasmus students. It was very much outside the city centre... And there we were, well,... only exchange students from abroad so there was no mix with... Swedish students. And then it happened that a couple of Dutch girls... moved in, to the campus... And they were telling me the same thing actually, that although they lived together with Swedes... in their first year of university in Stockholm itself... there was absolutely no mix... and if they went to the kitchen, the Swedes left the room and went away... so the foreign students will stick together.

Cosmopolitanism?

Another way of assessing the influence of the local in the lives of middle-class people might be to ask whether the educational credentials middle-class people tend to possess, or the kinds of jobs they perform, predispose them towards some form of cosmopolitanism.

Taking up Hannerz's idea of cultural openness – outlined in Chapter 1 – many observers see little evidence that this exists as a general tendency among middle-class populations whether in the UK or elsewhere. Here, Favell's (2003) work is worth a second visit. According to him, the historical development of modern nation-states and their institutions of law, education, social welfare and so on, especially in Europe, depended critically on winning the support of their emergent middle-class populations. This meant that modernizing elites had to appeal to the interests of educated people, enlist their support in constructing the building blocks of national unity and of course promise certain benefits particularly in respect to taxation, recognition of educational attainment and access to quality environments. Consequently, and still today, European societies remain largely built around 'sedimented structures of middle class social power' (423). Cities, too, are largely concerned with the 'self preservation' of a way of life designed to serve the interests of long-term residents rather than strangers (422). One legacy of all this is the persistently nationalistic outlook of most middle-class Europeans and a political environment which expects migrants to assimilate to the host culture. Although many of the migrants he interviewed were content to seek access to 'very average middle class satisfactions' and possessed 'averagely middle class ambitions' (423) themselves, these limited aspirations had not helped them to overcome resistance to outsiders.

There are few indications here that middle-class Europeans are particularly open to cultural difference. Moreover, if nationalistic leanings remain stubbornly evident in these internationalized cities, situated at the geographical and political heart of Europe, it is hard not to suspect their equal if not greater presence in the smaller cities across the continent (Favell 2003).

Savage et al. (2005: 186–7) also investigated the existence of cosmopolitan tendencies in their sample. A small minority (12 per cent) had lived abroad at some time mostly when they were children or as part of their education. Although more than a quarter of those interviewed also had family members living abroad these were mostly based in English speaking countries such as Canada or Australia. Small numbers of respondents were involved in other kinds of contacts overseas but these mostly tied them into the shared cultural history and the 'geography of the British empire' (202) with its predominantly white Anglo-Saxon leanings. Where their respondents did refer to places outside Britain, this mostly served to provide spatial reference points enabling them to make comparisons which helped to identify what was unique about their own locale and way of life. Local identities were affirmed rather than disturbed by knowledge of distant places. The tiny handful of individuals who did exhibit a genuinely global frame of reference had all been exposed to highly unusual life experiences, usually related to having lived in several countries.

If we apply Tomlinson's (1999) definition of cosmopolitanism as the capacity to assume a degree of moral responsibility for world problems and distant unknown others, what seems evident is either the limited or the ambivalent and inconsistent way in which people express such orientations. This is certainly one way of interpreting the complex findings generated by the research conducted in three British North Western cities by Szerszynski and Urry (2002) in 1999. They found that few respondents thought about citizenship and its responsibilities in global rather than national terms. Notions of 'moral connectedness' (471) were much more evident with respect to local communities and feelings of compassion decreased with physical and social distance. Many individuals admired global saints such Mother Theresa, Bob Geldorf or Nelson Mandela for their ability to extend compassion to all humans but regarded them as rare individuals. Nevertheless, where an expression of moral concern for distant others was evident it tended to revolve around the plight of specific individuals or social categories such as children or related to unique events and disasters. Their respondents found it much more difficult to think in terms of abstract ideas or to demonstrate empathy in the case of generalized concerns, such as those supported by charities. The authors argued that most people found it difficult to deal with 'abstraction' and were 'numbed' (471) by the complexity and generality of moral demands. Finally, and as with the study by Savage et al. (2005), regional North West identities remained strong even among young people who had travelled widely. Respondents might reveal a knowledge and concern about world affairs yet also express hostility to immigrants on the grounds of their cultural difference.

Clearly, inconsistency, ambivalence and skewed forms of local/national knowledge remain key ingredients in most people's thinking. In fact, Szerszynski and Urry (2002) argue that the multiple cultural ingredients brought by the mass media, consumer and other influences foster a 'banal' cosmopolitanism. These are an everyday and taken-for-granted set of stimuli on which individuals rarely reflect very deeply although it does leave them open to new influences. The impact of these cultural experiences is therefore often quite shallow. They provide exotic resources with which we can diversify our private consumption profiles, bodily expressions and self presentations but all this stops some way short of deepening our awareness and understanding of the 'other' or 'others'.

7.3 Enforced localization and working-class lives

In his book, *Globalization: The Human Consequences*, Bauman (1998) included several references to people whose lives have been detrimentally shaped by globalizing processes and who are compelled to find a perch somewhere near the bottom of the 'hierarchy of world mobility' (88). He alluded to one such group as 'vagabonds'; immigrants whose mobility was 'pushed from behind' (92) by poverty and oppression. But there is a second group harmed by globalization and these are 'locals by fate rather than choice' (100) who experience 'enforced localization' (99): their disadvantages render attempts to escape their condition highly problematic. Friedman (1997) added a further dimension to this scenario of enforced localization. He suggests that the decline of modernity has brought processes of cultural and social fragmentation propelling many to seek a 'return to roots' and to 'fixed identifications that are immune, in principle, from social change' (71). Friedman then identified three main responses to this fragmentation process: the resort to increased indigenization on the part of the native inhabitants, struggling to reassert their threatened sense of 'ethnic primordiality' in the face of rapid change; a move to resuscitate the regional or sub-national affiliations which flourished in the era before the nation-state acquired pre-eminence; and the attempts by migrants to re-establish their ethnic affiliations in the host society, including by forging transnational connections. In effect, therefore, the nation-state is undermined both from within and outside while processes involving the 'localisation of identification' (71) flourish. Much of this is clearly applicable to the experiences of some working-class people in the advanced societies both among the white native population and second generation migrants. In examining this theme we draw on empirical data from Britain which suggest that working-class meanings and identities remain largely shaped by and confined within the sphere of the local despite the impact of global flows.

As Bauman (1998) suggested, across the advanced societies during the period of modernity people engaged with their societies primarily as workers and soldiers. But now there is 'little need for mass industrial labour and conscript armies' (80) and instead even the less well-off are expected to function primarily as consumers. Thus, since the late 1970s working-class people have faced almost continuous deindustrialization – though less so in Germany and Japan – stagnant or falling real incomes, long periods of unemployment and the need to scramble for low-skilled service jobs once largely the preserve of female labour. Much of this was accompanied by declining welfare benefits, a reduction in the stock of social housing, especially in Britain, and the expansion of high-skilled employment whose beneficiaries have moved in and gentrified urban locations once occupied by better-off workers and especially in the larger global cities such as London and Paris.

Social belonging and the white working class

Several recent studies of working-class localities in and around London have explored the theme of localization against this backdrop. In his study of council house tenants living in a residential neighbourhood of the inner London borough of Camden, Watt (2006) discovered a strong working-class culture partly constructed around place and the importance of sociality and belonging. (O'Byrne's research (1997) on council estates in south London uncovered a very similar situation.) Whereas in the 1960s this area was a white, socially homogeneous area with abundant employment opportunities for men and women, by 2001 major shifts had occurred. The social housing sector had shrunk and was increasingly occupied by individuals on low incomes and without paid employment especially lone female households, minority ethnic groups and young people. The availability of manual jobs had collapsed and growing numbers now depended on welfare benefits and poorly paid formal and informal work. Also, first and second generation migrant ethnic communities were established in the vicinity, particularly Bengalis. Public services had also deteriorated as children's play areas were neglected and neighbourhood caretaking services had contracted leading to a general decline in the estate's physical appearance. Declining street markets, pubs and small shops and the privatization of public spaces, the growth of tourism and the gentrification of part of the borough by prosperous middle-class in-fillers all combined to reduce the opportunities for meeting people and engaging in social interaction. Struggling to make sense of their altered situation many interviewees provided a 'narrative of urban decline' and here two main themes recurred. First, there was a nostalgia for the lost community spirit and social togetherness which had supposedly once flourished. Such feelings were not confined to elderly tenants. Second, they insisted that a division had opened up between respectable people like themselves who maintained an orderly life in the face of difficulties and low-status, rough newcomers who were associated with violence, youth gangs, drugs consumption, excessive noise, graffiti and a general lack of cleanliness.

Despite these regrets, Watt found that nearly three-quarters of his sample also cited reasons for being satisfied with their neighbourhood. Only a minority believed that living there was unsafe. For the most part this satisfaction was linked to family life and the reality of continuing friendly relations with neighbours. Thus, some tenants had extended family members living nearby, especially those brought up on the estate. Chats with neighbours and small exchanges of mutual assistance were also common and sometimes these crossed ethnic boundaries. In addition, a network of tenants and residents associations existed and one-fifth of the residents had participated during the previous year. Those who felt threatened by rough elements, disruption and the 'visible signs of inner-city poverty' adopted 'geographies of exclusion' (9) to emphasize their own distinctiveness. For example, they tried to create enclaves of respectability by attending meetings of tenants associations and asking for certain people to be evicted or banned from moving into certain houses or areas. Others dreamt of escaping to gentler areas and a few withdrew behind their front door. Nevertheless, most compared their estate favourably with other neighbourhoods in Camden or London.

On the issue of inter-ethnic relations many white residents did make racist comments. Seeing migrants as the feared 'other' and a source of some anxieties was the dominant discourse (Watt 2007). The limited evidence of cosmopolitan openness by white working-class residents was in marked contrast to that displayed by the relatively low-paid, marginalized professionals, many of them women – teachers, social workers and so on – who were also local tenants. The latter engaged much more in social interaction and 'routine neighbouring' (2007: 15) across ethnic lines, demonstrated strong aesthetic interests in migrant culture and forged alliances with migrants through joint campaigning activity in tenants associations. However, the very different attitudes of the white working-class residents towards migrants were a response to the straightened circumstances they faced and their struggles to create social distance between themselves and the forces they perceived to be threatening their only resource; namely, a sense of social respectability. In any case, not all the perceived threats from migrant residents were completely imaginary. Inter-ethnic fights between local youth gangs did occur and there was competition for access to scarce resources, particularly social housing – although the allegations of unfair allocations to minorities and refugees by white tenants are hard to verify and probably untrue. Moreover, only a few claimed that the strangers had usurped their culture and former place. Similarly, many individuals made a clear distinction between the rough and respectable elements within the ethnic minorities and did not blame neighbourhood decline on the migrants and their families.

Racialized spaces and ethnic enclaves

Watt (1998) also explored the significance of a sense of place and the strength of ethnic social networks by examining how young Asian (mainly Muslims from Pakistan), Afro-Caribbeans and white middle-class youth, living in the suburbs, surrounding towns and villages outside London and in South East England constructed their leisure activities and spaces. White middle-class youngsters coming from prosperous up-market commuter towns and villages were the least likely to confine themselves to certain locations and spent their leisure time in towns away from their local neighbourhoods (692). They also displayed a weak sense of belonging in respect to the locations where their parents lived. In contrast, young Asians, especially males, felt strongly attached to the Asian spaces of safety where most members of their family and other ethnic members lived. Here, they felt secure from potential racist aggression, could defend their local territories, knew everyone and enjoyed a strong sense of Asian identity – though they were also exposed to other cultural influences coming from the mass media. Yet in respect to leisure activities, these Asian young men did not remain within these same parental locations. Rather they sought amusements together through visits to destinations away from home, especially though not just in Southall. This is an outer London town which during the past 50 years has become almost entirely inhabited by Sikh, Muslim and Hindu people from South Asia. Here they could easily retain a strong sense of Asian identity by linking the available cuisine, clothing styles, local shopping facilities and the availability of bhangra music – increasingly shared and enjoyed by young people from different south Asian backgrounds – to the home localities where their parents and families resided (694).

For Asian women, too, the home area of family and ethnic life offered safety. But it also exposed them to the continuous gaze of the people in the community and the risk of gossip if their actions contravened expected codes of Asian female demeanour or were regarded as threatening family honour, for example in respect to dress. To escape these communal pressures, they 'negotiated a range of public spaces' (695) sometime in different towns where they could experiment with wearing English clothing and enjoy the company of other young women both from their own and other Asian ethnic groups. In doing so they were not trying to break with community sexual codes or to rebel against their ethnic background but rather to construct a British-Asian identity across a range of social contexts and 'in a number of different spatial settings' (695).

Young Afro-Caribbeans also created their own leisure places and the men, in particular, were likely to seek out-of-town locations for their clubbing, drinking and shopping activities. Like the Asians, moreover, they evinced a clear sense of ethnic identity, as being 'black'. For example, many felt a strong allegiance towards the particular Caribbean island from which their parents had originally come. Moreover, in pursuing their weekend or evening leisure activities most tried to remain within their own social and spatial nexus not only by keeping together but also by visiting towns to the west of London such as Slough and Reading where there were large concentrations of black people. However, London was their most popular venue both because of the possible visits to family members and friends and the wealth of shops and clubs (Watt 1998: 697).

Considered as a whole, these studies by Watt demonstrate two main themes. One is that knowing people, the ability to rely on frequent contacts and help from others who share the same problems, along with an intricate absorption in the daily life and shared meanings of communities occupying the same territories, remain extremely important concerns for most working-class people of all ethnic/racial groups and even in the midst of vast changes and perhaps because of them. A second theme concerns the extent to which ordinary people living in multicultural localities and cities remain largely ensconced within their own ethnic/national social milieu whether because of shared communication and life worlds or their mutual fear of encountering prejudice.

Working-class cosmopolitan urbanism

Expanding on this second theme is there any evidence of 'cosmopolitan urbanism' (Binnie, Holloway, Millington and Young 2006) among working-class people? This is the everyday, routine, bottom-up engagement in small acts of mutual understanding and social engagement across ethnic lines. Watt's (1998) study of young people in South East England suggested that alongside the racial tension and the tendency for individuals to seek the safety of their ethnic milieu, there were also some indications of people forming inter-ethnic friendships. This was especially likely where young people had grown up in ethnically mixed estates and neighbourhoods and attended the same schools (697–8). Shared leisure interests in sport but especially music often played a key role here – a topic to which we return in Chapter 8. On the other hand, such friendships might wither when people moved into adult life built around employment and marriage. Also, such inter-ethnic friendships were far less likely to occur in the more socially homogenous white, middle-class suburbs and towns outside London. Indeed, most Asian and black youngsters perceived such locations as harbouring people with racist sentiments. Consequently, the geography of places held in the minds of these young minority individuals rarely included these white middle-class places.

Considered overall, therefore, these findings do not point convincingly either towards a clear scenario of emerging working-class ethnic border crossings or to a society openly ravaged by frequent inter-ethnic conflict and permanent separatism. However, two important caveats need to be added. One is that many individuals find it difficult to break the long-established and defensive localism embedded in working-class culture and social life, now strengthened or even intensified by massive economic and cultural uncertainties (Sandercock 2006: 40). In the face of these changes which threaten the stability of everyday economic and social life it is hardly surprising that we tend to find a 'society of cultural enclaves and de facto separatism' governed by 'a regime of differences that are non-interactive' (Sennett 2002: 47). Further, in responding to this situation, many native inhabitants in the host societies of the West – both those facing the same multiple disadvantages experienced by immigrants but also those who have escaped into white havens of nationalist identity (Amin 2002b) – may feel threatened by what they perceive as a series of 'invasions' from people apparently indifferent to their own culture. Instead of hybridity and border crossings therefore, we may find re-territorialization, a retreat into local affiliations and social fragmentation along the lines suggested by Friedman (1997).

Box 7   Populist radical right wing parties in Europe and Patriot Groups in America

Core values/concerns.   In the EU populist radical right parties share three concerns:

- Nativism – the belief that nations should be occupied exclusively by their original inhabitants. This is tantamount to a preference for a racially white population;
- A leaning towards authoritarianism or the desire to live in a highly ordered and disciplined society where leaders deserve obedience; and
- A reverence for the common-sense knowledge of ordinary people compared with the dubiously patriotic, more abstract thinking of elites. Politics should express the authentic views and will of ordinary people (Mudde 2007).

Enemies of the nation. These beliefs strongly incline populists to be suspicious or hostile towards those they believe threaten the nation from within including: immigrants (who steal our jobs and houses, cause crime and dilute the purity of national white culture), intellectual, political and cultural elites (who often ignore the innate knowledge of ordinary people), national ethnic minority groups, gays and feminists, among others.

Additional concerns. Populist radical right parties worry about Europe losing its pre-eminence in the world clash of cultures and fear that American culture will undermine authentic European culture (Liang 2007). They also distrust globalization for supposedly weakening nation-state power and allowing foreign capital to push out national businesses. Over the past 20 years economic globalization has helped to increase the electoral and popular support for radical right populist parties across Europe (Liang 2007).

Wider public support. Electoral support for these parties averaged 8 per cent during the 1990s but polls suggest that many citizens who would never vote for these parties nevertheless share similar attitudes. Thus, large minorities across the EU were equally antipathetic to EU enlargement in 2004, with 42 per cent opposed, and overall support for the EU has declined during the past two decades (Liang 2007). In Britain – and elsewhere – concern about migration is widespread and is often associated with racist tendencies and xenophobia (Griffin 2007). Nor are these confined to the tabloid press: the main political parties have often appealed to the patriotism and insularity of British people and particularly in the case of non-EU immigrants.

US Patriot groups. The Southern Poverty Law Center (2001) claimed there were 194 anti-government Patriot groups in the USA in 2000 though their numbers peaked in 1996. Declining membership was related to the stern government response in 1996 to the blowing up of the Oklahoma state building by Patriot supporter, Timothy McVeigh – when nearly two hundred people were killed. Castells (1997) argued that support for the Patriot groups or Militiamen occurred mostly among youngish, white men from Mid-West states living in small towns and rural areas. They tend to be either working or lower middle class in social origin or from small farming families – people who are downwardly mobile. Most believe in patriarchal family values and some are linked to fundamentalist Christian sects. Racist attitudes are often present and as in the EU close links to overtly neo-Nazi groups are not uncommon. Many adhere to conspiracy theories such as the belief that the United Nations constantly undermines the sovereign power of the USA (Munck 2007).

The second caveat is that in most EU countries, right wing populist movement and political parties have been present for several decades (Mudde 2007). Moreover, in recent years the widespread resentments felt towards the rise in migrant numbers, particularly Muslims, but also the fear that Europe is being progressively marginalized in a globalizing world and a suspicion of the growing integration of the EU itself, among other perceptions, have all helped far right parties to make a 'political comeback' (Liang 2007: 2) including in some of the new accession nations of Eastern Europe such as Hungary. Box 7 explores the attitudes of these far right groups in Europe and America. These movements are intensely nationalistic, resent globalization and usually regard non-native people as potentially threatening. Of course, these leanings are by no means confined to working-class people. The elderly are probably more likely to be attracted to these parties than the young. Also, it has long been suspected that the Front National in France has drawn much of its support from self-employed tradesmen and artisans as well as small farmers and business owners. Similar trends may also be evident in other countries. For example, Britain's United Kingdom Independence Party (UKIP) – with its strong opposition to the UK's membership of the European Union and fears about immigration – has links to sections of the mainstream Conservative Party (Griffin 2007) and some business owners. Nevertheless, some working-class individuals do provide an important reservoir of support for these parties as is clearly demonstrated in the case of the Danish People's Party. It gained 12 per cent of the votes in the election of 2001 (Andersen 2007: 103) and since 1994 this party and its predecessor have not only increasingly attracted working-class supporters but its membership is also more dependent on such support than any other Danish political party (106). In fact, the party has responded to this support by propounding social welfare policies which appeal to working-class people while retaining its strongly illiberal, nationalistic, xenophobic and anti-immigrant stance.

Faced with these uncertainties, inconsistencies and tensions in respect to working-class social life and culture under globalizing conditions, scholars and policy-makers suggest we value and encourage any evidence we can find of daily practices of civility and cooperation in streets, markets and work places among ordinary people. Similarly as Lamont and Aksartova (2002: 1) suggest we should recognize that faced with informal and institutional racism, some members of working-class immigrant minorities may not move much outside their own communities but this need not preclude them from possessing a 'cosmopolitan imagination'. Thus, in their study of North Africans working in France and Afro-Americans living in US cities, they found that these manual workers drew upon universal values, mostly of a religious or nationalist-republican nature, and utilized these to establish their affiliations to a common humanity. Meanwhile, policy-makers need to find ways to foster everyday social engagement across ethnic/national lines by creating sites – colleges, youth and community centres and so on (Amin 2002b) – where the inhabitants of the world's 'mongrel cities' (Sandercock 2006) can regularly interact and find common interests. If so, then it is possible that a more tangible and widespread kind of 'actually existing' (Malcomson 1998) cosmopolitan may emerge from the everyday lived experiences and real micro-encounters between members of different socio-cultural groups.

7.4   Social exclusion and the distortion of localism

Throughout this chapter we have explored case studies which suggest that across the social class spectrum many people continue to live primarily by depending on a local frame of reference. At the same time, most find it difficult to understand the changes engulfing them, even when these threaten their daily lives and identities. We have also argued that much of this arises from the sheer power of the local in all its forms and the way it absorbs and diverts us, filling our micro-worlds with loyalties, responsibilities and meanings which satisfy most of our needs. However, as we have seen the uneven and often destructive impact of globalization often provides part of the explanation concerning the resilience of local influences. Further, and as with many working-class people and others in the advanced societies, the adverse impact of globalization often falls more strongly on some individuals, localities, occupations or social groups than others. Here, the pull of the local may be even more overwhelming and difficult to resist just because of the protection and security it is perceived as providing. In this section we explore this argument in respect to those who have been largely by-passed and socially excluded from the global economy altogether.

Many writers (Bartolovich 2002, Hedetoft 2003, Massey 2005, Kiely 2005b, among others) suggest that despite several decades of intensified economic globalization, world inequality has increased overall. It has either created new victims of poverty and social marginalization or failed to improve the life chances of those people who were already poor. How are such individuals, North and South, likely to respond to their plight? As we will see in Chapter 8, many groups faced with worsening poverty and social exclusion and/or deep threats to their very culture and livelihoods have become linked into the growing networks of transnational activism spanning nations and continents which have massively grown – largely in response to neo-liberal economic globalization – since the 1990s. We discuss the associated rise of a global civil society in Chapter 9. In doing so they have offered support to, and mutual collaboration with, distant others facing similar problems. However, it is equally if not more likely that the responses by socially excluded people will sometimes involve sentiments completely opposite to those we associate with an emerging global consciousness including a retreat into primordial cultural bunkers (Castells 1997) and/or engaging in desperate attempts to return to their roots through re-indigenization, the assertion of subregional identities or re-ethnicization (Friedman 1997: 71). But such reactions to globalization can spill over into racial and inter-ethnic violence, genocidal civil wars or religious, nationalistic or ethnic fundamentalisms with the additional possibility that these will feed into national or global terrorism. Here, for many people, globalization, Western life and modernization are perceived as undermining the viability of traditional cultures and sacred beliefs and may culminate in dangerous reactions (for example, Munck 2007 and Steger 2008).

The plight of the poorest developing countries

Arguably all this points to the reality that like the working-class populations we discussed in the previous section, but probably much more so, many individuals in the developing world have little reason for welcoming globalization and far more for fearing or rejecting it, sometimes violently, while clinging to whatever remaining social support and cultural meaning the local can still provide even though this has been hollowed out (Bauman 1998: 2–3). Much of this is particularly – though not only – relevant to many in the least successful developing countries who, according to Massey (2005: 82), cannot follow in the path to prosperity promised by neo-liberalism precisely because of their very 'entanglement within the unequal relations of capitalist globalisation'. One major reason for this is that the livelihoods of more and more people depend on foreign investment and/or the presence of a cluster of flourishing local companies which are technically capable of catering for the subcontracting needs of large corporations. But this, in turn, depends very much on the levels of skill attainment among the population, the availability of sophisticated infrastructure and the ability of governments to offer tax and other inducements as well as political stability.

In the case of foreign investment, the 1990s saw an increased absolute flow into some Third World countries especially Latin America and South East Asia. But the already developed countries continued to receive approximately two-thirds of the world total while approximately three-quarters of the remaining went to around ten of the most industrialized developing countries such as Brazil, China and South Korea (Kiely 2005b: 108). This situation has continued into the present century. Thus, in 2002, Third World countries received $162 billion out of a world total for that year of $651 billion and while Asia and the Pacific attracted $95 billion only $11 billion flowed to the whole of Africa (Kiely 2005b: 108).

With little foreign investment and low skill levels, especially in science and technology, any manufacturing capacity possessed by the least developed countries is often confined to low-value-added activities such as garment making which large numbers of countries can provide. This intense competition means that neither the wage returns to the workers employed nor the profits obtained by local capitalist are likely to stimulate high rates of economic growth. Further, low wages and profits deprive governments of the tax returns for investment in education and infrastructure, further reducing the likelihood that TNCs and other investors will be attracted to the country. According to De Rivero (2001: 4–7), between 130 and 140 countries may be in this situation and it is now unlikely that most can overcome their underdeveloped condition without huge amounts of external assistance. For such countries, therefore, the idea of development has become a myth. He also argued that technological change is currently rendering approximately 30 per cent of the world's working population unemployed given the labour saving possibilities of computerization and automation. In the rich and some of the more developed Third World countries much of this labour can be, and is being, absorbed into low-wage, insecure service jobs (for example, Atkinson 2005: 57–8 and May et al. 2007). However this is more difficult in the poorest countries because in addition to low levels of economic growth the 'technological revolution' is on a 'collision course with the demographic explosion' taking place in these nations (De Rivero 2001: 6–7).

There are of course additional reasons why so many Third World countries and their populations remain poor: corrupt, incompetent governments; population increase; climate change and more frequent droughts; falling world prices for raw material exports alongside the rising prices of key commodities such as oil; and the impact of SAPs. Among other consequences, SAPs removed the subsidies and other support systems peasant farmers had previously enjoyed, forcing them to compete with agribusinesses and cheap food imports from rich countries (see also Chapter 8). Faced with economic distress, millions of peasants across the South have migrated to the already overcrowded cities thereby helping to fuel a historically unprecedented increase in urbanization (Davis 2006: 15–16). Thus, by 2015 there will be approximately 550 cities containing at least 1 million inhabitants, compared with 86 in 1950. Most of this urban growth is taking place in the South, including in the mega-cities, defined as those containing over 8 million people (Davis 2006: 1–2). In China alone, there were 166 cities with over a million people by 2005 though unlike most other countries the Chinese government has planned this urban expansion and ensured that much of it has been focused on the smaller and medium-sized ones. Indeed, more than half the world's population is already living in urban areas and according to many researchers this is set to rise dramatically.

Urban informal economies and the struggle for existence

In fact, this worldwide urban transformation raises yet other issues relating to economic marginalization. Here, Davis's recent book, *Planet of Slums* is useful. Drawing on the work of many scholars, including the findings generated by the international research team which produced *Understanding Slums: Case Studies for the Global Report on Human Settlements* (UN-HABITAT),[iv] Davis provided a picture of life in today's Third World mega-cities. A key theme concerns how the world's fast-growing urban populations can make a living, particularly since apart from the South East Asian economies, rapid urbanization is occurring without much or any industrialization. Accordingly, in South Asia, including India, most of Latin America, the Middle East and Africa, the capacity of most cities to generate employment, especially with respect to the less educated and poorer majority, is severely limited. Mainly because of globalization and neo-liberal economics, urbanization involves the 'reproduction of poverty, not the supply of jobs' (Davis 2006: 16). Two consequences follow. One is that perhaps as many as four-fifths of the city dwellers in the least developed countries are compelled to live in slums: either in shanty towns illegally occupied at the periphery of cities, in overcrowded inner-city private building, lacking access to sanitation, clean water or secure tenure, or simply by occupying streets, stations and other spaces. This constitutes one-third of the entire world urban population or one billion people. To give just one example, it is estimated that four-fifths of the half million people who migrate to Delhi every year end up in slum living conditions (18).

A second consequence is that most urban dwellers in the South depend on finding micro-niches in the informal economy. This consists of a vast range of tiny 'businesses' which lack legal or official recognition. They mostly involve unskilled activities, are clustered into overcrowded sectors such as street trade, rubbish removal, labouring or domestic work – and sometimes criminal activities – are intensely competitive and offer very low wages and no protection or social rights. Child employment requiring very long hours of work and offering little protection from abuse, form one central plank of the informal economy and involves sectors such as carpet and toy manufacturing in Indian and Pakistani cities. Here, some informal economic activities provide a 'stealth workforce' (178) at the edge of the subcontracting networks which produce the goods outsourced by large Western companies.

The informal economy is certainly not new. It flourished in many Western cities, such as London, in the nineteenth century and has provided a main source of economic survival in Third World cities for decades. However, neo-liberal policies and their impact on both urban industry and rural peasant agriculture in most world regions further increased informal sector employment. Indeed, according to the UN-HABITAT research, two-fifths of the entire economically active population of the developing countries and their families now depend upon it for their livelihood (cited in Davis 2006: 176). Nor is China exempt from this process since huge numbers of recent rural migrants cling precariously to an insecure and often illegal economic existence in many cities (177). Like de Rivero, therefore – and as the UN acknowledges – Davis argued that many Third World cities have become locations for depositing the world's 'surplus humanity' (174). Thus, many people across the South, but also some in the advanced economies, are in a sense structurally irrelevant to global capitalism (Hoogvelt 1997). They have little or nothing to offer and work at the cheapest possible wages when they work at all. They exist outside the global economy. Yet because there is nowhere else for them to go in search of a livelihood they also remain locked within it.

Some observers of the urban informal economy regard it as a training ground for future capitalist entrepreneurs and a source of capital, ideas and skills. However, most researchers view its growth differently. They argue that the extreme exploitation on which it is based, the sheer grinding poverty and insecurity it engenders for the vast majority and its intense competition – which constantly increases as more people are forced to depend on the informal economy for subsistence – mean that instead of bottom-up capital accumulation, the creation of jobs and poverty reduction, there is an endless subdivision of existing opportunities into tinier micro-niches. These support ever larger number of people who have to share or fight over the meagre returns.

The social costs of urban social exclusion

Returning to the argument that local life diverts people's attention from developing a degree of world consciousness, how does the experience of extreme economic marginality shape the way those in the urban informal economy experience social relationships and perceive people from cultures different from their own? Drawing on the research of other scholars, Davis (2006: 184–5) painted the following picture. Increasing competition tends to undermine the social solidarities which were once prevalent while devaluing the everyday social capital – reciprocal ties of mutual help, respect and hospitality – which formally held kinship groups and communities of poor households together. For example, as the burden of poverty on women increases and the struggle over scarce resources pitches individuals and families into ever more severe competition, many are less able or willing to care for another family's children, undertake small favours or lend or share food at times of extreme hardship. Similarly, increased economic rivalry often hardens into the formation of rival groups or gangs whose members carve out various symbolic or actual border lines and distinctions expressing difference. Sometimes these can turn into open conflicts expressed in the form of racial, ethnic or religious divisions. Moreover, since the struggle for urban space is so intense and access to work or niche markets is so minimal and fraught with tension, many have to rely on the patronage of local godfathers and/or seek membership of various exclusive networks to gain access. But in addition to fostering protectionist systems and the need for bribes and kickbacks, this 'semifeudal realm' can also breed or consolidate 'tribal loyalties', 'ethnic militia' and street gangs (Davis 2006: 185). None of this seems likely to generate sentiments of globality.

7.5 Football and local/national allegiances

All sports involve competition, arouse strong emotions between teams and supporters and presuppose winners and losers. Writing about football, Armstrong and Young (2000: 183) argued that it demands partisanship and the urgent necessity for our 'lads' to win; 'it isn't an "egalitarian" spectacle'. It is hardly surprising, therefore, that sport and the ritual warfare it sometimes involves embodies a kind of symbolic power through which individuals and groups define themselves and this may enhance local, communal, regional, ethnic, national or other identities. This does not apply only to football. Ice hockey in Canada, American football, cycling in France, cricket in India, marathon running in Kenya – the links to place and/or nations are many (Cohen and Kennedy 2007). Nor are such associations new. For example, towns, villages and even factories and streets across northern Britain financed their own cricket teams in the late nineteenth century and these became sites for expressing and boosting local pride (Hill 1994). Similarly, in the cities and barrios of Argentina, Brazil and Uruguay a few decades later football clubs with mass followings not only reflected different and often fierce attachments to particular parts of a city and class differences but also drew upon the ethnic/national rivalries between recent migrants from Italy, Spain and other European countries (Mason 1995). Meanwhile, for whatever motives – inculcating sentiments of national unity in their populations, declaring a symbolic autonomy from colonial powers or staking a claim to world leadership – governments have long invested in home teams, sought international sport achievement and exploited competitions, including the World Cup and the Olympic Games, as a way of engaging in 'patriot games' (Maguire 1999). This is a huge subject but here we focus on just a few examples demonstrating how football can provide powerful indications of the persistence of strong local, national or other primordial loyalties despite the vast changes that have re-shaped the game during recent decades. At other times the game itself creates or intensifies existing and new identities.

Like other sports, the organization, financing and the meanings of football for its supporters have all been transformed since the 1970s (Armstrong and Young 2000, Brick 2001, Maguire 1999). Among these changes are the following. The game in general, and particularly the leading world teams, has become increasingly commercialized, profit oriented and often owned by corporations while amateur football has become less appealing to many supporters. A celebrity culture now surrounds football as reflected in the rise of sport migration between teams and countries involving leading players. Further, a vast sports goods industry has helped to turn football into a consumerist industry. The mass media and especially the televisualization of sport (Miller, Lawrence, McKay and Rowe 2001) by satellite companies have helped to turn some competitions into global mega-events, attracting audiences of billions, while propelling spectators away from live matches and into pubs or private homes for viewing. The partial detachment of football from its local origins and personal bonding around match events is also demonstrated by the rise of national and global fanzines lined to famous clubs. For example, as early as 1985, one of Turin's two famous clubs, Juventus – with strong links to Fiat and its recruitment of migrant workers from southern Italy over decades – had more than 1100 fan clubs across the nation and internationally (Hazard and Gould 2001: 203).

Meanwhile, especially in Britain since the late 1980s, governments responded to football hooliganism, and a perception that the game needed to be cleansed of noisy chanting and bodily swaying by potentially unruly and mainly young working-class supporters, by encouraging clubs to introduce all-seater stadiums, more CCTV cameras, greater police and steward surveillance and a more family-friendly atmosphere (Armstrong and Young 2000). In addition, the price of attendance was pushed beyond the means of many ordinary supporters. This coincided with an increased interest in the game by post-modern middle-class supporters. Some of these fans evince a 'cool consumer spectator' involvement (Giulianotti 2002: 38). They are oriented more towards acquiring all the signifiers of the team and its grounds – the club couture and logo, the atmosphere of cosmopolitanism brought by multinational players, a TV presence – than to the assertion of solidarity with the team. Indeed, their loyalty is often thin and may disappear altogether if match performance declines as they transfer their 'allegiance' elsewhere. Giulianotti

(2002: 31–2) contrasted this person with 'traditional' 'hot' supporters for whom loyalty is 'obligatory' and who will never desert their team. They engage in 'thick' forms of solidarity based very much on a deep, emotional, 'topophilic' (Bale 1994), attachment not just to the club but also a particular place. They are also likely to belong to class or ethnic subcultures grounded in the locale. Employing Durkheim, Giulianotti further suggested that for these supporters the club is experienced as a 'totemic representation of the surrounding community' (33). Considered overall, however, the combination of the individualization and privatization of football spectatorship, higher ticket prices, increased stadium control and the limits placed on the ability of young, local men to express macho social solidarity every week towards each other, their team and town have combined to substantially neutralize the overt expression of such emotional attachments at the game though these probably survive outside the stadium.

The literature provides innumerable examples from across the world of football acting as a forum for expressing local, national or other identities while intensifying old or creating new divisions. For example, Hay (2001) described how young Croatian men fleeing from the political disruption and/or inter-ethnic conflicts of post-war communist Yugoslavia migrated to Australia in growing numbers in the 1950s. Most were from peasant or working-class backgrounds and many sought building or factory work in the cities. Prevented from gaining access to some Anglo clubs they formed their own football organization and clubs throughout Australian cities. But some of the migrants and their families were bitterly anti-communist so that playing against rival teams and clubs – especially those supported by Serbian migrants – became as much an assertion of political and national identity directed at their European roots as a leisure activity based on friendly rivalry. Indeed Croatian supporters and fans rapidly gained a reputation for violence and this has continued. Thus, even second generation young Croatians who formed a second version of the Bad Boy Blues club in Sydney during the 1990s 'clung to an image of their heritage' and in doing so 'adopted the hooligan style and some its substance' (89).

Hughson (2000) explored the changing character of premier team loyalties in Australian football clubs, which tended to coalesce around particular Southern European migrant nationalities, such as Croatia, Greece and Italy, during the 1950s, to the evolution of more recent teams where the links to ethnic communities are less evident. On the other hand, he refers to recent evidence suggesting that migrants from different countries still tend to cluster in particular cities and locations (25). One example of this is Perth which has always contained a high proportion of migrants from Britain. It was noticeable that when the Perth Glory team entered the premier Australian League in 1996 the home membership support which quickly built around it consisted almost exclusively of young people with a British background. They forged an 'exclusively male subculture' (26). There are also high concentrations of people from Britain in other cities, such as Sydney, where backpackers and tourists – who sometimes outstay their visa time – tend to congregate. These 'transient' young migrants of mixed gender often gravitate towards city pubs which show UK Premier League football matches by satellite. Here, imported British North-South and other regional identities and divisions are played out around the set. It seems that football is often capable of perpetuating or even reinvigorating both long-term migrant national affiliations and more recent, transient ones.

7.6   Appraisal

Focusing mainly on evidence drawn from the countries of the North, we have considered the tendency for people to remain deeply embedded within the locales where they live and be absorbed by the multilayered richness of their everyday lives, including the still strong pull of ethnic and/or national affiliations. This applies across the entire social class system, affecting rich, middle, low-income individuals and the poor alike. Moreover, it does so despite the increasing waves of global influences penetrating local-national boundaries and the intensifying interconnectivities which bind societies together. Of course this state of relative indifference to global influences, or the ability to remain more or less oblivious to them, is becoming increasingly difficult. Indeed, it may be that the world recession which began to hit most countries hard in the second half of 2008 may constitute not the least of the factors at work in inducing many people to become relatively more open to, and aware of, how global forces mutually impact on their lives. Moreover, social actors differ markedly in the degree to which their individual preferences and experiences may predispose them to become more responsive to globalizing influences perhaps as a result of particular experiences such as falling in love with a non-national or finding work overseas. We take up this theme in Chapter 9. Nevertheless, and at the present time, the evidence that local loyalties and ties remain powerful while global ones are relatively weak, or non-existent, for most people, seems rather overwhelming.

Asserting and Protecting Local Lives: Urban and Rural Resistance

8

This chapter focuses on four groups who possess and project strong local identities: indigenous peoples, peasants and small farmers, subaltern women and young migrants in northern cities. Despite the strikingly different patterns of their everyday lives, they nevertheless share broadly similar experiences and respond to these in not dissimilar ways. First, they all wish to assert and protect the particularity of their affiliations, territories and cultural meanings. In different ways, this requires them to redefine their identities and to project these as valid and viable. Second, they are responding to global flows that are adversely affecting their lives especially neo-liberal economic globalization. For example, peasants and small farmers have been exposed to greater economic competition from foreign agrarian businesses and the move towards free international trade in agricultural products while the livelihoods of many women have been damaged by reduced state spending on health and education. However, the cultural changes associated with globalization have also presented challenges and are undermining people's ontological being. But globalization has also brought resources which people have sometimes harnessed in the attempt to resist these same changes.

Third, globalization is not the only force with which they must contend. Thus, each also confronts the realities of inequality, oppression and marginalization which are endemic in their immediate local and national space. For urban migrants in global cities their situation is a result of job discrimination, being confined to the least secure sectors of the national economy and their representation by the mass media and sections of the host society as the frightening 'other'. While these experiences are relatively recent in origin, those to which subaltern women and indigenous peoples are exposed have a long history. Patriarchy and unequal gender relations inscribed in socio-cultural life have long defined women as subordinate and undeserving of the same respect as men. Pressures from ethnic majorities, Western colonialism and the development strategies pursued by modernizing governments have often jeopardized the survival of indigenous people, though development projects also threaten women's livelihood at times. Fourth, in attempting to defend their local lives each group has sometimes engaged in multi-scalar forms of resistance, whether as individuals and/or through collective actions, involving responses in their immediate localities, nationally and globally. It is their desire to resist the threats to their culture, livelihoods and place attachments that have propelled them to identify with others far away in similar situations, to respond to offers of external support or to participate in transnational protests. Yet these can be regarded as forms of protective localism.

Finally, these political responses take very different forms and are sometimes expressed through aesthetic and symbolic actions rather than overt forms of engagement. Here, we are reminded of Gramsci's argument that the hegemonic, all-pervasive power of ruling elites or classes – hegemonic because they have captured all the institutions which produce and disseminate society's discourses – can only be countered by building an alliance whose participants evoke equally powerful ideas and codes which can appeal to the popular imagination and conjure the picture of a viable but preferable alternative society (see also Melucci 1996).

Writing about forms of resistance in global cities, Sassen (2004) analysed the political actions in which mainly subaltern individuals, such as recent migrants, squatters and other marginalized groups, sometimes engage. Although they may be aware that people in the same situation as themselves are involved in similar struggles across the world there is little or no actual contact between them. Alternatively, these forms of activism may be targeted at international agencies such as the IMF and be linked together through a global network. However, in both cases these forms of politics are fundamentally oriented towards solving local problems; they are only global 'through the knowing multiplication of local practices' (2004: 662). Sassen refers to such actions as 'non-cosmopolitan' (2004: 656) or as forming 'non-cosmopolitan globalities' (2007: 6). In similar vein, Starr and Adams (2003) explored political actions in both the North and South which they delineate as 'autonomous movements'. What their participants share is a belief that economic activities must also 'fulfill social functions' (21) and this is only achievable at the local level where small communities or federations of such units can forge relations of mutual dependency. Equally this requires a partial or total disengagement from the commercialized, corporate world of neo-liberal global capitalism.

Both terms point usefully to the predicament facing our next three case studies of marginalized groups and to some extent the fourth as well. They also help to identify the reasons why local actions which sometimes engender transnational links and shared concerns often do so not because those involved possess a strong global consciousness, a well-defined global imaginary – which delineates clearly the shared path which humanity could take (Steger 2008) – or a sense of personal responsibility for the plight of distant unknown others. Rather, local protest is the result of desperate circumstances which people cannot resolve by acting in isolation.

8.1   Indigenous peoples

There are said to be approximately 5000 cultures across the world whose members fall within this category. Their total numbers are at least 350 million people or between 5 to 6 per cent of the world's population (Hall and Fenelon 2008: 6). Indigenous peoples are widely distributed and often live in areas remote from main centres of population. Many exist across the Americas from the Inuit of Alaska and Canada – though they also inhabit Siberia and Greenland – to the various Native American groups in the USA and the numerous Maya and other Indian peoples spread throughout South America including Mexico, Brazil, Bolivia and Ecuador. In South America they number between 40 and 55 million (Martin and Wilmer 2008: 585). Indigenous peoples are also found in Africa, Australia and New Zealand and throughout Asia. Indigenous peoples in India, for example, occupy approximately 7 per cent of its territory (Starr and Adams 2003: 33) while the census of 2001 classified over 84 million people as indigenous and belonging to perhaps 600 distinctive tribes. According to the International World Group for Indigenous Affairs (IWGIA 2009) this was equivalent to 8 per cent of the total population. As in other countries, India's indigenous peoples tend to be among the poorest with census data suggesting that more than half live below the official Indian poverty line. The proportion in poverty is higher than that for the lower castes and for other low-income groups. Though many now farm on marginal land, without practicing irrigation, most were once forest peoples who hunted animals and farmed forest products. But like other indigenous peoples, increased mining and logging businesses have led to deforestation and their displacement to less fertile farming areas.

Although in recent years the representatives of some indigenous peoples have become increasingly involved in transnational social movements, including joining with other indigenous peoples and participating in the Global Justice Movement (GJM) against neo-liberal globalization – discussed in Chapter 9 – their reasons for doing so have little to do with reforming or replacing global capitalism with some kind of socialist alternative. Rather, they wish to retain a 'political-cultural space to remain different' (Hall and Fenelon 2008: 2) so they can preserve their ancient cultures and livelihoods despite global transformations and the development goals pursued by governments. Thus, for them 'global society and culture and even polity are not so much causes, as opportunities and new tools to be harnessed to an old agenda' (2). How can this be explained?

The uniqueness of indigenous peoples

There have been several attempts to define the unique character of indigenous peoples. Both the ILO and the UN-Sub-Commission on the Prevention of Discrimination of Minorities emphasize that historically they are the descendents of people who have lived in particular areas for centuries and sometimes millennia (IWGIA 2009: 641). As such, their existence and cultures pre-date not only the establishment of nations, governments and economies on the territories they consider originally belonged to their ancestors by dominant peoples with very different cultures and agendas, but also the Spanish and Portuguese periods of colonization of South America (see also Martin and Wilmer 2008: 584). Consequently, much of their ancestral land has often been occupied and the survival of their languages, religious beliefs and customs has been threatened though not destroyed by these processes. However, what distinguishes indigenous peoples from other social groups who have been absorbed into modernizing processes is their determination to preserve much of their unique culture and forms of livelihood while continuing to transmit these and their ancestral territories to future generations (641).

The predicaments of indigenous peoples are interesting in others respects. First, they have struggled intermittently over long time periods against invaders, more dominant ethnic societies and nation-states whose governments often divided them by imposing territorial borders. Their societies were built around 'intense local interactions' (Hall and Fenelon 2008: 2) constructed around kinship and small, ideally self-sufficient communities. Consequently, state boundaries motivated them to engage in illegal crossings and these also brought them into conflict with state authorities. Thus, they have been participants in old as well as new social movements (Hall and Fenelon 2008: 2) for centuries (Schmidt 2007: 106).

Second, at least until now, the core beliefs and value systems common to indigenous peoples are quite different from those which emerged from Europe's Christian legacy, its era of nation-state building, the Enlightenment and modernity and which have since spread across the world. Thus, indigenous peoples believe that land is sacred and cannot be privately owned by individuals or companies. Land can only be protected and managed for future generations. Ancestor worship and/or the need to respect the particular burial places of the dead also tend to bring the agendas of indigenous peoples into conflict with modernizing states or those pushing for the commercialization of land or the exploitation of valuable natural resources such as timber or minerals. Further, animals, plants and other entities of the natural world are believed to exercise agency and possess a soul just as much as humans so that the latter's sole or central significance is not always justified or possible. Adding fuel to this sweeping set of epistemological and ontological challenges to Western values is the belief that human rights are innately embedded in the group not in the individual and the latter's main responsibility is to protect the group and its resources (Hall and Fenelon 2008: 7–8, Schmidt 2007: 104 and 110).

Third, the prioritization of cultural, political and economic autonomy does not mean that the indigenous peoples have remained fixed in time and are unable to adapt or change (Schmidt 2007: 105). In fact, within the space for manoeuvre left to them by powerful nations, they have always responded to new possibilities, adapted their livelihoods and found ways to minimize the restrictions imposed by states and businesses to retain their way of life. Hall and Fenelon (2008: 3) provide the example of the Navajo who over centuries indigenized the skills, animals and artefacts brought by the Spanish colonizers so successfully – including horse-riding and sheep-herding – that these accomplishments were eventually perceived as intrinsic to them. Alternatively, the pre-Columbian gods and religious practices in parts of South America were transmuted into a form more acceptable to the Spanish colonialists yet much of their traditional symbolism and beliefs remained concealed under the guise of Catholic saints and Christian festivals. As Schmidt suggested, flexibility 'has not been a luxury but a necessity for cultural survival' (105). Seeking the support of other indigenous peoples and groups nationally and the help provided by supranational organizations, especially the UN, provide concrete evidence for this assertion.

The clash with modernizing states and capitalist development

The core values concerning the nature of human existence held by indigenous peoples coupled to their determination to hand on their cultures, livelihoods and even ancestral lands have often placed them on a collision course with much that is accepted as 'normal' in the contemporary world. For one thing, the rationale of the sovereign state first developed in Europe and the system of international relations between governments which has grown up around it are undermined by the existence and aims of indigenous societies. Thus, their claims to autonomy fly in the face of the principle of state sovereignty. But they also challenge the entire framework of world affairs based on the idea that only states can operate as vehicles for managing human affairs (Hall and Fenelon 2008: 595, Martin and Wilmer 2008: 3). Further, the desire for self-determination sought by indigenous peoples is also diametrically opposed to the agendas of state-led modernization and capital with their inevitable drive to pursue vast development projects. These conflicting agendas are especially evident where the territories inhabited by indigenous peoples are needed for dam and motorway construction, energy supplies, large-scale agribusiness, mining and logging enterprises and so on (IWGIA 2009: 231, Martin and Wilmer 2008: 595–6).

Thus, neo-liberal globalization is only the last in a stream of events and processes which have displaced indigenous peoples or undermined their autonomy. In fact, indigenous peoples have struggled for centuries against those who threatened their local existence. But from the late nineteenth century, many sought national allies – workers, peasants and so on – and brought their demands to the attention of national governments. However, this strategy was rarely successful particularly in non-democratic countries or where their number in the population was not substantial. The creation of the WB, the IMF and the UN, particularly the latter, after the Second World War, however, encouraged indigenous peoples to partly shift their concerns to the global level (Passy 1999: 149–50). Passy argued that the UN provided a framework in which organizations and movements could share information, appeal to public opinion, with the help of the mass media, get their agendas recognized and legitimize their demands within the context of international normative regimes – such as the declaration of human rights – established by member states and upheld by UN agencies. The UN gained from these interactions since its agencies urgently needed on-the-ground knowledge and allies who would support their attempts to build acceptance for various normative principles, policies and declarations (155–6). Following two conferences held under the auspices of the UN in 1977 and 1981, worldwide indigenous people's representatives reached a consensus regarding their shared concerns. Later, during the 1980s and 1990s they established transnational networks and common interests (Passy 1999: 160–4).

In the meantime, neo-liberalism exposed Southern economies to increased foreign investment and open trade regimes and thinned down or removed legal, welfare and economic systems which had previously insulated vulnerable people from the full force of market competition whether in terms of access to land or forests, agricultural livelihoods or employment. In doing so neo-liberal economics intensified the need for indigenous peoples to continue their strategy of seeking external allies (Passy 1999) as a way of protecting their autonomy and identity. Section 9.4 in Chapter 9 examines Mexico's Zapatista movement, first established by the indigenous Chiapas people, as a response to economic globalization and the impact this had on the rise of the Global Justice Movement.

8.2 Peasants and small farmers

Despite more than two hundred years of industrialization and urbanization, peasants and small farmers continue to make up nearly half of the world's economically active population (Edelman 2003: 215). For several decades most scholarly work on agrarian socio-economic relations distinguished between peasants and small capitalist farmers (see Jacobs 2009). Peasants were seen as oriented to subsistence production although most also marketed some of their crops, probably to pay rents or taxes. Their aim was to preserve the family farm and their life worlds revolved around the village community. In contrast, small farmers were regarded as much more driven by the competitive pressures of the capitalist market and were likely to become specialized producers. They aimed to make a reasonable living and to earn a sufficient return on their investment in land and equipment with a view to perhaps expanding their business. However, the fundamental worldwide transformations taking place in agriculture over a long period, but especially since the 1970s, have increasingly exposed small farmers everywhere to the same problems and so the distinction between these two categories now seems less significant.

Particularly since the early 1990s, this shared susceptibility to agricultural change has encouraged farmers to forge regional and transnational alliances as a more effective way to protect their local and national interests. The networking and political activism to which this led included a remarkable degree of North-South collaboration despite cultural and other differences. Similarly, farmers' organizations have forged alliances with environmentalists, women's groups, consumer interests, anti-dam protesters, indigenous peoples and others where their interests in preserving the autonomy and uniqueness of particular places, local resources, ecologies and cultures have converged.

The crises facing small agricultural producers worldwide

During the past 150 years, large and small farmers have often passed through periods of economic insecurity. Mostly this was due to two enduring problems. First, under capitalist market conditions the interests of urban and industrial dwellers as against those of rural agricultural groups were often in conflict. In the cities capitalist factory owners wished to pay the lowest possible wages and growing armies of workers needed cheap food. But farmers needed crop prices sufficient to earn a living and to pay the interest on their loans for machinery and other investments. A second source of agricultural insecurity arose because of increased farm international trade: export competition, the rising cost of agricultural inputs, falling world crop prices or some combination of these. In the nineteenth century, for example, technological developments such as steamships and refrigeration enabled not only the USA and Canada but also Argentina, Australia and New Zealand to export huge quantities of cereals, meat and dairy produce at prices lower than European farmers could normally offer. Such differences of national interest continue today as demonstrated by the tendency for North American and EU governments – with the tacit support of the WTO – to subsidize their farmers and then permit the latter to dump cheap produce on countries in the South. Clearly this undercuts domestic food prices and damages local farmers in the Southern countries.

Such conflicts of interest rendered the task of uniting farmers and workers, or with their counterparts in different nations, highly problematical. Nevertheless, especially from the 1980s, the sheer weight of difficulties bearing down on small farmers encouraged many to combine forces in joint protest. Moreover, economic globalization converged with additional transformations affecting agriculture and these also squeezed small farmers hard: corporatization, advanced technological development, the establishment of regional trade groupings and growing land concentration. How and why did these factors intensify and interact?

1. During the 1980s, many governments in the South were compelled to accept SAPs in return for assistance with debt rescheduling and gaining new loans, foreign aid and so on. These involved a package of neo-liberal measures including privatization of public resources, reduced subsidies, the liberalization of capital and foreign investment flows and more open trade. Together these policies worsened the material conditions of many farmers whose

landholdings were small and whose conditions of land tenure were insecure. Thus, many governments reduced or eradicated earlier programmes designed to preserve the small farm sector and rural communities. These included not only low-interest loans, subsidized fertilizers, rural extension services and guaranteed produce prices (Edelman 2003: 189) but also the legal insulation of public or communal lands from commercial sale – as in Mexico prior to the 1980s – and trade protection from foreign food imports.

2. During the 1990s regional trade agreements were established in Central America, North America, as in the case of NAFTA, and the EU. This was accompanied by moves on the part of the WTO (formed in 1995 out of the General Agreement on Tariffs and Trade or the GATT) to extend the same regime of freer trade to agriculture and services that had been introduced to manufacturing during the previous decades. Many small farmers resented these changes because they feared that increased foreign competition from cheaper imports would reduce their earnings and place their already precarious livelihoods in jeopardy, for example through increased indebtedness (Reitan 109–11 and 120–1). However, it seemed likely that a more open and competitive agricultural system would have the opposite effect on large farmers, enabling them to further consolidate their share of national and global markets.

Responses to the WTO and regionalization by farmers were many and widespread. In France, for example, farmer's associations participated in several meetings and protests, in association with farmers not only from other EU countries but also from Japan, North America and elsewhere. In 1992 when the EU's price support system for wheat, milk and other products was under discussion, French farmers lobbied strongly for the introduction of a ceiling on these payments. This would have prevented the largest farms from gaining the greater advantage merely because they produced a lot more output – a benefit that enabled them to become even larger so increasing farm concentration (Edelman 2003: 203). One particular incident with strong anti-American undertones occurred in 1999 when Josè Bové and members of the Confédération Paysanne, dismantled a new McDonald's restaurant in south west France – attracting wide national and international attention (Reitan 2007: 161–4).

3. Huge corporations have increased their grip on the various stages and processes involved in agriculture often through undertaking a series of mergers and amalgamations. The result, according to Hendrickson and Heffernan (2002: 347), has been the forging of global food chain clusters. In effect, each of these clusters control a huge part of the decision-making involved in the global food system – 'from gene to supermarket shelf' – (350) leaving farmers as little more than suppliers of labour (350). Even if they own some of the capital, they no longer own the products moving through the food system. Instead, farmers have to accept the specialized roles and price rulings imposed on them by the corporate giants.

Global supermarkets have also become gigantic players in this world food system. For example, Wal-Mart not only bought two leading German supermarkets and the UK's third largest supermarket, Asda, in 1999 but also owns retail outlets in Brazil, Argentina and Mexico and has joint ventures in China and South Korea. This concentration of market share by supermarkets has increased their capacity to bargain lower prices with farm suppliers and to squeeze out the smaller farmers who cannot cope with the demand for ever cheaper products and more stringent regulations (Hendrickson and Heffernan 2002: 357–8). Blythman (2007: 238) explains how for supermarkets '[q]uality is not the point. The secret of success is to supply a big volume of some generic, anonymous, bottom-of-the-range, own-label produced product such as block cheese, sliced ham' or chicken. Clearly, even large farmers are likely to be severely damaged by such tactics.

4. Many farmers have also felt threatened by developments in biotechnology pioneered largely by corporations. Here, some companies have purchased the genetic material associated with various plants and then claimed international patent rights or trade related intellectual property rights (TRIPS). These confer exclusive rights to monopolize whatever products are later developed. TRIPS became a core part of the new GATT/WTO trade rules in the mid-1990s. To many small farmers this move to effectively privatize genetic material seemed to threaten their access to the vast stock of natural resources – or the commons – which had formally belonged to everyone and consisting of 'the earth's water, forests, air, land, and seeds' (Reitan 2007: 150). In India, this became a key issue in the struggles undertaken by a coalition of farmers who later joined with tribal peoples, anti-dam protestors, women's groups and fisherfolk to form a coalition in 1991. This was soon after the Indian government adopted trade liberalization along with a range of other neo-liberal policies. The government also repealed a national patent law enacted in 1970. This had been designed specifically to protect national environmental resources and plants from being owned by foreign interests. However, after 1991 it became necessary to repeal this act so that India could comply with the GATT/WTO trade rules (Reitan 2007: 156–8). The particular instance which sparked mass protest against TRIPS in India was the acquisition by a major corporation of American patent rights on the seeds of the neem tree – widely used for everyday medical and other purposes (Edelman 2003: 203). This then focused discontent on wider issues.

Towards transnational networking and activism

Whether in Brazil, where the Landless Rural Workers' Movement (MST) helped to organize land invasions, in India, or in the case of the peasant and rural worker's resistance to SAPs in Costa Rica or Honduras, and elsewhere, farm resistance to the changes outlined above generally began at the grass-roots level (Reitan 2007: 164–5). Soon, however, farm leaders and their organizations realized that national governments were increasingly unable or unwilling to deal with their concerns at the domestic level. Moreover, the threats to their survival had shifted to the sphere of the global whether this concerned free trade, neo-liberal economics or competition from powerful corporations. National farmer's groups recognized that effective resistance required them to 'broker ties with one another and diffuse information, first macro-regionally, and eventually across continents' (165). Indeed, the volume and intensity of such transnational networking and cooperation escalated from the early 1990s. For example, Canadian, American and Mexican farming organizations increasingly collaborated in the attempt to resist NAFTA, due to begin in 1994.

The second national congress organized by the National Union of Agriculturalists and Livestock Producers in Nicaragua in 1992 proved to be a key event. Representatives were invited from farm organizations across Europe and North and South America. Those present drew up the Managua Declaration which agreed on future coordination designed to resist neo-liberal policies and the GATT proposals. After some initial disagreements, Via Campesina (VC) – The Peasant Road – was established in Belgium a year later with the support of organizations from 36 countries. From its inception the VC was determined to remain autonomous and permitted membership only to organizations representing the interests of farmers, peasants, rural women and indigenous people (Desmarais 2002: 93–6, Edelman 2003: 192–3, Reitan 2007: 166–70). Since that time VC members have been important players at several major world events: for example, the Rome World Food Summit organized by the Food and Agricultural Organization in 1996 and the WTO conference in Seattle in December 1999.

Transnational action but for local ends

Despite many years of transnational activism, the organizations involved in VC have retained the primary concerns which motivated their members from the beginning. To demonstrate this claim here are two sources. The first comes from an interview conducted in 2002 with Nettie Wiebe who was formerly a president of the National Farmers Union of Canada and later a VC activist. She alluded to the fundamentally similar nature of farming practice, irrespective of whether those involved are Western producers or peasants mainly engaged in subsistence production, and therefore the need for all agriculturalists to combine together. But her statement also reveals the inescapably grounded demands of farm life.

> If you actually ask what 'peasant' means, it means 'people of the land'. Are we Canadian farmers 'people of the land'? Well, yes, of course…We too are peasants and it's the land and our relationship to the land and food production that distinguishes us. We're not part of the industrial machine. We're much more closely

linked to places where we grow food and how we grow food, and what the weather is there. (Cited in Edelman 2003: 187)

Second, a visit to the current VC website (www. viacampesina.org/main_en/index) immediately reveals its members' central priorities. Thus, under the heading of 'Organization' part of the introductory preamble states that

> The principal objective of La Via Campesina is to develop solidarity and unity among small farmer organizations in order to promote gender parity and social justice in fair economic relations: the preservation of land, water, seeds and other natural resources; food sovereignty; sustainable agricultural production based on small and medium-sized producers.

However, a strong preference for preserving local and traditional life is clearly evident. Thus, agriculture should be based on the family farm operating in 'harmony with local culture and traditions', rely on 'locally available resources' rather than 'external' ones and should provide mainly for 'family consumption and domestic markets'. Here, the dominant 'industrialized agribusiness model', with its construction of global supply chains, is rejected and replaced with decentralized farm production where 'production, distribution and consumption are controlled by the people and their communities themselves and not by transnational corporations'. There is also a commitment to 'food sovereignty' where each nation pursues its own independent agriculture so it can meet the food needs of local communities. To this end, each nation has the right to protect its domestic market from agricultural imports, including the dumping of cheap subsidized food. Thus, VC's struggle against economic globalization in all its forms is basically about returning as far as possible to the local.

Observers of VC have recognized this primary desire to recover and protect the local. Reitan (2007: 177), for example, argued that the VC's members 'remain consciously and necessarily rooted in local places...its alternative model of development based on agrarian reform seeks to amplify and revalorize local, traditional knowledge'. Similarly, Munck (2007) included the VC and the recent peasant and small farmer movement under the general heading of 'local transnationalisms'. Moreover, in their analysis and critique of the current global food system, some researchers see the need to return to the kind of agriculture desired by the VC and which is 'rooted in the local context' (Baker 1999: 257 but see also Field 1999, Gibson-Graham 2005 and Hendrickson and Heffernan 2002).

8.3   Women against neo-liberalism and patriarchy

Continuing the theme that the need to protect the local is a major reason for transnational action, this section considers why some women have also resisted globalization partly through global activism. Women have always faced constraints on their ability to make personal choices or exercise social agency because of the gender hierarchies existing in virtually all societies. These societies assigned certain roles primarily to women on the grounds of their biological difference from men when, unlike sexual differences, gender is socially acquired and imposed not genetically inherited. These female gender roles were then evaluated as inferior to those of men. The resulting systems of patriarchal domination and female subordination meant that women's work and social contribution were persistently undervalued, they were often denied access to the same rights as men and their lives were confined more or less to the private-domestic sphere (for example, Peterson and Runyan 1993). The extent of patriarchy and the particular social forms to which it gave rise have varied (Harcourt and Escobar 2005: 4). Nevertheless, the current situation facing educated, middle-class women – particularly those living in Western societies – has improved in certain ways. Thus, they now enjoy greater economic, social and geographical mobility. Also their capacity to make autonomous decisions concerning their private, domestic and sexual lives is greater now than it was even 40 years ago and is certainly much more extensive than anything available to most women elsewhere. Accordingly, this discussion focuses primarily, though not entirely, on the experiences of subaltern rural and urban women living in the South.

Patriarchy is a major reason why despite globalization women are usually more constrained than men by the pull of the local and conduct most of their lives within its orbit (Harcourt and Escobar 2005: 9, Jacobs 2004: 178, Rowbotham and Linkogle 2001: 4). By the same token, place and the local also become the focus for resistance when women perceive that the resources and relationships available to them are at risk. Yet, while women's political actions tend to be 'place-based' this does not mean that they are always 'place-bound' (Harcourt and Escobar 2005: 5). What is it about women's relation to the local that has increasingly driven many to act to protect it from external threats?

The local as a sphere of resistance for subaltern women

1. One obvious and compelling factor is the reality that most subaltern women are mothers with wide-ranging domestic responsibilities including the care of children and the household. As Sassen (2004: 655) suggested in the context of global cities: 'women can emerge as political and civic subjects without having to step outside of these domestic worlds' if their situation is precarious or threatened. The same is equally true of rural women.

2. Poor and often marginalized women invariably contribute to the family economy so that seeking and maintaining some kind of a livelihood is a vital and unavoidable extension of their role as mothers. Accordingly, any changes that upset the already fragile balance of economic life and further weaken their capacity to pursue a livelihood may push women into political action.

3. This, in turn, means that their lives and concerns are 'enmeshed with what happens to landscapes and ecosystems' (Harcourt and Escobar 2005: 10).

Clearly, the local environment is even more crucial for rural women whose land rights are precarious, who only have access to marginal farmland – steeply sloped, arid or subject to drought – or who are dependent upon common land threatened by privatization. A similar situation may prevail where women's livelihoods are tied up with forest products, fishing or craft production based on natural products.

4. It is our bodies more than anything else that bind us to places as we saw in Chapter 6: bodies are inescapably emplaced. But this is even more compelling for women whose bodies have always been key sites where power struggles take place. In particular, issues relating to power are closely linked to female fertility and the capacity to produce the next generation of kinsmen, tribesmen, citizens and so on. But women's sexuality and men's wish to gain access to it and/or to control it adds a further dimension. Yet another is associated with bio-politics where modernizing nineteenth-century states developed institutions, laws and policies designed to ensure future citizens would be healthy, trained, disciplined workers and warriors (Foucault 1976). However, more recently, modernizing governments in the South have been equally determined to engage in a kind of bio-politics focused specifically around women. Thus, as 'maternal bodies', women need protection from disease, death in childbirth and unplanned pregnancies. As 'productive bodies, women have been redefined as the new workforce that needed management and care' while as 'sexualized bodies', subject to domestic violence and rape, they require protection and empowerment in home, community and social life (Harcourt 2005: 42–3). Much of this is worthy yet often strategies designed, in part, to improve women's situation become yet another form of control. Women must collaborate and confront the numerous ways in which men, kin groups, society, governments and international agencies manage the emplaced female body (44–6). Indeed, the determination to resist such moves has provided part of the motivation for women's acts of resistance.

5. Subaltern women's political actions also tend to be partly expressed within the local because their domestic roles leave them more embedded than men in local networks and therefore they depend on contiguous social relations and the cooperative, community life these provide. Here, women may draw on rights permitting them to utilize public resources and can call on the assistance of kin and neighbours. Similarly, practical knowledge is shared and passed on through family, kinship and community socialization to each generation. All of this requires and engenders affective bonds and close interpersonal ties that help communities to cohere while creating an entity which can empower women in their struggles. As Grueso and Arroyo (2005: 102) explain: place or 'territory is the space where the social matrix is woven generation after generation, linking past, present, and future'. Similarly, places 'are entangled in personal and collective identities' (Underhill-Sem 2005: 23). Consequently, whether in rural and urban areas, women's capacity to resist the demands of landlords, slum clearance programmes, government officials, logging, quarry, mining or other companies, and so on, depends at least in part on the support

of the local community (Marchand 2005: 222). Yet, community solidarity is also bound up with the specifics of shared language, ethnic culture, tradition and the meanings associated with 'ancestral and kinship relations', the sites where 'security and affirmation and renewal' have always been possible and where 'the voices and ideas and visions' of a people are located in particular places (Kothari and Harcourt 2005: 115–16). Thus, when the 'development juggernaut' (116) pushes into the lives of poor families and communities – particularly those whose members possess few alternative livelihoods or locations to which they can retreat – those taking the lead in resisting the bulldozers have often been women.

There have been many cases where all these factors came into play and motivated women to resist economic change or development projects. Kothari and Harcourt's (2005) analysis of tribal communities in the Bihar state of India is especially revealing. Here, women have played major and sometimes leading roles – beginning in the mid-1970s – in the resistance to hydroelectric projects involving dams on the Koel and Karo rivers. The many collective actions in which men and women have engaged include ploughing up and blockading road access to the sites and forming human barricades against police intervention. Kothari argued that the livelihoods of almost 70 per cent of India's population depend on natural resources such as land, forests, lakes and rivers (118). But the relentless commitment of India's governments to economic modernization since 1947 has inevitably led to large-scale development projects. These frequently require the privatization of natural resources and this is liable to disrupt local ecosystems and place previously communal resources outside the control of local people. Indeed, since 1947 between 20 and 30 million women have been displaced (124) because the 'place-based interests of local communities' conflicted with those of 'national and global capital' (121). The latter fail to understand that for tribal and other marginalized peoples, poor farmers and subaltern women, the places where they live are not items of 'real estate' but constitute 'the ground where body, home, community, and habitat are joined in everyday experiences, as well as in history' (122).

In short, the actions women take to protect their livelihoods 'are never simply about economics' (Rowbotham and Linkogle 2001: 4). Moreover, when women embark on collective political actions these are likely to be based on 'interlocking and mutually constituted relationships of the body, household, neighbourhood city' and nation. But it is also possible that they will generate transnational solidarities and move onto a global level (Wekerle 2005: 96). We now explore the reasons for this.

Patriarchy and economic globalization: multiple oppressions

The livelihoods and local situations of numerous subaltern women have been adversely affected by neo-liberal policies. Because the well-being and sometimes the existence of their families, communities and cultures are under threat many have combined at the local, regional or national level to resist change. For most subaltern women, individual escape routes are either non-existent, especially if they have children, or fraught with even greater risks, for example, migrating to cities where they may become exposed to exploitation in the sex industry.

The range of scenarios women face varies markedly as do their modes of response (Barndt 1999, Harcourt and Escobar 2005, Rowbotham and Linkogle 2001). The overriding variables at work include the following: the degree of ethnic/cultural homogeneity characteristic of their rural community and/or whether they are subject to additional forms of discrimination as members of tribal, ethnic or caste minorities; the impact of development projects; the rural or urban nature of their location; their residence in the cities of the South or North – in the latter case probably as recent migrants; and whether those living in cities are employed in factories or depend on the informal economy. Before exploring some of these different scenarios it is important to recall how gender inequalities interact with women's parallel exposure to neoliberal policies and/or large-scale development projects. The need to cope with both phenomena may worsen their already difficult situation as the following examples illustrate.

Women employed in factories in the South have to contend with other issues besides low wages, job insecurity, unpaid overtime or unhealthy working conditions. The need to deal with sexual harassment or violent threatening behaviour from male supervisors or bosses are two such difficulties. Others include the requirement that young women live in dormitories under the close supervision of employers often under dangerous conditions and in clear violation of nationally validated laws relating to human rights. In addition, women workers have often found it difficult if not impossible to gain the support of male-dominated trade unions. In other words, women workers have been abused not just as workers but crucially as women workers, too (Hale 2004).

Faced with this double experience of abuse, women have sometimes resisted in subtle ways which register their discontent but without withdrawing their labour and incurring the risk of unpleasant employer or police retribution. Hale (2004: 157) gave the example of garment workers in the Philippines who arranged the symbolic, mock funerals of enterprises which operated with especially unpleasant and exploitative work arrangements. But this double oppression may also intensify the determination to seek improvements. Resistance may also be easier than it would be if they were self-employed as home workers or had remained at home in their village. The factory also offers more opportunities for socializing than rural life. Another possibility is that factory women will look to sympathetic external organizations and networks for assistance.

The situation confronting rural women is often more difficult in respect to countering the combined impact of traditional patriarchal relations and economic globalization. In Pakistan, for example, the Woman's Resource Centre (Shirkat Gah) has tried to empower women and influence policy-makers since the 1970s (Mumtaz and Harcourt 2005). The Centre has long campaigned on behalf of women's rights in respect to such issues as honour killings, access to contraceptives, marriage choice, the right to pol-itical representation and gaining custody of children in the case of divorce. Recently, Shirkat Gah participated in a large survey across Pakistan, com-missioned by the government and designed to investigate the insights of poor people themselves concerning the causes and consequence of their marginal-ized existence and how it might be improved. The research revealed that the poorest women continued to deal with the traditional 'prescribed roles' and 'mechanisms of control' (65) to which they had long been subject as well as the new burdens linked to economic globalization. This included increased outward male migration in search of wages and women's need, therefore, to compensate for falling household income by seeking arduous, poorly paid domestic work. As one of the organizers, Khawar Mumtaz, declared when interviewed by Wendy Harcourt:

> A political defense of place by women focuses not just on the defense of a commu-nity's land or environment or traditional culture in the face of global change, but also on a struggle for women's freedom – often from traditional culture itself – and right to bodily integrity, autonomy, knowledge, and identity, that is a mix of modern and traditional discourses. (63)

From local to transnational resistance

At some point many women's organizations realized that confining their operations solely to the immediate situation is not always effective. Even in the Pakistan case, the Woman's Resource Centre gradually extended the scope of its operations and forged external links (Mumtaz and Harcourt 2005) follow-ing a period when it formalized its organization and built links to cities such as Karachi. Later it brought women's organizations together to form a national platform which championed their human rights by drawing on internation-ally established conventions. Then in the 1990s the Centre established links with Asian regional and global networks such as Development Alternatives for Women in a New Era (59–61). It is also important to note that women played a central role in the establishment of VC in 1993. One-quarter of the representatives and farm leaders present at the inaugural meeting were women (Desmarais 2002: 95). Moreover, these same women forced a debate on how to increase women's participation and to foster gender equality in VC's activities. This led to the setting up of special workshops for women's peas-ant groups in South America and later in Asia and an international women's assembly in 2000 (Reitan 2007: 173).

We conclude by exploring two case studies examining the circumstances which led women's groups to add global action to their existing forms of networking and resistance.

Factory workers and international networks

A considerable proportion of female workers are employed in garment factories and provide inputs into the chains of outsourcing companies stretching across Central America and much of Asia. Hale (2004: 159) described how women workers quickly realized that given the reality of 'globalised production, power does not lie with the local employer but with multinational companies, based mainly in the US, Europe and Japan'. Combating low wages, chronic insecurity and appalling work conditions therefore required a degree of cross-national employee and indeed global solidarity. Consequently, cross-border alliances and networking became an increasingly significant element in the political actions of female factory workers. In Mexico, Canada and the USA, for example, an alliance of women's organizations sprang up in the early 1990s opposed to NAFTA. In Asia a network of regional women's organizations began to emerge from the mid-1980s, the Committee for Asian Women (CAW), though from the outset it included self-employed women. By 2004, CAW incorporated organizations from 13 countries including the women's sections of trade unions. It campaigned both against the particular injustices that women faced as female workers and the consequences of an unjust world economy (160).

During the same period, several networks were formed in Europe. Part of their remit involved supporting garment workers in the South. Women Working Worldwide in the UK and the Clean Clothes Campaign, initially founded in the Netherlands, were two such organizations. Quite quickly they cooperated to mount public campaigns in Europe and North America designed to increase popular understanding of the conditions faced by garment workers in the South. They also developed the Ethical Trading Initiative (ETI). This was targeted particularly at the large corporations based in the North – such as Nike which obtained their output by subcontracting production through long global supply chains (Hale 2004: 161–2). The ETI aimed to pressurize these corporations into imposing codes of labour conduct onto their numerous suppliers. The European Clean Clothes Campaign also organized a four-year programme of education in conjunction with women workers organizations in India, Bangladesh, Indonesia and Thailand among other countries (162).

The informal urban economy

Despite widespread industrialization most urban women in the South depend on the informal economy. Unlike factory employment, such livelihoods exist largely outside and beyond the reach of regulation (Rowbotham and Linkogle 2001). Women in the informal economy eke out a living in highly overcrowded and low-skilled service activities such as domestic work or street trading. Alternatively, they are home workers at the bottom of the global manufacturing supply chain dependent on the work brought to them by small subcontractors. Meagre earnings form only one aspect of their concerns over livelihood. Other issues include: the price of everyday necessities, rent, essential foodstuffs, cooking fuel and so on; the condition of the local environment; the availability of clinics, family-planning programmes and other health resources;

the quality and costs of schools; the attitudes of local officials and the police towards informal business operations and squatter settlements; whether socio-economic support is available through kin or informal community networks such as social credit schemes; or the availability, if any, of small loans from banks or other agencies (Rowbotham and Linkogle 2001: 2).

Faced with the sheer scale of these difficulties, the capacity of desperately poor women with little or no education to organize self-help systems, protest against the rising price of water or establish cooperative projects based on social need rather than market forces is remarkable. One such organization is the Self Employed Women's Association (SEWA) which was founded in 1972 in Ahmedabad, in India, and now has 700,000 women members. Its website (SEWA.org) claims that in India more than 90 per cent of the Indian female labour force works in the unorganized sectors of the economy and their contributions are largely uncounted and unacknowledged. SEWA's aim has always been to help women become organized as a path to self-reliance so that together in local, national and cross-campaign struggles they can attain a degree of security in the spheres of income, work, food, health and child-care. In 1999 alone, SEWA ran ten major campaigns covering such issues as improved security for forest workers, better childcare facilities and a minimum wage for women in the informal economy. The organization also helps members gain access to capital independently of male kinsmen and to build associations and cooperatives.

Although most of SEWA's work is focused on women in India, it has long attracted the attention of women's networks in the North. It also has strong links to the United Nations, organizes internationals conferences and maintains close links to similar organizations such as HomeNet (2009). The latter is a South Asian network representing 50 million home workers in Sri Lanka, Pakistan, Bangladesh, Nepal and India (Homenetsouthasia.org).

8.4   Young migrants: music, identity and urban localism

So far the majority of people we have considered are rural dwellers living in the South. Here, in contrast, we focus on young migrants living in the towns and global cities of the North. Sassen (2004 and 2007) has argued that although global cities constitute key sites where powerful capitalist interests are bound into a grid of trans-city networks they also provide spaces where resource-poor individuals, particularly migrants, can construct transnational linkages to their home societies and perhaps other kinds of cross-border connections. But global cities also provide 'thick enabling environments' (2004: 651) where very 'concrete' (653), localized forms of distinctly 'place-centered' (652), 'micro-politics' (653) involving marginalized people are also played out. These actions may also generate solidarities between a potentially wide swathe of local groups – including not only illegal, poorly paid or female migrants but also squatters and gay people among others – or between people occupying a particular urban locale and others like themselves living in distant cities and countries. However, such solidarities are mostly formed as a way of resisting threats to the immediate local situation and/or may be expressed symbolically rather than through concrete connections or overt political actions. Here, there is little or no intention to express a global consciousness or a moral concern for distant, unknown others. Young migrants who have grown up in the host society – whether born there or brought when very young – provide one very interesting example of these possibilities.

Global music-scapes: a case of cultural imperialism?

During the 1980s, some observers argued that globalization was leading to the Westernization, or more specifically the Americanization, of global cultures whether in the sphere of cuisine, branded consumer goods, the arts or media products (for example, Janus 1986, Mattelart 1983, Ritzer 1993, Ritzer 2004). Consequently there was a growing worldwide trend towards cultural homogenization. Most scholars are now sceptical of these claims (Hannerz 2003, Sahlins 2000, Sklair 1995, Tomlinson 1991 and 1999). Contemporary anthropologists argue that people everywhere have become more self-conscious about their own culture. Similarly, all cultures increasingly coexist in relation to each other (Robertson 1992). Consequently, there is now a world system of cultures (Sahlins 2000) characterized by interconnecting scapes and flows where – as with some world religions, particularly the different Christian churches – cultures demonstrate mutual respect for their differences and acknowledge commonalities (Hannerz 2003). But this does not mean that cultures have lost their particularities or that American life worlds are about to dominate everywhere. As Sahlins argued:

> The traditional culture has its superior values, but refrigerators, outboard engines, and television sets are not among them. Defenders of the indigenous order are prepared to make useful compromises with the dominant culture … in the course of distinguishing their own … The local people articulate with the dominant cultural order even as they take their distance from it, jiving to the world beat while they make their own music. (2000: 493)

Sahlin's quote leads us to music and how it relates to the theory of American cultural domination.

Anglo-American pop rock

Regev (2002) has argued that since the mid-1950s pop rock has attained a kind of world dominance in the sense that virtually everywhere youth have fallen under its influence to a greater or lesser extent. Pop rock originated in America and Britain and Anglo-American influences have continued to provide much of its vigour as it has evolved through numerous genres and subgenres. From the outset, pop rock was thoroughly commercial, oriented towards capturing a mass youth market, based around a star system (Frith 1983) and largely controlled by a few Western media corporations but including Japanese capital (Negus 1992). In respect to pop rock's distinctive and winning aesthetic or style, Regev (2002) points to additional characteristics. One concerns the extensive use of electronic instruments and sophisticated sound techniques combined with the manipulation of vocal delivery. Together these endowed pop rock with an immediacy of expression and spontaneity that has wide appeal and distinguishes it from all other kinds of music. Further, pop rock has acquired its own authenticity by insisting on the importance of musical authorship and the willingness to canonize certain key individuals and their performances. Moreover, musicians have been supported by a galaxy of professionals: critics, DJs, journalists, TV shows, cultural entrepreneurs, recording studios, designers, sound specialists and many others (see also Frith 1983).

These features have allowed pop rock to spread and invade all other genres and styles: we see the 'pop-rockization' of the world and the rise of a 'global meta-category of popular music' (Regev: 275). This is taken for granted everywhere and has tended to marginalize other kinds of music or force these to accept some of pop rock's cultural aesthetics – such as incorporating its musical instruments, its strong beat or electrical sound amplification (Barrett 1996). Accordingly, pop rock's influence seems to point irrefutably towards Western/American cultural hegemony in the sphere of music. However, there is another side to this argument.

1. Anglo-American musical influence is undeniable but it is important to recognize that the music along with its supporting worldwide technical, market and business networks have created a framework of opportunity which other kinds of music, and their artists and entrepreneurs, have utilized in their own right. Thus, deploying both the commercial and technical resources set up by pop rock and the diasporic routes established by fellow migrants, Southern musicians have moved North, founded recording studios and catered for minority audiences, thereby adding to the rich mélange of hybridized styles available in the worldwide music market. Alternatively, they have incorporated elements of pop rock into their national music. The saturation of musical culture by global commercial influences has provided 'an effective means of receiving and sending messages' (Lipsitz 1997: 13) outside the Anglo-American sphere.

2. Music has always flowed easily across borders especially when it lacked text or its meaning did not rely on a particular language. This means that music intrinsically lends itself to hybridization and cannot be static; there is no such thing as culturally pure musical sound. However, globalization has further intensified the fluid and hybrid potential of all music, not just pop rock, and its capacity to break away from the locations where it originated. Consequently, musicians, musical artists and consumers can readily draw

from the growing repertoire of genres and scapes. Most music has acquired a trans-local quality (Peterson and Bennett 2004: 8–9).

3. Yet, while music increasingly circulates it still comes from recognizable places and speaks to the particularities of its origins. Indeed, in the case of diasporic musicians far from their homelands this might include 'laments for lost places and narratives of exile' (Lipsitz 1997: 25). Thus, music is increasingly purchased, flows away from its original place attachments, may merge with other genres and is likely to alter. However, none of this can entirely eradicate the marks of its origins (4). Indeed, as we have argued throughout this book, the reality of global flows and increased cross-national connections have 'problematized traditional understandings of place' but they do not mean that people's 'local identities and affiliations' disappear (Lipsitz 1997: 4); in fact, the need for these may increase. Similarly, the arrival of new musical experiences may alert local inhabitants to the particularities of their own musical heritage (18).

4. Like other cultural products, musical fragments can easily be appropriated by musicians, artists or consumers and re-embedded into new locations – or glocalized – to meet their various needs including the desire to resist certain changes or express discontent. Lull (1995) and Bennett (2000: 138) described this process as 'cultural re-territorialization': the re-embedding of selected global ingredients back into the local situation as a way of asserting something concrete about a particular situation.

5. However, global music flows may be accessed by many different groups across the world who face very similar situations and problems. Thus, they can become a powerful medium for expressing shared discontents and needs and in this way certain types of music may help to generate a transnational politicized culture (Lipsitz 1997: 10–13).

Rap and hip hop: global flows and local appropriation

Hip hop culture involves graffiti, break-dancing, rap music and characteristic dress styles while rap itself combines the rhythmical speaking of lyrical statements against a sound system which mixes musical fragments drawn from a vast range of styles. Commentators normally identity its origins as occurring in the Bronx, New York, during the early 1970s when a street gang member calling himself Afrika Bambaataa set up the 'Zulu Nation'. The name was a deliberate allusion to a film in which the Zulus of southern Africa were portrayed as savage warriors resisting British imperialism (Lipsitz 1997: 25–6). Lipsitz argued that Bambaataa was trying to celebrate the expressive, popular culture emanating from the neglected areas of American cities and their racially and economically oppressed inhabitants. Rap's musical roots have been described as 'culturally, eclectically, and syncretically wide ranging' (Mitchell 2001: 4) because many streams fed into it including 1950s Black jive, reggae and Rastafarianism through the Jamaican diaspora, house music and Hispanic influences, especially in Los Angeles. However, most observers refer to the central importance of Afro-American influences (Lipsitz 1997, Mitchell 2001, Toop 1991).

Box 8   Hip hop in Germany: 'A foreigner in my own country'

Bennett (2000) explored hip hop culture among young migrants in Frankfurt Am Main, where approximately one-quarter of the population are of foreign origin. Although migrants were from southern Europe, Africa and South East Asia, Turks and Moroccans formed the largest groups and many were born in Germany of parents who came in the 1950s and 1960s as Gastarbeiter (guest workers) when labour was in short supply. Hip hop arrived in Germany through American soldiers stationed at Frankfurt and many were Afro-Americans. Germans heard the music either via the US Armed Forces radio network, films and TV or through personal contact with black soldiers at local clubs or army bases. The migrants also encountered other musical styles through these mediums such as heavy metal and soul.

Second class citizens.   Some migrants had grown up in Germany, were highly edu-cated or skilled and had acquired citizenship. Nevertheless, many held occupational positions below their educational level and resented being stigmatized as asylum seekers or treated as second-class citizens. In addition, and particularly after German reunification in 1990 – when racism and neo-Fascist violence increased – many migrants felt increasingly insecure and likely to be singled out for attacks because of their physical difference from native Germans. Others believed they were ridiculed or distrusted if their command of the German language was less than perfect. In short, many felt their German-ness was being undermined or questioned. The song title of one rap group sums up this wider predicament exactly: 'A foreigner in my own country' (143). Many responded by following the example of young disadvantaged Afro-Americans in the 1970s and 1980s who had faced a similar situation in the USA by adopting hip hop and rap as a way of claiming their own unique identity and place within German society.

Carving out an ethnic German identity.   Bennett also showed how particularly in Frankfurt, where ethnic migrants formed such a large proportion of the popula-tion, some rap groups eventually criticized both the anti-Fascist white rap groups and groups formed of migrants like themselves. They argued that in both cases the possession of a German passport assumed too much significance and, even more crucially, that admission to a native German identity was all that was being offered when it should be acceptable to 'rediscover' and 'reconstruct notions of identity tied to traditional ethnic roots' (144). Thus, some groups began rapping in Turkish and imported cassettes from Turkey through family contacts or personal visits. This allowed them to introduce traditional songs and to mix these with Afro-American and German-Turkish rap styles. In this way they claimed an alternative to white German host culture, expressed their preferred hybridized ethnic identity and clearly asserted their own place within the space of German city life.

Like previous Black musical forms, early rap articulated the dissatisfaction of young, inner-city, Afro-American males 'who found themselves unwanted as students...as citizens or users of city services...and even unwanted as consumers by merchants increasingly reliant on surveillance and police power to keep urban "have-nots" away from affluent buyers' (Lipsitz 1997: 26). Girl rappers were also increasingly successful. Later, some American rap artists increasingly evoked violence, criminality, misogynic and homophobic sentiments. Others, in the 1990s, were seduced by wealth and became involved in businesses selling hip hop merchandise. Alternatively, the sheer mass popularity of rap led corporations to pay huge sums to some artists – for example, 50 Cents and Busta Rhymes – for drawing attention to their brands when rapping (Doward 2003).

As with earlier kinds of popular music originating in black culture, rap music's appeal reached far wider than young Afro-Americans and other marginalized inner-city groups both in America and elsewhere. As it spread across the world, it was taken up by middle-class youth but was also increasingly popular among young people who, like the original Afro-American audiences in US cities, perceived themselves to be oppressed and exploited by dominant majorities. Mitchell (2001) explained how some observers regarded this global dissemination as evidence for the continuing validity of the cultural imperialism thesis. However, like other researchers – including Bennett (2000), Peterson and Bennett (2004) and Sernhede (2005) – Mitchell saw this nearly worldwide acceptance by youth audiences as evidence of something quite different: namely, the process of cultural re-territorialization. Thus, following an initial period of imitating American rap, the music was transformed into a 'vehicle for youth affiliations and a tool for reworking local identity' (2) and a way of expressing the protests of young ethnic minorities in 'different local contexts' (10). In the process, 'vernacular' musical traditions and others imported from the migrants' homelands were blended with Afro-American music and enjoyed by multicultural audiences in each country.

Mitchell's 'tour guide' (12–33) of world rap performances roamed across Europe, Asia, Africa, Australasia and Central America including the following countries: Senegal, South Africa, Morocco, Algeria – with an estimated 100 groups in the city of Algiers alone in the late 1990s, mixing French, Arabic and English language sources – Japan, South Korea, New Zealand, Cuba, Spain, Palestine, Italy, Croatia, Sweden and France, to name but a few. In France, for example, rap groups emerged from the mid-1980s and quickly drew on the various musical traditions, political ideas and concerns of North African Muslims, migrants from the French African colonies or Quebec and who mostly lived in the outer suburbs of French cities (12–14). Some rap groups expressed resentment not at being treated as second-class migrant citizens but because they belonged to ethnic or national minorities whose demand for some form of political autonomy had been denied, such as Basque rappers in Spain and Maori groups in New Zealand. Other native rap groups, as in Italy, used music to express their allegiance to particular regions by using local dialects.

The plight of young migrants in global cities

It is misleading to regard young migrants as confused victims caught between the two cultures of their parent's homeland and the host society and there is rarely one uniform response evident among migrant youth to their predicament (Lithman and Andersson 2005). Thus, writing about Oslo in Norway, Andersson (2005: 42) suggested that while some young migrants form gangs based on neighbourhood territories and grounded in their own ethnic community, others pursue a more individualistic path of educational achievement, see themselves as belonging to a broader youth body consisting of both native and other foreign youngsters and reject 'communitarian identity-politics'. Further, young migrants are generally only too aware that the homeland their parents left decades earlier no longer exists in the same form: permanent return is probably impossible. Nor can they relate to the intricate rivalries between kin, clan, village, sectarian and political groups, parties or ideologies which once absorbed their parents' generation and were then imported to the host society. Eade and Garbin (2006), for example, explored the changing intergenerational dynamics among Bangladeshi migrants living in East London and elsewhere in the UK. They showed how the more secularist politics and concerns of the first generation have been largely replaced among their children, born in Britain, by a strong Islamist sense of identity and reflected in the rise of several different influential Islamic associations. Indeed, young migrants are not trapped between two radically different cultures – in a state of confusion and pulled in different directions – but rather they wish to participate on their own terms in both the host society and the changing one associated with their parents while juggling various transnational affiliations.

Nevertheless, most young migrants do face difficulties though these have less to do with cultural marginality than their position in respect to the host economic and political situation. In East London, the Young Muslim Organization which emerged at the end of the 1970s tried to increase the self-esteem of young Bangladeshis in the face of unemployment and discrimination by offering a comprehensive and authentic religious ethos covering all aspects of daily life (Eade and Garbin 2006). A similar story can be found in Germany, Sweden, Norway, France and elsewhere: much higher rates of unemployment among young migrants and a general scarcity of jobs of all kind, even insecure and low-paid ones; schools to which migrant children often cannot relate and a high incidence of educational failure; and the experience of living in very heterogeneous, run-down metropolitan areas where building even fragile community solidarity is often problematic (Sernhede 2005). But what renders the lives of migrant youth equally difficult is their representation as criminalized and probably dangerous minorities by the police, a sensationalist mass media and politicians trying to escape criticism by blaming migrants for social problems. It is in the space that arises between their ethnic backgrounds and the othering practices of the host society where most young migrants work out their identities and forge strategies in response to their immediate, local situation including through music (Andersson 2005: 31–2). It is against this background that the riots by young migrants, which took place across 300 French cities in 2000, become readily comprehensible.

A case study of Göteburg in Sweden

Sernhede's (2005) research on Angered, an immigrant suburb in Göteburg, Sweden, brought out clearly the themes of alienation and territoriality among young migrants and the role of music in expressing these. But his work also drew attention to the potential for migrants to cross ethnic barriers within the urban ghetto and to identify with other people they regard as equally oppressed in distant locations through music even if there are few possibilities of meeting them or engaging in transnational protest.

He stressed that, as in other European countries, migrants in Sweden's cities tend to be hugely over-represented among the economically marginalized. Surveys indicate that two-fifths of young people under the age of 18 live in relatively deprived metropolitan districts and the majority are from foreign backgrounds on very low incomes. In some urban areas more than half the children under the age of seven have migrant parents who are unemployed (273). In addition, most migrants are clustered together in well-defined ghetto areas or neighbourhoods which are stereotyped by the media as riven with criminality and racial or religious divisions. In fact, Sernhede (2005) observed that extreme ethnic/national heterogeneity is often common within these metropolitan districts. Finding this difficult to cope with, many first generation parents remain bound to their own ethnic group and this makes the formation of wider communities problematic (274). On the other hand, the young, mostly born in Sweden, experience this ethnic mixing quite differently. Growing up on the same streets, exposed to the same media imagery and stigma from the host society they find it easier and indeed highly conducive to forge cross-ethnic friendships. Though this possibility is less clear-cut in the case of Watt's findings (1998 and 2006) for young migrants in London, discussed in Chapter 7, and the Bangladeshi youngsters interviewed by Eade and Garbin (2006), outlined above, these examples do bear some comparison with Sernhede's findings.

Sernhede (2005: 275) also discovered that most young migrants were highly open to 'absorbing and testing' the ideas and outlooks of people from different cultures. Most also shared a strong sense of alienation from Swedish society. They argued that neither native individuals nor Sweden's institutions showed any interest in interacting with them as migrants: they were excluded and therefore could not belong. However, neither could they return to their parent's homeland. This sense of 'non-belonging' left them believing that it was their common identity as immigrants that most readily defined who they were and which brought them together irrespective of origins. As one youngster graphically suggested: 'alienation is our nation' (277). Particularly among young men, there was also a strong focus on their neighbourhood, as a key source of security, protection, identity and sociality. This was their own place or homeland and for them it existed separately from Sweden (178).

The research looked closely at the views, music and interactions among a particularly active hip hop group based in one of the ghetto areas within Angered and consisting of around fifty young men with Middle Eastern, African and Latin American backgrounds. They regarded themselves as forming an 'ethnic alliance' whose task was to speak not only for all immigrant youth living in Sweden's city suburbs but also for the entire emergent migrant underclass across Europe. In similar vein they regarded their music not just as an aesthetic protest but also an explicitly political weapon in their struggle against racism, police brutality and marginalization. Moreover, some lyrics expressed their resentment against the history of white European aggression in Africa and Latin America while songs sometimes celebrated the cultural achievements and political resistance demonstrated, for example, by Indian tribes in the Andes who were never completely conquered by the Spanish (281–2). Finally, Sernhede explained how despite their strong sense of territory and 'ghetto identity' (283), this group felt connected to people living in cities across the world. They were also relatively informed about the conditions under which such people lived – for example, Chicanos in Los Angeles – they bought CDs and videos from these other countries and exchanged musical ideas with others through the world wide web. As one respondent declared: '[h]ip hop people all over the world have the same language so it is easy to live with them. Hip hop is a language for those that live in ghettos' (283).

8.5   Appraisal

Despite their obvious differences these social categories share much in common. They are all deeply bound to the local – as defined in Chapter 6 – by a combination of socio-ethnic affiliations, economic need, personal preference and a resilient cultural orientation. Second, at some point, local and then regional, national and sometimes transnational links and actions became possible, whether as a result of their own initiatives and/or the assistance of others and as some people recognized the potential significance of drawing on wider support. Third, although transnational involvement has a potential for heightening their global consciousness, these groups and their members sought international support primarily as a vehicle for protecting their local situation and/or expressing their shared discontent.

It is important, therefore, to be circumspect concerning the possibility that the predominantly local concerns of these groups – who together probably constitute more than two-thirds of humanity – can and will rapidly morph into, or merge with, much stronger forms of globality. Thus, it is the leaders and organizers of these social movements who are probably most acutely attuned to the problems they share with similar groups worldwide. They may also possess or acquire a greater degree of literacy or computer skills than those they represent as well as better opportunities to attend workshops, forums, conferences, concerts and so on. We should not assume that all peasants, subaltern women and indigenous peoples have been equally empowered or informed by transnational experiences. In the case of urban migrants, too, it is probable that artists are more likely than their audiences to desire personal contacts with musicians in other countries and to engage in cosmopolitan social situations with other creative people through the diasporic connections forged by intellectuals and artists or through travelling to concerts and so on.

Further, indigenous peoples, peasants/small farmers and subaltern women have been exposed to forms of oppression and/or economic insecurities which long preceded the recent surge of economic globalization and it has been against these as much as anything else that their struggles have been directed. These ancient oppressions or long-standing uncertainties are highly complex and do not lend themselves easily to resolution. Paradoxically, too, while economic globalization has generated widespread resistance and the demand for reform, it has simultaneously provided a worldwide framework of real resources which even severely disadvantaged people can potentially harness in their struggles both against neo-liberalism and these much older injustices. In the long term, the success of such struggles may create further possibilities for greater cross-cultural understanding and globality. However, in the meantime these continuing experiences of oppression, made bearable by persisting local affiliations and identities, suggest that most people's preoccupations and priorities do not lie primarily with the development of a global consciousness at this time.

Part Three

Paths towards a World Society

Introduction to Part Three

In Part One we saw how powerful globalizing forces are shaping and intervening in our lives. They bring undoubted benefits, at least for some people. But their impact is often disruptive and they may even endanger all our futures in certain respects. Further, economic globalization and the neo-liberal policies which accompanied and served to deepen it have often worsened rather than improved the conditions of large minorities while inequality both within and between societies has increased.[i] Yet, in Part Two it was suggested that most people, most of the time, are unable to think, feel or act as if the world mattered very much in their lives and this is partly explicable in terms of the powerful centripetal pull of the local, drawing our attention, actions and thoughts inwards. Even when people do look to the world outside their immediate situation in search of transnational allies their primary reason for doing so is to protect their own local situation. As we saw in Chapter 8, this may provide one very important avenue into the formation of a world society where increasing numbers of people develop a global consciousness. However, it also seemed likely that this prospect applies much more strikingly to small groups of leaders or creative artists, attending international events and conferences, rather than to the large majorities of mainly non-privileged people whose interests they are trying to represent and who remain behind in their communities absorbed in the daily struggle for existence.

Referring to the impact of globalization, and echoing the perceptions of Albrow and Robertson,[ii] Robbins (1998) articulated this dilemma in the following terms:

> An existing global condition ought not to be mistaken for an existing mass-based feeling of belonging to a world community (cosmopolitanism) because the globality of the everyday does not necessarily engender an existing popular global political consciousness. (7)

This worrying contradiction surely calls for some attempt to indicate where the possible escape routes or paths out of this impasse might lie. Yet, thinking about what might be involved in the making of a world society and the deepening of a global consciousness deserves, of course, to be the theme of an entire book, if not several. Consequently, the arguments in Chapter 9 are tentative and exploratory. Moreover, the discussion focuses not on the role of various global elites but on the micro-actions, interpersonal relationships, motivations and sources of empowerment that impel a small but growing number of ordinary people to act in ways that contribute towards building a world society that is 'for itself' and not just 'of itself' (Robertson 1992) through their everyday choices and actions. Here, I suggest that such individual social actors are not escaping from the local, or caring about it less than before. Nor are they working to diminish its significance: rather they are harnessing the resources provided by both the local and the global while at the same time trying to bring them into alignment.

Some attention in Chapter 9 is also given to the continuing actual or potential role of nation-states, and the political processes that are grounded within them, as arenas through and from which effective global actions can also be mounted. Of course, in developing this analysis there is no intention to suggest that the actions of various political, economic, cultural and academic elites and their institutions, associations and networks have been, or are now, in any way marginal to the formation of a world society 'for itself'. Neither am I suggesting that the global terrain and forms of collective action are any less efficacious as avenues for conducting protest or pursuing global goals compared with the national arena or to individual's actions. In fact, quite the opposite is true. But these key themes have been thoroughly investigated elsewhere – and they do receive some attention here. This focus on the sphere of interpersonal, micro-relations and actions and on the possible role of national spaces in helping to provide some of the energy and resources for building a world society is prioritized because so far these avenues and arenas for change have not received the attention from researchers and theorists that they manifestly deserve. Arguably, they also raise some interesting theoretical as well as practical questions that point to the need for further research and analysis in their own right.

Globality and World Society: Micro-Actions and Interpersonal Relations

9

The discussion begins by indicating what might constitute the minimum requirements for a world society where a critical mass of social actors are able and willing to think, feel and act, at least some of the time, as if the world existed 'for itself' and had some right to claim a portion of their loyalty while requiring that they assume a degree of personal responsibility for its plight and the situation faced by some of its less fortunate inhabitants. Accordingly, we need to identify and outline what kinds of orientations and actions might help to underpin and foster a strengthened global consciousness, or globality. Then we explore some of the possible energizing resources which may dispose at least some individuals to act in ways that might promote these orientations. In doing so, the discussion draws on recent attempts to theorize the changing nature of contemporary socio-cultural life and its impact on social actors – changes which operate in parallel with globalization. Third, we consider what dispositions on the part of social actors might provide pathways towards a world society which moves beyond aesthetic curiosity or the extension of interactions across territorial borders. These orientations and actions may involve solitary decisions or they may require individuals to interact with others including participation in large-scale collective protests at the national or global level. The final section focuses on two case studies which allow us to explore more fully some of the discussion developed in earlier sections.

9.1 Criteria for defining world society and a global consciousness

Globalization has already provided the technical, institutional and to some extent the social framework of a world society. Thus, we can say that world society today is equivalent to the totality of all social relations that are 'not integrated into or determined by national-state politics' (Beck 2000a: 10) and that an increasing volume of these are indeed taking place outside the national level (Shaw 2000: 11–12). But in themselves these extensions across territorial borders tell us little concerning how their participants actually experience them and what significance, if any, they attach to such relations and actions. Transnational criminals moving drugs along international supply routes, paedophiles using the Internet and world networks to entrap children, crews of freighter ships ferrying components from China's workshops to factories in Bangkok or Los Angeles for assembly into finished goods or first generation migrants remitting money to their home villages are all engaged in forging and extending social relations across borders. However, it is doubtful whether these actions contribute to building the kind of world society where some people possess a growing global consciousness. Instead, it seems more likely that these mobilities constitute an accumulation of separate actions, driven by immediate and narrow motives, which require actors to cross territorial borders – dragging their local baggage with them – but little else. Instead, what are required are not just territorial but also cultural border crossings where people interact and develop mutual affections and commitments despite their primordial cultural differences. Further, such trans-social relations need to generate situations where in place of 'single-stranded' (Mitchell 1969: 48) interactions which encompass only one life sphere – for example, enjoying music when attending a gig or working in the same office or factory – an increasing number occur which engender bridge building activities and inclusiveness where 'broader identities' and forms of 'reciprocity' (Putnam 2000: 23) are created.

A second way of thinking about world society is in terms of the growing interconnectivities between nations and societies. Many scholars, quite rightly, have regarded these as the quintessential heart of globalization. However, as suggested in Chapter 2, these interconnectivities are often most compelling, in terms of their capacity to penetrate our lives, when they operate through abstract, impersonal interdependencies linked to a money economy. But most people either do not understand these or find it hard to accept how and why these shape their lives rather than local or national influences. Accordingly, interconnectivities could be said to form what is only 'the minimalist core' (Calhoun 2007: 170) of globalization; a set of objective linkages which do not necessarily feed into or influence people's subjectivity.

Then there is the argument that our exposure to global cultural flows whether through consumerism, media, cyber or tourist experiences provides another way of thinking about the preconditions for world society. However, there is little evidence to suggest that such experiences equip us with greater understanding of the plight of distant unknown others or that they motivate us to pressurize governments and other leading agents to act so as to avert world crises. What evidence exists is either insubstantial, contradictory or both (for example, Szerszynski and Urry 2002 and Woodward, Skrbis and Bean 2008). Holidays in Morocco, investigating web sites on Inca art or eating in Sri Lankan restaurants are certainly good indications of Beck's cosmopolitanization process[i]: the shallow internalization of global cultural fragments into our subjectivity. Of course, it would be foolish to deny that cultural flows, media influences, foreign holidays, cyber interactions, and so on, probably do help to propel many people in this direction and future research may tell us much more about the specific situations in which this occurs. For example, it is highly likely that they constitute the main source of the empathy and knowledge that motivate a growing number of people to make donations for disaster victims, from time to time, or to decide to recycle more of their domestic waste because of their fears concerning climate change, and so on. But, arguably, they neither lead inevitably towards, nor constitute in themselves, a global consciousness or habitus which forms a constant and driving element in an actor's subjectivity – as is borne out by some of the research on the lifestyles of global elites (see Chapter 7). But, in addition, what social actors learn through intimate and mutually dependent micro-interactions with others is sometimes equally or even much more crucial as a lever for widening their horizons and motivating them towards caring for distant others and this has largely been ignored by globalization theorists. Certainly, it has always been assumed by social scientists that what humans learn through their personal interactions with other humans, in daily, close social relationships, provides the most salient elements shaping, if not constituting, each individual's social being and persona.

Arguably, therefore, we need to imagine and create a different world society that moves beyond the mere extension of interactions across territorial borders, the forging of 'objective' interconnectivities and the continuing growth of banal cosmopolitanism: a world 'of itself' but which does not behave, as yet, as a world 'for itself' (Robertson 1992). Instead, this second version of a world society would contain a growing minority of people who are willing to care and act, sometimes, as if the lives of distant, unknown others mattered and as if the planet and its peoples possessed certain needs in their own right which deserved some of our attention and support. We develop this theme, and what kinds of orientations and actions this might entail, later in the chapter. But for the moment here are two more caveats to this argument.

For one thing, as previously argued, we need to accept that most people find it hard to satisfy their 'primal need for belonging' while at the same time pursing forms of social solidarity that are sufficiently 'global in scope' to be effective in dealing with world challenges (Hollinger 2002: 231). Putting this another way, trying to become or to act like a cosmopolitan, and to demonstrate greater openness to the world, is something which most people find problematic. Indeed, much recent thinking on cosmopolitanism has come to terms with the 'honest difficulties that even virtuous people have in achieving solidarity with persons they perceive as very different from themselves' (230).

Second, and allied to this, is the view that nationalism, or patriotism, and cosmopolitanism have never been, nor are they now, 'logical antagonists' (Cheah 1998: 36). Neither inevitably precludes or cancels out the other. If we are inclined to believe that the problems brought by globalization cannot be resolved by the nation and nationalism, since these are now outdated and even dangerous given their parochialism, then we would be misguided – particularly when nation-states are prepared to collaborate to solve global problems. This is because realistic alternatives beyond the nation-state for organizing large-scale human endeavour, guaranteeing the welfare and protection of citizens, albeit imperfectly, and for harnessing popular consciousness (Cheah 1998: 31) are as yet poorly developed or non-existent in some spheres of human activity. Alternatively, where they do operate in the form of regional federations of states– as in the case of the EU – they seem incapable, at present, of mobilizing the same intensity of support from citizens as do the individual member nation-states forming the alliance (see also Calhoun 2007). As Robbins (1998: 3) suggested, the implications of all this are that cosmopolitan behaviour usually needs to be 'located and embodied'. Even relatively privileged middle-class individuals often begin their journey towards cosmopolitanism and/or the development of something akin to a global consciousness because their own personal situation, rooted in their life course and immediate predicament, first impels them in this direction.

9.2   Towards globality – sources of individual empowerment

Many influences may empower individuals to become more open to other societies and/or to develop a heightened sense of ethical or political responsibility beyond their local situation. Here, we focus on three possible scenarios: the ability to draw on what we might call cosmopolitan capital or a cosmopolitan habitus originating in particular background experiences; the possibility that becoming a social outsider propels some individuals to compensate by forging alliances with 'strangers' while discovering, at the same time, that their displacement creates an environment in which openness to the other is more permissible and possible; and the implications of the individualization process which some sociologists claim has become one of the dominant axes around which many people increasingly construct their lives.

The role of cosmopolitan capital

Generally speaking, young middle-class professionals share common life experiences. Should circumstances bring them together – for example, as migrant students (King and Ruiz-Gelices 2003) or as co-workers in a global company team (for example, Bozkurt 2006 and Kennedy 2005) – they may, potentially, find it easier than people with lower levels of education to form relationships and to discover commonalities that cross over different ethnic/national borders and backgrounds. First, a middle-class background (Colic-Peisker 2002) provides a cultural and personality toolkit conferring confidence and adaptability. It also tends to generate an individual frame of reference where self-direction and being accountable to oneself, rather than to a collective identity determined by family, ethnic group, church or nation, are paramount. This depiction of the middle-class person strongly resonates with the emphasis Beck and Beck-Gernsheim (2002) place on the desire for individuals living under late-modern and globalizing conditions to construct their own biographies (see below). But, second, social class is also shaped by education and here, by definition, middle-class individuals tend to possess high educational credentials or their equivalent. These also generate shared orientations: the ability to think analytically and the willingness to ask questions; an awareness of the limits to one's own knowledge but an ability to seek additional skills; a preference for a self-reliant lifestyle and for work experiences providing autonomy and creativity; and a curiosity with respect to new experiences and ideas.

Third, membership of the same generation may provide further ingredients, ready to hand, for constructing a cosmopolitan lifestyle and perhaps, in certain circumstances, a shared transnational life space and especially among today's young people. Here, there is a formidable reservoir of shared resources, interests and experiences on which they can draw. Here we could include participation in cyberspace through such fora as Facebook, an interest in local or international art, literature, holidays, a range of possible consumer and leisure interests, including old and new sports – for example, white water rafting, snowboarding – global popular music and films. All these items tend to transcend local and national cultural differences and therefore they can be mobilized by individuals to help cement trans-cultural friendships. Finally, a tendency to travel, whether in pursuit of short-term educational or employment goals, as a gap year of self-discovery or over a longer time period, is becoming increasingly commonplace among a minority of young people. Favell (2006: 247), for example, refers to educated young 'free movers' in search of adventure while Recchi (2006: 76) claims that moving overseas may increasingly appeal to young middle-class Europeans because it offers a 'shortcut to capital accumulation' and the opportunity to follow a 'nomadic and globalizing lifestyle'.

Cosmopolitan capital may also stem from much earlier socialization experiences which remain embedded in the individual's persona. This resilience may predispose them towards behaviour in adult life with implications for building world society. For example, a recent study (Kennedy 2005: 178–9) of transnational professionals who worked for large building-design companies with strong global connections found that approximately one-quarter were exposed during their childhood to additional cosmopolitan experiences not available to the majority. They had either lived abroad as a child because, for example, a parent had worked for an IGO, a foreign government or company, and/or been exposed to family and parental friends with significant overseas experience where people talked about international affairs and overseas cultures. Moreover, not only had they acquired a highly credentialized education and a repertoire of technical and cultural skills, including a proficiency in two or more languages, but they also enjoyed a wealth of social capital in the form of well-connected family networks which might later open doors to national and international opportunities. These additional resources predisposed them to explore cultures different from their own with confidence. They also provided access to the kinds of detailed knowledge which could later be exploited in pursuing multinational career avenues if and when the opportunity arose. Access to cosmopolitan capital may also result from childhood socialization involving exposure to strong religious, political or other ideological values calling for social justice, equality or moral responsibility. These may fuel action in defence of these values in adult life although – as in the case of charitable acts driven by religious belief – they may be directed primarily towards the local situation or those sharing the same deeply rooted outlook.

Possessing a cosmopolitan habitus, though, is not always a guarantee of openness to the world or a sense of globality. Even fortunate individuals coming from the kinds of social backgrounds outlined above face the same constraints on their career and lifestyle opportunities as everyone else working and living in the same milieu. Thus, in Kennedy's study (2005) the choices exercised by this subgroup were strongly shaped by circumstances largely beyond their control: for example, periods of economic downturn and the need to follow the ebb and flow of building cycles as these moved unevenly across the world, both of which placed serious restraints on their actions and mobility. Also, their preferences had to comply with the demands created by each new project and the kinds of people – their nationality, preferences, age and so on – with whom they found themselves working at any one time as clients, colleagues, partners, local officials or suppliers.

However, in any case, as we saw in Chapter 8, even those who are poorly educated and who are compelled to survive in the face of ancient forms of oppression sometimes become sufficiently empowered to join with others in resisting those who are responsible for their plight. They may even, at times, be able to signal their support for transnational protests especially when they can count on the cooperation of external transnational networks whose members enjoy access to privileged resources and the global public media. Such cross-class and trans-cultural interaction is particularly likely in the case of women because of their shared and universal exposure to patriarchy. However, peasants and small farmers, indigenous peoples, second generation migrants and workers may also be drawn towards forging transnational alliances whether as individuals or as groups. The difficulty, of course, is to develop the ideological cement and practical strategies capable of drawing and then holding all these different disadvantaged groups together into viable global alliances across vast distances, while also straddling the North-South divide, and especially given their heavy dependence on the local. Compared with more privileged individuals, their ability to deploy the local as a springboard for becoming involved in the sphere of the global presents formidable obstacles. Indeed, even more challenging from the perspective of creating a world society capable of acting 'for itself', would be the attempt to forge alliances between these latter groups and the more privileged individuals discussed above: educated, middle-class, contemporary youth, transnational professionals and those sharing similar cosmopolitan social backgrounds and lifestyles.[ii]

Being or becoming a social outsider

Some people experience social displacement in that they move by choice or necessity outside their early or original national, regional, ethnic or social class position. This sense of being an outsider need not have any obvious consequences. On the other hand, it is also possible that despite the insecurities it engenders, social displacement provides a certain freedom from 'normal' social expectations and therefore an opportunity to reinvent one's persona and/or life course. But such situations may also leave people more exposed than they might otherwise have been to socio cultural influences originating outside their main frame of reference. They might even be positively attracted to these precisely because they have moved outside their social orbit and need new allegiances. These possibilities may work themselves out in a number of ways. But we now consider three examples of social displacement with a propensity to propel social actors along a personal trajectory leading to new or intensified cosmopolitan orientations: marginalized professionals, members of the gay community and certain kinds of skilled migrants.

'Marginalized professionals'.   This term was employed by Watt (2007) in reference to a particular subcategory of middle-class professionals living in London (see Chapter 7). These were people employed mainly in third or public sector occupations, for example, as teachers, social or probation workers, care workers or nurses. Clearly, these individuals occur widely across the advanced countries but also in the South whether as volunteers working for a host of NGOs and INGOs or as indigenous professionals probably employed in the public sector. In the case of Britain, and despite possessing high educational qualifications, their relatively low salaries often mean they cannot afford to buy property. Many therefore live, instead, in social housing located in poor working-class areas or in rented accommodation. The combination of high education, working in caring jobs and being placed by their low incomes outside their 'normal' social class location appears to leave many strongly disposed towards holding ethical values and/or left-of-centre political concerns. Some were also inclined to become involved in the local social life of the estates where they lived. Though Watt's study did not investigate this aspect, it is possible, too, that members of this group also tend disproportionately to donate money to charities – including some concerned with poverty and oppression in the South – to buy organic or vegetarian foods and/or to support local protests concerned with such issues as environmental pollution or the low wages imposed by global supply chains on Third World workers and whose products are ultimately sold by supermarkets.

Gay communities.   Most writers on gay cultures and experiences insist on the need for extreme caution before claiming that there is such a thing as ' "the global gay" ' (Altman 1996: 77). Moreover, local, ethnic, national and religious differences in how gayness is practiced in everyday life are evident everywhere while the ability to move across national borders is also strongly 'gendered, classed and racialized' (Binnie 2004: 84). Income inequalities, too, often create as many divisions among gays as in the heterosexual world (Binnie 2004: 62–6). Nevertheless, in most societies homosexuals were – and often still are – denigrated if not persecuted, their actions are sometimes liable to severe punishment and even in relatively tolerant societies they remain subject to social ostracism and may feel it necessary to conceal their sexuality from mainstream society. There is a sense, too, in which the threat of being an outsider means that many gay people cannot feel at home if they remain in the localities of their birth. Indeed, they may find it difficult to feel at home anywhere: unlike other 'migrants' they have no 'homeland' to which they can dream of returning. Thus, migration – whether within their country, often to the relative anonymity provided by cities, or across territorial borders – is often necessary to claim a clear and distinctive gay identity, to be yourself, and as a means of becoming 'full citizens in a queer world' (Binnie 2004: 85). Such actions may partly compensate for the reality that the gay person nevertheless remains an 'outsider' who shares with others a sense of 'disenfranchisement rather than entitlement' (Binnie 2004: 105).

Globalization has increased the opportunities for gay people to communicate within as well as across ethnic/national cultures and borders whether through information technology, co-present relations or both. Important here as loci and milieus are capitalist businesses catering for the pink pound, cheap tourist travel, international gay festivals, newspapers and other media forums dedicated to gay concerns, the claiming of particular gay sites within cities such as bars, restaurants and so on. The need to move together across borders to share information and resources has also been intensified by the international pandemic of AIDS (Nardi 1998). Gay political and cultural movements that began originally within countries such as the USA, Australia and Germany in the 1960s quite soon began to unite in international political protest culminating in the formation of the International Lesbian and Gay Association in 1978. Indeed, in recent decades and despite the continuing vitality of local gay movements there has been a clear sense of a 'globalizing…gay community and political identity struggling for equality' (Nardi 1998: 571). According to Altman (2001: 86–7), globalization 'has helped create an international gay/lesbian identity…by no means confined to the western world' while the 'gay world' is an example of 'emerging global subcultures where members of particular groups have more in common across national and continental boundaries' than with those from their own countries. However, it is by no means clear whether the experience of social displacement has led some or most gay people to express their sense of belonging to a global community in respect to additional oppressed or marginalized groups whose members are not gay. This is one of many areas where research would be invaluable.

Skilled, educated migrants. Skilled migrants provide yet another possible example of social displacement especially where they move overseas alone under their own steam, without a family and are not part of a pre-existing company team – as was the case with the professionals working for British law firms who were assigned with their families and colleagues to work in affiliated companies in New York and studied by Beaverstock et al. (1999). In contrast, the former type of migrant is likely to feel relatively isolated especially in the early stages of their stint overseas. This was the situation faced by the postgraduates from 13 EU countries interviewed for the 2005 Manchester EU migrant study who arrived in search of further education or employment. We now draw upon their accounts.

Many described their sense of having escaped from the social pressures in which they had previously been immersed when at home. They discovered a social space for reinventing their persona and perhaps their life course because they now enjoyed more freedom to make choices than had been available at home. One respondent described this as *'cutting off strings'*. Yet, as migrants they were also social outsiders in respect to Manchester's social life, at least until they joined new social networks. The following remarks illustrate this point well and echo similar points made by others. Oscar was a German national who had lived in Britain for 12 years and who had recently set up his own business following a long period working as a language teacher.

> *I don't have the same pressures other Germans have ... my experience of England has been different ... slightly on the outside. And ... none of the measurements ... totally apply to me ... you are in this strange cultural middle position of not being judged by your own country because I don't live there, so I'm in a sense a bit the odd one out over there ... well, he lives in England – and of course the same applies here ... this sort of middle ground ... And that seems to give me some kind of strange sense of freedom.*

In addition, the exposure of these EU migrants to new cultural influences, not through the media but as a result of interpersonal relationships, was probably more intense than anything they might have encountered had they remained at home encapsulated within a homogeneous, national middle-class life world. This neither would have encouraged them to become exposed to new influences nor would they have needed to do so. Thus, approximately three-fifths of the sample claimed that through meeting people of different nationalities they had become much more knowledgeable about and tolerant of other cultures. For example, a Greek man who came to Manchester to study and later started his own business suggested:

> *I mean recently I have been describing myself as a European to various people. But I don't know, I think I am just a leftwing citizen of the world really who happens to be behind the so-called gates of the European Union ... Yeah, I have changed, I have been meeting people from many different places and that has shaped my views on the world, you know I am much more aware of what the world is now.*

Finally, more than one-third of the respondents suggested that they were now more capable of forming their own picture of the world. Again, this was primarily the result of meeting and sometimes forming emotive attachments to people from different cultures. Elvira, for example, was Norwegian. Before coming to Manchester to study she had boarded for two years in a French school containing pupils of many nationalities. Talking about herself and these fellow students in France, she said:

> *they are so adaptable that I think they feel less threatened by globalization than people who are very stuck in their own country, because that's where you get prejudice…where people are scared of other cultures and haven't been out exploring them…I feel I belong to a set of international people, I've lived in many places.*

Individualization processes

Alongside the structural transformations we associate with globalization other changes are said to be occurring much closer to the personal lives of individuals. In an introductory chapter to the book written by Beck and Beck-Gernsheim (2002), Lash argued that whereas during the earlier period of modernity social actors were largely formed by their functional roles in respect to social institutions, today those remnants of tradition on which people could still depend till recently – class, unambiguous gender divisions, family, local communities, church and the nation-state – have finally retreated or partly dissolved. Consequently, the impetus for taking and choosing social action has moved 'much more intensively and closer to the individual' (xi). Similarly, according to Giddens (1991: 5), 'self actualization' and 'the tightly confined personal realm' have become the key resources for engaging in 'life planning and daily activity'.

In this analysis individualization entails several elements. On one hand, it involves the widespread and strong desire, particularly in the advanced societies, to live 'a life of one's own' (Beck and Beck-Gernsheim 2002: 22); to pursue an 'ethic of self-fulfilment'. Self-realization becomes our primary goal and perhaps duty. But, on the other hand, this freedom to be the author of our own lives – a realistic possibility for the first time in human history – is also necessary. Thus, the declining influence of traditional support systems such as kinship, coupled to the risks and insecurities brought by environmental degradation (Beck 1992), economic globalization and reduced welfare protection (Beck 2000a) all compel us to create our own personal life biography and identity whether we like it or not since we can no longer rely on other forces to do this for us. Moreover, legal, market and bureaucratic institutions are arranged so as to force people to take charge of their own lives; 'they compel the self-organization and self-thematization of people's biographies' (Beck and Beck-Gernsheim 2002: 24).

The individualization thesis can be criticized. For example, it exaggerates the erosion of social institutions (Heelas 1996: 7–11) and neglects the continuing influence of gender, ethnicity, social class, age and national differences in shaping people's life choices (Mythen 2005: 138–43, Tulloch and Lupton 2003: 123–9) – or what we have referred to in this book as the sphere of the local. Further, Beck (1994) argued that individuals increasingly need to exercise reflexivity through continuous self-confrontation; monitoring the impact of their actions on others and on the world around them. Yet it is doubtful whether everyone is equally equipped to do this. Moreover, this version of reflexivity almost certainly plays down the continuing importance of social relationships and commitments (Mason 2004: 164–6).

Nevertheless, the individualization thesis helps us see how individuals exist both as micro-causal agents, whose minute decisions feed into and augment globalization processes, and as the often-reluctant recipients of the vast forces generated by the latter – albeit without always fully understanding the nature of this dual involvement. Moreover, Beck (2000a and 2000b) and Beck and Beck-Gernsheim (2002) utilized the individualization thesis to throw light on the emergence of new forms of politics which have important implications for issue relating to globality and the rise of a world society. Democratic politics in the advanced societies was once constructed around the demand for material progress but also for social justice and questions concerning the responsibilities citizens should accept in respect to their nation, family and social class. But the goal of self-fulfilment has become more significant today. Consequently, it might seem as if our drive for self-realization will undermine older ideas of moral and political duty. Yet, this is not the case. Rather, we still exercise these virtues but in different ways that enable us to pursue a life of self-realization – exploring our identities, having adventures, acquiring new skills, enhancing our future employment opportunities – at the same time.

These arguments about individualization were taken a step further by Berking (2000). The insecurities accentuated by neo-liberal policies and economic globalization coupled to the de-traditionalization of social life have certainly left us more alone to organize our own economic future as well as our private life space. But there is much more to this than simply managing our pensions, mortgages, employment opportunities and future career prospects. We are also expected to take responsibility for our bodies, health, sexuality, personality and relationships. It is anticipated that we will be slim, fit, attractive, fashionably dressed, amusing, humanitarian and culturally interesting as well as successful and financially independent. But, again, this seems likely to create manipulative, narcissistic and self-interested individuals who demand personal liberty but are reluctant to demonstrate a compensatory degree of responsibility towards collective life. Meanwhile, the culture of self-realization further accelerates the destruction of older forms of social solidarity.

However, what may also emerge is an unexpected re-moralization and strengthening of social life built around what Berking described as 'solidary individualism'. How can this paradox be explained? First, because we increasingly live in an interconnected world where multiple, dispersed actions influence the health of the biosphere, the fluctuations of the global economy, the possibility that terrorism, international crime and disease will reach us from collapsing states and regions of poverty, and so on, we have no choice – if we truly wish to preserve our bodies, personal health, lifestyle opportunities, our futures – but to take actions which contain some possibility of removing or ameliorating these threats. Since under globalizing conditions everything impinges on our lives so everything must become the object of our concerns or we forfeit the possibility of realistically pursuing our project of self-realization. It is pointless spending money on expensive health centres or gyms, in the attempt to live a healthy, sexually active life till we are 90, if the moment we move outside the building we inhale toxic fumes from passing vehicles or risk getting skin cancer because of ozone depletion. In short, many people do not lose their political orientation because of their goals of self-realization: it simply shifts in a different direction towards issues relating to life politics (Giddens 1991). Second, we need to form cooperative alliances if we are to act effectively to improve the living space around us; drawing our friends, for example, into joining a protest against an additional airport runway or a supermarket which sells clothing produced by child labour. Moreover, without an audience we cannot meaningfully play out our chosen lifestyle especially since presentation forms such a central part of our quest for self-realization.

Berking's theory therefore reinforces the theme of this chapter. The microsphere of intimate social interactions and private life worlds, grounded in the immediacy of the local, may encourage some individuals to act in ways that contribute towards the creation of a world society and the pursuit of globality. Moreover, these spheres have a potential to become highly politicized.

9.3   Making world society – modes of operation

In recent years an impressive literature has explored the different entities which together are creating the architecture of global governance. This includes intergovernmental institutional structures (for example, Archibugi and Held 1995, Held 2004), the accumulation of world cultural scripts (Lechner and Boli 2005), the influence exercised by global imaginaries (Steger 2008) and the widespread engagement in powerful discourses – for example the human rights agenda (O'Byrne 2003, Sklair 2002). This emerging, global, cosmopolitan, socio-economic order and system of governance needs to be strengthened if it is to become more effective and fairer. Most of the responsibility for building this architecture is down to the role played by various collaborating national and international elites who have provided initiative, leadership and specialist knowledge and continue to do so. But the global policies and actions pursued by these elites would be more politically achievable if they could harness the potential energy and support bubbling up from the multiple micro-actions of everyday life and even if, at times, the global concerns of ordinary individuals diverged somewhat from the preferred agendas of such elites. For one thing, elites would have more chance of realistically implementing global policies if these were accepted by at least minority groups in different countries. An obvious example here would be dealing with carbon omissions by encouraging people to modify their lifestyles: use public transport more often, consume less meat, recycle their household waste or insulate their houses more effectively. But there is also the question of democracy and ensuring that the majority of ordinary people are able to exercise some control over how global agendas are prioritized and implemented. Without such grass-roots influence, the design and implementation of global policies may by-pass the needs of a large number of powerless people or be skewed towards the needs and concerns of a few.

Against this context, we now focus on some of the ways in which ordinary social actors can contribute to the making of a world society and the strengthening of a global consciousness. Arguably, there are three major avenues through which this is most likely and possible: certain kinds of political activity; adopting an ethical stance in respect to global issues; and becoming more willing to cross cultural borders and forge trans-social relationships. In practice these are not at all mutually exclusive. In fact, they may reinforce each other so that it is sometimes more difficult to distinguish between them. Yet, although each may engender or strengthen the others, there can be no certainty of this. For example, social actors may become increasingly absorbed in intercultural exchanges but remain politically inactive and unconcerned in respect to wider global issues. The opposite is obviously equally possible.

A further distinction can be made between situations where individuals act alone and collective actions designed to affect some kind of global change. In practice, the line between these is often blurred as individuals may engage in both types of actions simultaneously, they may move from one condition towards the other or collectivities may dissolve leaving only the actions of separate actors in place. Both political and ethical actions may involve lone individual decisions and/or joining a collectivity to express a concern more effectively. Moreover, organizations can also decide to adopt an ethical position. On the other hand, crossing cultural borders is very much an informal individual activity where the possibility for developing a collectivized momentum is much less evident. We now explore each of these orientations in greater detail bearing in mind that the focus here is primarily on interpersonal and micro-actions.

Collective political actions with global implications

In recent years, two major political transformations have been mapped and explored by scholars: the eruption of social movements onto the global scene and the rise of a global civil society. Each feeds into the other and both have frequently formed the central pivot around which global actions are being woven. Both have attracted the lion's share of scholarly attention from those interested in transnational political action. Global civil society has attracted interest because it has a potential for contributing to global governance in ways that may help to make the world a fairer, more peaceful and environmentally sustainable place (for example, Keane 2003 and Anheier, Glasius and Kaldor 2001). Many agents are helping to form a global civil society. Some of these engage in short-lived or occasional activities while others have permanent organizations such as INGOs. Then there are information networks mainly based in cyberspace, diasporic and immigrant groups and organizations, large social movements pursuing particular issues such as resisting development programmes which increase carbon omissions and a myriad of much smaller informal groupings (Anheier and Themudo 2002: 196). What all these share is a capacity for engaging in joint action and their desire to shape world political and public opinion beyond the confines of the nation-state by influencing powerful agents such as IGOs, TNCs and governments. Although the activities encompassed by global civil society have many historical precedents, what is new is their 'sheer scale and scope' while the 'range and type of fields in which they operate has never been wider' (Anheier, Glasius and Kaldor 2005: 4).

The second transformation, developing in parallel with global civil society, has been the tendency for political protest taking the form of social movement activities to increasingly shift scales from the national to regional and/or global levels (della Porta and Kriese 1999, della Porta and Tarrow 2005, Gills 2000, Hamel, Lustiger-Thaler, Nederveen Pieterse and Roseneil 2001, Keck and Sikking 1998, Munck 2007, Reitan 2007). Social movements and social movement organizations are forms of political action where participants are normally concerned with single issues or a bundle of closely related concerns, as in the case of joint opposition to the spread of neo-liberal economic policies. Participants tend to operate outside the normal institutions and organizations of democratic politics and engage, instead, in such activities as mass demonstrations, boycotts, occupying sites or plants and so on. Global social movements have formed alliances which cross both national borders and different issues. They have also drawn increasingly on a widening repertoire of protests, particularly the move towards cyber-activism. Till now, the most significant of these transnational social movements has been the GJM which crystallized out of many smaller movements during the late 1990s.

One view of the GJM is that it was nothing less than a vast countermovement of worldwide resistance to the spread of neo-liberal capitalism (for example, Kiely 2005a, Munck 2007 and Reitan 2007). Its participants variously intended either to reform neo-liberalism, persuade governments and IGOs to retreat from economic globalization altogether – to effectively de-globalize – or to replace it with socialist, anarchist or deep green alternatives. During the 1990s, a growing number of transnational protest movements merged to form larger networks as we saw in the case of Via Campesina. Other examples were the alliance formed by trade unionists, peasant organizations and others across Mexico, the USA and Canada against NAFTA in the early 1990s, the Jubilee 2000 anti-debt movement and the alliance of groups making up Our World Is Not For Sale. Eventually, at Seattle in December 1999, the widespread discontent concerning neo-liberal globalization crystallized around the protests against the WTO to form the anti-globalization movement or the GJM. This was then followed by a series of major global protests directed against the WTO, WB and IMF or the G7 group of nations. These continued till 2002.

Ironically, the spread of neo-liberal capitalism deepened and fleshed-out the available framework of worldwide resources that could be utilized effectively –to strike back against the very source of this discontent through transnational action. This, perhaps, provides 'a more positive reading of globalization' (Munck 2007: 64). These resources included the following: the diffusion of ICTs; cheaper, faster travel and therefore improved opportunities for mobility; the thickening supply chains and other conduits of market exposure which also provided a shared motive for action and the possibility of establishing linkages between previously remote peoples; and the enhanced ability to appeal to the UN, other INGOs and global public opinion while drawing on widely accepted discourses such as human rights (Tarrow 1998: 179–81).

The literature on how and why these transnational movements surged across the world between the mid-1990s and the early years of the new millennium is impressive but cannot be repeated here. Instead, I want to make two points which relate to the theme of this chapter. First, it is important to highlight the key role of co-present micro-interactions in contributing to the spread and efficacy of transnational political actions. This contrasts with the more typical emphasis most observers have placed on the undoubtedly crucial role played by information technology and the media in enabling protest to shift towards multi-scalar levels. Three arenas where personal relationships played key supporting roles in strengthening transnational collective protest were the following: the widening public support for Jubilee 2000, which is examined below; the success of the Mexican Zapatista movement and its role in providing a key arena for cementing relationships and consolidating values which fed into subsequent movements, explored in Section 9.4; and Via Campesina. To some extent the understandable interest in global civil society, the GJM and its sister movements has distracted scholarly attention from the potential role of micro-actions in rendering transnational collective protest more effective and the continuing significance of local and national arenas as spaces where global struggles are also being fought and won. Second, despite their undoubted successes in helping to radicalize global public opinion and to induce IGOs such as the WB to modify aspects of their economic programmes, among other achievements, global civil society and the GJM encountered real constraints. Also, both have been dogged by fractures along ideological, class, religious, North-South, generational and other lines. Here, we outline three of the most salient difficulties encountered by the GJM which in the end limited its effectiveness though there are several others.

An assessment of global civil society and transnational movements

Perhaps the most formidable division emerged along North-South lines. Thus, on occasions activists from the South denounced their alliance with Northern groups on the grounds that the latter were 'self-appointed representatives of their plight' in what was in reality a 'one-way relationship characterized by paternalism and inequality' (Reitan 2007: 52–4). Increasingly, Southern NGOs and networks rejected the 'altruism' offered by the North, and preferred to organize their own protests based on mutual solidarity with other Southern groups. One example of a clear rift along these lines occurred when the anti-debt coalition, Jubilee 2000, exacted promises from world leaders at the G8 meeting in Cologne in 1999 concerning partial debt relief and reform of SAPs. This was immediately denounced by many participating organizations – mostly from the South – on the grounds that they fell 'far short' (Reitan 2007: 87) of what was necessary to improve the real lives of their citizens and failed to acknowledge the responsibility of the North for the conditions prevailing in the South following years of colonial and post-colonial exploitation. Indeed, in November 1999, Jubilee South split from the main coalition and formed a separate alliance based on Third World groups which then decided to try and persuade governments in the South to repudiate their debts. Further, a central characteristic of the discourse on global civil society is its 'irredeemably Eurocentric bias' (Munck 2007: 55). This is clearly evident in the emphasis placed on the universality of such values as democracy, civility and rationality. Munck is surely right to argue that these underling concerns take little account of the very different cultures and histories of non-European peoples – or even those within Europe itself – nor do they accept that the countries of the South may need to pursue quite different 'paths to modernity' (2007: 55).

Second, the efficacy and legitimacy of global civil society and transnational movements have been called into question (for example, Anderson and Rieff 2005). For one thing, global civil society is assumed to be analogous to civil society at the national level. But this is misleading because no equivalent world democratic system exists to act as a check on global civil society's bid to shape global governance. Moreover, by claiming to speak for the world's population its participants, especially NGOs, risk alienating governments, IGOs and ordinary people while placing in jeopardy the legitimacy of their claim to provide technical expertise and to accumulate intimate knowledge of local peoples – both of which have proved indispensable. Anderson and Rieff (2005) further suggested that in the aftermath of the destruction of the WTC twin towers in New York, in September 2001, world politics changed dramatically and revealed the continuing power of the nation-state particularly American power. What remained, they enquired, of global civil society discourse 'in a world in which security is back on the table, and with it the value of sovereignty' (35)? Thus, during the 1990s, global civil society and various IGOs were conducting a 'love affair…each legitimizing the other' (35). Similarly, in 2000, the United Nations Secretary General, Kofi Annan, addressed the Millennium Forum of NGOs and declared that they 'represented the world's peoples' (36). However, after 9/11 and the Iraq War it became apparent that the dialogue that really mattered was taking place between leading governments, especially the USA, and the United Nations and that the latter's real legitimacy 'comes from the capitals of the leading nation states' (36). Nation-states remain crucial in global affairs. Consequently, the political battles fought at the domestic level in the attempt to shape government policies with respect to global problems must form a key part of any attempts to alter and improve the parameters of global life. We expand this point below.

A third argument is that in drawing numerous actors into the global arena, transnational collectivities and global civil society tend to create a situation where each participant's cause is transformed into a kind of abstraction while the actual people they represent become mere social categories (Drainville 2005: 169). In fact, each group's representatives run the danger of becoming what Drainville called, 'cosmopolitan *proxies*' (author's italics) who believe they can stand in for humanity – all women, the workers of the world and so on. A danger, here, however, is that in this 'puffed up' role these representatives will allow themselves to be persuaded that the gestures and reforms offered them by powerful world elites posses a greater potential to improve the lives of their supporters than they actually do. They will be taken in by a 'mollifying consensus' (169) which cannot genuinely challenge global inequalities and injustices or revolutionize the world's economy. In contrast, far less 'sensational' but more capable of producing significant benefits might be those numerous campaigns which are being fought everyday – against everything from sex tourism and 'union-busting' to the destruction of localities by the rapacious actions of global oil companies in countries such as Nigeria and Ecuador – by ordinary people who are 'rooted in indefinite communities of struggle' on the ground (179–80).

Individual political actions and global change

Individual political acts can obviously take many forms. Examples here might include writing to a political representative or the media, demanding that government takes political action in respect to a global issue such as Third World debt, joining a public demonstration aimed at pressurizing supermarkets to firm-up the codes of social conduct they impose on their chains of suppliers or subscribing to the national branch of Greenpeace or Amnesty International. The individual may also direct his/her opinion towards organizations such as the WTO, perhaps for its complicity in not tackling the EU and the USA in respect to the imposition of grossly unfair trade regimes on poor countries. Alternatively, it is possible for individuals to act against a corporation which is implicated in selling arms to a repressive regime or engaging in unsustainable deforestation enterprises, for example, by withdrawing personal investments from a company or boycotting their products through some form of ethical consumption. Other individual acts with global intent include the following: seeking a career with NGOs, charities and similar organizations; joining Internet chat rooms to lobby a government, IGO or TNC; buying fair trade or cruelty free products or recycling domestic waste; or simply attending music festivals, concerts or discos where young people from different ethnic backgrounds dance to alternative, 'underground' music that tries to speak to and for other cultures. Individual political actions might also involve teaming up temporarily with others or with large organizations engaged in the same action, for example, signing petitions against supermarkets or other corporate practices or joining a mass demonstration as in the anti-Iraq war campaign in 2003.

Many such activities may not be regarded as 'political' or 'global' by conventional political parties and journalists or they may be defined as 'ethical' rather than 'political' both in intent and effect. Indeed, the line between these is often difficult to draw. However, where individuals exercise them with the deliberate intention of effecting local or international change they could be said to have political and global implications. Part of the problem here is that such actions are frequently unnoticed or unrecorded as political acts because they take place within people's individual domestic and personal lives or are perceived as being ethical rather than political in intent. Box 9 provides some recent empirical data showing the growing incidence of individual ethical actions some of which clearly have political implications too.

It is important to note that many individual political actions with global implications are directed at local or national agents rather than international organizations or policies. Yet, whether intended or not they may also exercise a global impact. This may seem an obvious point but it needs repeating because the rise of transnational collective movements during the 1990s, especially the GJM, focused most attention on large-scale protests taking place on a global stage while strengthening the assumption that only such actions could be effective in the face of advancing economic globalization. But there are two sources of confusion here. First, although collective action is immensely important in tackling global agencies so, too, are multitudes of individual actions many of which are conducted outside the context of social movements. Indeed, there is an 'iceberg effect' at work here since underpinning the overt mass mobilizations we associate with events attracting worldwide publicity at the global level – such as the action at Seattle against the WTO – are millions of continuous, individual, everyday decisions and actions which, whether by accident or design, support these larger collective actions but which remain hidden or unnoticed. Second, a large proportion of political acts, whether involving discreet individuals, small groups or large collectivities, are conducted at the local or national level. But this need not mean that they are any less effective in registering disapproval of the policies pursued by powerful global agents or in empowering global public opinion than mass events and transnational collective movements. Partly this is because global communication and media systems guarantee that the majority of local or national actions are immediately relayed across the world; they cannot remain solely national events. But more crucially, it is necessary to remember that nation-states and their governments remain extremely important players and their actions, whether at the national or international levels, continue to shape world as well as local affairs.

Any one who doubts this should recall the often astonished reaction of many media and public spokespersons – individuals who had perhaps absorbed too much globalization theory announcing the relative decline of nation-states – during the autumn and winter of 2008–9 when government after government overturned years of unrelenting commitment to pro-market and anti-state-regulation ideology in response to the near collapse of the world's financial system. Almost overnight, in the attempt to regain control over markets and banks, governments rediscovered that only they possessed the authority, the policy instruments and the will to at least attempt to prevent a world recession escalating into a depression by reversing policies that only months before, and for decades, they had rejected and even vilified. These acts included bailing out corporations, mounting almost unprecedented programmes of government spending, drawing up re-regulatory schemes and partially nationalizing huge private banks. In addition, we saw governments rapidly trying to collaborate on an equally unprecedented scale by synchronizing their spending, tax and monetary responses to crisis. In addition, the governments of the most wealthy and/or the most successful developing countries convened the G20 London conference in April 2009 to discuss, and hopefully agree, coordinated policies in respect to such issues as dealing with tax havens and corporate tax evasion, how to rein in the excesses of financial businesses, channelling large amounts of additional funding to the poorer countries via the IMF – a belated recognition that world poverty and inequality undermine capitalist growth and stability – and so on. What was also notable about this occasion was not just the presence of many countries from the Global South but their undoubted capacity to make their voices and intentions count.[iii]

This last point is particularly important. To deal effectively with many global problems, and not just the insecurities, volatility and inequalities associated with economic globalization, governments will almost certainly need to leverage the scale and intensity of their attempts at interstate collaboration to much higher levels than has previously been apparent, though this is obviously fraught with difficulties. This, in turn, points to the potential significance, for global problem-solving, of campaigns and political actions which take place at the national level and which are directed at pressurizing governments to accept the need to seek more inter-government cooperation.

A neglected argument offered by Beck is useful, here. He suggested that democratic nations need to develop cosmopolitan political parties (1998 and 2000c) whose participants would reinvent party politics by 'representing transnational interests transnationally, but also work within the arenas of national politics' thereby becoming 'national global movements' (2000c: 29). It seems likely that such democratically accountable parties with a wide global policy remit might prove especially attractive to some young voters who at present seem relatively disenchanted with conventional political party systems across the advanced countries. As Beck suggested:

> Young people are moved by that which national politics largely rules out: how can global environmental destruction be resolved? How can one live and love with the threat of AIDS? What does tolerance and social justice mean in the global age? These questions slip through the political agendas of national states. The consequence is that freedom's children practice a highly political disavowal of politics. (1998: 29)

Perhaps, though, cosmopolitan political parties with global agendas might also capture the imagination of older voters. Thus, in political systems constructed around some version of proportional representation such a party would only need to obtain a small proportion of overall votes to negotiate a voice in a government of coalition parties thereby bringing global issues very much to the centre of government agendas at the national level.

Ethical actions

Here Tomlinson's term, 'ethical glocalism' (1999: 194) is useful. While it refers to the willingness to assume some responsibility for people and problems beyond one's own society there is also the suggestion that this does not preclude us from remaining concerned about our own local sphere, too. As suggested earlier, it is often difficult to distinguish political from ethical acts or intentions. It is also important to note that ethical acts are often conducted on an individual basis much of the time. Thus, people make choices – for example, whether to donate to certain charities, buy green products or desist from buying clothes sold by companies whose suppliers are known to engage in dubious labour practices – and then act within the confines of their private, domestic or family situation.[iv]

Ethicality may also be closely linked to consumerism. Thus, some sociologists have argued that consumerism has become the core area of concern and the most meaningful area in the lives of many citizens, especially those living in the advanced societies.

Box 9 Ethical consumer and investment behaviour and trends

Ethical consumption and investment involve avoiding companies which do the following:

Environmental – invest in nuclear power, dubious animal testing and welfare practices or activities that worsen global warming or cause pollution and toxic poisoning (oil, timber etc);

Social – invest in countries with a poor human rights record or where worker's rights are not recognized or which sell arms and military hardware to oppressive regimes;

Political – invest in genetic engineering or offer bribes to corrupt governments.

Ethical investment

Ethical investment took off in the 1980s, partly linked to the anti-apartheid campaign against South Africa. Churches and charities were in the forefront and remain important though pension funds, insurance companies and others are also big investors, now. Investments with an element of ethicality have grown rapidly. In 2007, UK ethical funds reached £8.9 billion. Equivalent figures for Europe, 2006, were $1 trillion and for the USA, $2 trillion. There are also ethical funds in Asia. In the UK, only approximately 4 per cent of this investment is conducted by individuals buying shares; far more is purchased as components of unit trusts (EIRIS 2009).

Ethical consumerism

According to the 2007 report prepared by *The Ethical Consumer* for the Cooperative Bank, total UK household spending in 2006 equalled £600 billion and approximately 5.3per cent of this involved ethical goods and services – or £32.3 billion. This was £664 for every UK household compared with £366 in 2002 and includes all goods and services such as clothing, appliances, investment, savings, transport, energy use and food and drink.

The report identifies different types of ethical consumer in the UK.

1. **'Committed'** ethical consumers now amount to 2.8 million people – or 6 per cent of adults. They shop on a weekly basis, spending approximately £1600 per year. Most are middle class and aged between 30 and 44.
2. **'Regular'** – they buy some ethical goods every month, spend an average of £360 per year and equal 11per cent of the adult population.
3. **'Passive'** consumers – or 31per cent of the adult population – are infrequent ethical consumers and spend an estimated £170 per year.

Food and drink

In the UK, of total household spending in 2006 on food and drink (£71billion) approximately 7 per cent involved purchases of ethical goods (£4.8 billion). Some of the detail is interesting:

■ Approximately 2.4 per cent of this spending involved organic produce.
■ The consumption of Fairtrade products is rising rapidly as more consumers recognize these goods. It was worth approximately £285 million in 2006.
■ The incidence of consumer boycotts – mainly by switching brands to avoid a company of whom people disapprove – is also rising fast and involved goods worth £1214 million in 2006 or 2 per cent of total spending (does not include Fairtrade and organic produce).

Other notable features

- People over 60 are the least likely to engage in ethical consumption.
- In 2007, 83 per cent of consumers claimed they tried to shop locally sometimes.
- The young aged between 18–29 are the group most likely to actively seek information on companies so they can make informed decisions on which brands to buy.
- They are also the most likely group to engage in active campaigning on these issues for example by phoning, writing or otherwise lobbying their local political representatives.
- In 2007, this willingness to campaign involved one-quarter of the population at some time during the year.

Bennett (2004) argued that one consequence is that citizen-consumers expect their democratic politics to be a version of the personalized, market-driven communication they anticipate in their shopping and lifestyle adventures. Politicians must find new ways of motivating citizens which imitate the personal attention and the cultivation of personal appeal provided by commerce; a kind of 'supermarket state'. While this obviously creates difficulties for politicians and may trivialize political discourse, there is a flip side in that consumerism offers opportunities for displaying ethical awareness, knowledge and power. In many respects, issues over the management of consumerism, and related themes such as the environment, animal rights, the conditions under which food is produced and distributed, and so on, have become central themes in the relationship between governments and citizens, largely replacing earlier struggles between workers and their employers. Helped by information technology and the reality that so much consumer behaviour now depends on economic globalization, consumer politics is also global politics. As such it offers a huge potential for activism which is both ethical and political and irrespective of whether it is undertaken by individuals, social movements, organizations or all of these. But consumer politics also turns the weapons of capitalism against itself especially the exercise of buying power, ICTs and investor nervousness in the event of falling corporate asset values related to media exposure or a consumer boycott (Bennett 2004). Nor can consumer or investor choices be easily controlled by governments or corporations: these kinds of ethical actions get under the radar net of mainstream powerful organizations.

Finally, certain institutions such as trade unions and churches are likely to uphold values which anticipate that their members will engage in acts intended to express personal sacrifices for unknown others. One example where entire institutions made ethical decisions occurred during the anti-apartheid campaigns of the 1980s and early 1990s. Then, some large organizations, such as colleges and municipal authorities, used their huge spending power and procurement policies to boycott businesses which invested in or traded with South Africa. Another more recent and important case is shown by the Jubilee 2000 anti-debt campaign to which we now turn and where the Christian churches played a crucial role.

Reitan (2007: 66–79) showed how many influences helped the anti-debt campaign to ultimately attain worldwide significance in the later 1990s. These included the contribution of celebrities such as Bono, Geldorf and Pope John Paul II, the volume of information relayed through the Internet and the ability to capture wide media interest. Moreover, many highly influential humanitarian, environmental and alternative development NGOs participated alongside the Christian churches of North America and Europe as well as Jewish and Muslim communities (77). Nevertheless, the role played by church organizations and their leaders and complex hierarchies was crucial in massively spreading the campaign and in helping to coordinate national actions so that transnational action became increasingly possible and effective. How was this possible? For one thing, the churches were able to activate the ready-made social networks already available within each congregation though it seems likely that this partly depended on the personal enthusiasm and commitment exercised by particular pastors and leading figures within each parish, diocese and so on. Second, church organization provided a forum for 'popular education' because it was accustomed to transmitting information and moral arguments – presented in terms of Christian values – through pamphlets, books, sermons, missionary messages and so on (71). Third, the churches belonged to vast international organizations and hierarchies spread not only across the North but which also reached out to the parishes of Africa, South America and elsewhere and which enjoyed close links with NGOs, IGOs, governments and other powerful agencies. These networks obviously provided vehicles for disseminating ideas and moral messages, transmitting and pooling information and for arranging coordinated national and transnational actions. For example, church missionaries and aid workers based in the South relayed information and images concerning the impact of debt on those they were trying to help back to church congregations in the North. Last, but not least, the churches not only evoked the familiar message of charity and 'sympathy for the poor', as intrinsic duties attendant upon all Christians, but they also reframed the argument about Third World debt in terms of 'economic justice', claiming that it was morally necessary and right to correct the hitherto exploitative relationship that had prevailed for centuries between North and South. According to Reitan (2007: 78–9), this way of presenting the case reached people who would not normally have supported political action because it succeeded in ratcheting up their 'normal' concerns about poverty and the desire to be seen as responsible Christians to a higher level. Again, we see here the tendency for ethical and political motivation and action to merge and engender the other.

Openness to other cultures and trans-sociality

Some individuals may become much more open towards, and interested in, the lives of people from other cultures. This may lead to genuine intercultural dialogue which involves not simply crossing territorial but also cultural borders where the partners involved engage in mutual exploration of each other's meanings based on the articulation of different 'cultural models' (Delanty 2006: 37) and respect for difference. This process is also likely to involve 'critical mutual evaluation' (Turner 2006: 142). Such interactions are very different from aesthetic curiosity because unlike the latter they depend on the creation of enduring sociality between the partners to flourish. Where genuine intercultural relations are formed, a number of changes become possible. For example, those involved may interrogate their own primordial identity and affiliations (Delanty 2006) and may ultimately become partially socialized into the life worlds of people hailing from ethnic or national cultures very different from their own. As we will see, this may occur in the case of certain kinds of skilled migrants. Alternatively, it may occur where individuals become romantically involved with someone from another country. It seems likely, therefore, that one of the building blocks for constructing a world society consists of the emergence of just such overlapping and thickening clusters of trans-cultural interactions.

Trans-cultural interactions also have the potential to awaken or intensify a global conscience. Indeed, this happened in the case of a minority of the skilled migrants interviewed for the Manchester 2005 study and their experiences are discussed next. But there is no certainty this will occur. Similarly, it is perfectly possible to remain always at home, largely encapsulated within a homogeneous social milieu, never exposed to trans-cultural relationships involving foreigners, and yet assume a degree of ethical or political responsibility extending far beyond the confines of one's local life.

9.4   Case studies

Trans-sociality and taking moral responsibility for the 'other(s)': Europeans in Manchester

Employing empirical data provided by the 2005 Manchester study of skilled migrants this case study demonstrates how even highly educated individuals often find it hard to identify meaningfully with distant 'others' and to assume some responsibility for them unless they first forge close affective ties with individuals drawn from this social group. As we saw in Section 9.2 approximately three-fifths of those interviewed referred at some point to the central role that meeting particular people and forming new relationships had played in helping them to become more knowledgeable about, and tolerant, of other cultures though this was usually implicit in the narratives of the remainder as well. However, during their interviews, a subgroup – 15 individuals – volunteered information which suggested that through their personal involvement with individuals from other cultures they had also became empathetic towards that person's society and the conditions experienced by its members and even though they had no initial or any actual contact with these more distant others. As such, these accounts are revealing because they bear directly on the issue of how globality may arise or be intensified through interpersonal relations rather than media or commercial cultural influences.

The degree of empathy and its possible outcomes varied a good deal among these respondents. In some instances it simply involved a realization that it was mainly or only through such personal bonding that they could develop this wider understanding. For example, Annette was French and had previously been an Erasmus student in Dublin. Now, after living in Ireland and Manchester, she observed:

> I'm much more interested in different countries but I realized that if I'm interested in Italy a lot it's because I've met some Italian people. Like, I've not met some people from Hungary and I'm not very interested in Hungary. So when I meet someone from a country – a person I really like – I will be interested in their country...Because I need something real to give me a connection, otherwise it's something very far from me that I don't understand...I'm more interested in the world...France was the world for me but now it's getting bigger and bigger.

Beatriz was Spanish and worked in a health-food emporium. When asked if living abroad had changed her she said:

> I think because I have met people from different kinds of environment. I have a friend from Malawi and I think how difficult it must be for her and how it is over there in her country. Because, one thing is what you read in newspapers and the other thing is what you really know through people and their experiences, you get the truth. You can put yourself in the skin of other people.

Several respondents became empathetic towards distant others through their contact with an intermediary – usually a close friend – who then relayed the feelings of intimate knowledge and sympathy they themselves had gained. Francesca's account also shows how her later concrete experience of meeting those she was drawn into helping, further deepened her sense of ethical responsibility. Other respondents reported similar experiences.

Francesca had lived in Britain for more than twenty years working as a language teacher. Although she had provided financial support to poor families in India for some years her sense of globality had intensified to the point where she began spending several weeks at her own expense, during her summer vacations, working in Lima, Peru, teaching poor children through the auspices of an INGO. When asked what had prompted this venture she replied:

> Because one of my friends, she went there before, and then I was talking a lot to her and I said 'wow, that's really interesting'. Because I've done TEFALv and I think God reminded me of my TEFAL and they desperately need English to better themselves...it was very scary...but I was so pleased I have done it. I've learned a lot, I've changed as a person...I think I have to go back. They are waiting for me.

When asked whether she would have gone to Peru without her friend's influence she said probably not. On her Peruvian experience she suggested it was: *'indescribable. Yes ... I thought I knew but you don't know, I did not know, no one knows. You have to go and see ... it is amazing what I saw. So Peru is my heart'.*

Francesca's account raises the question of what concrete steps, if any, are considered or actually undertaken with the intention of improving the lives of distant others. For example, this might require spending time in one or more of the countries involved – as Francesca did – to provide practical help. But other actions might involve giving financial assistance, placing political pressure on relevant bodies capable of effecting concrete improvements or simply trying to offer personal support over time. Alternatively, the individual may undertake a current, or prepare a future concrete action which expresses a sense of ethical glocalism.

Hans's case illustrates how some of this can work out in practice. He was an Austrian university lecturer whose classes included non-Europeans to whom he lectured in international business and economics. In Vienna, he had held strong neo-liberal, free-market views about Third World development. However, after teaching *'very clever'* Chinese and other Asian/Third World postgraduate students while in Manchester, he observed:

> *I am more liberal than before and more critical of this American slash Blair work view. It seems to be very dangerous ... if you are teaching in another country, the fact that you are teaching with a different audience with a different background it makes you more reflective of what you are doing ... and it becomes like a silent dialogue ... there is a process going on that is a reconfiguration of your original ideas.*

He claimed that he had now changed some of his teaching materials in response to the insights and accounts he had absorbed from his Third World students.

Massimiliano was an Italian anthropologist in his early thirties. He came to Manchester in 1998 to begin his doctorate studies but this had involved spending some time in Namibia.

> *I feel loyalty to the places I've been and I've worked in ... Yes, I have strong links with the place I did my research, the people I worked with (in Namibia) ... I went back already two times after I finished my research and I'm going back again ... I feel very strongly attached to it, emotionally. Because of the human side of it – I left behind a lot of good friends and feel for the things they had to go through.*

Finally, the response to a heightened sense of globality may induce the individuals to seek a better understanding of the explanations for the predicament faced by those whose relationship has induced this empathy. This might involve immediate investigations designed to enhance the ability to provide assistance or embarking on a long-term educational programme that might enable the learner to provide practical help at a later date. Frederik's case illustrates both outcomes while Elvira's is more clearly oriented towards the latter situation.

The response of Frederik a German doctoral student was as follows:

A very important experience of my life was when I worked in the Netherlands social services. I was involved in asylum, refugee work…I read a lot about the personal histories of these persons…and the development of their countries…It can work in different ways, I mean, either you know something about a specific country from books or from videos or television…and then you meet people from this country and that's a good opportunity to um, both get to know more about their country from a personal point of view or maybe change perceptions you have. But also…this happened to me when I met people from different countries…I didn't know anything about them and then through this personal contact you get more interested in that specific country or culture and then you start, er, reading about it.

Finally, Elvira, whose experiences were discussed earlier, explained why she had eventually chosen to follow a development studies course at a Manchester university:

But the reasons I do development studies are that there's got to be some sort of socially conscious way of globalizing so that you don't divide the world into rich and poor…it's possible to go about it in a less exploitative way…Because I'm interested so much in learning about regions I don't know anything about…I became so interested in regions because I went abroad and met so many different people.

It is important to make a final point concerning expressions of globality that result from the dynamics of interpersonal relationships. In themselves, as single isolated cases, they make only a modest contribution to the development of a global consciousness and a world 'for itself'. Yet, they possess a potential to disseminate much more widely through the continuous processes of socialization that are intrinsic to all human sociality and in which these individuals themselves, of course, are also engaged and implicated. These interactions then ripple outwards further through multiplier effects.

The Zapatistas, transnational action and interpersonal relations

More has been written about the exploits of the Zapatistas of Chiapas in southern Mexico than any other indigenous people or any single Southern transnational movement (Burbach 2001, Castells 1997, Cid Aguayo 2008, Munck 2007, Oeleson 2005, Paulson 2000 and Reitan 2007, to name but a few). The movement's name derives from Zapata, one of two leaders who led an armed peasant uprising and marched into Mexico City in 1914. On 1 January 1994 – the day that NAFTA formally began – the Zapatista National Liberation Army (EZLN) took control of the region's army barracks, radio station, some large landholdings and five cities near the Lacandonian Forest, including San Cristóbal. These actions captured the national imagination because they evoked a powerful 'historical folk memory' of the Mexican Revolution eight decades earlier (Munck 2007: 66). Led by Subcommandante Marcos, EZLN's actions also gained support from other Mayan Indian communities.

The Chiapas and others in nearby indigenous communities had several grievances. For example, one related to the government's decision to remove the protection established during the Mexican Revolution for communal, peasant landownership. Another was linked to the increased opening of the Lancandonian Forest to logging companies and the government's eventual decision to declare it a protected bio-reserve which further reduced the possibility that local people could obtain an income from forest lands (Cid Aguayo 2008: 549). However, these and other policies were exacerbated by the neo-liberal policies adopted by the Mexican government from the mid-1980s, including the decision that Mexico should join NAFTA. The Chiapas and other local Indian peoples also wanted the right to exercise a degree of autonomy within Mexico and this, too, was further threatened by neo-liberalism. This idea of autonomy included the preservation of cultural uniqueness and communal self-government and the rights of indigenous women (Paulson 2001: 280–2). Underlying these demands was a desire to retain the choice to reject the capitalist market and its values and therefore the importance of retaining territorial independence so that alternative sources of livelihood remained possible (Paulson 2001).

The Zapatista rebellion rapidly attained wide support across the world during 1994, giving rise to 'international Zapatismo' (Munck 2007: 65, Reitan 2007: 195). But this tends to obscure the extent to which the EZLN's roots were firmly grounded within Mexican history, the politics of the 1970s and 1980s and the impact of neo-liberal globalization. Thus, the original rebellion began in the 1980s with a small group of Marxists and this eventually became focused around the EZLN in 1983. But as discontent grew among nearby indigenous peoples, the Zapatistas gained wider support. The EZLN also became more involved in local Indian concerns and consulted local communities (Munck 2007: 63). Further, as with other such movements in South America, the Zapatistas were helped by the actions of various individuals and groups in the years preceding the 1994 rebellion and afterwards: for example, sections of the Catholic Church in Mexico, whose members drew on Liberation Theology, urban Marxists, intellectuals and academics, students, trade unions and local NGOs.

Several factors account for the speed and intensity with which worldwide support gathered for the EZLN following the 1994 insurgency. Certainly, the actions of EZLN leaders were key in that they quickly acknowledged the importance of international networks in helping their cause and presented their own domestic situation as part of the wider global struggle against the social injustices of globalization (Paulson 2000: 285–6, Reitan 2007: 193–5). Also, sympathetic Mexican individuals and organizations formed supporting organizations and used mainstream newspapers and the Internet to express solidarity. They also presented the events in Chiapas as a struggle against economic globalization. But these same groups had also established previous networks with like-minded collectivities in other countries. Similarly, Mexican NGOs were able to diffuse information and appeal for wider support through their links to international organizations such as Amnesty International and Human Rights Watch. These, in turn, utilized their yet wider links to peace groups, anti-debt networks, universities and so on (Reitan 2007: 193). Third, many observers (for example, Castells 1997) have emphasized the significance of the advances in ICTs which were reaching new levels of sophistication in the mid-1990s. This is because they facilitated rapid, extensive and cheap information-pooling among all those involved including the EZLN, Mexican organizations, INGOs and other worldwide networks contesting globalization.

However, the interpersonal relationships between EZLN members and the many foreign sympathizers and political activists who visited Chiapas during this time were also fundamental. On returning home these visitors generated further support. Indeed, these interactions were actively fostered by the EZLN when in 1996 it organized a seminar in Chiapas and called on activists worldwide to join them. This was intended to prepare the way for the establishment of an Intercontinental Encounter for Humanity and Against Neoliberalism later that year (Reitan 2007: 200). According to Reitan approximately three thousand people attended from 43 countries. Most were young Europeans but trade unionists and members of the MST from Brazil and other South American activists also came as did environmentalists, communists, left wing artists and intellectuals. A later seminar in support of the Zapatistas was held in Spain. Reitan argued that the personal ties established at these Zapatista-inspired seminars, along with the wider networks they helped to make possible, prepared the way for the establishment of the People's Global Action (PGA) network in 1997 and 1998. This involved a massive joining of movements focused around opposition to neo-liberal globalization (202–4). But the ties forged within the PGA during this period among activist groups, such as the indigenous people's, peasant's and fisherfolk movements, support groups for the EZLN, women organizing against sweatshops, peace, ecological groups and so on, in turn, helped prepare the way for the crystallization of transnational action focused around the GJM at the WTO conference in December 1999.

9.5 Appraisal

The huge impact of the transnational collective movements which gathered pace during the 1990s and beyond has received much less attention than it deserved in this chapter. This was deliberate as I wanted to focus on the relatively neglected but potentially important cumulative impact of the dispositions, micro-interactions and personal behaviour displayed by a growing number of individuals in helping to construct a world society which has some meaning – at least for them. But individual acts which are intended to register protest and demand change and those pursued in a more directed way by people coming together to form social movements are part and parcel of the same phenomenon: each feeds into the other and they form a seamless web of potentially effective global influences. Not only did the GJM and its sister movements create a critique which enhanced global public understanding of the inequalities and economic failures caused by the imposition of a one-size-fits-all neo-liberal straightjacket on so many countries – while helping to eventually tone down some of the hubris demonstrated by WB and IMF officials – but they also undoubtedly exercised an informing not to say galvanizing effect on numerous individuals who never participated in mass demonstrations or other collective events during those years and perhaps never will in future. At the same time, the increasing yet unnoticed everyday actions of millions of people, acting as consumers, investors, cyber-activists, church members, boycotters, workers, charity donors, music and entertainment-makers and so on, constantly challenge governments, TNCs and IGOs and underpin the actions of social movements. Individual actions and social interactions are also helping to build a world society whenever those involved cross cultural and not just territorial borders and forge trans-cultural mutual understandings. Moreover, local actions directed primarily at national agents, especially governments, may be potentially just as significant in shaping global events, policies and agents as those which ostensibly occur within transnational political spaces and which are intended to influence global agents. Similarly, local action which is focused on persuading national governments to collaborate much more extensively and deeply than in the past with other governments, in the management of global problems, is likely to make an equally essential contribution to the making of a world society capable of acting and thinking, at times, 'for itself'.

Looking Forward

10

A central theme explored throughout this book has been the continuing power and appeal of the local in the lives of most people in the face of globalizing processes. Moreover, the local, in turn, is constantly enacted, sustained and regenerated in large part by episodes of co-presence taking place in innumerable micro-relationships. In the case of those dispositions and relationships which sustain the present situation, namely a world which operates primarily 'of itself', it is the meanings, social affiliations and loyalties rooted in family, village, ethnicity, locality, region or nation that provide a large portion of the resources making possible a wide range of large and small acts of transnational interaction extending beyond territorial borders and into global space. These same, largely, primordial ties also generate much of the motivation driving such transnational actions in the first place: for example, maintaining family survival in distant homelands and furnishing much of the support poor migrants need overseas or providing the mutual trust required to sustain certain kinds of legal or illicit business transactions.

However, when it comes to forging relationships, performing collaborative actions or taking responsibility for distant unknown others which engender genuine elements of trans-sociality, here, too, it is micro-relationships forged out of local situations and their resources – grounded partly in the affectivities made possible at some point by co-presence – that frequently underpins much, though not all, of what is possible in the making of a world society capable of acting 'for itself'. Thus, in certain situations, friendships, romantic partnerships, shared professional skills and experiences, the pursuit of educational goals or youthful travels may all generate concrete, immediate arenas that bring individuals who were previously strangers into conjunction and press them into crossing cultural borders and navigating new forms of understanding because only by doing so can they overcome their personal loneliness, manage urgent and immediate projects or cope with the social indifference emanating from local insiders. Alternatively, many other experiences, singly or in combination, may tip social actors into developing a global consciousness of one kind or another: the drive to self-realization and therefore the need to counter those surrounding and distant dangers pushing into one's immediate domestic situation which clearly threaten to negate it; becoming a parent and worrying about a child's safety or future prospects; the particular experiences stemming from childhood and household relationships that suggest cultural openness is enjoyable and manageable or which endow individuals with an ideological propensity to resist what they perceive as the injustices heaped on distant others later in life; reaching a point in the life course where social displacement becomes an overriding force driving the individual to look outwards in the search for new allies; or becoming aware that unknown others face the same forms of oppression which they too, cannot resist alone. All these depend on the resources and motivations that grow out of situations rooted at least partly, and often mainly, in local alliances, needs, orientations, opportunities or dangers.

Yet, at the present time we are also living through what may turn out to be the worst world economic crisis since the 1930s. This engulfed the world from 2007 onwards and with growing intensity. The question, therefore, arises as to whether and in what ways it may unravel much or even most of the multiple interconnectivities that have knitted the fates of human beings together through globalization during recent decades, albeit, without apparently penetrating the subjective life worlds of most people very far. Clearly, this is a large issue beyond the remit of this book and which is widely engaging the full attention of many global theorists and others.

What can be said, however, is that it quickly became apparent that some governments and politicians representing regional and other interests were trying to protect national employment through various forms of covert economic protectionism (for example, allowing currency values to fall) while workers in France, Britain and elsewhere have engaged in confrontations designed to preserve national jobs. In addition to the alarming speed with which the recession took hold, first in finance and then spreading rapidly into the 'real' economy, it also soon became clear that economic retrenchment in a few countries was erupting in many others, too. For example, in the early months of the crisis some observers stated that the strength of the South East Asian economies, and particularly China, would enable them to remain largely unaffected by what was happening in the already advanced economies. Moreover, Asian economic autonomy and dynamic growth, it was thought, might blunt the edge of economic crisis in North America, Japan and Europe. However, fairly quickly the degree to which globalization has done its work, in tying North and South, East and West firmly together in powerful coils of economic interdependency, became apparent when the unemployment rate in China spiralled upward – as the markets for its exports collapsed across America and elsewhere, along with the available credit to buy them – and its rate of growth fell well below recent achievements. Similar reverberations could be listed for countries such as Russia, plagued by falling oil prices, many Third World countries facing a near collapse in the value of their exports, and so on.

Moreover, it is perfectly possible, as many spokespersons have suggested or urged, that whether through purposive policy design, populist demand or sheer economic contraction, a prolonged recession will both undermine the credibility of the market fundamentalism that has dominated thinking for so long and encourage, and in fact drive, governments to enact substantial measures designed to permanently reduce their previous dependence on an open global economy and foreign capital. Along with this they may attempt to resuscitate economic sectors and industries which were long ago hollowed out by the mobility of capital and the relocation of work to the South. In other words, de-globalization – driven by popular national demand, economic necessity or a revival of quasi-socialist/nationalist ideology singly or in combination – may become the new reality.

However, we can also construct another story entirely and we end on this note even though at this moment the only point on which it is possible to be certain is that there are probably few grounds for holding any kind of certainty: only time and the particularity of unfolding events will reveal outcomes. In constructing a counter argument to the scenario outlined above, the following points deserve some consideration. First, alongside and often accompanying certain moves by governments towards protectionism there have also been encouraging and indeed unprecedented signs of international collaboration. These include the following: joint actions to stimulate economic activity; shared policies designed to re-regulate large swathes of the global financial system and bring tax havens under international control; an apparent recognition that inequality is partly responsible for the crisis and therefore the need to boost the poorest economies so that their economic growth will create demand in the wider world economy; and coordinated declarations of intent stating that the market fundamentalism that was allowed to rampage through the world economy in recent decades is no longer viable and needs to be reined in. Second, it is possible that the sheer magnitude of the recession, the risks it has generated for virtually everyone and above all its manifestly global character – in an age of Internet activity, global media reach, tourism, and much else besides – will have launched a further tranche of world citizens, who were previously indifferent to or immune from global influences, along a path towards the acquisition of a global consciousness. Perhaps, here, their local life worlds and their desire to protect these will provide some of the resources, motivations and loyalties, embedded in personal relationships, that will help to maintain this trajectory.

Last, even if substantial amounts of economic de-globalization occur, accompanied, perhaps, by a marked ideological shift towards the desire for socialist or nationalist autarky or a deep green, much more self-sufficient though poorer economy by millions of people, it is arguable that powerful interconnectivities will remain as threats to the present and future lives of humans everywhere. Possible examples of these are legion: global warming and climate change; world population growth; deepening inequalities, entrenched unemployment or increasing numbers of meaningless jobs that do not allow people to construct a life and which instead engender widespread alienation among ever larger minorities, both within the advanced and more successful developing countries and the poorer ones; and the continuing stark inequality between the poorest countries of the South and the rest of the world and the likely effects of this in terms of transnational crime, spreading wars and health risks, the fostering of terrorist breading grounds, unmanageable levels of migration and so on. In these areas, globalization is not about to go away whatever may occur in the economic realm. It follows that the struggle to engender and deepen the vitality of a world capable of acting 'for itself', supported by a critical, growing mass of individuals who participate in and share a global consciousness, remains an urgent, unfinished project.

Notes

1. Introduction: Global *and* Local

i. See Scholte's thorough analysis of this burgeoning international, transnational and global network of agencies (2005).
ii. In the summer of 2008, the price of oil reached $150 a barrel though it later fell dramatically – and probably temporarily – as the world recession accelerated. China's growth has been especially important in pushing up cereal prices. In 1980, with a population of approximately 1 billion, average annual meat consumption was 20 kilos but by 2007 this had risen to 54 kilos – by which time population had risen by 300 million (Watts 2008). It will be the poorest people living in the least developed countries, where governments are often ineffective, who will be least able to afford basic foodstuffs. This will further diminish their life prospects and perhaps aggravate responses which contribute to world disorder – mass migration, spreading health epidemics, crime, etc. Even rich countries like Britain face a precarious future food situation because UK consumers require six times more land and sea for food production than they actually possess (Lawrence 2008).

2. Theorizing Globalization: Linking the World

i. James may well be right about this but his claim can at least be contested and certainly deserves to be subjected to some examination in the light of empirical work. We take up this point in Section 2.6 and in Chapter 6.
ii. We return to these themes in Chapters 8 and 9.
iii. The huge and likely role of language barriers in constraining global social life, and the need to overcome them, has been strangely ignored by most globalization scholars.

3. The Global Economy: Fragmented Workers – Mobile Capital

i. On the other hand, approximately one-third of the world's working-age population (De Rivero 2001: 6) seem barely to possess a foothold in the world economy at all. Yet, there is nowhere else they can go. Thus, given their struggles to forage some kind of meagre and often semi-legal livelihood at the margins of the global economy – increasingly in Third World cities – there is a sense in which even those 'excluded' from the global economy are very much 'included'. We discuss this theme in more detail in Chapters 7 and 8.

ii. The current global recession has, of course, prompted some observers to argue that governments are now being forced to retreat from this era where markets were virtually given a free rein and regarded as almost the sine qua non of human destiny. However, it remains to be seen whether and how far governments will indeed alter these orientations and practices.

4. Migrants: key Agents of Globalization

i. Of course, the opposite situation may also transpire where different migrant groups find ways to cross cultural boundaries and collaborate against, or symbolically resist, what they perceive as host society injustices (Sassen 2007). We explore this possibility in Chapter 8.

5. Transnational Criminals and Terrorists: New Insecurities

i. Chapter 9 includes a case study of the Zapatista movement in Mexico which can be seen, in part, as a response to these SAP policies and their effects on land distribution and ownership.
ii. One consequence of the financial collapse which gathered pace across the world during 2008 was that at the G20 London meeting in April 2009, the governments present resolved to work together to bring offshore tax havens under stricter control as one of several collaborative policies designed to avoid the excesses that had led to this crisis in the first place. Whether their intentions will become reality remains to be seen.

Introduction to Part Two

i. In stark contrast, the same book also includes a chapter on working-class people living in a South West London housing estate whose sense of being at home in their locale and experience of living all aspects of their life as a coherent whole, despite massive changes, remained relatively intact (O'Byrne 1997, 73–89).

6. The Resilient Local: Critiquing the Idea of the Hegemonic Global

i. As the authors make clear, there is a striking parallel here with the way in which women have invariably been constructed in patriarchal thought as the feeble 'other' in and by a male-dominated world.
ii. Of course, it is extremely difficult to avoid referring to the 'local' and the 'global' or to engage in any discussion of globalizing processes without invoking these terms. The answer lies in deploying them purely in a heuristic sense as tools designed to

aid the exploration of certain empirical materials while avoiding turning them into abstractions or reifications where terms become concepts and the latter are then used as if they were objective realities.

iii. The discussion will draw upon the evidence from this study at several points during this and later chapters. It is referred to as the '2005 Manchester EU migrant research'.

iv. Box 6 examines the evidence suggesting that theorists have also tended to exaggerate the similarities between global cities, ignoring or underplaying the continuing influence of national history and culture on their contemporary character.

v. On the other hand, respondents in Mexico and Krugyzstan reported rather higher world identities: 14.8 per cent and 11.1 per cent respectively in 2001.

vi. This notion is very close to the idea of 'banal' or everyday cosmopolitanism elaborated by Szerszynski and Urry (2002) in their study of North West Britain and discussed in Chapter 7.

7. The Continuing Appeal of Local, Bubble Lives: Case Studies

i. Chan (1997) described hypermobile, 'astronaut' families who settled a husband/wife and children in the host country while one partner managed the home business and shuttled back and forth. This also fulfilled minimum residency requirements for immigration in the host country and ensured excellent education for children. But straddling nations and creating a 'multiplicity of selves and identities in motion' led to uncertainty (207) with families breaking up and a loss of control over teenage children (Ley 2004: 158).

ii. Such emotional attachments to particular areas and cultures and positioned sharply against rival regions, the capital city or even the nation as a whole, are of course far from being unique to Britain. Belgium's deep regional, cultural and linguistic division between the Flemish and French-speaking Walloon communities – and represented strongly within the capital city, Brussels, through a system of multiple governance in addition to demarcated areas of residence – provides an additional European example.

iii. There are of course other strands in the British middle class including those Watt (2006) referred to as the 'marginalized middle class', mostly public sector workers on low incomes, who tend to be much more open to the 'other' (see the next section and Chapter 9).

iv. This research was conducted and the report was prepared by the Development Planning Unit at University College London. But the project was financed and commissioned by the UN Human Settlements Programme (UN-HABITAT) in 2002 to be submitted in 2003.

Introduction to Part Three

i. Indeed, in America the combination of growing inequality and exposure to widespread stagnant or falling real wage levels across the economy were inextricably bound up with the financial crisis which has swept the world since 2008 in that, for many, incurring large personal debts was their only avenue into the consumer society and given that over-lending and over-borrowing were central factors in the crisis. Similarly, many families were too poor or financially insecure to afford a mortgage without being offered special loan conditions via the sub-prime market which, it eventually transpired, neither the lenders nor the economic system could sustain.

ii. See the beginning of Chapter 1.

8.   Globality and World Society: Micro-Actions and Interpersonal Relations

 i. This is discussed in Chapters 1 and 6.
 ii. Investigating whether, to what extent and how all this may occur will, hopefully, be tasks that other researchers will take up in the near future.
 iii. Among other things, many commentators saw this as a powerful indication of the long term, relative economic decline of America but also of the Northern economies in contrast to the rise to global prominence of many Southern nations.
 iv. Of course, self-preservation is also a significant motive behind some or all ethical decisions. The discussion of individualization theory points strongly in this direction. For example, a switch to organic or vegetarian food may reflect personal lifestyle concerns – becoming healthier, improving the taste of food, prolonging longevity – as much or more than a wish to express concern for animal welfare or to reduce one's carbon footprint. Similarly, actions to combat global warming, such as using public transport, contain an unavoidable element of self-preservation including the desire to create a safer world for one's children. Yet, few actions are purely altruistic as is recognized by most religious thinking. Nor – apart from a few saints and holy people – can they be if everyday social life is to continue.
 v. TEFLE qualifications equip people to teach English abroad.

Bibliography

M. Albrow (1996), *The Global Age*, Cambridge: Polity.

M. Albrow (1997), 'Traveling beyond local cultures: socioscapes in a global city', in J. Eade (ed.), *Living the Global City: Globalization as a Local Process*, London: Routledge, 37–55.

D. Altman (1996), 'The internationalization of gay identities; rupture or continuity?', *Social Text*, 14, 3, 77–94.

D. Altman (2001), *Global Sex*, Chicago: University of Chicago Press.

A. Amin (2002a), 'Spatialities of globalization', *Environment and Planning A*, 34, 3, 385–399.

A. Amin (2002b), 'Ethnicity and the multicultural city: living with diversity', *Environment and Planning A*, 34, 3, 958–980.

J. G. Andersen (2007), 'Nationalism, new right and new cleavages in Danish politics: foreign and security policy of the Danish People's Party', in C. S. Liang (ed.), *Europe for the Europeans: The Foreign and Security Policy of the Populist Radical Right*, Aldershot: Ashgate, 103–124.

B. Anderson (1983), *Imagined Communities: Reflections on the Origins and Spread of Nationalism*, London: Verso.

K. Anderson and D. Rieff (2005), ' "Global civil society": A skeptical view', in M. Kaldor, H. Anheier and M. Glasius (eds), *Global Civil Society 2004/5*, London: Sage, 26–39.

M. Andersson (2005), 'Individualized and collectivized bases for migrant youth identity work', in M. Andersson, Y. G. Lithman and O. Sernhede (eds), *Youth, Otherness and the Plural City: Modes of Belonging and Social Life*, Göteborg: Bokförlaget Daidalas A. B, 27–51.

P. Andreas (1999), 'When policies collide: market reform, market prohibition, and the narcotization of the Mexican economy', in H. R. Friman and P. Andreas (eds), *The Illicit Global Economy and State Power*, Oxford: Rowman and Littlefield, 125–142.

P. Andreas (2002), 'Transnational organized crime and economic globalization', in M. Berdal and M. Serrano (eds), *Transnational Organized Crime and International Security*, London: Lynne Rienner, 37–52.

N. Anheier and N. Themudo (2002), 'Organisational forms of global civil society: implications of going global', in M. Glasius, M. Kaldor and H. Anheier (eds), *Global Civil Society Yearbook 2002*, Oxford: Oxford University Press, 192–216.

H. Anheier, M. Glasius and M. Kaldor (eds) (2001), *Global Civil Society Yearbook 2001*, Oxford: Oxford University Press.

H. Anheier, M. Glasius and M. Kaldor (2005), 'Introducing global civil society', in H. Anheier, M. Glasius and M. Kaldor (eds), *Global Civil Society Yearbook 2004/05*, London: Sage, 3–22.

A. Appadurai (1990), 'Disjuncture and difference in the global cultural economy', in M. Featherstone (ed.), *Global Culture: Nationalism, Globalization and Modernity*, London: Sage, 295–310.

A. Appadurai (1991), 'Global ethnoscapes: notes and queries for a transnational anthropology', in R. G. Fox (ed.), *Recapturing Anthropology: Working in the Present*, Sante Fe: School of American research Press, 191–200.

K. A. Appiah (1998), 'Cosmopolitan patriots', in P. Cheah and B. Robbins (eds), *Cosmopolitics: Thinking and Feeling beyond the Nation*, Minneapolis: University of Minnesota Press, 91–114.

K. Archer, M. Martin Bosman, M. Mark Amen and E. Schmidt (2007), 'Hegemony/Counter-hegemony: imagining a new, post-nation-state cartography of culture in an age of globalization', *Globalizations*, 4, 1, 115 –135.

D. Archibugi and D. Held (eds) (1995), *Cosmopolitan Democracy: An Agenda for a New World Order*, Cambridge: Polity.

G. Armstrong and M. Young (2000), 'Fanatical football chants: creating and controlling carnival', in G. P. Finn and R. Giulianotti (eds), *Football Culture: Local Contests, Global Visions*, London: Frank Cass, 173–211.

R. D. Atkinson (2005), 'Inequality in the new knowledge economy', in A. Giddens and P. Diamond (eds), *The New Equalitarianism*, Cambridge: Polity, 52–68.

M. Auge (1995), *Non-places: Introduction to an Anthropology of Super-modernity*, London: Verso.

A. Aviveros (2008), 'Female migration increases and spurs development: World Bank Research', http://web.worldbankd.org/WBSITE/EXTERNAL/NEWS/0,contentsMDK:21561028, accessed February 2008.

L. Baker (1999), 'A different tomato: crating vernacular foodscapes', in D. Barndt (ed.), *Women Working the NAFTA Food Chain*, Toronto: Second Story Press, 249–260.

J. Bale (1994), *Landscapes of Modern Sport*, Leicester: Leicester University Press.

B. Barber (1996), *Jihad vs McWorld*, New York: Random House.

D. Barndt (1999), *Women Working the NAFTA Food Chain: Women, Food and Globalization*, Toronto: Second Story Press.

J. Barrett (1996), 'World music, nation and postcolonialism', *Cultural Studies*, 10, 2, 237–247.

C. Bartolovich (2002), 'Introduction: Marxism, modernity, and postcolonial studies', in C. Bartolovich and N. Lazarus (eds), *Marxism, Modernity and Postcolonial Studies*, Cambridge: Cambridge University Press, 1–17.

L. Basch, N. G. Schiller and C. S. Blanc (1994), *Nations Unbound: Transnational Projects, Postcolonial Predicaments and Deterritorialized Nation States*, New York: Gordon and Breach.

Z. Bauman (1998), *Globalization: The Human Consequences*, Cambridge: Polity.

M. E. Beare (2003), 'Organized corporate criminality: corporate complicity in tobacco smuggling', in M. E. Beare (ed.), *Critical Reflections on Transnational Organized Crime, Money Laundering, and Corruption*, Toronto: University of Toronto Press, 183–206.

J. V. Beaverstock, R. G. Smith and P. J. Taylor (1999), 'The long arm of the law: London's law firms in a globalizing world-economy', *Environment and Planning A*, 31, 10, 1857–1876.

J. V. Beaverstock, R. G. Smith and P. J. Taylor (2000), 'Geographies of globalization: United States law firms in world cities', *Urban Geography*, 21, 2, 95–120.

J. V. Beaverstock, M. A. Doel, P. J. Hubbard and P. J. Taylor (2002), 'Attending to the world: competition, cooperation and connectivity in the World City network', *Global Networks: A Journal of Transnational Affairs*, 2, 2, 111–132.

U. Beck (1992), *The Risk Society: Towards a New Modernity*, London: Sage.

U. Beck (1994), 'The reinvention of politics: towards a theory of reflexive modernization', in U. Beck, A. Giddens and S. Lash (eds), *Reflexive Modernization: Politics, Tradition and Aesthetics in the Modern Social Order*, Cambridge: Polity, 110–175 and 198–215.

U. Beck (1998), 'The cosmopolitan manifesto', *New Statesman*, March 20, 28–30.

U. Beck (2000a), *What Is Globalization?*, Cambridge: Polity.

U. Beck (2000b), *The Brave New World of Work*, Cambridge: Polity.

U. Beck (2000c), 'The cosmopolitan perspective: sociology of the second age of modernity', *British Journal of Sociology*, 51, 1, 79–105.

U. Beck (2004), 'Cosmopolitical realism: on the distinction between cosmopolitanism in philosophy and the social sciences', *Global Networks: A Journal of Transnational Affairs*, 4, 2, 131–156.

U. Beck (2006), *The Cosmopolitan Vision*, Cambridge: Polity.

U. Beck and E. Beck-Gernsheim (2002), *Individualization*, London: Sage.

W. Bello (2001), *The Future in the Balance: Essays on Globalization and Resistance*, Oakland, CA: Food First Books.

W. Bello (2002), *Deglobalization: Ideas of a New World Economy*, London: Zed.

L. Benedictus and M. Godwin (2005, 'Every race, colour, nation and religion on earth', the *Guardian*, 21 January.

A. Bennett (2000), *Popular Music and Youth Culture: Music, Identity and Place*, London: Macmillan.

W. L. Bennett (2004), 'Branded political communication: lifestyle politics, logo campaigns, and the rise of global citizenship', in A. Føllesdal, M. Micheletti and D. Stolle (eds), *Politics, Products and Markets: Exploring Political Consumerism Past and Present*, New Brunswick, NJ: Transaction Books, 101–125.

M. Berdal and M. Serrano (2002), 'Transnational organized crime and international security: the new topography', in M. Berdal and M. Serrano (eds), *Transnational Organized Crime and International Security*, Boulder, CO: Lynne Rienner, 197–207.

M. Berdal and M. Serrano (2002), 'Introduction', in M. Berdal and M. Serrano (eds), *Transnational Organized Crime and International Security*, Boulder, CO: Lynne Rienner, 1–9.

P. L. Berger, B. Berger and H. Kellner (1973), *The Homeless Mind: Modernization and Consciousness*, Harmondsworth: Penguin.

A. J. Bergesen and O. Lizardo (2004), 'International terrorism and the world-system', *Sociological Theory*, 22, 1, 38–52.

H. Berking (2000), 'Solidary individualism', in S. Lash, B. Szersynski and B. Wynne (eds), *Risk, Environment and Modernity: Towards a New Ecology*, 185–201.

M. Bienefeld (2007), 'Suppressing the double movement to secure the dictatorship of finance', in A. Buğra and K. Ağartan (eds), *Reading Karl Polanyi for the Twenty-First Century: Market Economy as a Political Project*, Basingstoke: Palgrave, 13–32.

J. Binnie (2004), *The Globalization of Sex*, London: Sage.

J. Binnie, J. Holloway, S. Millington and C. Young (eds) (2006), *Cosmopolitan Urbanism*, London: Routledge.

D. Black (2004), 'The geometry of terrorism', *Sociological Theory*, 22, 1, 14–25.

H-P. Blossfeld, E. Klijzing, M. Mills and K. Kurz (2005), *Globalization, Uncertainty and Youth in Society*, London: Routledge.

J. Blythman (2007), *Shopped: The Shocking Power of Britain's Supermarkets*, London: Harper Perennial.

D. Boden and L. Molotch (1994), 'The compulsions of proximity', in R. Friedland and D. Boden (eds), *Space, Time and Modernity*, Berkeley: University of California Press, 257–280.

P. Bourdieu (1990), *The Logic of Practice*, Stanford, CA: Stanford University Press.

P. Bourdieu (1993), *Sociology in Question*, London: Sage.

P. Bourdieu (2000), *Pascalian Meditations*, Cambridge: Polity.

P. Bourdieu and L. J. D. Wacquant (1992), *An Invitation to Reflexive Sociology*, Cambridge: Polity.

O. Bozkurt (2006), 'Highly skilled employment and global mobility in mobile telecommunications multinationals', in M. P. Smith and A. Favell (eds), *The Human Face of Global Mobility*, New Brunswick, NJ: Transaction Publishers, 247–274.

N. Brenner (1999), 'Beyond state-centrism? Space, territoriality, and geographical scale in globalization studies', *Theory and Society*, 28, 1, 39–78.

R. Brenner (2002), *The Boom and the Bubble: The US in the Global Economy*, London: Verso.

C. Brick (2001), 'Can't live with them. Can't live without them: Reflections on Manchester United', in G. Armstrong and R. Giulianotti (eds), *Fear and Loathing in World Football*, Oxford: Berg, 9–22.

British Broadcasting Corporation (2005), 'Born abroad: an immigrant map of Britain'. www.bbc.co.uk/bornabroad, accessed February 2008.

R. Burbach (2001), *Globalization and Postmodern Politics: From Zapatistas to High-Tech Robber Barons*, London: Pluto Press.

R. Burbach, O. Núñez and B. Kagarlitsky (1997), *Globalization and Its Discontents: The Rise of Postmodern Socialisms*, London: Pluto Press.

T. Butler (2003), 'Living in the bubble: gentrification and its "others" in North London', *Urban Studies*, 40, 12, 2469–2486.

C. Calhoun (2002), 'The class consciousness of frequent travellers: towards a critique of actually existing cosmopolitanism', in S. Vertovec and R. Cohen (eds), *Conceiving Cosmopolitanism: Theory, Context, and Practice*, Oxford: Oxford University Press, 86–109.

C. Calhoun (2007), *Nations Matter: Culture, History, and the Cosmopolitan Dream*, London: Routledge.

D. Campbell and O. Bowcott (2008), 'Drug cartels running rampant, says UN', the *Guardian*, 5 March, 19.

S. Campbell (2004), 'Lost in transit', *New Internationalist*, 369, 20–22.

W. K. Carroll and C. Carson (2003), 'The network of global corporations and elite policy groups: a structure for transnational capitalist class formation?', *Global Networks: A Journal of Transnational Affairs*, 3, 4, 29–59.

D. L. Carter (1997), 'International organized crime: emerging trends in entrepreneurial crime', in P. J. Ryan and G. E. Rush (eds), *Understanding Organized Crime in Global Perspective*, London: Sage, 131–148.

M. Caselli (2006), 'On the nature of globalization and its measurement. Some notes on the *A. T. Kearney/Foreign Policy Magazine Globalization Index* and the *CSGR Globalisation Index*', UNU-CRIS Occasional Papers, 0–2006/3, 1–25.

E. Casey (1993),*Getting Back into Place: Towards a Renewed Understanding of the Place-World,* Bloomington, IN: Indiana University Press.

M. Castells (1996), *The Rise of the Network Society,* Oxford: Blackwell.

M. Castells (1997), *The Power of Identity,* Oxford: Blackwell.

M. Castells (1998), *End of Millennium,* Oxford: Blackwell.

N. Castree, N. M. Coe, K. Ward and M. Samers (2004), *Spaces of Work: Global Capitalism and Geographies of Labour,* London: Sage.

M. de Certeau (1984), *The Practice of Everyday Life,* translated by S. Rendall, Berkeley: University of California Press.

M. de Certeau, L. Giard and P. Mayol (1994), *Practice of Everyday Life, Volume 2: Living and Cooking,* translated by T. J. Tomasik, Minneapolis: University of Minnesota Press.

M. de Certeau, L. Giard and P. Mayol (1998), *The Practice of Everyday Life,* Volume II, Minneapolis: University of Minnesota Press.

B. K. Chan (1997), 'A family affair: migration, dispersal and the emergent identity of the Chinese cosmopolitan', *Diaspora,* 6, 2, 195–213.

G. Chang (2000), *Disposable Domestics: Immigrant Women Workers in the Global Economy,* Cambridge, MA: South End Press.

H-J. Chang (2008), *Bad Samaritans: The Guilty Secrets of Rich Nations and the Threat to Global Prosperity,* Croydon: Random House Business Books.

P. Cheah (1998), 'The cosmopolitical today', in P. Cheah and B. Robbins (eds), *Cosmopolitics: Thinking and Feeling beyond the Nation,* Minneapolis: University of Minnesota Press, 20–43.

P. Cheah and B. Robbins (eds) (1998), *Cosmopolitics: Thinking and Feeling beyond the Nation,* Minneapolis: University of Minnesota Press.

B. E. Cid Aguayo (2008), 'Global villages and rural cosmopolitanism: exploring global ruralities', *Globalizations,* 5, 4, 541–554.

A. P. Cohen (1985), *The Symbolic Construction of Community,* Chichester and London: Ellis Horwood and Tavistock Publications.

R. Cohen (1987), *The New Helots: Migrants in the International Division of Labour,* Aldershot: Gower.

R. Cohen (2008), *Global Diasporas: An Introduction,* 2nd edition, Oxford: Routledge.

R. Cohen and P. Kennedy (2007), *Global Sociology,* 2nd edition, Basingstoke: Palgrave.

V. Colic-Peisker (2002), 'Migrant communities and class: Croatians in Western Australia', in P. Kennedy and V. Roudometof (eds), *Communities Across Borders: New Immigrants and Transnational Cultures,* London: Routledge, 29–40.

O. Contreras and M. Kenney (2002), 'Global industries and local agents: becoming a world-class manager in the Mexico-USA border region', in P. Kennedy and V. Roudometof (eds), *Communities Across Borders: New Migrants and Transnational Cultures,* London: Routledge, 129–142.

M. Davis (2006), *Planet of Slums,* London: Verso.

O. De Rivero (2001), *The Myth of Development,* London: Zed.

D. della Porta and H. Kriese (1999), 'Social movements in a globalizing world: an introduction', in D. della Porta, H. Kriesi and D. Rucht (eds), *Social Movements in a Globalizing World,* Basingstoke: Macmillan, 3–22.

D. della Porta and S. Tarrow (2005), 'Transnational processes and social activism: an introduction', in D. della Porta and S. Tarrow (eds), *Transnational Protest and Global Activism,* Lanham, MD: Rowman and Littlefield, 1–17.

G. Delanty (2006), 'The cosmopolitan imagination: critical cosmopolitanism and social theory', *British Journal of Sociology*, 57, 1, 25–48.

G. Deleuze and F. Guattari (1988), *A Thousand Plateaus: Capitalism and Schizophrenia*, translated by B. Massuma, London: Athlone Press.

A. Desmarais (2002), 'The Via Campesina: consolidating an international peasant and farm movement', *Journal of Peasant Studies*, 29, 2, 91–124.

F. J. Desroches (2003), 'Drug trafficking and organized crime in Canada: a study of high-level drug networks', in M. E. Beare (ed.), *Critical Reflections on Transnational Organized Crime, Money Laundering, and Corruption*, Toronto: University of Toronto Press, 237–255.

Development Planning Unit, University College London (2003), *Understanding Slums: Case Studies for the Global Report on Human Settlements*, United Nations Human Settlement programme (UN-HABITAT).

P. Dicken (2007), *Global Shift: Mapping the Changing Contours of the World Economy*, 5th edition, London: Sage.

A. Dirlik (2001), 'Place-based imagination: globalism and the politics of place', in R. Prazniak and A. Dirlik (eds), *Places and Politics in an Age of Globalization*, Oxford: Rowman and Littlefield Publishers, 15–52.

J. Dombrink and J. Huey-Long Song (1997), 'Hong Kong after 1997: transnational organized crime in a shrinking world', in P. J. Ryan and G. E. Rush (eds), *Understanding Organized Crime in Global Perspective*, London: Sage, 214–219.

J. Doward (2003), 'Rappers put the bling into business', the *Observer*, 11 November, 8.

A. C. Drainville (2005), 'Québec City 2001 and the making of transnational subjects', in L. Amoore (ed.), *The Global Resistance Reader*, London: Routledge, 169–189.

J. Eade and D. Garbin (2006), 'Competing visions of identity and space: Bangladeshi Muslims in Britain', *Contemporary South Asia*, 15, 2, 181–193.

J. Eade (ed.) (1997), *Living the Global City: Globalization as a Local Process*, London: Routledge.

M. Edelman (2003), 'Transnational peasant and farmer movements and networks', in H. Anheier, M. Glasius and M. Kaldor (eds), *Global Civil Society 2003*, Oxford: Oxford University Press, 185–218.

S. Edgell (2001), *Veblen in Perspective: His Life and Thought*, London: M. E. Sharpe, 117–136.

B. Ehrenreich and A. Russell Hochschild (2003), 'Introduction', in B. Ehrenreich and A. Russell Hochschild (eds), *Global Woman: Nannies, Maids and Sex Workers in the New Economy*, London: Granta Books, 1–13.

L. Elliot and D. Atkinson (2008), *The Gods That Failed: How Blind Faith in Markets Has Cost Us Our Future*, London: The Bodley Head.

A. Escobar (2001), 'Culture sits in places. Reflections on globalism and subaltern strategies of globalization', *Political Geography*, 20, 139–174.

Ethical Investment Research Service (EIRIS) (2009), *Key Ethical/Socially Responsible Investments (SRI) Statistics*, www.eiris.org/pages/top%20menu, accessed March 2009.

T. Faist (2000), *The Volume and Dynamics of International Migration and Transnational Society*, Oxford: Clarendon Press.

A. Favell (2001), 'Migration, mobility and globaloney: metaphors and rhetoric in the sociology of globalization', *Global Networks: A Journal of Transnational Studies*, 1, 4, 389–398.

A. Favell (2003), 'Games without frontiers? Questioning the transnational social power of migrants in Europe', *European Journal of Sociology*, XLIV, 3, 397–427.

A. Favell (2006), 'London as a Eurocity: free movers in the economic capital of Europe', in M. P. Smith and A. Favell (eds), *The Human Face of Global Mobility*, New Brunswick, NJ: Transaction Publishers: 247–274.

A. Favell, M. Feldblum and M. P. Smith (2006), 'The human face of global mobility: a research agenda', in M. P. Smith and A. Favell (eds), *The Human Face of Global Mobility*, New Brunswick, NJ: Transaction Publishers, 1–25.

M. Featherstone (1990), 'Global culture: an introduction', in M. Featherstone (ed.), *Global Culture: Nationalism, Globalization and Modernity*, London: Sage, 1–14.

M. Featherstone and S. Lash (1999), 'Introduction', in M. Featherstone and S. Lash (eds), *Spaces of Culture: City-Nation-World*, London: Sage, 1–13.

D. Field (1999), 'Putting food first: women's role in creating a grassroots system outside the market place', in D. Barndt (ed.), *Women Working the NAFTA Food Chain*, Toronto: Second Story Press, 193–208.

M. Findlay (1999), *The Globalization of Crime*, Cambridge: Cambridge University Press.

S. Flusty (2004), *De-Coca-Colonization: Making the Globe from the Inside Out*, London: Routledge.

M. Foucault (1976), *The History of Sexuality*, Volume 1, Harmondsworth: Penguin.

B. F. Frederiksen (2002), 'Mobile minds and socio-economic barriers: livelihoods and African-American identities among youth in Nairobi', in N. N. Sørenson and K. Fog Olwig (eds), *Work and Migration: Life and Livelihoods in a Globalizing World*, London: Routledge, 23–44.

R. B. Freeman (2007), 'The challenge of the growing globalization of labor markets to economic and social policy', in E. Paus (ed.), *Global Capitalism Unbound: Winners and Losers in Offshore Outsourcing*, Basingstoke: Palgrave, 23–40.

J. Friedman (1986), 'The world city hypothesis', *Development and Change*, 17, 69–83.

J. Friedman (1994), *Cultural Identity and Global Process*, London: Sage.

J. Friedman (1997), 'Global crises, the struggle for cultural identity and intellectual porkbarrelling: cosmopolitans versus locals, ethnics and nationals in an era of de-hegemonisation', in P. Werbner and T. Modood (eds), *Debating Cultural Hybridity*, London: Zed, 70–89.

T. L. Friedman (2005), *The World Is Flat: The Globalized World in the Twenty-First Century*, London: Penguin.

H. Friese and P. Wagner (1999), 'Not all that is solid melts into air: modernity and contingency', in M. Featherstone and S. Lash (eds), *Spaces of Culture: City-Nation-World*, London: Sage, 101–115.

H. R. Friman and P. Andreas (1999), 'Introduction: international relations and the illicit global economy', in H. R. Friman and P. Andreas (eds), *The Illicit Global Economy and State Power*, Oxford: Rowman and Littlefield Publishers, 1–24.

S. Frith (1983), *Sound Effects: Youth, Leisure and the Politics of Rock*, London: Constable.

J. K. Gibson-Graham (1996), *The End of Capitalism (as We Knew It)*, Oxford: Blackwell Publishers.

J. K. Gibson-Graham (2002), 'Beyond global vs. local: economic policies outside the binary frame', in A. Herod and M. W. Wright (eds), *Geographies of Power: Placing Scale*, Oxford: Blackwell Publishing, 25–60.

J. K. Gibson-Graham (2005), 'Building community economies: women and the politics of place', in W. Harcourt and A. Escobar (eds), *Women and the Politics of Place*, Bloomfield, CT: Kumarian Press, 130–157.

A. Giddens (1990), *The Consequences of Modernity*, Cambridge: Polity.

A. Giddens (1991), *Modernity and Self-Identity: Self and Society in the Late Modern Age*, Cambridge: Polity.

A. Giddens (2002), *Runaway World: How Globalization Is Reshaping Our Lives*, London: Profile Books.

B. K. Gills (2000), 'Introduction: globalization and the politics of resistance', in B. K. Gills (ed.), *Globalization and the Politics of Resistance*, Basingstoke: Macmillan, 3–11.

R. Giulianotti (2002), 'Supporters, followers, fans and *flaneurs*: a taxonomy of spectator identities in football', *Journal of Sport and Social Issues*, 26, 1, 25–46.

D. Gow (2006), 'Fears for UK car plants as factories shift east', the *Guardian, Business*, 2 March, 26.

P. Gowan (1999), *Global Gamble: Washington's Faustian Bid for World Dominance*, London: Verso.

P. Gowan (2009), 'Crisis in the heartlands: Consequences of the New Wall Street System', *New Left Review, 55*, January to February, 5–28.

M. Granovetter (1983), 'The strength of weak ties: a network theory revisited', *Sociological Theory*, 1, 201–233.

K. Grayson (2003), 'Discourse, identity, and the US "War on drugs"', in M. E. Beare (ed.), *Critical Reflections on Transnational Organized Crime, Money Laundering, and Corruption*, Toronto: University of Toronto Press, 145–170.

R. Griffin (2007), 'Non Angeli, sed Angli: The Neo-populist foreign policy of the "New" BNP', in C. S. Liang (ed.), *Europe for the Europeans: The Foreign and Security Policy of the Populist Radical Right*, Aldershot: Ashgate, 239–260.

R. Grimm (2008), *Belsunce, a Place in the French-Algerian Transnational Social Space*, unpublished PhD, Manchester Metropolitan University.

L. Grueso and L. A. Arroyo (2005), 'Women and the defense of place in Columbian Black Movement struggles', in W. Harcourt and A. Escobar (eds), *Women and the Politics of Place,* Bloomfield, CT: Kumarian Press, 100–114.

A. Hale (2004), 'Globalised production and networks of resistance: Women Working Worldwide and new alliances for the dignity of labour', *Journal of Interdisciplinary Gender Studies*, 8, 1 and 2, 153–170.

S. Hall (1992), 'The question of cultural identity', in S. Hall, D. Held and T. McGrew (eds), *Modernity and Its Futures*, Cambridge: Polity and Blackwell, 273–323.

T. H. Hall and J. V. Fenelon (2008), 'Indigenous movements and globalization: What is different? What is the same?', *Globalizations*, 5, 1, 1–12.

P. Hamel, H. Lustiger-Thaler, J. Nederveen Pieterse and S. Roseneil (2001), 'Introduction: the shifting frames of collective action', in P. Hamel, H. Lustiger-Thaler, J. Nederveen Pieterse and S. Roseneil (eds), *Globalization and Social Movements*, Basingstoke: Macmillan, 1–18.

C. Hamnett (2003), 'Gentrification and the middle-class remaking of inner London 1961–2001', *Urban Studies*, 40, 12, 2401–2426.

U. Hannerz (1990), 'Cosmopolitans and locals in world culture', in M. Featherstone (ed.), *Global Culture: Nationalism, Globalization and Modernity*, London: Sage, 237–252.

U. Hannerz (2003), *Transnational Connections: Culture, People, Places*, London: Routledge.

W. Harcourt (2005), 'The body politic in global development discourse: a woman and the politics of place perspective', in W. Harcourt and A. Escobar (eds), *Women and the Politics of Place*, Bloomfield, CT: Kumarian Press, 32–47.

W. Harcourt and A. Escobar (2005), 'Introduction: practices of differences', in W. Harcourt and A. Escobar (eds), *Women and the Politics of Place*, Bloomfield, CT: Kumarian Press, 1–17.

N. Harris (1983), *Of Bread and Guns*, Harmonsworth: Penguin.

N. Harris (2002), *Thinking the Unthinkable: The Immigration Myth Exposed*, London: I. B. Tauris.

D. Harvey (1989), *The Condition of Postmodernity*, Oxford: Blackwell.

D. Harvey (2003), *The New Imperialism*, Oxford: Oxford University Press.

R. Hay (2001), ' "Those bloody Croatians": Croatian soccer teams, ethnicity and violence in Australia, 1950–99', in G. Armstrong and R. Giulianotti (eds), *Fear and Loathing in World Football*, Oxford: Berg, 77–90.

P. Hazard and D. Gould (2001), 'Three confrontations and a coda: Juventus of Turin and Italy', in G. Armstrong and R. Giulianotti (eds), *Fear and Loathing in World Football*, Oxford: Berg, 199–219.

U. Hedetoft (2003), *The Global Turn: National Encounters with the World*, Aalborg: Aalborg University Press.

P. Heelas (1996), 'Introduction: de-traditionalization and its rivals', in P. Heelas, S. Lash and P. Morris (eds), *De-traditionalization*, Oxford: Blackwell, 1–20.

D. Held (2004), *Global Covenant*, Cambridge: Polity.

D. Held, A. McGrew, D. Goldblatt and J. Perraton (1999), *Global Transformations*, Cambridge: Polity.

E. Helleiner (1999), 'State power and the regulation of illicit activity in global finance', in H. R. Friman and P. Andreas (eds), *The Illicit Global Economy and State Power*, Oxford: Rowman and Littlefield, 53–90.

M. K. Hendrickson and W. D. Heffernan (2002), 'Opening spaces through relocalization: locating potential resistance in the weaknesses of the global food system', *Sociologia Ruralis*, 42, 4, 347–369.

J. Hill (1994), 'Cricket and the imperial connection; overseas players in Lancashire in the inter-war years', in J. Bale and J. Maguire (eds), *The Global Sports Arena: Athletic Talent Migration in an Interdependent World*, London: Frank Cass, 49–62.

E. Hobsbawm (1994), *Age of Extremes: The Short Twentieth Century, 1914–1991*, London: Michael Joseph.

A. R. Hochschild (2000), 'Global care chains and emotional surplus value', in W. Hutton and A. Giddens (eds), *On the Edge: Living with Global Capitalism*, London: Jonathon Cape, 130–146.

D. A. Hollinger (2002), 'Not universalists, nor pluralists: the new cosmopolitans find their way', in S. Vertovec and R. Cohen (eds), *Conceiving Cosmopolitanism: Theory, Context, and Practice*, Oxford: Oxford University Press, 227–239.

HomeNet (2009), http://www.homenetsouthasia.org, accessed February 2009.

A. M. Hoogvelt (1997), *Globalization and the Post-colonial World: The New Political Economy of Development*, Basingstoke: Macmillan.

J. Hughson (2000), 'A tale of two tribes: expressive Fandom in Australian soccer's A-League', in G. P. Finn and R. Giulianotti (eds), *Football Cultures: Local Contests, Global Visions*, London: Frank Cass, 10–30.

S. Huntington (1996), *The Clash of Globalizations and the Remaking of World Order*, New York: Simon and Schuster.

J. Hurley and D. Miller (2005), 'The changing face of the global garment industry', in A. Hales and J. Wills (eds), *Threads of Labour,* Oxford: Blackwell, 16–39.

W. Hutton (2007), 'Low wage competition isn't to blame for western job losses and inequality', the *Guardian,* 9 January, 25.

Institute for Public Policy Research (2005), *Press Release on Migration in Britain,* September, www.ippr.org/pressreleases/?id=1688, accessed February 2008.

International Work Group for Indigenous Affairs (IWGIA) (2009), (http//www. iwgia.org/sw.asp, and www.iwgia./org/sw18239.asp, www.iwgia.org/sw641.asp and www.iwgia.org/sw231.asp). www.iwgia.org/sw231.asp), accessed February 2009.

P. Iyer (2001), *The Global Soul: Jet-Lag, Shopping Malls and the Search for Home,* London: Bloomsbury.

M. Jackson (1996), 'Introduction: phenomenology, radical empiricism and anthropo-logical critique', in M. Jackson (ed.), *Things as They Are: New Directions in Phenomenological Anthropology,* Bloomington and Indianapolis, IN: Indiana University Press, 1–50.

S. Jacobs (2004), 'New forms, longstanding issues, and some successes: feminist net-works and organising in a globalising era', *Journal of Interdisciplinary Gender Studies,* 8, 1 and 2, 171–194.

S. Jacobs (2009), *Gender and Agrarian Reform,* London: Routledge.

P. James (2005), 'Arguing globalizations: propositions towards an investigation of glo-bal formation', *Globalizations,* 2, 2, 193–209.

N. Janus (1986), 'Transnational advertising: some considerations on the impact of peripheral societies', in R. Atwood and E. G. McAnany (eds), *Communications and Latin American Society: Trends in Critical Research 1960–85,* Madison, WI: University of Wisconsin Press, 127–142.

B. Jordan and F. Düvell (2003), *Migration: The Boundaries of Equality and Justice,* Cambridge: Polity.

S. Kaplan (2001), 'Between a rock and hard place: women's self-mobilization to over-come poverty in Uganda', in S. Rowbotham and S. Linkogle (eds), *Women Resist Globalization: Mobilizing for Livelihood and Rights,* London: Zed, 28–45.

J. Keane (2003), *Global Civil Society?,* Cambridge: Cambridge University Press.

M. E. Keck and K. Sikking (1998), *Activists Beyond Borders: Advocacy Networks in International Politics,* Ithaca, NY: Cornell University Press.

P. Kennedy (2004), 'Making global society: friendship networks among transnational professionals in the building design industry', *Global Networks: A Journal of Transnational Affairs,* 4, 2, 157–180.

P. Kennedy (2005), 'Joining, constructing and benefiting from the global work-place: transnational professionals in the building-design industry', *Sociological Review,* 53, 1, 172–197.

P. Kennedy (2007a), 'Global transformations but local, "bubble" lives: taking a reality check on some globalization concepts', *Globalizations,* 4, 2, 267–282.

P. Kennedy (2007b), 'The subversive element in interpersonal relations – cultural border crossings and third spaces: skilled migrants at work and play in the global system', *Globalizations,* 4, 3, 341–354.

P. Kennedy (2008), 'The construction of trans-social European networks and the neu-tralization of borders: skilled EU migrants in Manchester – re-constituting social and national belonging', *Space and Politics,* 12, 1, 109–133.

J. Kenway, A. Kraack and A. Hickey-Moody (2006), *Masculinity Beyond the Metropolis*, Basingstoke: Palgrave.

R. Kiely (2005a), *The Clash of Globalizations: Neo-liberalism, the Third Way and Anti-globalisation,* Leiden: Brill.

R. Kiely (2005b), *Empire in the Age of Globalization: US Hegemony and Neoliberal Disorder,* London: Pluto Press.

R. King and E. Ruiz-Gelices (2003), 'International student migration and the European "year abroad": effects on European identity and subsequent migration behaviour', *International Journal of Population Geography,* 9, 3, 229–252.

N. Klein (2001), *No Logo,* London: Flamingo.

T. Köppel and A. Székely (2002), 'Transnational organized crime and conflicts in the Balkans', in M. Berdal and M. Serrano (eds), *Transnational Organized Crime and International Security*, Boulder, CO: Lynne Rienner, 129–140.

S. Kothari and W. Harcourt (2005), 'Women displaced: democracy, development, and identity in India', in W. Harcourt and A. Escobar (eds), *Women and the Politics of Place,* Bloomfield, CT: Kumarian Press, 115–128.

Y. Kong Chu (2002), 'Global triads: myth or reality?', in M. Berdal and M. Serrano (eds), *Transnational Organized Crime and International Security*, Boulder, CO: Lynne Rienner, 183–193.

La Via Campesina: International Peasant Movement (2009), http//www.viacampesina.org/main_en, accessed February 2009.

M. Lamont and A. Aksartova (2002), 'Ordinary cosmopolitans: strategies for bridging racial boundaries among working class men', *Theory, Culture and Society,* 19, 4, 1–25.

S. Lash (2002), 'Foreword: Individualization in a non-linear mode', in U. Beck and E. Beck-Gernsheim (eds), *Individualization,* London: Sage, vii–xiii.

S. Lash and J. Urry (1987), *The End of Organized Capitalism,* Cambridge: Polity.

S. Lash and J. Urry (1994), *Economies of Signs and Spaces,* London: Sage.

B. Latour (1993), *We Have Never Been Modern,* Cambridge, MA: Harvard University Press.

F. Lawrence (2008), 'Food crises could swing future UK elections, says think tank', the *Guardian,* 7 October, 14.

F. J. Lechner and K. Boli (2005), *World Culture: Origins and Consequences,* Oxford: Blackwell Publishing.

H. Lefebvre (1991), *The Production of Space,* translated by D. Nicholson-Smith, Oxford: Blackwell.

H. Lefebvre (2004), *Rhythmanalysis: Space, Time and Everyday Life,* translated by S. Elden and G. Moore, London: Continuum.

P. Levitt (2001), *The Transnational Villagers,* Berkeley: University of California Press.

D. Ley (2004), 'Transnational spaces and everyday lives', *Transnational Institute of British Geographers,* 29, 151–164.

C. S. Liang (2007), 'Europe for the "Europeans"; the foreign and security policy of the populist radical right', in C. S. Liang (ed.), *Europe for the Europeans: The Foreign and Security Policy of the Populist Radical Right,* Aldershot: Ashgate, 1–32.

P. Lilley (2006), *Dirty Dealing,* London: Kogan Page.

G. Lipsitz (1997), *Dangerous Crossroads: Popular Music, Postmodernism and the Poetics of Place,* London: Verso.

Y. G. Lithman and M. Andersson (2005), 'Introduction', in M. Andersson, Y. G. Lithman and O. Sernhede (eds), *Youth, Otherness and the Plural City: Modes of Belonging and Social Life,* Göteborg: Bokförlaget Daidalas A. B, 1–24.

N. Lovell (1998), 'Introduction', in N. Lovell (ed.), *Locality and Belonging*, London: Routledge, 1–24.

J. Lull (1995), *Media, Communications, Culture: A Global Approach*, Cambridge: Polity.

E. MacAskill and D. Glaister (2008), ' "We do all their work and they don't like us" – how migrants became an election issue', the *Guardian, International*, 18 January, 27.

M. Magatti (1999), 'Globalization as a double disconnection and its consequences: an outline'. Paper given at the conference, *Globalization and Identities*, Manchester Metropolitan University, 30 June–2 July.

J. Maguire (1999), *Global Sport: Identities, Societies, Civilizations*, Cambridge: Polity.

S. L. Malcomson (1998) 'The varieties of cosmopolitan experience', in P. Cheah and B. Robbins (eds), *Cosmopolitics: Thinking and Feeling Beyond the Nation*, Minneapolis: University of Minnesota Press, 233–245.

A. Mansoor and B. Quillan (2006), *Migration and Remittances: Eastern Europe and the Former Soviet Union*, Washington DC: World Bank,

M. H. Marchand (2005), 'Some theoretical "musings" about gender and resistance', in L. Amore (ed.), *The Global Resistance Reader*, London: Routledge, 215–225.

P. Marcuse and R. van Kempen (2000), *Globalizing Cities: A New Spatial Order?* Oxford: Blackwell.

S. A. Marston, K. Woodward and J. P. Jones III (2007), 'Flattening ontologies of globalization: the Nollywood case', *Globalizations*, 4, 1, 45–64.

H-P. Martin (2007), 'The European trap: jobs on the run, democracy at stake', in E. Paus (ed.), *Global Capitalism Unbound: Winners and Losers in Offshore Outsourcing*, Basingstoke: Palgrave, 131–145.

P. Martin and F. Wilmer (2008), 'Transnational normative struggles and globalization: the case of indigenous peoples in Bolivia and Ecuador', *Globalizations*, 5, 4, 583–598.

J. Mason (2004), 'Personal narratives, relational selves: residential histories in the living and telling', *The Sociological Review*, 52, 2, 162–179.

T. Mason (1995), *Passion of the People? Football in South America*, London: Verso.

D. Massey (1993), 'Power geometry and a progressive sense of place', in J. Bird, B. Curtis, T. Putnam, G. Robertson and L. Tickner (eds), *Mapping the Futures: Local Cultures, Global Change*, London: Routledge, 59–70.

D. Massey (1994), *Space, Place and Gender*, Cambridge: Polity.

D. Massey (1995), 'The conceptualization of place', in D. Massey and P. Jess (eds), *A Place in the World?*, Oxford: Open University, 45–86.

D. Massey (2005), *For Space*, London: Sage.

M. Mattelart (1983), *Transnationals and the Third World: The Struggle for Culture, in the South*, Hadley, MA: Bergin and Garvey.

J. May, J. Wills, K. Datta, Y. Evans, J. Herbert and C. McIlwaine (2007), 'Keeping London working: global cities, the British state and London's new migrant division of labour', *Transnational Institute of British Geography*, 32, 151–167.

M. McCluhan (1962), *The Gutenberg Galaxy: The Making of Typographical Man*, Toronto: University of Toronto Press.

R. McKie (2008), 'Arctic "could be free of ice in five years" ', the *Observer*, 10 October, 17.

P. McMichael (1996), *Development and Change: A Global Perspective*, Thousand Oaks, CA: Pine Forge.

A. Melucci (1996), *Challenging Codes: Collective Action in the Information Age*, Cambridge: Cambridge University Press.

M. Merleau-Ponty (1962), *Phenomenology of Perception*, London: Routledge and Kegan Paul.

A. Middleton, A. Murie and R. Groves (2005), 'Social capital and neighbourhoods that work', *Urban Studies*, 42, 10, 1711–1738.

Migration Policy Institute (MPI) (2007), 'Data hub: Migration facts, stats and maps', www.migrationinformation.org/datahub/charts/1.2, 5.1, 6.1 and 6.2; accessed February 2008.

F. T. Miko (2007), 'International human trafficking', in K. L. Thachuk (ed.), *Transnational Threats: Smuggling and Trafficking in Arms. Drugs and Human Life*, Westport, CT: Praeger Security International, 36–52.

T. Miller, G. Lawrence, J. McKay and D. Rowe (2001), *Globalization and Sport: Playing the World*, London: Sage.

M. Mills and H-P. Blossfeld (2005), 'Globalization, uncertainty and the early life course: A theoretical framework', in H-P. Blossfeld, E. Klijzing, M. Mills and K. Kurz (eds), *Globalization, Uncertainty and Youth in Society*, London: Routledge, 1–24.

J. C. Mitchell (1969), 'The concept and use of social networks', in J. C. Mitchell (ed.), *Social Networks in Urban Situations*, Manchester: Manchester University Press, 1–50.

K. Mitchell (1995), 'Flexible circulation in the Pacific Rim: capitalism in cultural context', *Economic Geography*, 71, 4, 364–382.

T. Mitchell (2001), 'Another root – hip-hop outside the USA', in T. Mitchell (ed.), *Global Noise: Rap and Hop-Hop Outside the USA*, Middletown, CT: Wesleyan University Press, 1–38.

C. Mudde (2007), *Populist Radical Right Parties in Europe*, Cambridge: Cambridge University Press.

K. Mumtaz and W. Harcourt (2005), 'The politics of place and women's rights in Pakistan', in W. Harcourt and A. Escobar (eds), *Women and the Politics of Place*, Bloomfield, CT: Kumarian Press, 59–70.

R. Munck (2007), *Globalization and Contestation*, Oxford: Routledge.

R. Munck and D. O'Hearn (2001), 'Preface', in R. Munck and D. O'Hearn (eds), *Critical Development Theory: Contributions to a New Paradigm*, London: Zed, xiv–xx.

A. Murie and S. Musterd (2004), 'Social exclusion and opportunity structures in European cities and neighbourhoods', *Urban Studies*, 41, 8, 1441–1459.

G. Mythen (2005), 'Employment, individualization and insecurity: rethinking the risk society perspective', *The Sociological Review*, 53, 1, 129–149.

L. Napoleoni (2004), *Terror Inc: Tracing the Money behind Global Terrorism*, London: Penguin.

P. M. Nardi (1998), 'The globalization of the gay and lesbian socio-political movement', *Sociological Perspectives*, 41, 3, 569–585.

K. Negus (1992), *Producing Pop: Culture and Conflict in the Popular Music Industry*, London: E. Arnold.

P. Norris (2000), 'Global governance and cosmopolitan citizens', in J. S. Nye and J. D. Donahue (eds), *Governance in a Globalizing World*, Cambridge, MA: Brookings Institute Press, 155–177.

M. Nowicka and M. Rovisco (eds) (2009), *Cosmopolitanism in Practice*, Farnham: Ashgate.

D. O'Byrne (1997), 'Working-class culture: local community and global conditions', in J. Eade (ed.), *Living the Global City: Globalization as a Local Process*, London: Routledge, 73–89.

D. O'Byrne (2003), *Human Rights: An Introduction,* Harlow: Longman.

T. Oeleson (2005), *International Zapatismo: The Construction of Solidarity in the Age of Globalization,* London: Zed.

Office of the Chief Economist of the World Bank (2008), 'Remittances: Not Manna from Heaven', www.worldbank.org/WEBSITE/EXTERNAL/COUNTRIES, accessed February 2008.

A. Ong and D. M. Nonini (1997), *Ungrounded Empires: The Cultural Politics of Modern Chinese Transnationalism,* London: Routledge.

S. O'Riain (2000), 'Net-working for a living: Irish software developers in the global workplace', in M. Burawoy et al., (eds) *Global Ethnography: Forces, Connections, and Imaginations in a Postmodern World,* Berkeley and Los Angeles: University of California Press, 175–202.

R. Parreñas (2001), *Servants of Globalization,* Stanford, CA: Stanford University Press.

F. Passy (1999), 'Supranational political opportunities as a channel of globalization of political conflicts: the case of the rights of indigenous peoples', in D. della Porta, K. Hanspeter and D. Rucht (eds), *Social Movements in a Globalizing World,* Basingstoke: Macmillan, 148–169.

J. Paulson (2001), 'Peasant struggles and international solidarity: the case of Chiapas', in L. Panitch and C. Leys (eds), *Socialist Register 2000,* London: Merlin, 275–288.

E. Paus (2007), 'Winners and losers from offshore outsourcing: what is to be done?', in E. Paus (ed.), *Global Capitalism Unbound: Winners and Losers in Offshore Outsourcing,* Basingstoke: Palgrave, 3–20.

R. A. Peterson and A. Bennett (2004), 'Introducing music scenes', in A. Bennett and R. A. Peterson (eds), *Music Scenes: Local, Translocal, and Virtual,* Nashville: Vanderbilt University Press, 1–30.

V. S. Peterson and A. S. Runyan (1993), *Global Gender Issues,* Boulder, CO: Westview Press.

C. Porter (2008), 'Manchester United, global capitalism and local resistance', *Belgeo,* 2, 181–191.

A. Portes (1997), 'Globalization from below: the rise of transnational communities', Working Paper Series No. 1 of the *Transnational Communities Project* at the Faculty of Anthropology and Geography, Oxford University.

P. L. Price (2007), 'Cohering culture on *Calle Ocho*: the pause and flow of *Latinidad*', *Globalizations,* 4, 1, 81–100.

L. Pries (ed.) (2001), *New Transnational Social Spaces: International Migrations and Transnational Companies in the Early 21st Century,* London: Routledge.

R. Putnam (2000), *Bowling Alone,* New York: Simon and Schuster.

D. Ratha (2009), 'Remittance flows to developing countries are estimated to exceed $300 billion in 2008', http://peoplemove.worldbank.org/en/comment/reply/130, accessed April 2009.

A. Rawnsley (2009), 'Well done, Gordon. Now it's time to come back to earth', the *Observer,* 5 April, 27.

E. Recchi (2006), 'From migrants to movers: citizenship and mobility in the European Union', in M. P. Smith and A. Favell (eds), *The Human Face of Global Mobility,* New Brunswick, NJ: Transaction Publishers, 53–77.

M. Regev (2002), 'The "pop-rockization" of popular music', in D. Hesmondhalgh and K. Negus (eds), *Popular Music Studies,* London: Arnold, 251–264.

R. Reich (1991), *The Work of Nations: Preparing Ourselves for Twenty-First Century Capitalism,* New York: Simon and Schuster.

R. Reitan (2007), *Global Activism*, London: Routledge.

X. Rice (2008), 'They risk everything to escape', the *Guardian*, G2, 21 April, 2.

R. Rifkin (1996), *The End of Work*, New York: G. P. Putnam's and Sons.

G. Ritzer (1993), *The McDonaldization of Society: An Investigation into the Changing Character of Social Life*, Thousand Oaks, CA: Pine Forge.

G. Ritzer (2004), *The Globalization of Nothing*, London: Pine Forge.

B. Robbins (1998), 'Actually existing cosmopolitanism', in P. Cheah and B. Robbins (eds), *Cosmopolitics: Thinking and Feeling beyond the Nation*, Minneapolis: University of Minnesota Press, 1–19.

R. Robertson (1992), *Globalization: Social Theory and Global Culture*, London: Sage.

R. Robertson (1995), 'Glocalization: time-space and homogeneity-heterogeneity', in M. Featherstone, M. S. Lash and R. Robertson (eds), *Global Modernities*, London: Sage, 25–44.

R. Robertson (2001), 'Globalization theory 2000+: Major problematics', in C. Ritzer and B. Smart (eds), *Handbook of Social Theory*, London: Sage, 458–471.

W. I. Robinson (2001), 'Social theory and globalization: the rise of a transnational state', *Theory and Society*, 30, 2, 157–200.

W. I. Robinson (2002), 'Capitalist globalization and the transnationalization of the state', in M. Rupert and H. Smith (eds), *Historical Materialism and Globalization*, London: Routledge, 210–229.

W. I. Robinson and J. Harris (2000), 'Towards a global ruling class? Globalization and the transnational capitalist class', *Science and Society*, 64, 1, 11–54.

M. W. Rofe (2003), ' "I just want to be global": theorising the gentrifying class as an emergent elite global community', *Urban Studies*, 40, 12, 3511–3526.

J. G. Ronderos (2003), 'The war on drugs and the military: the case of Columbia', in M. E. Beare (ed.), *Critical Reflections on Transnational Organized Crime, Money Laundering, and Corruption*, Toronto: University of Toronto Press, 207–236.

S. Rowbotham and S. Linkogle (2001), 'Introduction', in S. Rowbotham and S. Linkogle (eds), *Women Resist Globalization: Mobilizing for Livelihood and Rights*, London: Zed, 1–12.

V. Ruggiero (1993), 'The *Camorra*: "clean" capital and organized crime', in F. Pearce and M. Woodiwiss (eds), *Global Crime Connections: Dynamics and Control*, Basingstoke: Palgrave, 141–161.

V. Ruggiero (2003), 'Global markets and crime', in E. Beare (ed.), *Critical Reflections on Transnational Organized Crime, Money Laundering, and Corruption*, Toronto: University of Toronto Press, 171–182.

M. Sahlins (2000), *Culture in Practice: Selected Essays*, New York: Zone Books.

L. Sandercock (2006), 'Cosmopolitan urbanism: a love song to our mongrel cities', in J. Binnie, J. Holloway, S. Millington and C. Young (eds), *Cosmopolitan Urbanism*, London: Routledge, 37–52.

S. Sassen (1991), *The Global City: New York, London, Tokyo*, Princeton, NJ: Princeton University Press.

S. Sassen (2000), *Cities in a World Economy*, Thousand Oaks, CA: Pine Forge.

S. Sassen (2002), 'Introduction: locating cities on global circuits', in S. Sassen (ed.), *Global Networks: Linked Cities*, New York: Routledge, 1–37.

S. Sassen (2004), 'Local actors in global politics', *Current Sociology*, 52, 4, 649–670.

S. Sassen (2007), *A Sociology of Globalization*, New York: W.W. Norton and Co.

M. Savage, G. Bagnall and B. Longhurst (2005), *Globalization and Belonging*, London: Sage.

N. G. Schiller (1999), 'Transmigrants and nation-states: something old and something new in the US immigrant experience', in C. Hirschman, P. Kasinitz and J. De Wind (eds), *The Handbook of International Migration: The American Experience*, New York: Russell Sage Foundation, 94–119.

E. Schmidt (2007), 'Whose "culture"; Globalism, localism and the expansion of tradition: the case of the Hñähñu of Hidalgo, Mexico and Clearwater, Florida', *Globalizations*, 4, 1, 101–114.

J. A. Scholte (2005), *Globalization: A Critical Introduction*, Basingstoke: Macmillan.

A. Schutz (1964), *Collected Papers Volume II: Studies in Social Theory* (edited and introduced by A. Brodersen), The Hague: Martinus Nijhoff, 92–105.

A. Schutz (1974), *The Structures of the Life-World*, London: Heinemann Educational Books.

J. Scott (2000), *Social Network Analysis: A Handbook*, London: Sage.

Self Employed Women's Association (SEWA), http://www.sewa.org/aboutus/index.asp, and http://www. sewa.org/links/index.asp, accessed February 2009.

R. Senechal de la Roche (1996), 'Collective violence as social control', *Sociological Forum*, 11, 97–128.

R. Senechal de la Roche (2004), 'Towards a scientific theory of terrorism', *Sociological Theory*, 22, 1, 1–4.

R. Sennett (2002), 'Cosmopolitanism and the social experience of cities', in S. Vertovec and R. Cohen (eds), *Conceiving Cosmopolitanism: Theory, Context and Practice*, Oxford: Oxford University Press, 42–47.

O. Sernhede (2005), '"Reality is my nationality" – the global tribe of hip hop and immigrant youth in "The New Sweden"', in M. Andersson, Y. G. Lithman and O. Sernhede (eds), *Youth, Otherness and the Plural City: Modes of Belonging and Social Life*, Göteborg: Bokförlaget Daidalas A. B, 271–289.

M. Serrano (2002), 'Transnational organized crime and international security: business as usual?', in M. Berdal and M. Serrano (eds), *Transnational Organized Crime and International Security*, Boulder, CO: Lynne Rienner, 13–36.

M. Serrano and M. C. Toro (2002), 'From drug trafficking to transnational organized crime in Latin America', in M. Berdal and M. Serrano (eds), *Transnational Organized Crime and International Security*, Boulder, CO: Lynne Rienner, 155–182.

M. Shaw (2000), *Theory of the Global State – Globality as an Unfinished Project*, Cambridge: Cambridge University Press.

L. I. Shelley (2007), 'The rise and diversification of human smuggling and trafficking into the United States', in K. L. Thachuk (ed.), *Transnational Threats: Smuggling and Trafficking in Arms. Drugs and Human Life*, Westport, CT: Praeger Security International, 194–210.

W. R. Schroeder (2001), 'Money laundering: a global threat and the international community's response', *FBI Law Enforcement Bulletin*, 70, 5, 1–9.

B. J. Silver and G. Arrighi (2003), 'Polanyi's "Double movement": The *Belle époques* of British and U.S. Hegemony compared', *Politics and Society*, 31, 2, 325–355.

G. Simmel (1950), 'The field of sociology', in K. H. Wolf (editor and translator), *The Sociology of Georg Simmel*, New York: The Free Press, 3–25.

L. Sklair (1995), *Sociology of the Global System*, London: Prentice Hall, Harvester Wheatsheaf.

L. Sklair (2001), *The Transnational Capitalist Class*, London: Blackwell.

L. Sklair (2002), *Globalization: Capitalism and Its Alternatives,* Oxford: Oxford University Press.

A. D. Smith (1995), *Nations and Nationalism in a Global Age*, Cambridge: Polity.

D. Smith and B. Montague (2007), 'Do migrants make or break us?', the *Sunday Times*, 4 November.

M. P. Smith and L. E. Guarnizo (1998), 'The locations of transnationalism', in M. P. Smith and L. E. Guarnizo (eds), *Transnationalism from Below: Comparative and Community Research, NO. 6*, New Brunswick, NJ: Transaction Publishers, 3–34

R. C. Smith (1998), 'Transnational localities: community, technology and the politics of membership within the context of Mexico and US migration', in M. P. Smith and L. E. Guarnizo (eds), *Transnationalism from Below: Comparative and Community Research, NO. 6*, New Brunswick, NJ: Transaction Publishers, 196–238.

Southern Poverty Law Centre (2001), 'Intelligence report: the rise and decline of the "Patriots" ', http://www.splcenter.org/intel/intelreport/article.jsp?aid=195, accessed January 2009.

G. Standing (2007), 'Labour recommodification in the global transformation', in A. Buğra and K. Ağartan (eds), *Reading Karl Polanyi for the Twenty-First Century: Market Economy as a Political Project*, Basingstoke: Palgrave, 67–94.

A. Starr and J. Adams (2003), 'Anti-globalization: the global fight for local autonomy', *New Political Science*, 25, 1, 20–42.

M. B. Steger (2008), *The Rise of the Global Imaginary: Political Ideologies from the French Revolution to the Global War on Terror*, Oxford: Oxford University Press.

J. E. Stiglitz (2002), *Globalization and Its Discontents*, London: Allen Lane.

M. Storper (1997), 'The city: centre of economic reflexivity', *The Service Industries Journal*, 17, 1, 1–27.

N. Suri (2007), 'Offshore outsourcing of services as a catalyst of economic development: the case of India', in E. Paus (ed.), *Global Capitalism Unbound: Winners and Losers in Offshore Outsourcing*, Basingstoke: Palgrave, 163–180.

E. Swyngedouw (1997), 'Neither global nor local: "glocalization" and the politics of scale', in K. R. Cox (ed.), *Spaces of Globalization: Reasserting the Power of the Local*, New York: Guildford Press, 137–166.

M. Swyngedouw, K. Abts and M. van Craen (2007), 'Our own people first in a Europe of peoples: the international policy of the *Vlaams Blok*', in C. S. Liang (ed.), *Europe for the Europeans: The Foreign and Security Policy of the Populist Radical Right*, Aldershot: Ashgate, 81–102.

B. Szerszynski and J. Urry (2002), 'Cultures of Cosmopolitanism', *The Sociological Review*, 50, 4, 461–481.

B. Szerszynski and J. Urry (2006), 'Visuality, mobility and cosmopolitanism: inhabiting the world from afar', *The British Journal of Sociology*, 57, 1, 113–132.

S. Tarrow (1998), *Power in Movement: Social Movements and Contentious Politics*, Cambridge: Cambridge University Press.

I. Taylor (2002), 'Liberal markets and the Republic of Europe: contextualizing the growth of transnational organized crime', in M. Berdal and M. Serrano (eds), *Transnational Organized Crime and International Security*, Boulder, CO: Lynne Rienner, 119–128.

P. J. Taylor (2004), *World City Network: A Global Urban Analysis*, London: Routledge.

B. Teschke and C. Heine (2002), 'The dialectics of globalization: a critique of social constructivism', in M. Rupert and H. Smith (eds), *Historical Materialism and Globalization*, London: Routledge, 165–188.

K. L. Thachuk (2007), 'An introduction to transnational threats', in K. L. Thachuk (ed.), *Transnational Threats: Smuggling and Trafficking in Arms. Drugs and Human Life*, Westport, CT: Praeger Security International, 3–22.

The Economist (2007), 'Economic and financial indicators', 21 April, 121.

The Economist (2007), 'Has globalization hurt workers in rich economies? The IMF wades in', 7 April, 84.

The Ethical Consumer Research Association (2007), *The Ethical Consumer Report for the Co-operative Bank*, Manchester: The Co-operative Bank.

J. Tomlinson (1991), *Cultural Imperialism: A Critical Introduction*, London: Pinter.

J. Tomlinson (1999), *Globalization and Culture*, Cambridge: Polity.

D. Toop (1991), *Rap Attack 2: African Rap to Global Village*, London: Serpent's Tail.

A. Travis (2007), 'Migrants – the verdict: hardworking and skilled but with social problems in tow', the *Guardian*, 17 October.

I. Traynor (2008), 'EU sets up centre in Africa to fight illegal migration', the *Guardian*, 7 October.

J. Tulloch and D. Lupton (2003), *Risk and Everyday Life*, London: Sage.

B. Turner (2006), 'Classical sociology and cosmopolitanism: a critical defense of the social', *The British Journal of Sociology*, 57, 1, 133–152.

UNCTAD (2007), *World Investment Report 2007: Transnational Corporations, Extractive Industries and Development*, New York: United Nations, 229–234

Y. Underhill-Sem (2005), 'Bodies in places, places in bodies', in W. Harcourt and A. Escobar (eds), *Women and the Politics of Place*, Bloomfield, CT: Kumarian Press, 20–31.

United Nations Office for Drug Control and Crime Prevention (2005), *World Drug Report 2005*, New York: United Nations Publications.

J. Urry (2000), *Sociology Beyond Societies*, London: Routledge.

J. Urry (2003), *Global Complexity*, Cambridge: Polity.

J. Urry (2004), 'Small Worlds and the new "social" physics', *Global Networks: A Journal of Transnational Affairs*, 4, 2, 109–130.

M. Vaattovaara and M. Kortteinen (2003), 'Beyond polarisation versus professionalism? A case study of the development of the Helsinki region, Finland', *Urban Studies*, 40, 11, 2127–2145.

S. Vertovec (1999), 'Conceiving and researching transnationalism', *Ethnic and Racial Studies*, 22, 2, 447–462.

S. Vertovec (2001), 'Transnational social formations: towards conceptual cross-fertilization', Working paper 01–16 for the ESRC *Transnational Communities Project* at Oxford University.

S. Vertovec (2007), 'Super-diversity and its implications', *Ethnic and Racial Studies*, 30, 6, 1024–1056.

S. Vertovec and R. Cohen (eds) (2002), *Conceiving Cosmopolitanisn: Theory, Context, and Practice*, Oxford: Oxford University Press.

Via Campesina (2009), 'The International Peasant's Voice', http://www.viacampesina. org/main_en/index, accessed February 2009.

R. Wade (2001), 'The US role in the long Asian crisis of 1990–2000', in F. Batista-Rivera and A. Lukauskis (eds), *The East Asian Crisis and Its Aftermath*, London: Edward Elgar.

R. Wade (2004), 'Is globalization reducing poverty and inequality?', *World Development*, 32, 4, 567–589.

R. Waldinger and D. Fitzgerald (2004), 'Transnationalism in question', *American Journal of Sociology*, 109, 5, 1177–1195.

P. Waley (2000), 'Tokyo: patterns of familiarity and partitions of difference', in P. Marcuse and R. van Kempen (eds), *Globalizing Cities: A New Spatial Order?* Oxford: Blackwell, 127–157.

J. Walker (1999), 'Measuring the extent of international crime and money laundering', paper given at the Budapest conference, *KriminálExpo*, June.

W.O. Walker III (1999), 'The limits of coercive diplomacy: US drug policy and Columbian state stability, 1978–1997', in H. R. Friman and P. Andreas (eds), *The Illicit Global Economy and State Power*, Oxford: Rowman and Littlefield, 143–172.

P. Watt (1998), 'Going out of town: youth, "race", and place in the Sough East of England', *Environment and Planning D: Society and Space*, 16, 687–703.

P. Watt (2006), 'Respectability, roughness and "race": neighbourhood place images and the making of working-class social distinctions in London', *International Journal of Urban and Regional Research*, 30, 4, 776–797.

P. Watt (2007), ' "There aren't many school teachers hanging around council estates": everyday cosmopolitan urbanism in London council housing', paper presented at the conference, *'Everyday life in the global city'*, Manchester Institute for Social and Spatial Transformations, Manchester Metropolitan University, July, 2007.

J. Watts (2008), 'Global food crisis. More wealth, more meat. How China's rise spells trouble', the *Guardian*, 30 May, 22.

G. Wearden and D. Stanway (2008), 'China slowdown: after years of boom', the *Guardian*, 21 October, 8.

G. R. Wekerle (2005), 'Domesticating the neoliberal city: invisible genders and the politics of place', in W. Harcourt and A. Escobar (eds), *Women and the Politics of Place*, Bloomfield, CT: Kumarian Press, 86–99.

B. Wellman (1999), 'The network community: an introduction', in B. Wellman (ed.), *Networks in the Global Age: Life in Contemporary Communities*, Boulder, CO: Westview Press, 1–47.

W. Welsch (1999), 'Transculturality: the puzzling form of cultures today', in M. Featherstone and S. Lash (eds), *Spaces of Culture: City-Nation-World*, London: Sage, 194–213.

S. Westwood and A. Phizacklea (2000), *Transnationalism and the Politics of Belonging*, London: Routledge.

P. Williams and G. Baudin-O'Hayon (2002), 'Global governance, transnational organized crime and money laundering', in D. Held and A. McGrew (eds), *Governing Globalization: Power, Authority and Global Governance*, Cambridge: Polity: 127–144.

J. Wills and A. Hale (2005), 'Threads of labour in the global garment industry', in A. Hales and J. Wills (eds), *Threads of Labour*, Oxford: Blackwell, 1–15.

M. Woodiwiss (1993), 'Crime's global reach', in F. Pearce and M. Woodiwiss (eds), *Global Crime Connections: Dynamics and Control*, Basingstoke: Palgrave, 1–31.

M. Woodiwiss (2003), 'Transnational organized crime: the strange career of an American concept', in M. E. Beare (ed.), *Critical Reflections on Transnational Organized Crime, Money Laundering, and Corruption*, Toronto: University of Toronto Press, 3–32.

I. Woodward, Z. Skrbis and C. Bean (2008), 'Attitudes towards globalization and cosmopolitanism: cultural diversity, personal consumption and national economy', *The British Journal of Sociology*, 59, 2, 207–226.

World Bank (2004), World Bank Indicators, Washington: World Bank, http//www.wprldbank.org/data

N. Yeates (2004), 'Global care chains: critical reflections and lines of enquiry', *International Feminist Journal of Politics*, 6, 3, 369–391.

Y. Zhou and Y-F. Tseng (2001), 'Regrounding the "Ungrounded Empires": localization as the geographical catalyst for transnationalism', *Global Networks: A Journal of Transnational Affairs*, 1, 2, 131–154.

Index